GO FOR IT, NAKAMURA!

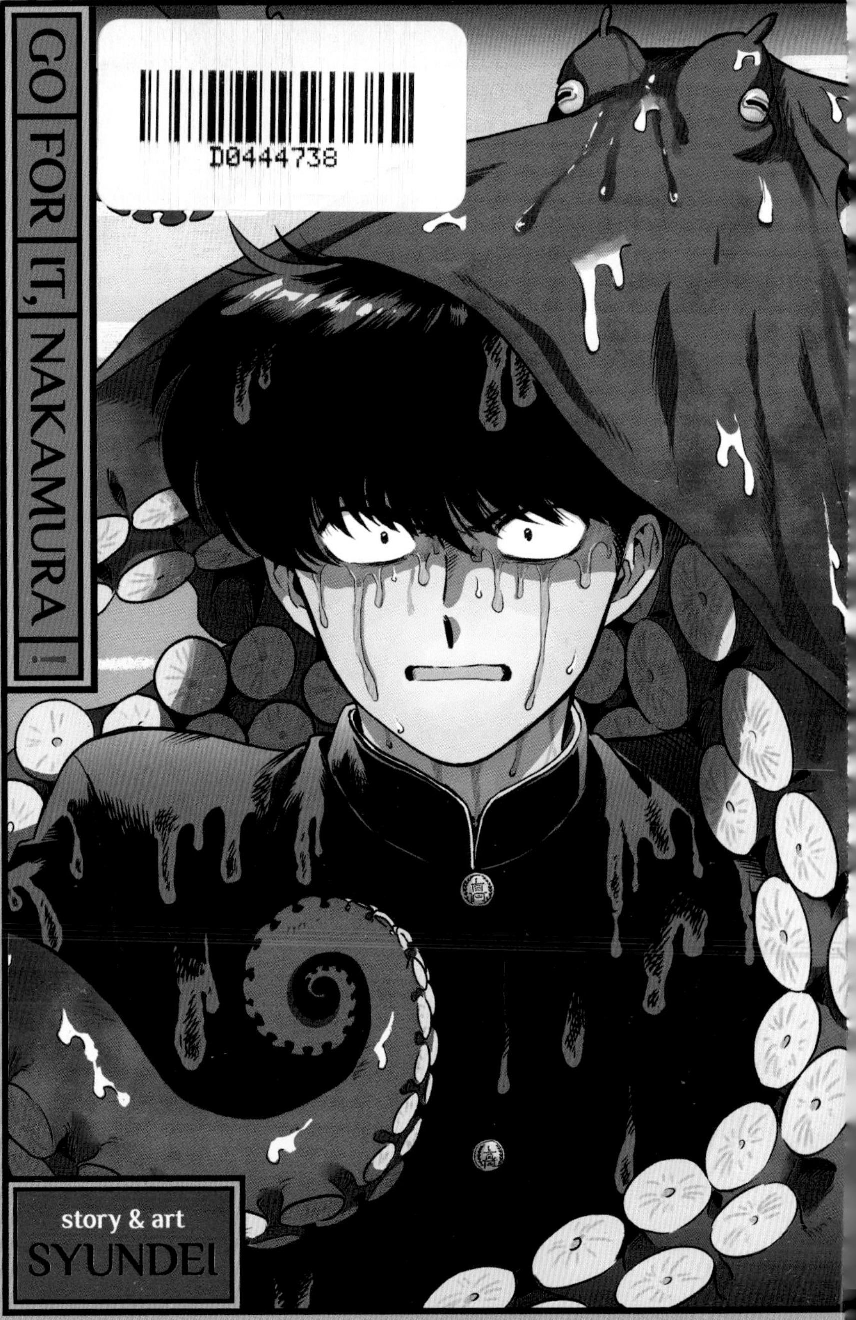

story & art
SYUNDEI

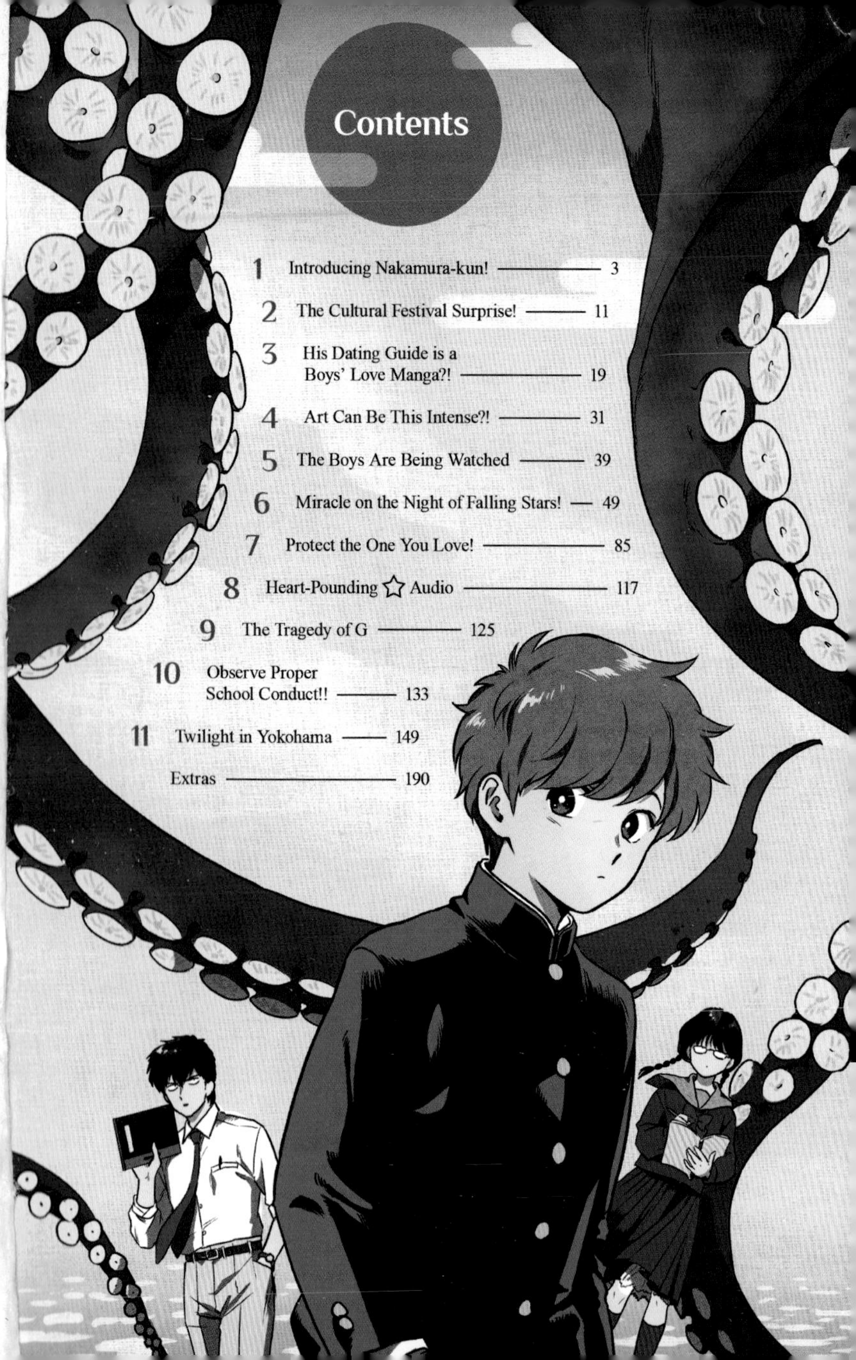

Contents

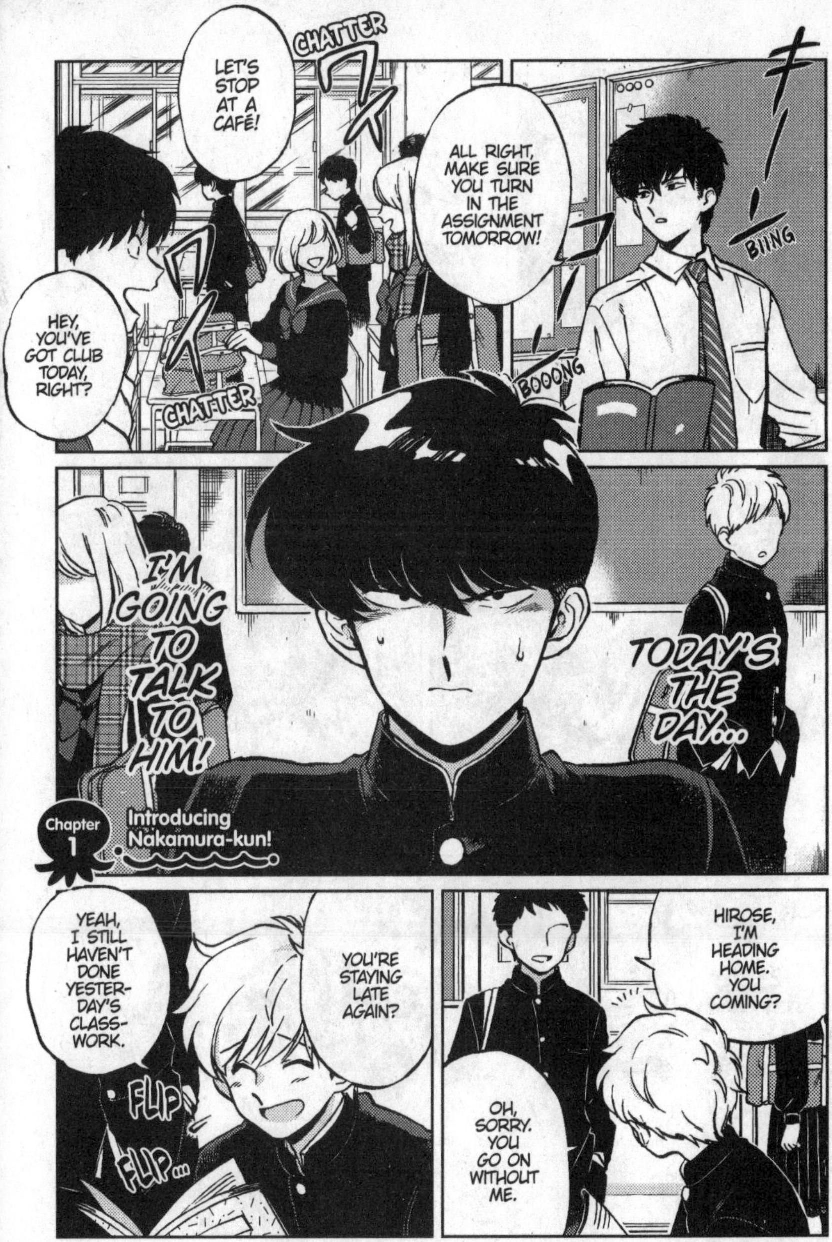
ALL RIGHT, MAKE SURE YOU TURN IN THE ASSIGNMENT TOMORROW!
BIING
BOOONG
LET'S STOP AT A CAFÉ!
CHATTER
HEY, YOU'VE GOT CLUB TODAY, RIGHT?
CHATTER
TODAY'S THE DAY...
I'M GOING TO TALK TO HIM!
Chapter 1
Introducing Nakamura-kun!
HIROSE, I'M HEADING HOME. YOU COMING?
OH, SORRY. YOU GO ON WITHOUT ME.
YOU'RE STAYING LATE AGAIN?
YEAH, I STILL HAVEN'T DONE YESTER-DAY'S CLASS-WORK.
FLIP
FLIP...

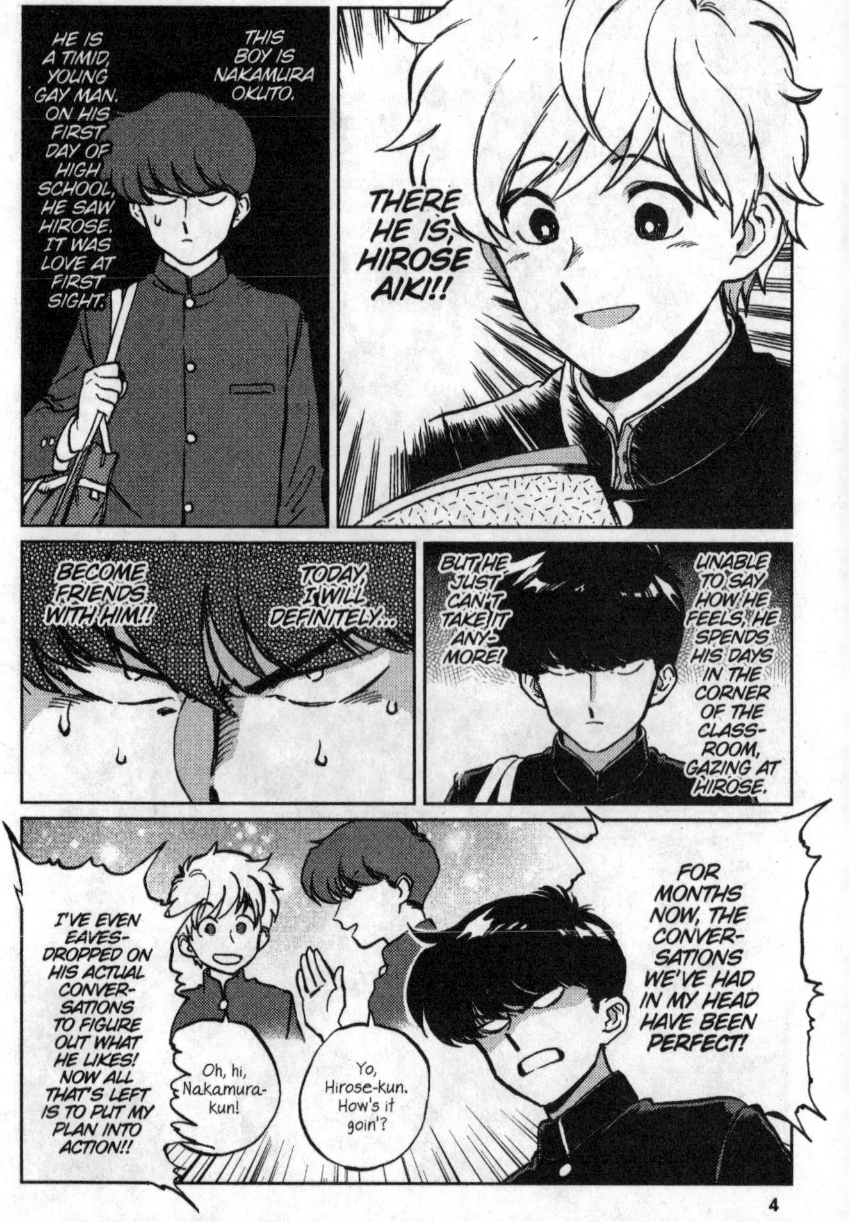
THERE HE IS, HIROSE AIKI!!
THIS BOY IS NAKAMURA OKUTO.
HE IS A TIMID, YOUNG GAY MAN. ON HIS FIRST DAY OF HIGH SCHOOL, HE SAW HIROSE. IT WAS LOVE AT FIRST SIGHT.
UNABLE TO SAY HOW HE FEELS, HE SPENDS HIS DAYS IN THE CORNER OF THE CLASSROOM, GAZING AT HIROSE.
BUT HE JUST CAN'T TAKE IT ANYMORE!
TODAY, I WILL DEFINITELY...
BECOME FRIENDS WITH HIM!!
FOR MONTHS NOW, THE CONVERSATIONS WE'VE HAD IN MY HEAD HAVE BEEN PERFECT!
Yo, Hirose-kun. How's it goin'?
Oh, hi, Nakamura-kun!
I'VE EVEN EAVESDROPPED ON HIS ACTUAL CONVERSATIONS TO FIGURE OUT WHAT HE LIKES! NOW ALL THAT'S LEFT IS TO PUT MY PLAN INTO ACTION!!

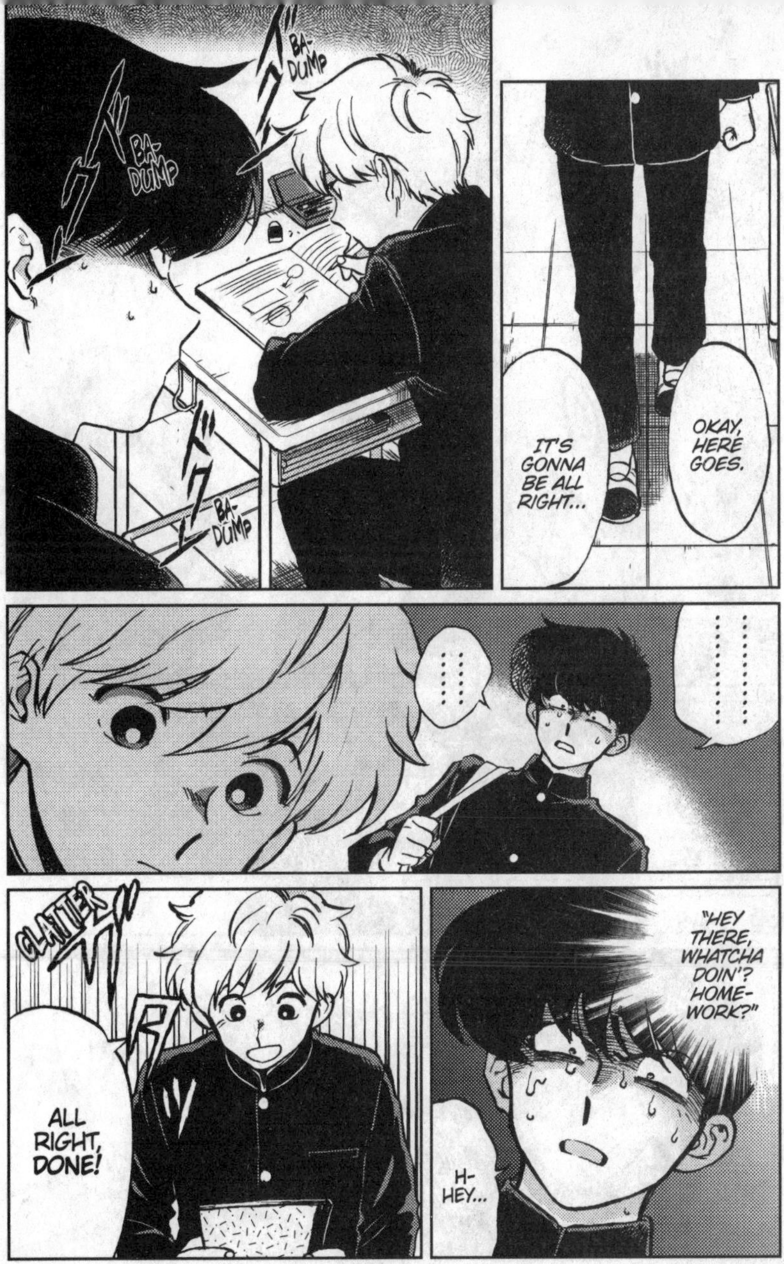
OKAY, HERE GOES.
IT'S GONNA BE ALL RIGHT...
BA-DUMP
BA-DUMP
BA-DUMP
......
......
"HEY THERE, WHATCHA DOIN'? HOME-WORK?"
H-HEY...
CLATTER
ALL RIGHT, DONE!

HM?
ZOOOM
I-I-I-I CAN'T DO IT!!
HUFF!
HUFF!
HUFF!
AS SOON AS I WAS FACE TO FACE WITH HIROSE, MY BRAIN WENT COMPLETELY BLANK!
HUFF!
BUT...
HM?
THAT WAS THE FIRST TIME I'VE EVER LOOKED HIM IN THE EYE.
HE... HE'S SO CUTE!

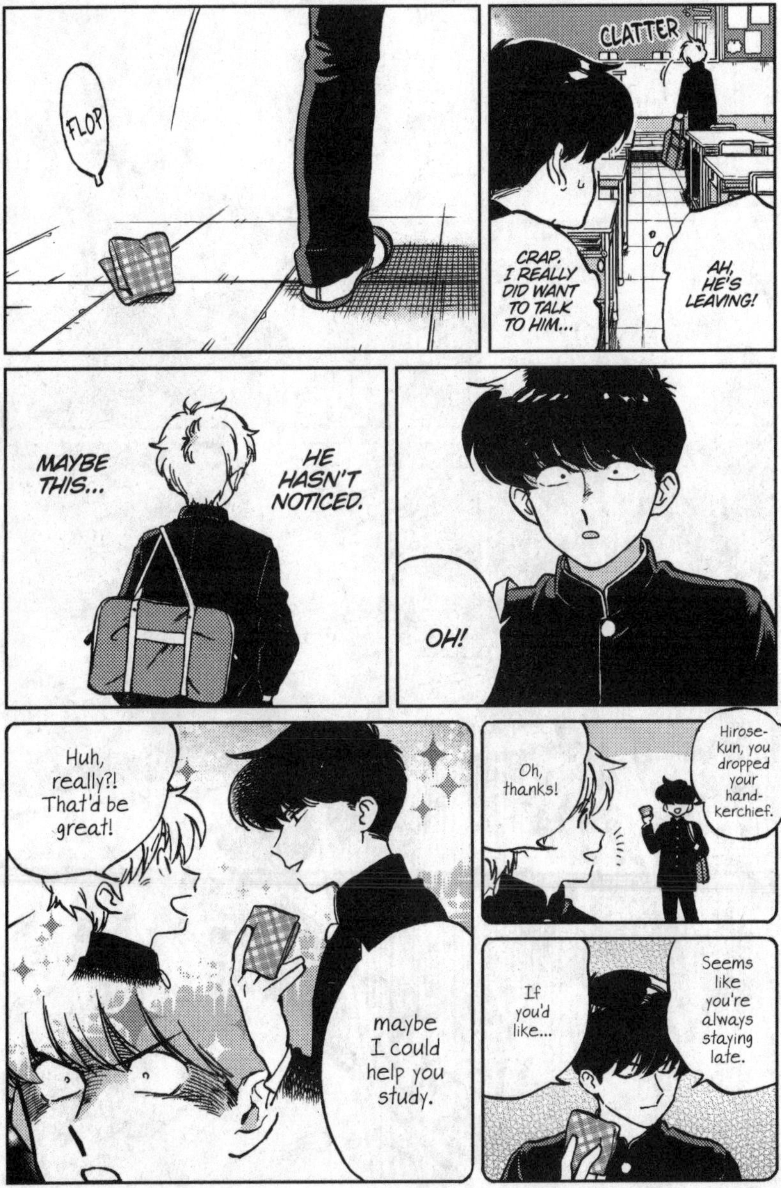
CLATTER
AH, HE'S LEAVING!
CRAP. I REALLY DID WANT TO TALK TO HIM...
FLOP
OH!
HE HASN'T NOTICED.
MAYBE THIS...
Hirose-kun, you dropped your handkerchief.
Oh, thanks!
Seems like you're always staying late.
If you'd like...
maybe I could help you study.
Huh, really?! That'd be great!

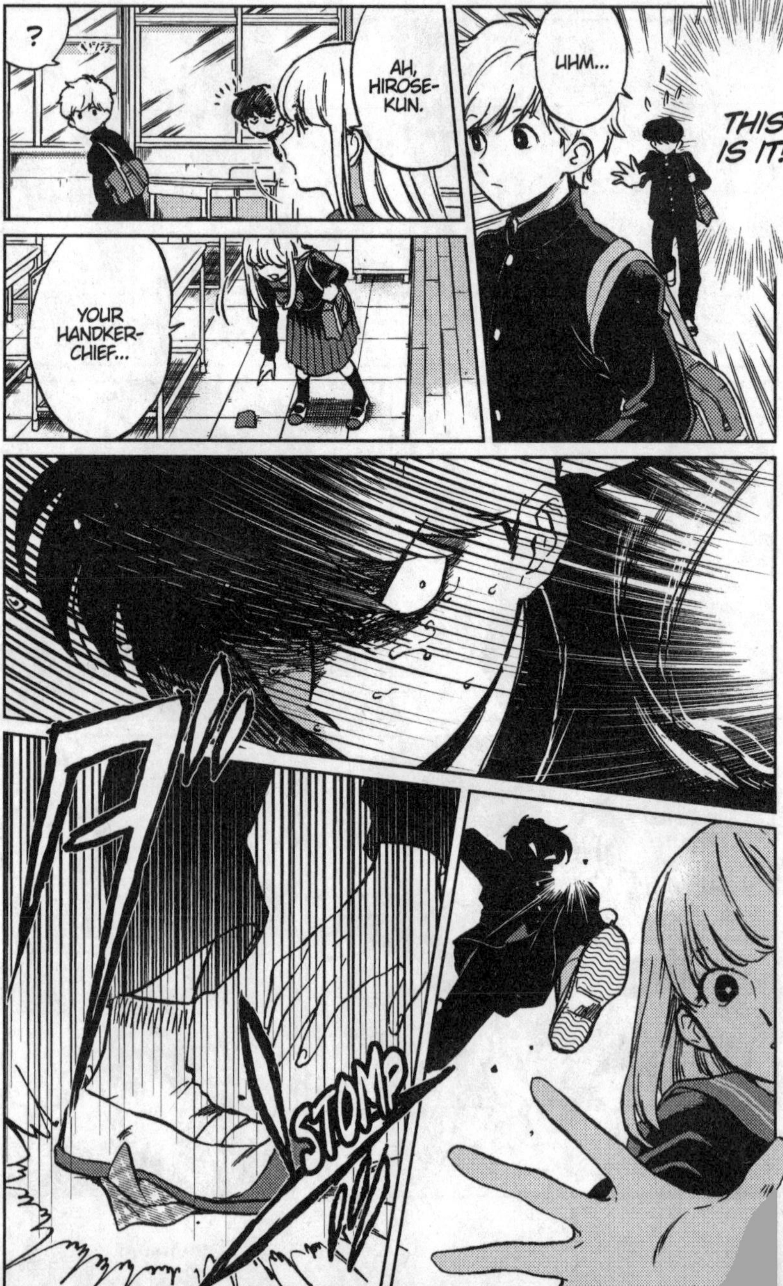
UHM...
THIS IS IT!
AH, HIROSE-KUN.
?
YOUR HANDKER-CHIEF...
STOMP

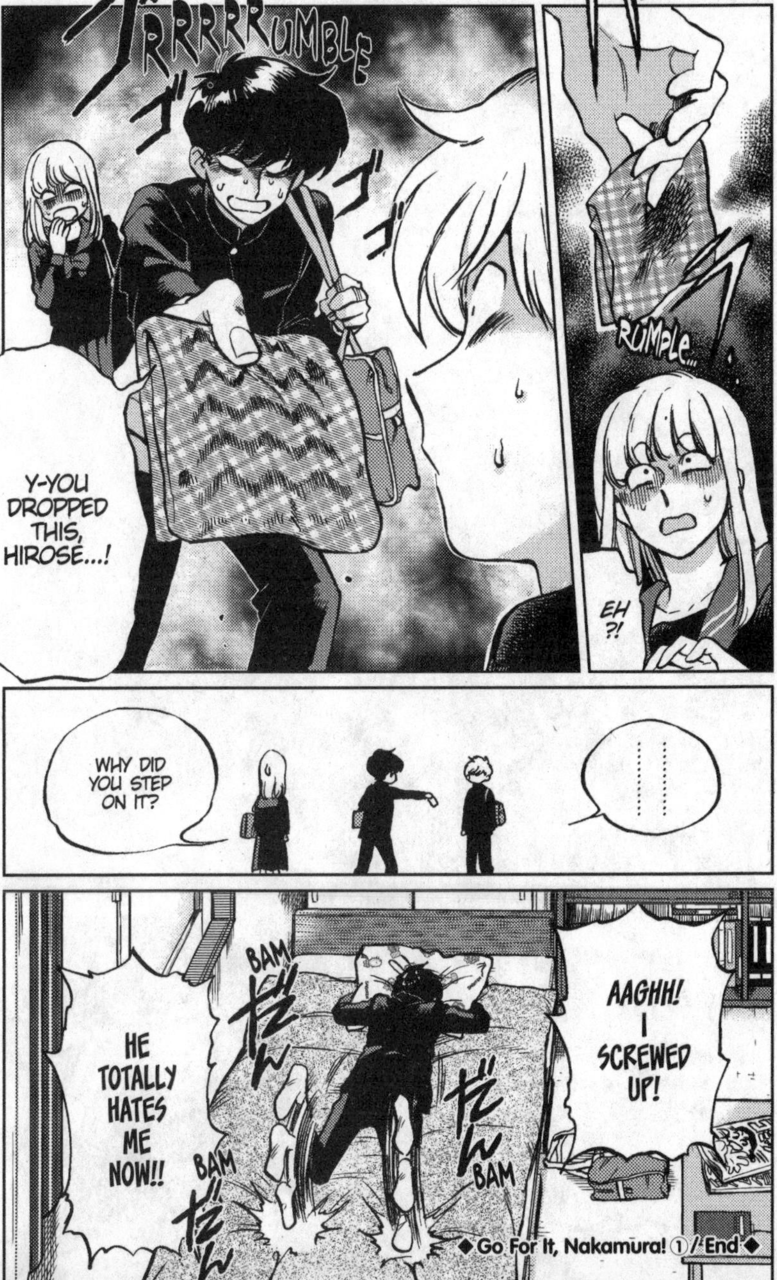
RUMPLE...
EH ?!
RRRRRUMBLE
Y-YOU DROPPED THIS, HIROSE...!
......
WHY DID YOU STEP ON IT?
AAGHH! I SCREWED UP!
BAM
BAM
HE TOTALLY HATES ME NOW!!
BAM

◆Go For It, Nakamura! ① / End◆

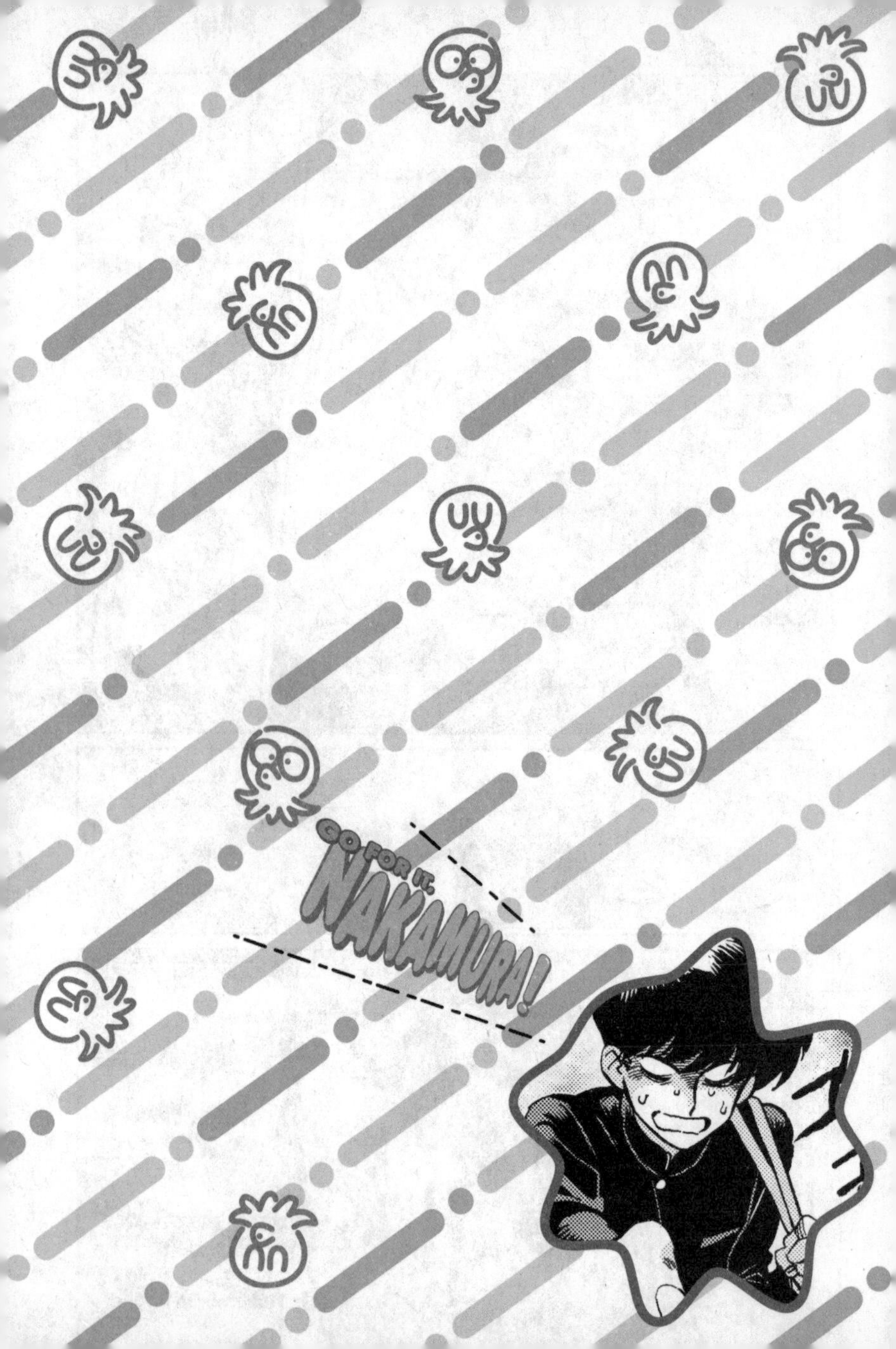
GO FOR IT, NAKAMURA!

Chapter 2 The Cultural Festival Surprise! ☆

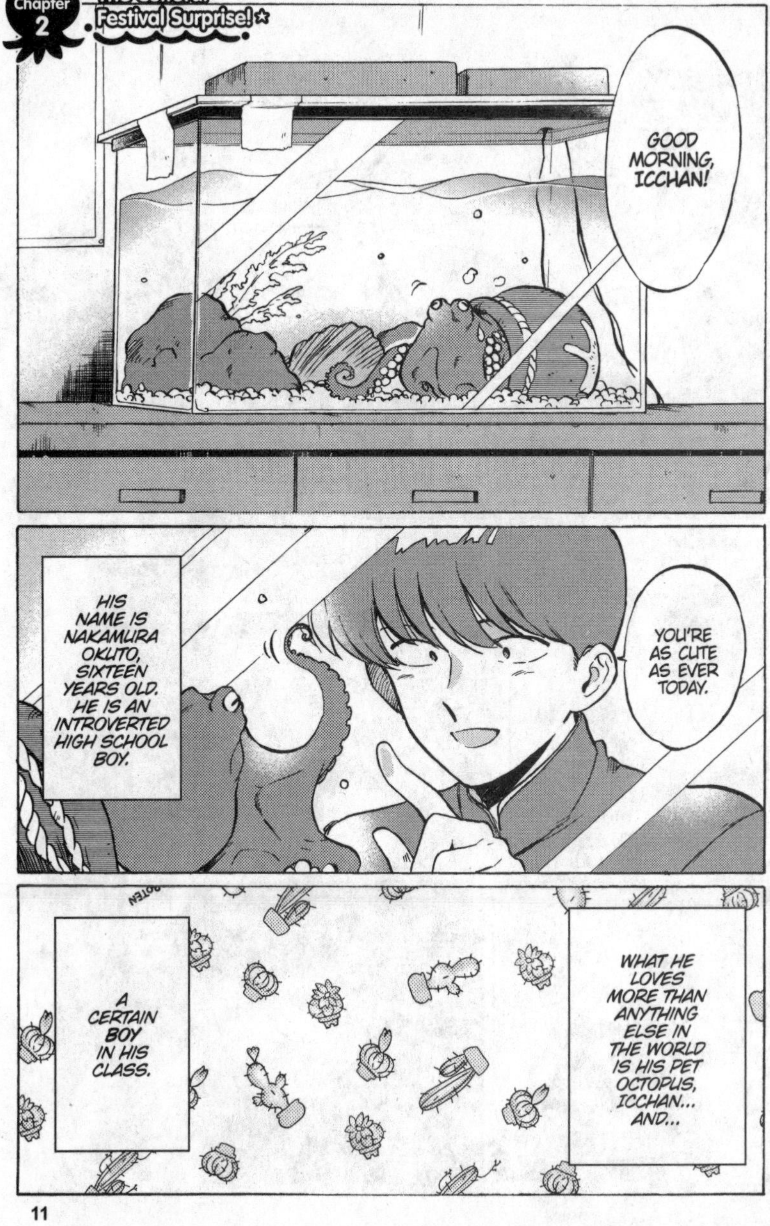

GOOD MORNING, ICCHAN!
YOU'RE AS CUTE AS EVER TODAY.
HIS NAME IS NAKAMURA OKUTO, SIXTEEN YEARS OLD. HE IS AN INTROVERTED HIGH SCHOOL BOY.
WHAT HE LOVES MORE THAN ANYTHING ELSE IN THE WORLD IS HIS PET OCTOPUS, ICCHAN... AND...
A CERTAIN BOY IN HIS CLASS.

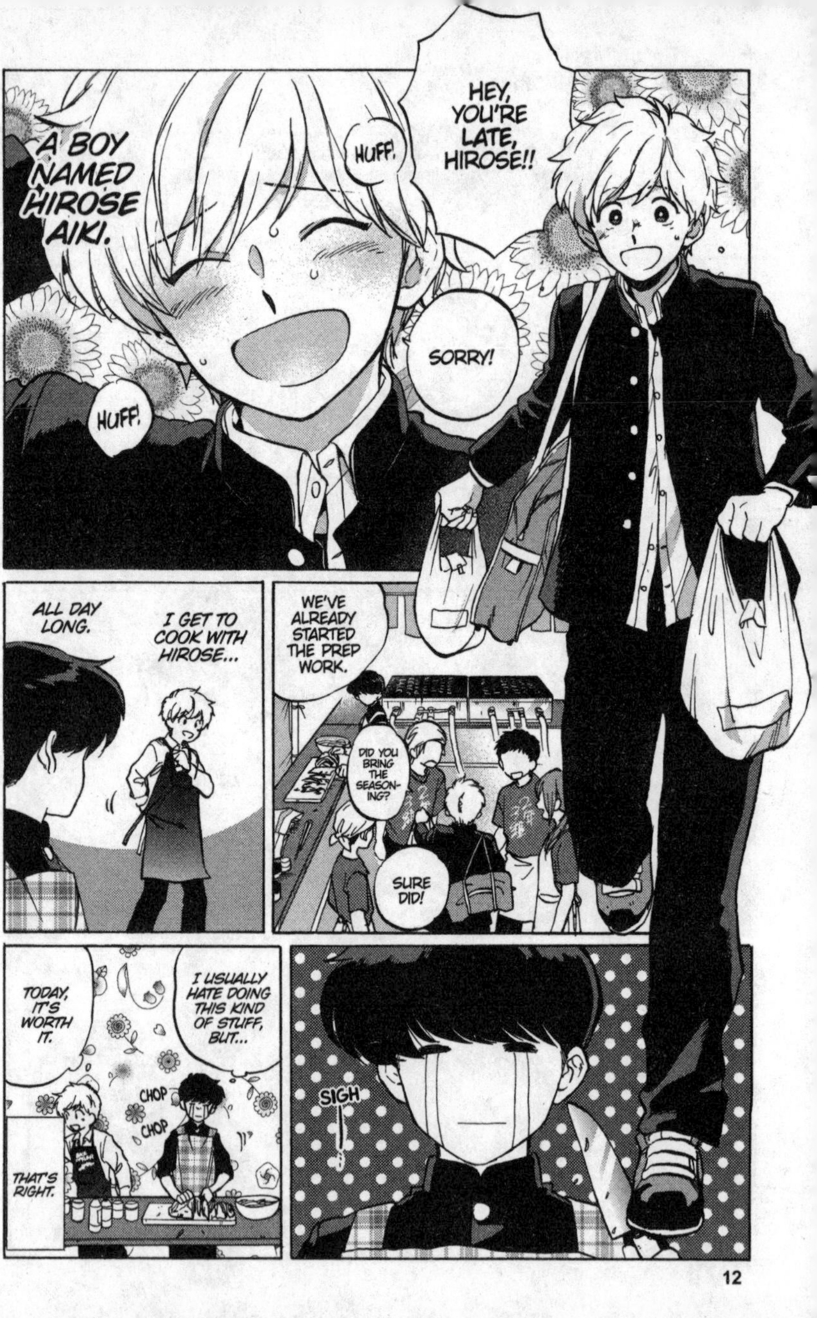
HEY, YOU'RE LATE, HIROSE!!
HUFF!
SORRY!
HUFF!
A BOY NAMED HIROSE AIKI.
WE'VE ALREADY STARTED THE PREP WORK.
DID YOU BRING THE SEASON-ING?
SURE DID!
I GET TO COOK WITH HIROSE...
ALL DAY LONG.
SIGH
I USUALLY HATE DOING THIS KIND OF STUFF, BUT...
TODAY, IT'S WORTH IT.
CHOP
CHOP
THAT'S RIGHT.

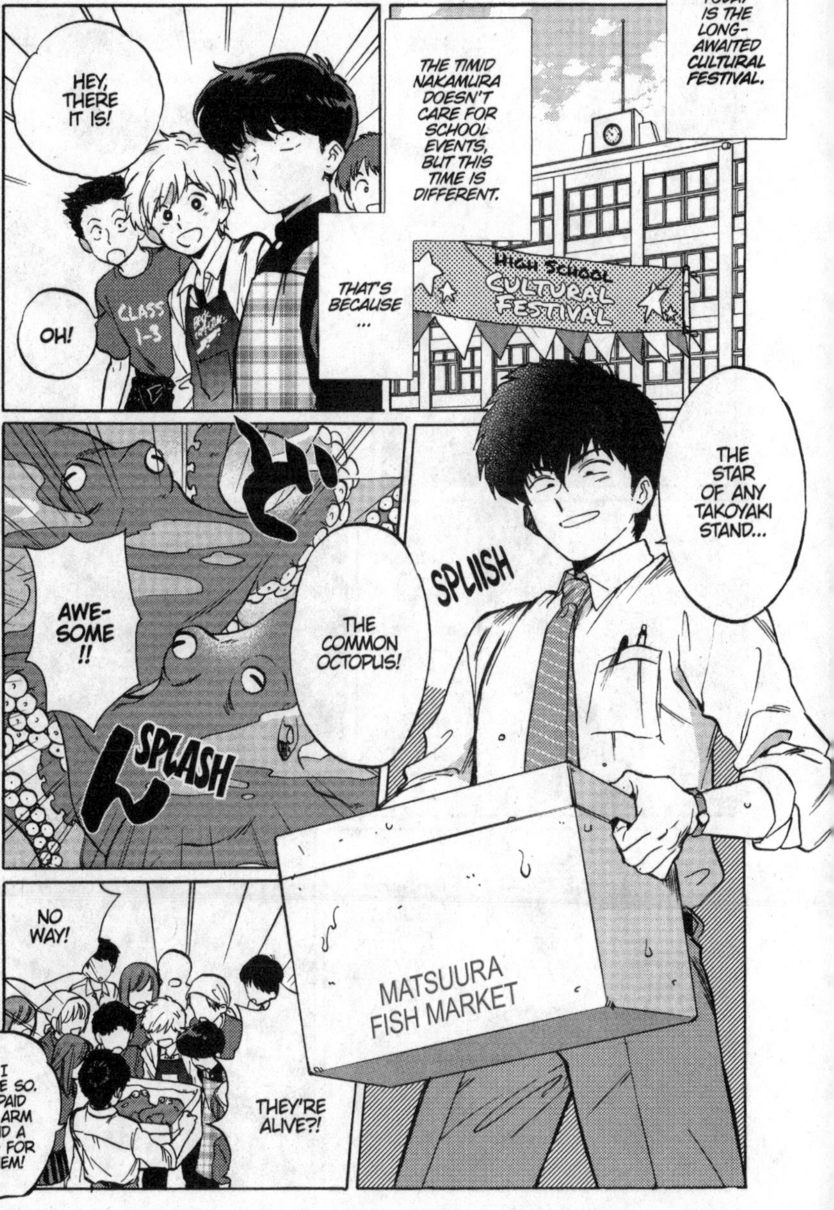
TODAY IS THE LONG-AWAITED CULTURAL FESTIVAL.
THE TIMID NAKAMURA DOESN'T CARE FOR SCHOOL EVENTS, BUT THIS TIME IS DIFFERENT.
THAT'S BECAUSE ...
HIGH SCHOOL CULTURAL FESTIVAL
HEY, THERE IT IS!
CLASS 1-3
OH!
THE STAR OF ANY TAKOYAKI STAND...
SPLIISH
THE COMMON OCTOPUS!
MATSUURA FISH MARKET
AWE-SOME !!
SPLASH
NO WAY!
THEY'RE ALIVE?!
I HOPE SO. I PAID AN ARM AND A LEG FOR THEM!

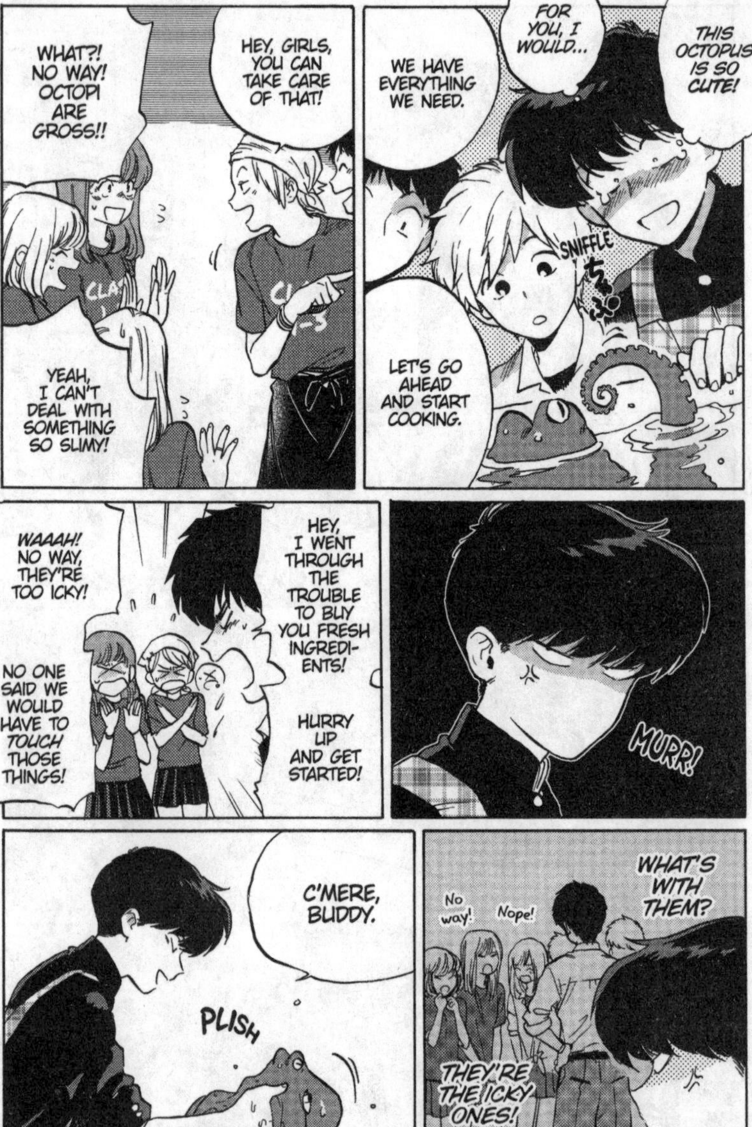
THIS OCTOPUS IS SO CUTE!
FOR YOU, I WOULD...
SNIFFLE
WE HAVE EVERYTHING WE NEED.
LET'S GO AHEAD AND START COOKING.
HEY, GIRLS, YOU CAN TAKE CARE OF THAT!
WHAT?! NO WAY! OCTOPI ARE GROSS!!
YEAH, I CAN'T DEAL WITH SOMETHING SO SLIMY!
MURR!
HEY, I WENT THROUGH THE TROUBLE TO BUY YOU FRESH INGREDI-ENTS!
HURRY UP AND GET STARTED!
WAAAH! NO WAY, THEY'RE TOO ICKY!
NO ONE SAID WE WOULD HAVE TO TOUCH THOSE THINGS!
WHAT'S WITH THEM?
Nope!
No way!
THEY'RE THE ICKY ONES!
C'MERE, BUDDY.
PLISH

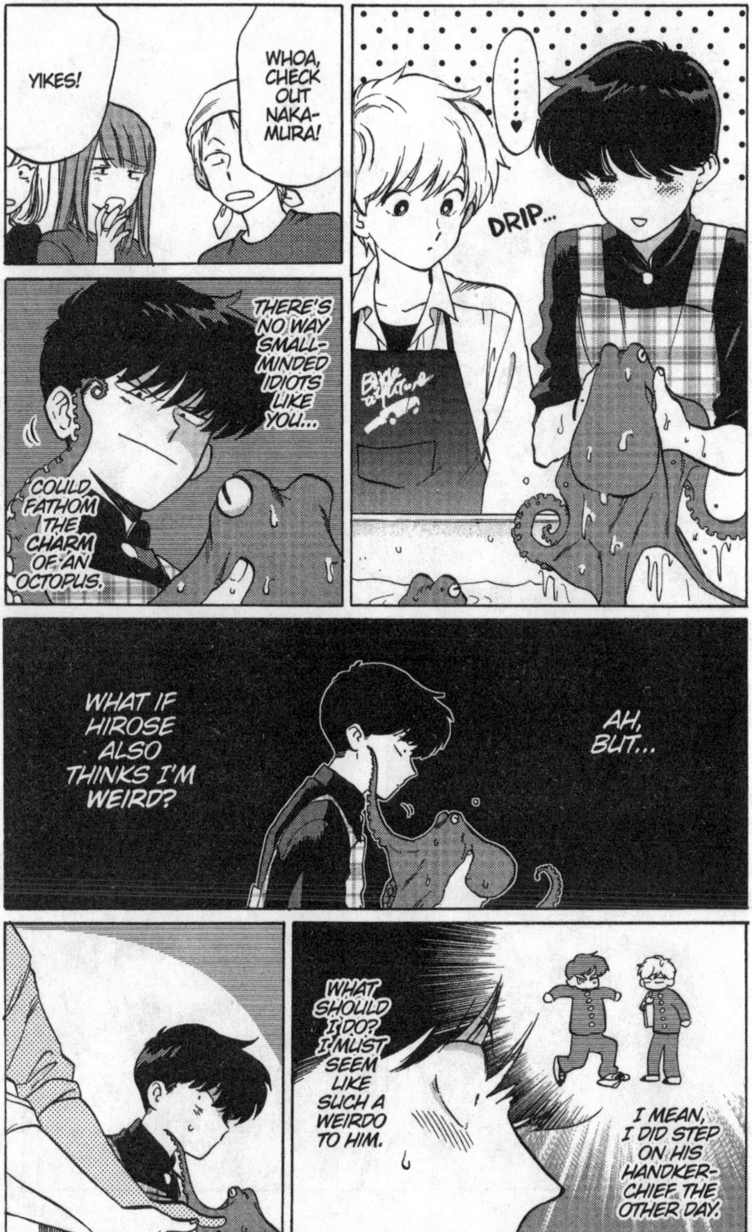
......♥
DRIP...
WHOA, CHECK OUT NAKA-MURA!
YIKES!
THERE'S NO WAY SMALL-MINDED IDIOTS LIKE YOU...
COULD FATHOM THE CHARM OF AN OCTOPUS.
AH, BUT...
WHAT IF HIROSE ALSO THINKS I'M WEIRD?
I MEAN, I DID STEP ON HIS HANDKER-CHIEF THE OTHER DAY.
WHAT SHOULD I DO? I MUST SEEM LIKE SUCH A WEIRDO TO HIM.

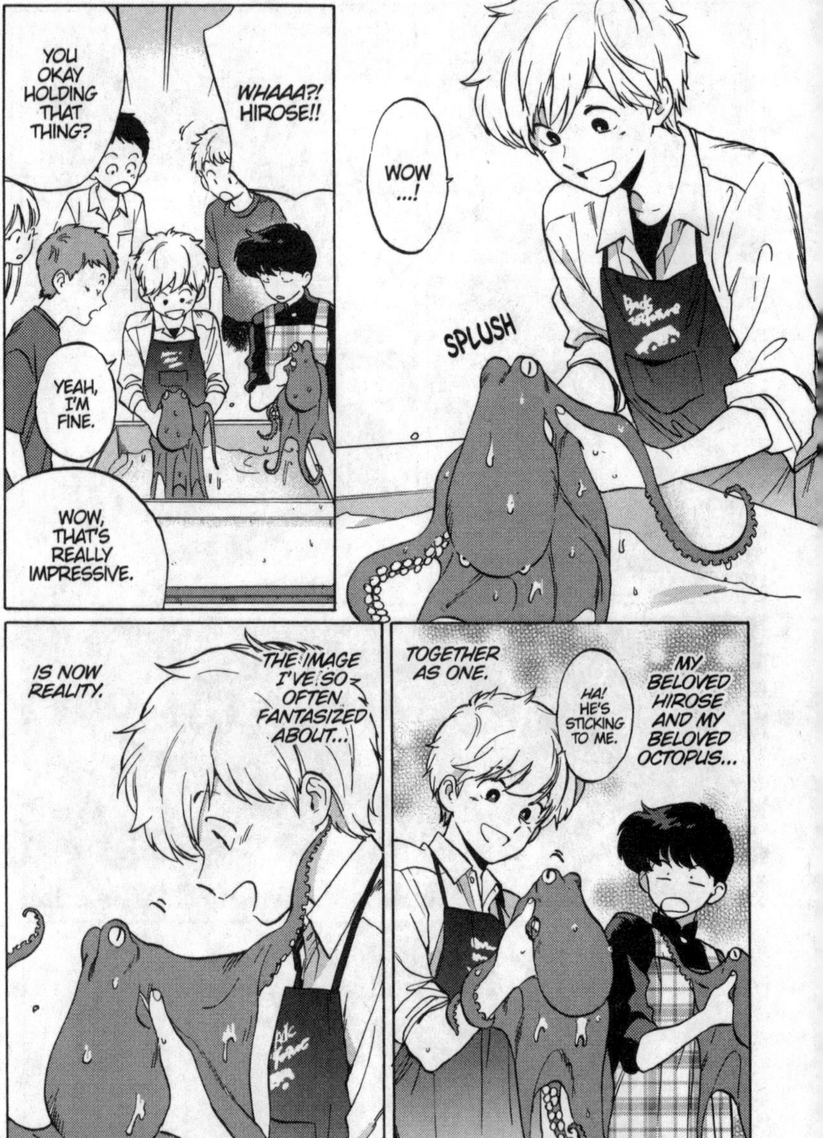
WOW ...!
SPLUSH
WHAAA?! HIROSE!!
YOU OKAY HOLDING THAT THING?
YEAH, I'M FINE.
WOW, THAT'S REALLY IMPRESSIVE.
MY BELOVED HIROSE AND MY BELOVED OCTOPUS...
HA! HE'S STICKING TO ME.
TOGETHER AS ONE.
THE IMAGE I'VE SO OFTEN FANTASIZED ABOUT...
IS NOW REALITY.

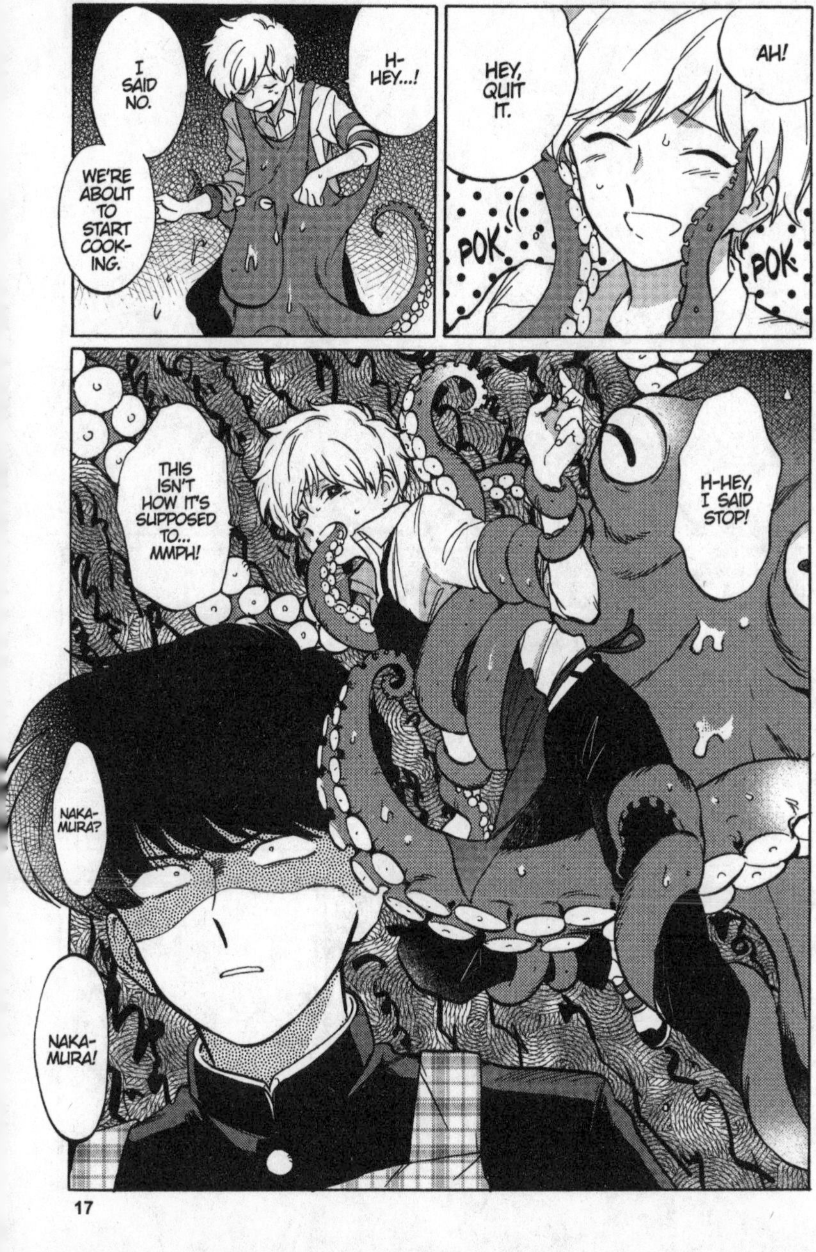
AH!
HEY, QUIT IT.
POK
POK
H- HEY...!
I SAID NO.
WE'RE ABOUT TO START COOK- ING.
H-HEY, I SAID STOP!
THIS ISN'T HOW IT'S SUPPOSED TO... MMPH!
NAKA- MURA?
NAKA- MURA!

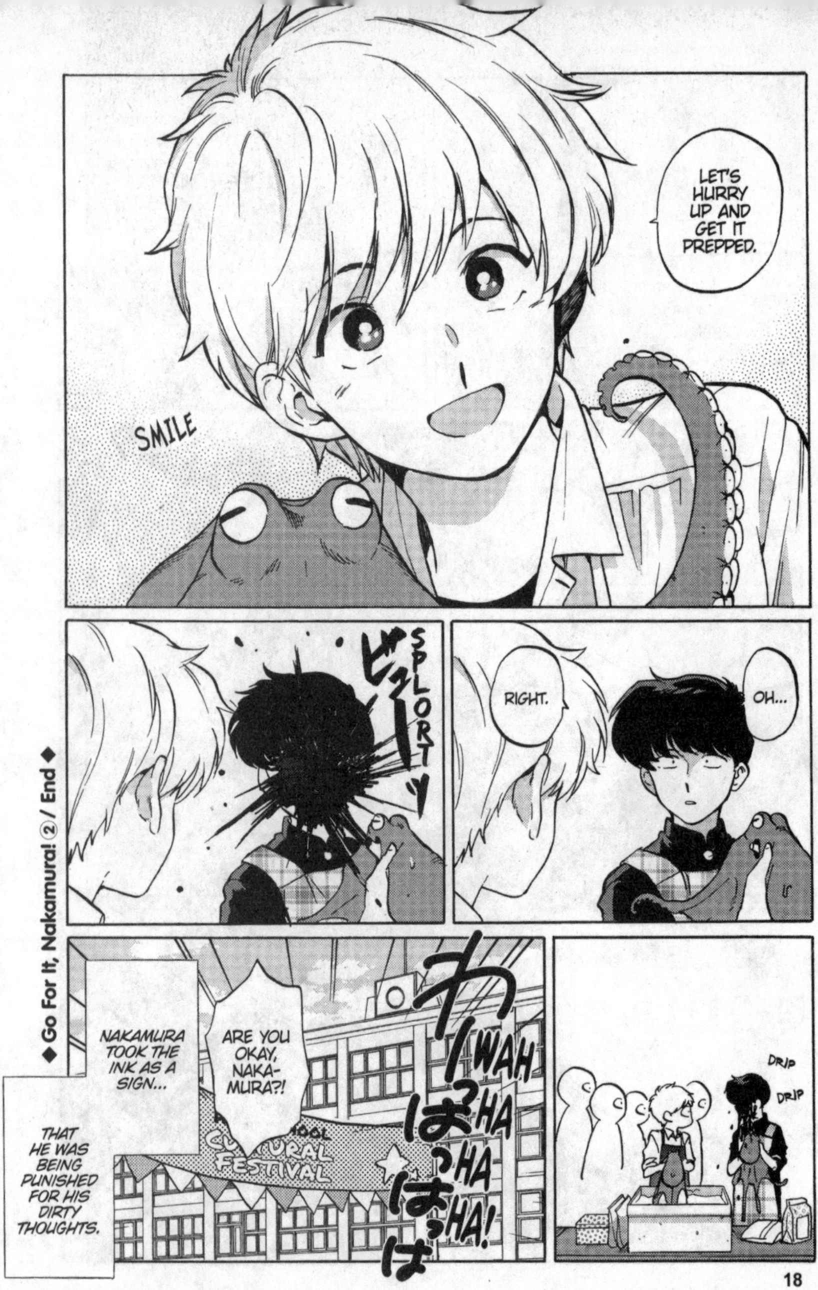
LET'S HURRY UP AND GET IT PREPPED.
SMILE
OH...
RIGHT.
SPLORT
DRIP
DRIP
WAH HA HA HA!
ARE YOU OKAY, NAKA-MURA?!
NAKAMURA TOOK THE INK AS A SIGN...
THAT HE WAS BEING PUNISHED FOR HIS DIRTY THOUGHTS.

◆ Go For It, Nakamura! ② / End ◆

Chapter 3 His Dating Guide is a Boys' Love Manga?!

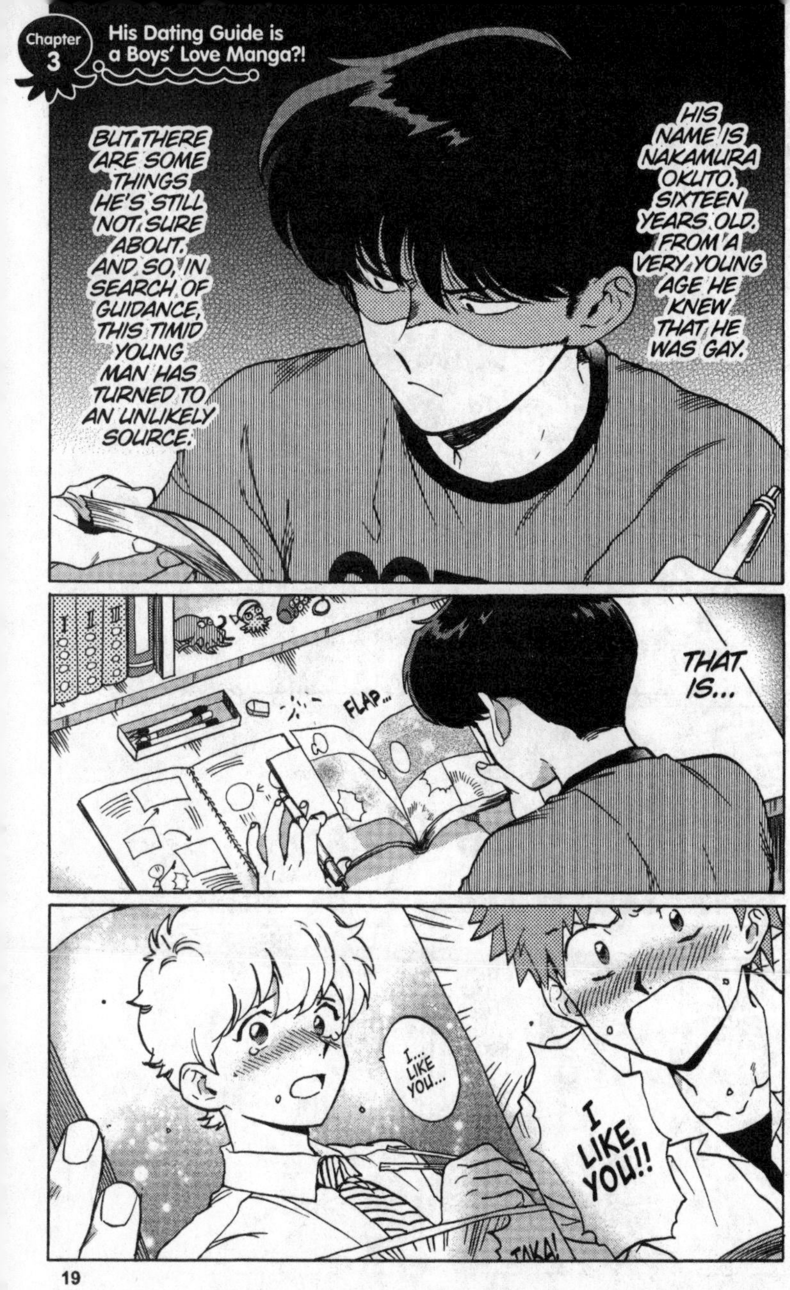
HIS NAME IS NAKAMURA OKUTO. SIXTEEN YEARS OLD. FROM A VERY YOUNG AGE HE KNEW THAT HE WAS GAY.
BUT THERE ARE SOME THINGS HE'S STILL NOT SURE ABOUT. AND SO, IN SEARCH OF GUIDANCE, THIS TIMID YOUNG MAN HAS TURNED TO AN UNLIKELY SOURCE.
THAT IS...
FLAP...
I LIKE YOU!!
I... LIKE YOU...
TAKA!

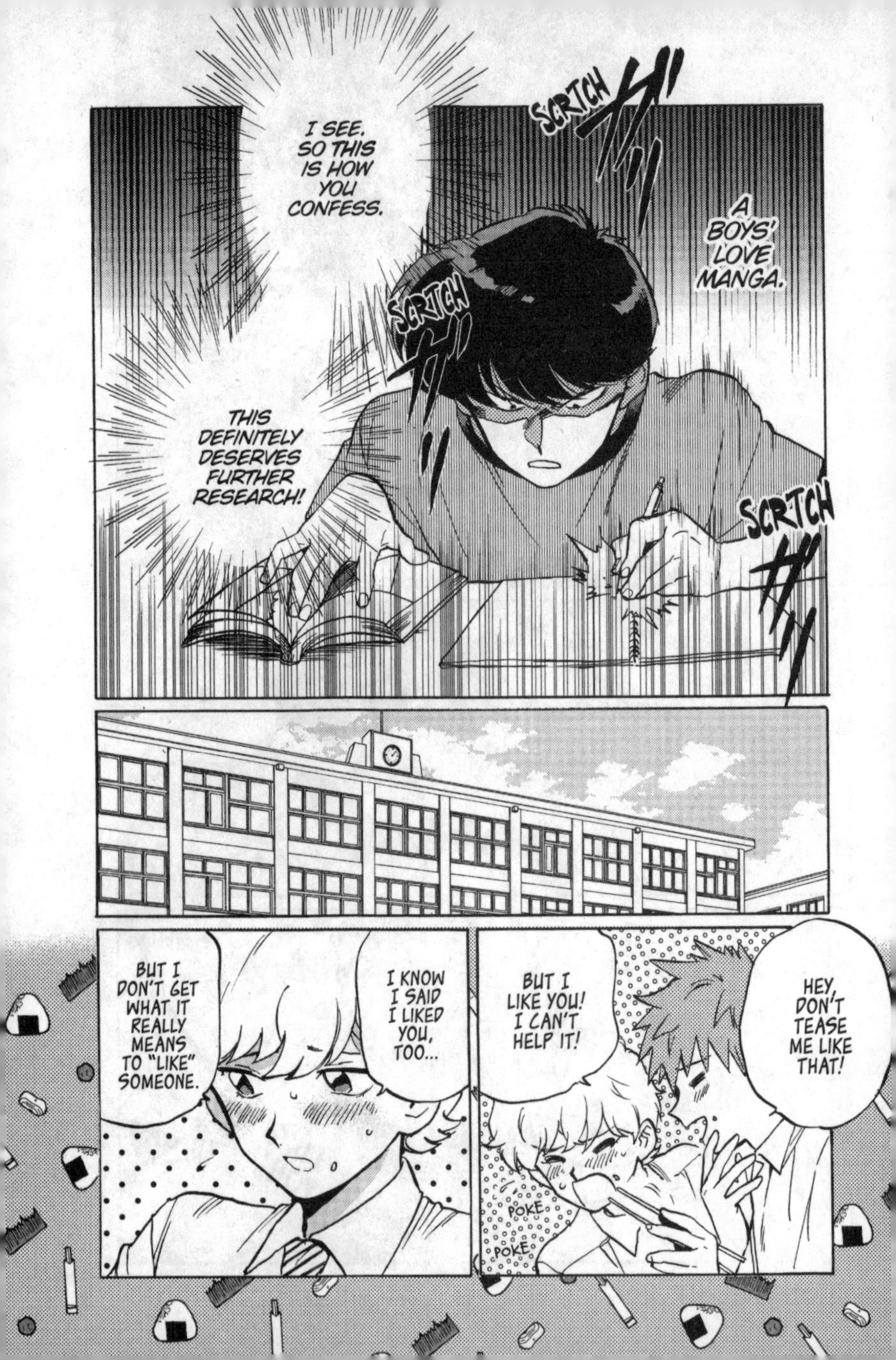
SCRTCH
A BOYS' LOVE MANGA.
I SEE. SO THIS IS HOW YOU CONFESS.
SCRTCH
THIS DEFINITELY DESERVES FURTHER RESEARCH!
SCRTCH
HEY, DON'T TEASE ME LIKE THAT!
BUT I LIKE YOU! I CAN'T HELP IT!
POKE
POKE
I KNOW I SAID I LIKED YOU, TOO...
BUT I DON'T GET WHAT IT REALLY MEANS TO "LIKE" SOMEONE.

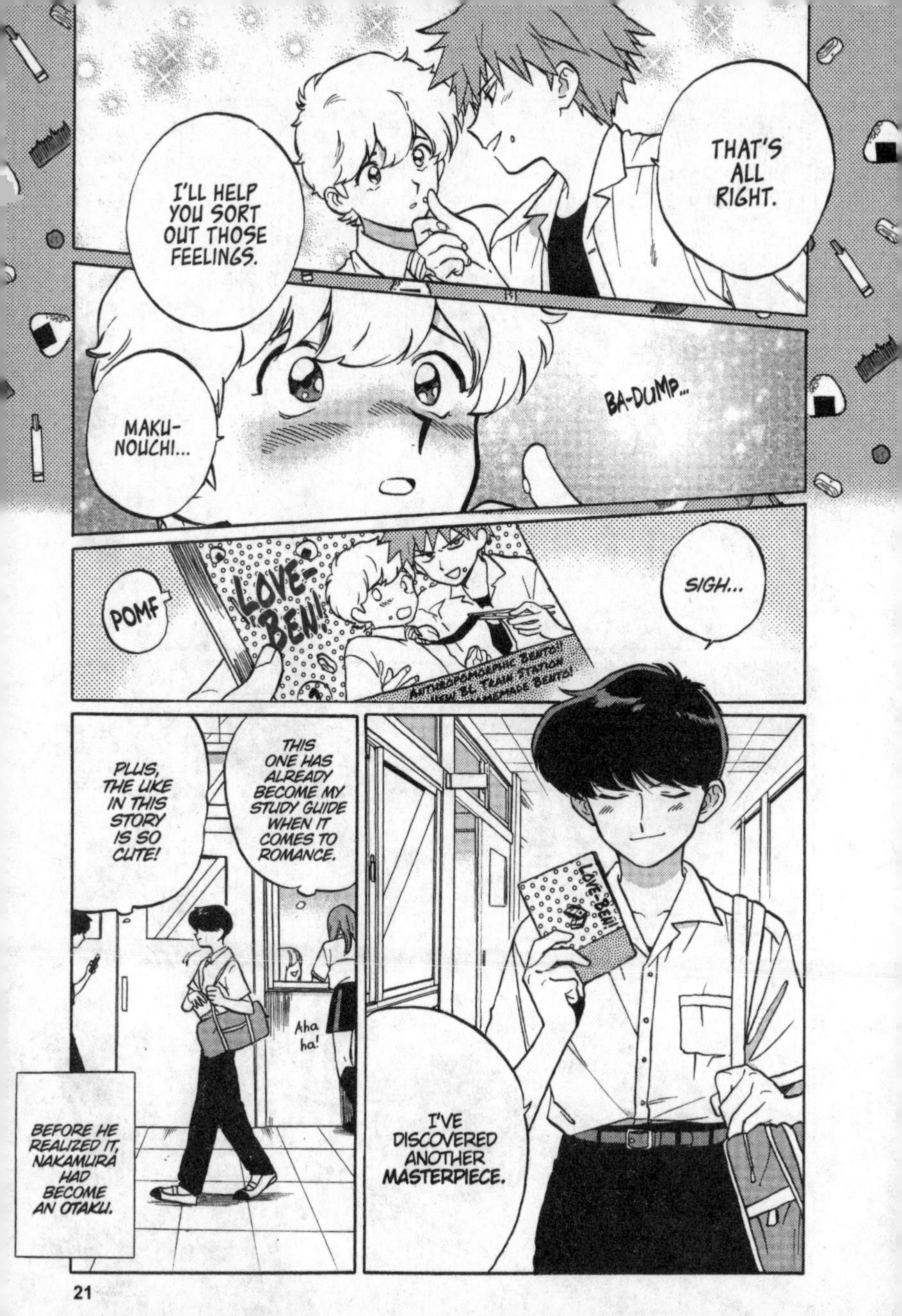
THAT'S ALL RIGHT.
I'LL HELP YOU SORT OUT THOSE FEELINGS.
BA-DUMP...
MAKU-NOUCHI...
SIGH...
LOVE-BEN!!
POMF
ANTHROPOMORPHIC BENTO!!
I'VE DISCOVERED ANOTHER MASTERPIECE.
THIS ONE HAS ALREADY BECOME MY STUDY GUIDE WHEN IT COMES TO ROMANCE.
PLUS, THE LIKE IN THIS STORY IS SO CUTE!
Aha ha!
BEFORE HE REALIZED IT, NAKAMURA HAD BECOME AN OTAKU.

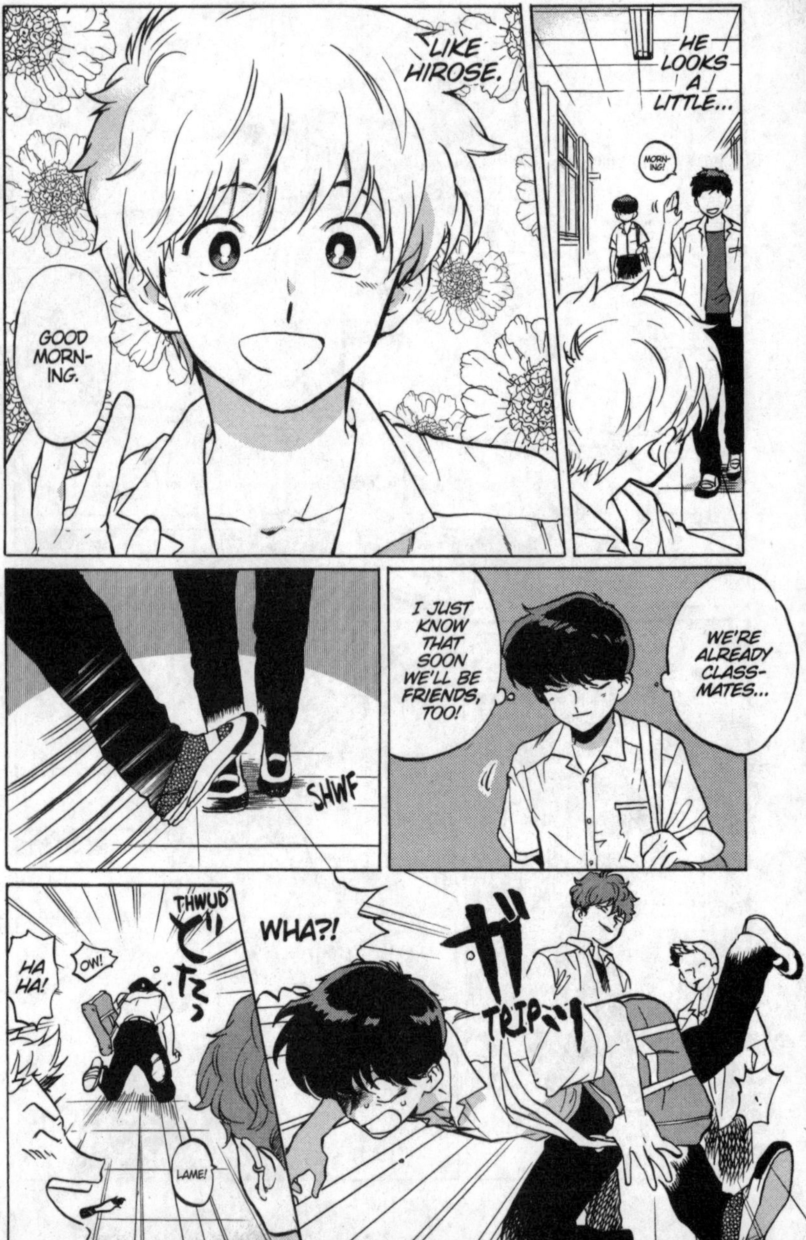
HE LOOKS A LITTLE...
MORNING!
LIKE HIROSE.
GOOD MORNING.
WE'RE ALREADY CLASSMATES...
I JUST KNOW THAT SOON WE'LL BE FRIENDS, TOO!
SHWF
WHA?!
TRIP
THWUD
OW!
HA HA!
LAME!

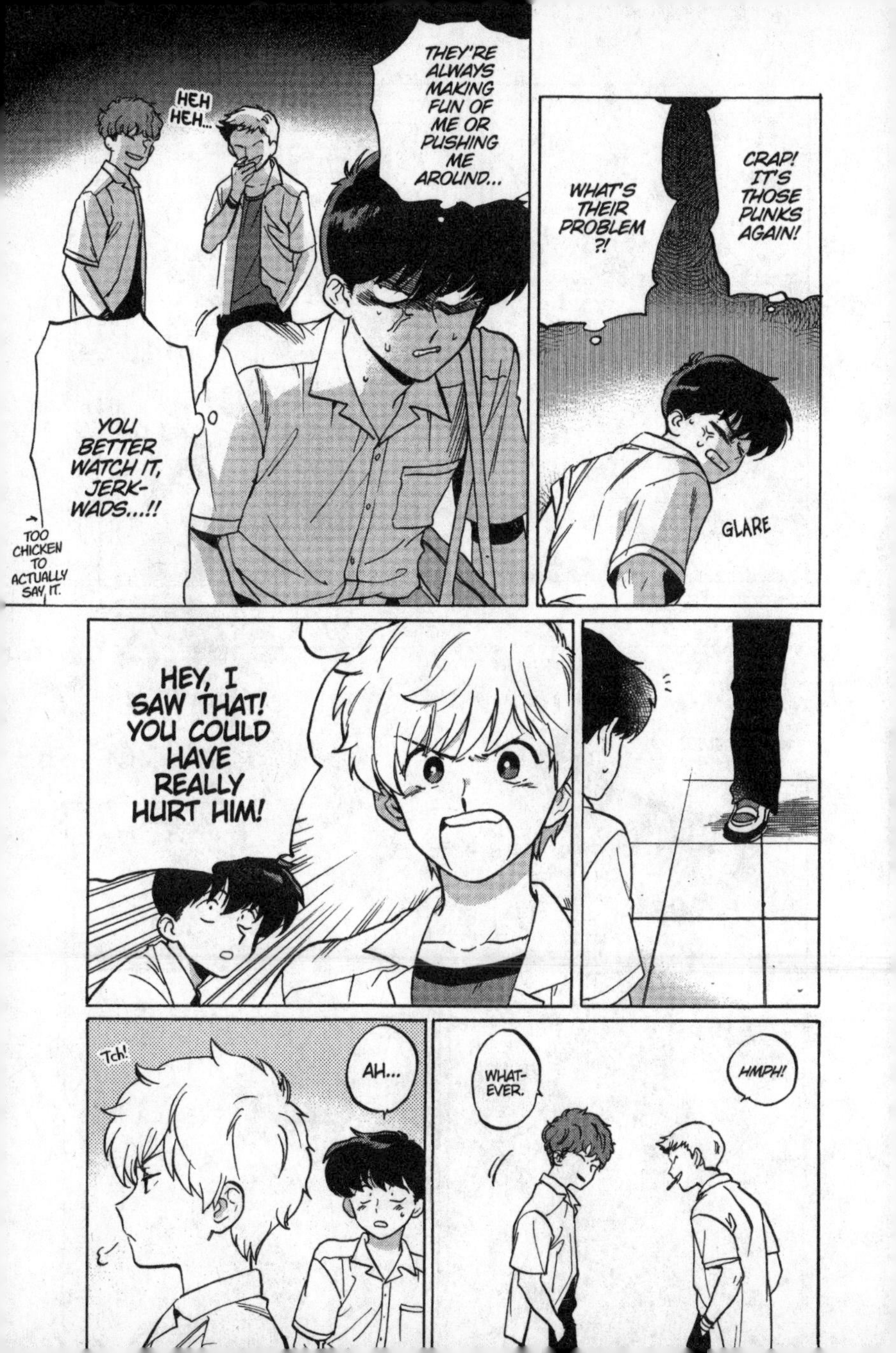
CRAP! IT'S THOSE PUNKS AGAIN!
WHAT'S THEIR PROBLEM ?!
GLARE
THEY'RE ALWAYS MAKING FUN OF ME OR PUSHING ME AROUND...
HEH HEH...
YOU BETTER WATCH IT, JERK-WADS...!!
TOO CHICKEN TO ACTUALLY SAY IT.
HEY, I SAW THAT! YOU COULD HAVE REALLY HURT HIM!
HMPH!
WHAT-EVER.
AH...
Tch!

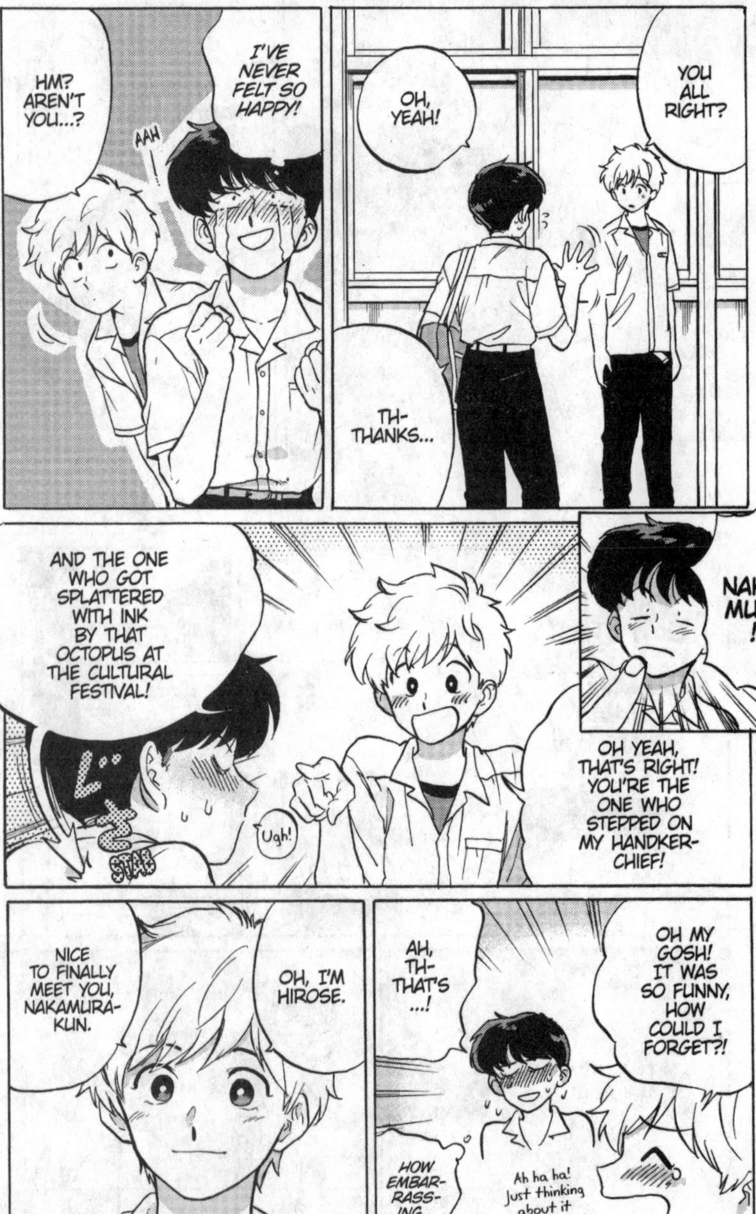
YOU ALL RIGHT?
OH, YEAH!
TH- THANKS...
I'VE NEVER FELT SO HAPPY!
AAH
HM? AREN'T YOU...?
NAKA-MURA!!
OH YEAH, THAT'S RIGHT! YOU'RE THE ONE WHO STEPPED ON MY HANDKER-CHIEF!
AND THE ONE WHO GOT SPLATTERED WITH INK BY THAT OCTOPUS AT THE CULTURAL FESTIVAL!
Ugh!
STAB
OH MY GOSH! IT WAS SO FUNNY, HOW COULD I FORGET?!
AH, TH- THAT'S ...!
Ah ha ha! Just thinking about it cracks me up!
HOW EMBAR-RASS-ING...
OH, I'M HIROSE.
NICE TO FINALLY MEET YOU, NAKAMURA-KUN.

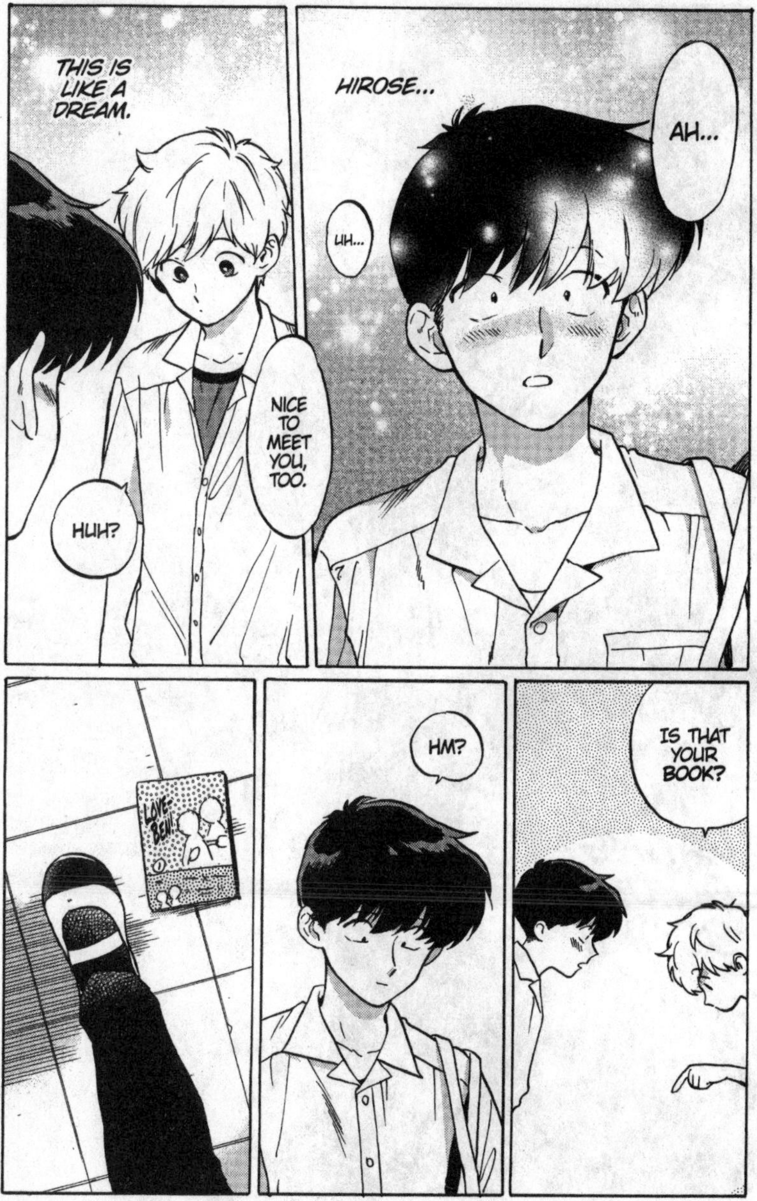
AH...
HIROSE...
UH...
THIS IS LIKE A DREAM.
NICE TO MEET YOU, TOO.
HUH?
IS THAT YOUR BOOK?
HM?
LOVE BEN!

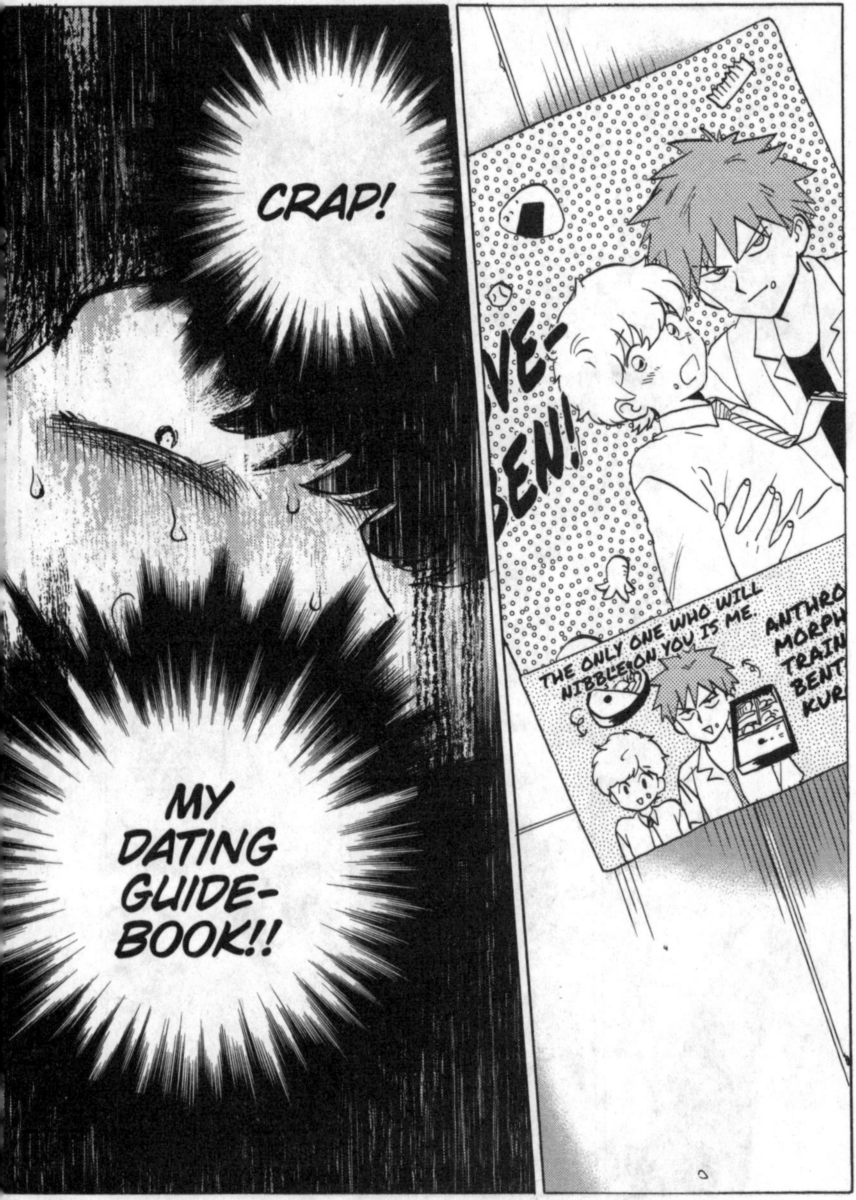
VE-
BEN!
THE ONLY ONE WHO WILL NIBBLE ON YOU IS ME.
ANTHRO
MORPH
TRAIN
BENT
KUR
CRAP!
MY DATING GUIDE-BOOK!!

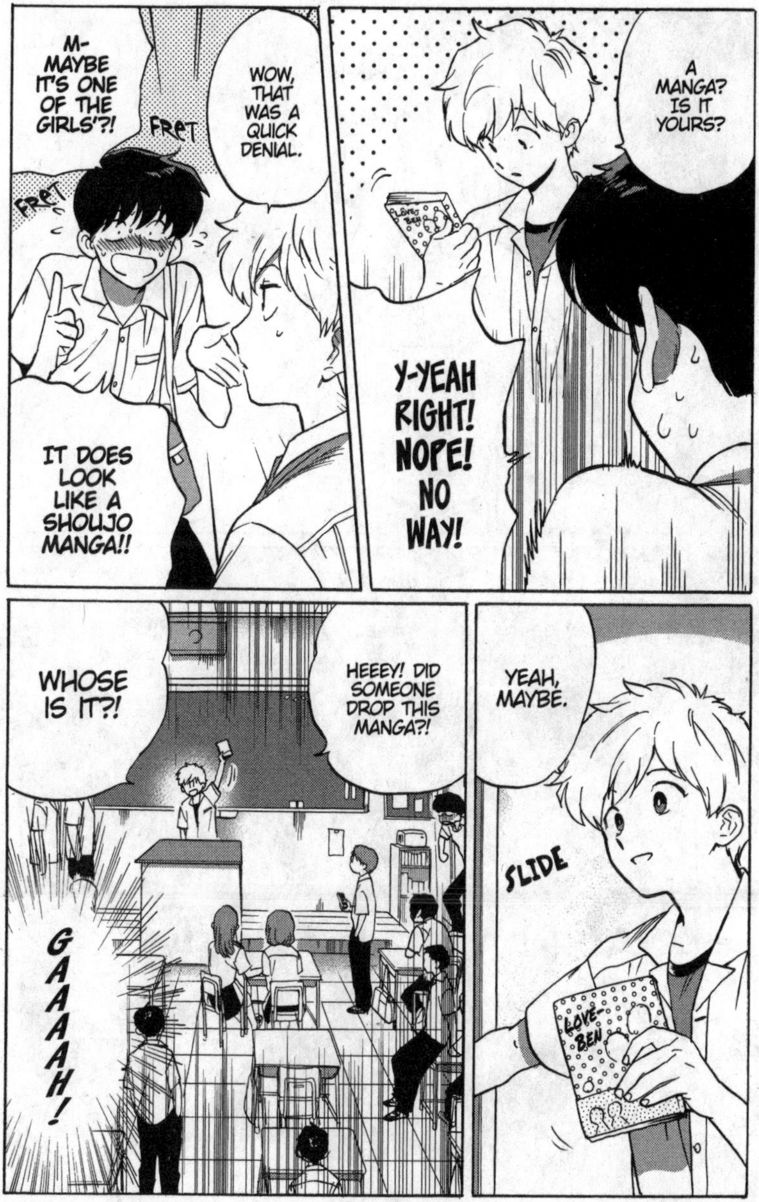
A MANGA? IS IT YOURS?
LOVE BEN
Y-YEAH RIGHT! NOPE! NO WAY!
WOW, THAT WAS A QUICK DENIAL.
M-MAYBE IT'S ONE OF THE GIRLS'?!
FRET
FRET
IT DOES LOOK LIKE A SHOUJO MANGA!!
YEAH, MAYBE.
SLIDE
LOVE-BEN
HEEEY! DID SOMEONE DROP THIS MANGA?!
WHOSE IS IT?!
GAAAAAH!

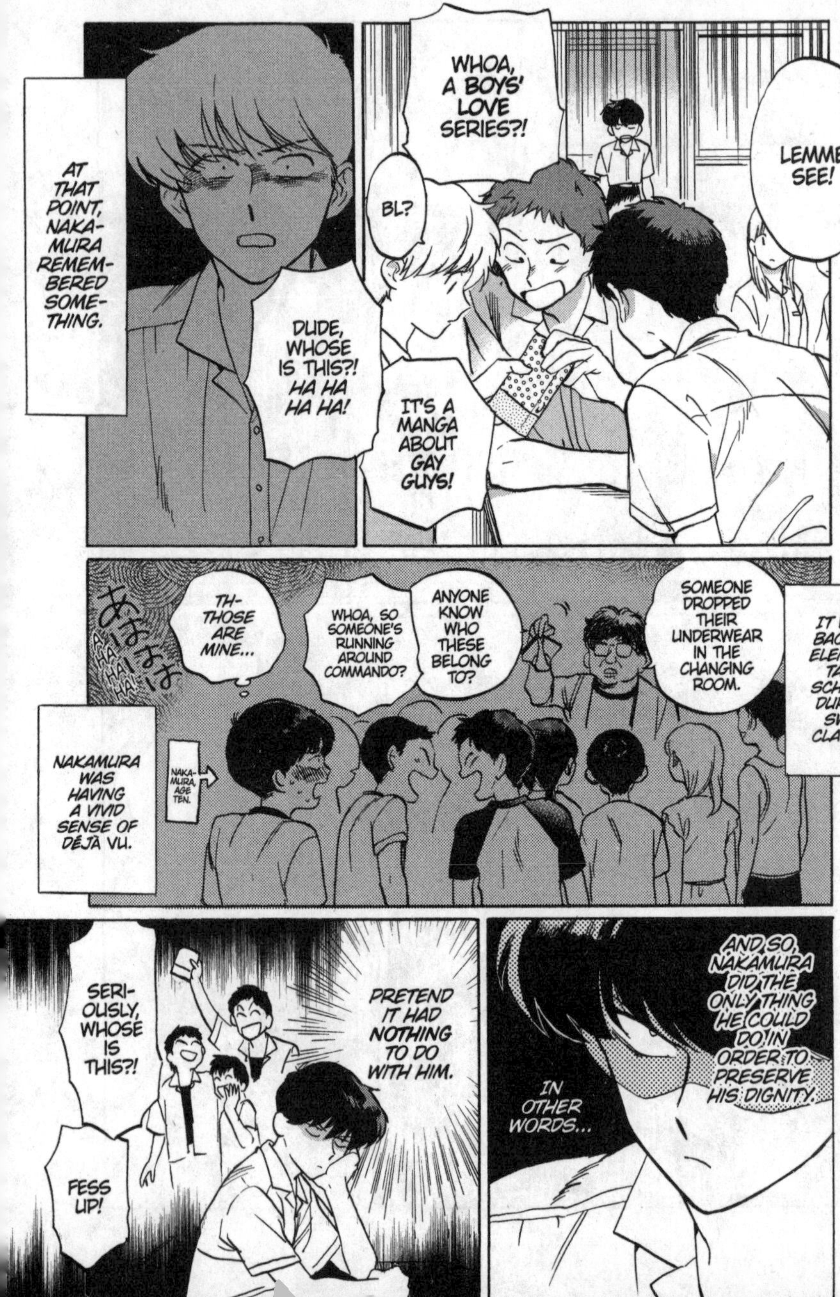
LEMME SEE!
WHOA, A BOYS' LOVE SERIES?!
BL?
DUDE, WHOSE IS THIS?! HA HA HA HA!
IT'S A MANGA ABOUT GAY GUYS!
AT THAT POINT, NAKAMURA REMEMBERED SOMETHING.
IT WAS BACK IN ELEMENTARY SCHOOL, DURING SWIM CLASS...
SOMEONE DROPPED THEIR UNDERWEAR IN THE CHANGING ROOM.
ANYONE KNOW WHO THESE BELONG TO?
WHOA, SO SOMEONE'S RUNNING AROUND COMMANDO?
TH-THOSE ARE MINE...
あははははは
A HA HA HA!
NAKAMURA, AGE TEN.
NAKAMURA WAS HAVING A VIVID SENSE OF DÉJÀ VU.
AND SO, NAKAMURA DID THE ONLY THING HE COULD DO IN ORDER TO PRESERVE HIS DIGNITY.
IN OTHER WORDS...
PRETEND IT HAD NOTHING TO DO WITH HIM.
SERIOUSLY, WHOSE IS THIS?!
FESS UP!

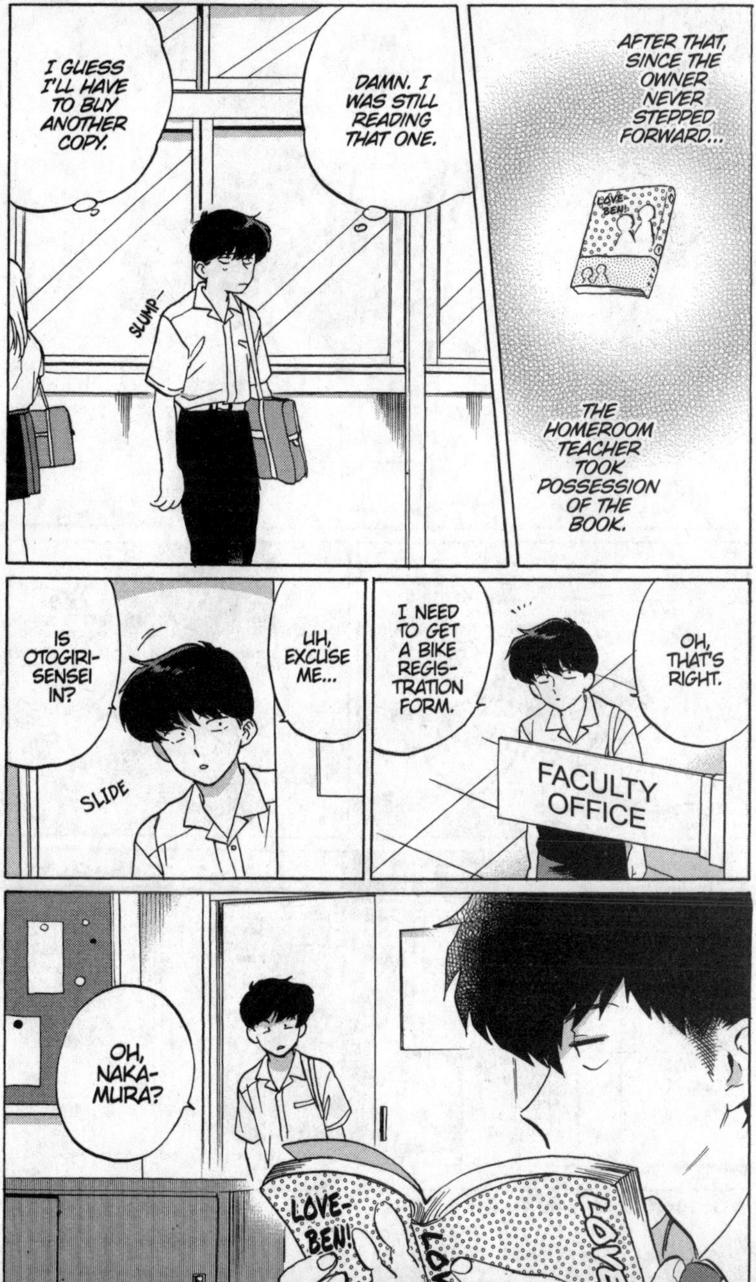
AFTER THAT, SINCE THE OWNER NEVER STEPPED FORWARD...
LOVE-BEN!
THE HOMEROOM TEACHER TOOK POSSESSION OF THE BOOK.
DAMN. I WAS STILL READING THAT ONE.
I GUESS I'LL HAVE TO BUY ANOTHER COPY.
SLUMP—
OH, THAT'S RIGHT.
I NEED TO GET A BIKE REGISTRATION FORM.
FACULTY OFFICE
UH, EXCUSE ME...
IS OTOGIRI-SENSEI IN?
SLIDE
OH, NAKAMURA?
LOVE-BEN!
LOVE
LOV

WHAT'S UP?
HE'S READING IT!
SENSEI, THAT'S...!
OH, SOMEONE LEFT IT BEHIND. IT'S PRETTY INTEREST-ING!
IT'S SOME WEIRD SHOUJO MANGA.
THE OWNER IS PROBABLY TOO EMBAR-RASSED TO COME AND COLLECT IT.
STILL, THOUGH ...
FLIP
FLIP
FLIP
LOVE-BEN!
THEY'RE GOING TO GET REALLY WARPED IDEAS ABOUT ROMANCE IF THIS IS ALL THEY READ!
They're both boys, after all!
SHUT UP!
No one asked you!
AFTER THAT, NAKAMURA STOPPED USING BOYS' LOVE MANGA AS DATING GUIDES.
I DIDN'T REALIZE VOLUME TWO WAS OUT ALREADY.
I'M GLAD I STOPPED OFF AT THE BOOK-STORE.
BUT HE STILL READ THEM FOR FUN.

CHAPTER 4

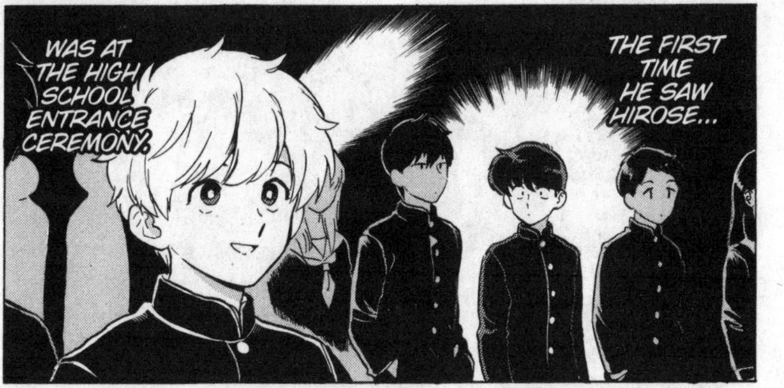
THE FIRST TIME HE SAW HIROSE...
WAS AT THE HIGH SCHOOL ENTRANCE CEREMONY.

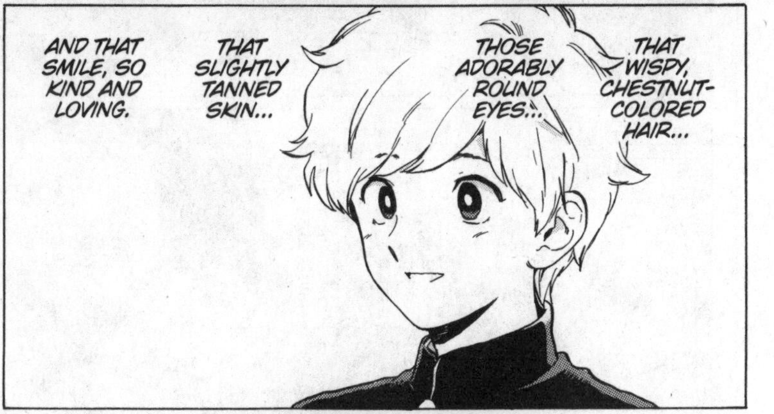
THAT WISPY, CHESTNUT-COLORED HAIR...
THOSE ADORABLY ROUND EYES...
THAT SLIGHTLY TANNED SKIN...
AND THAT SMILE, SO KIND AND LOVING.

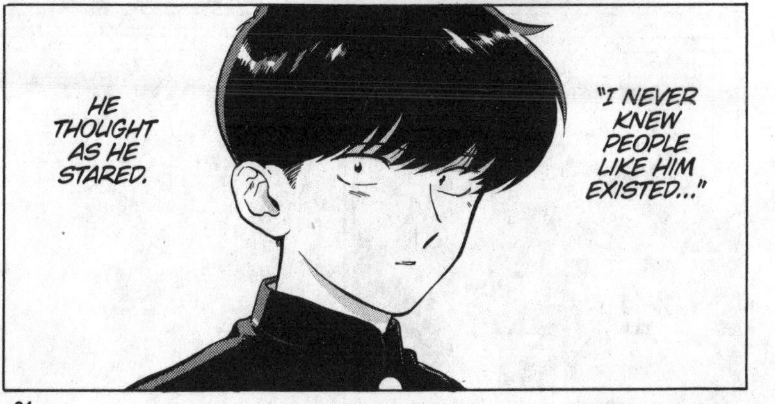
"I NEVER KNEW PEOPLE LIKE HIM EXISTED..."
HE THOUGHT AS HE STARED.

Chapter 4 Art Can Be This Intense?!

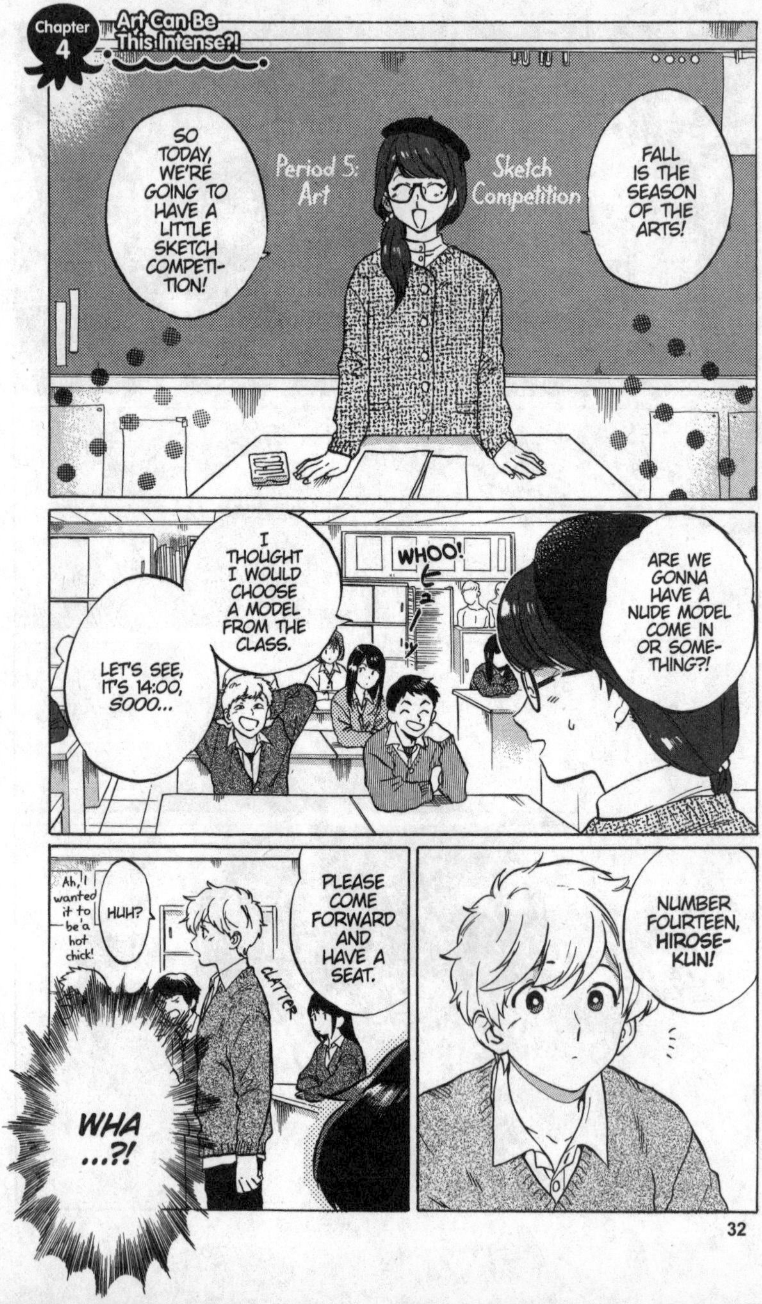

FALL IS THE SEASON OF THE ARTS!
Sketch Competition
Period 5: Art
SO TODAY, WE'RE GOING TO HAVE A LITTLE SKETCH COMPETITION!
ARE WE GONNA HAVE A NUDE MODEL COME IN OR SOMETHING?!
WHOO!
I THOUGHT I WOULD CHOOSE A MODEL FROM THE CLASS.
LET'S SEE, IT'S 14:00, SOOO...
NUMBER FOURTEEN, HIROSE-KUN!
PLEASE COME FORWARD AND HAVE A SEAT.
CLATTER
HUH?
Ah, I wanted it to be a hot chick!
WHA...?!

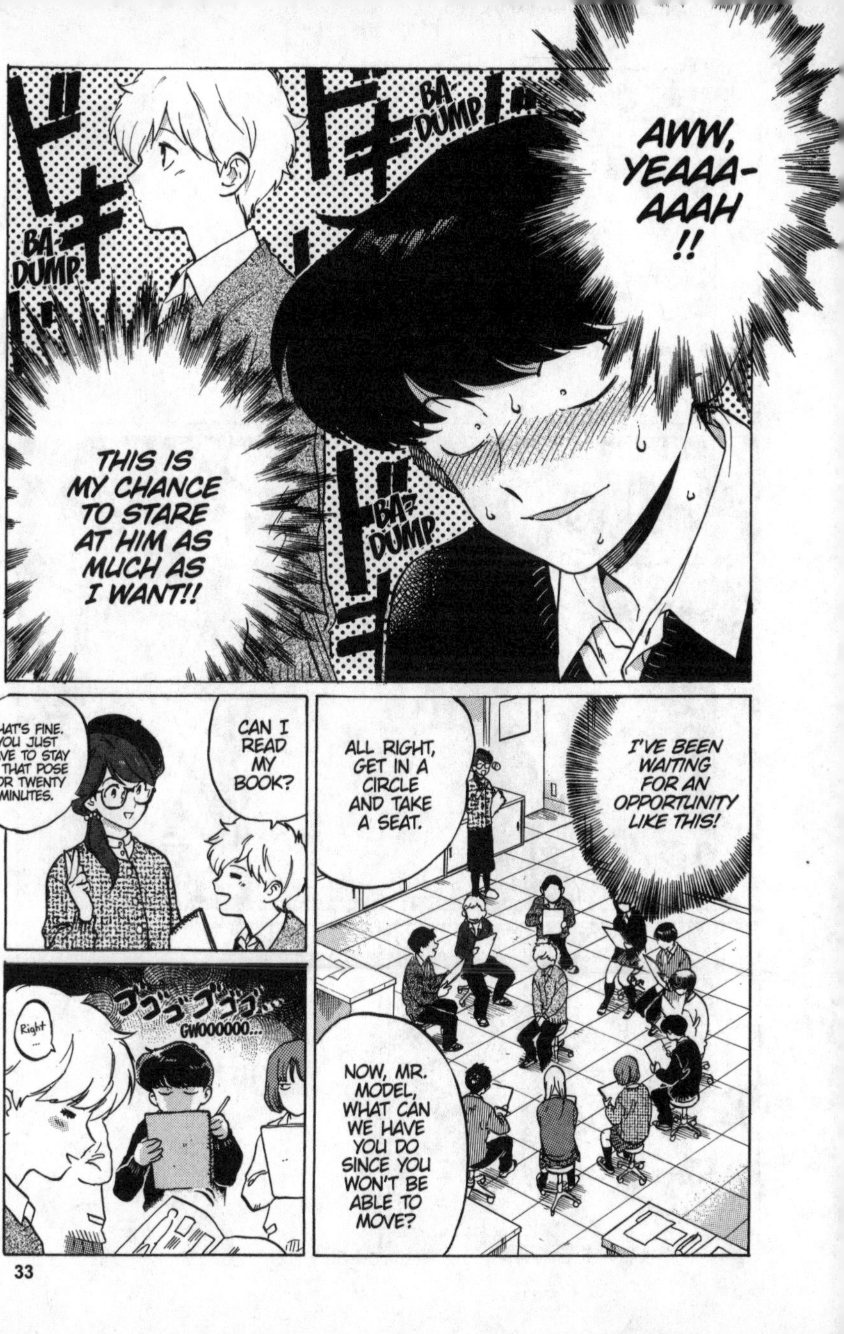
AWW, YEAAAA-AAAH!!
BA-DUMP
BA-DUMP
BA-DUMP
THIS IS MY CHANCE TO STARE AT HIM AS MUCH AS I WANT!!
I'VE BEEN WAITING FOR AN OPPORTUNITY LIKE THIS!
ALL RIGHT, GET IN A CIRCLE AND TAKE A SEAT.
NOW, MR. MODEL, WHAT CAN WE HAVE YOU DO SINCE YOU WON'T BE ABLE TO MOVE?
CAN I READ MY BOOK?
THAT'S FINE. YOU JUST HAVE TO STAY IN THAT POSE FOR TWENTY MINUTES.
GWOOOOOO...
Right...

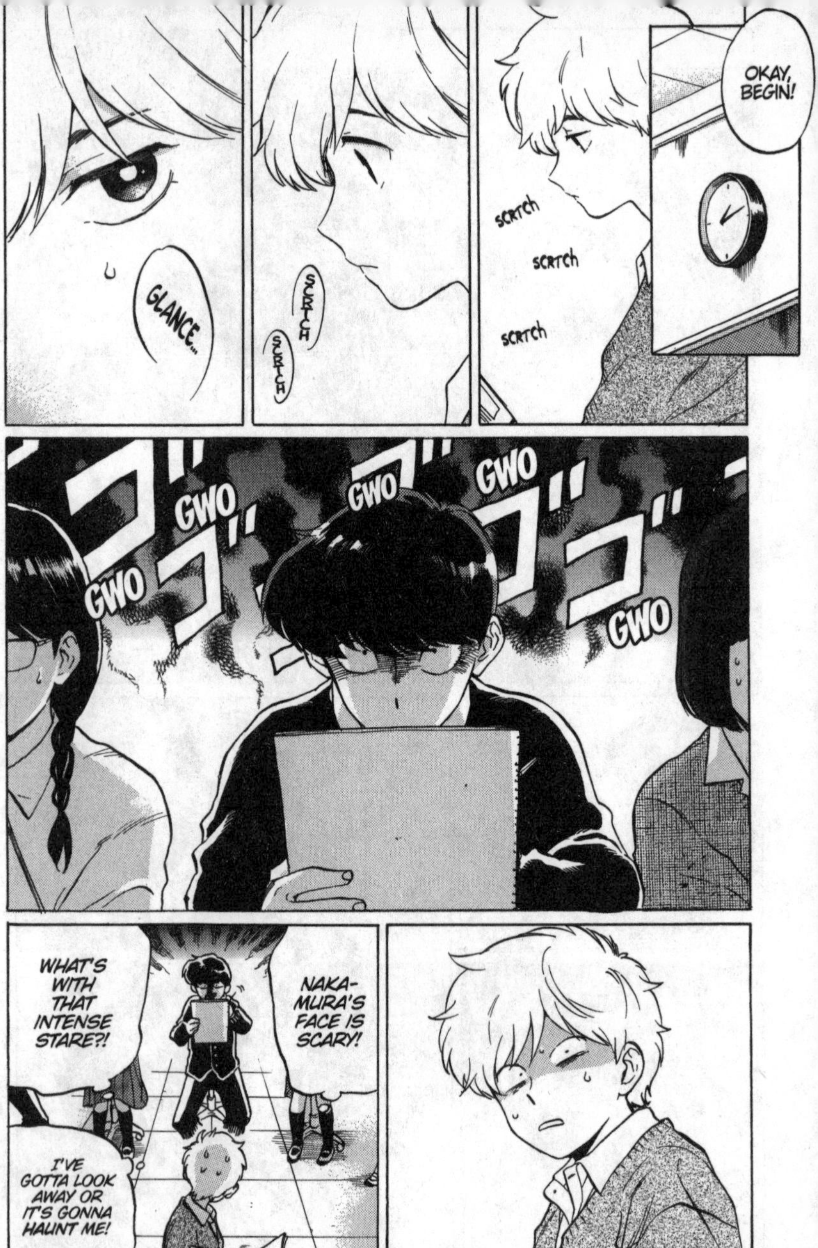

OKAY, BEGIN!
SCRTCH
SCRTCH
SCRTCH
SCRTCH
SCRTCH
GLANCE...
GWO
GWO
GWO
GWO
GWO
NAKA-MURA'S FACE IS SCARY!
WHAT'S WITH THAT INTENSE STARE?!
I'VE GOTTA LOOK AWAY OR IT'S GONNA HAUNT ME!

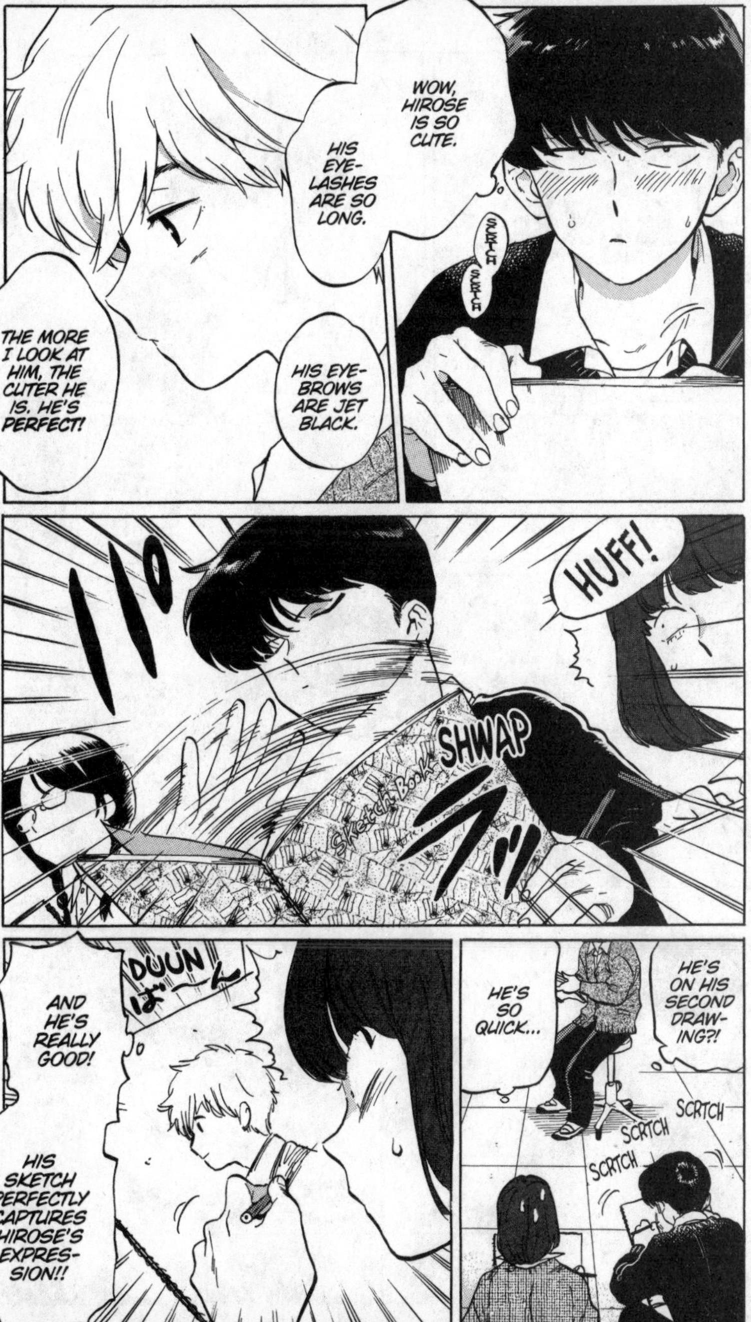
SCRTCH SCRTCH
WOW, HIROSE IS SO CUTE.
HIS EYELASHES ARE SO LONG.
HIS EYEBROWS ARE JET BLACK.
THE MORE I LOOK AT HIM, THE CUTER HE IS. HE'S PERFECT!
HUFF!
SHWAP
Sketch Book
HE'S ON HIS SECOND DRAWING?!
HE'S SO QUICK...
SCRTCH
SCRTCH
SCRTCH
DUUN
ばーん
AND HE'S REALLY GOOD!
HIS SKETCH PERFECTLY CAPTURES HIROSE'S EXPRESSION!!

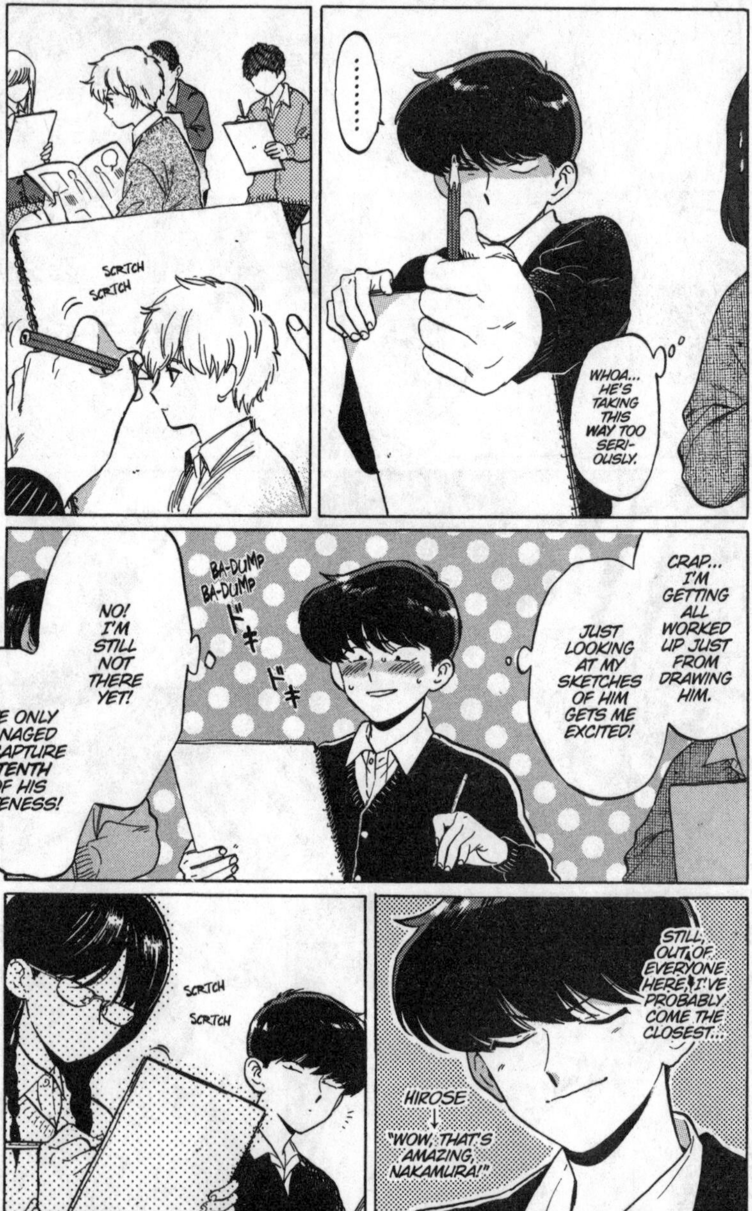
......
WHOA... HE'S TAKING THIS WAY TOO SERI-OUSLY.
SCRTCH
SCRTCH
CRAP... I'M GETTING ALL WORKED UP JUST FROM DRAWING HIM.
JUST LOOKING AT MY SKETCHES OF HIM GETS ME EXCITED!
BA-DUMP BA-DUMP
ドキドキ
NO! I'M STILL NOT THERE YET!
I'VE ONLY MANAGED TO CAPTURE A TENTH OF HIS CUTENESS!
STILL, OUT OF EVERYONE HERE, I'VE PROBABLY COME THE CLOSEST...
HIROSE
"WOW, THAT'S AMAZING, NAKAMURA!"
SCRTCH
SCRTCH

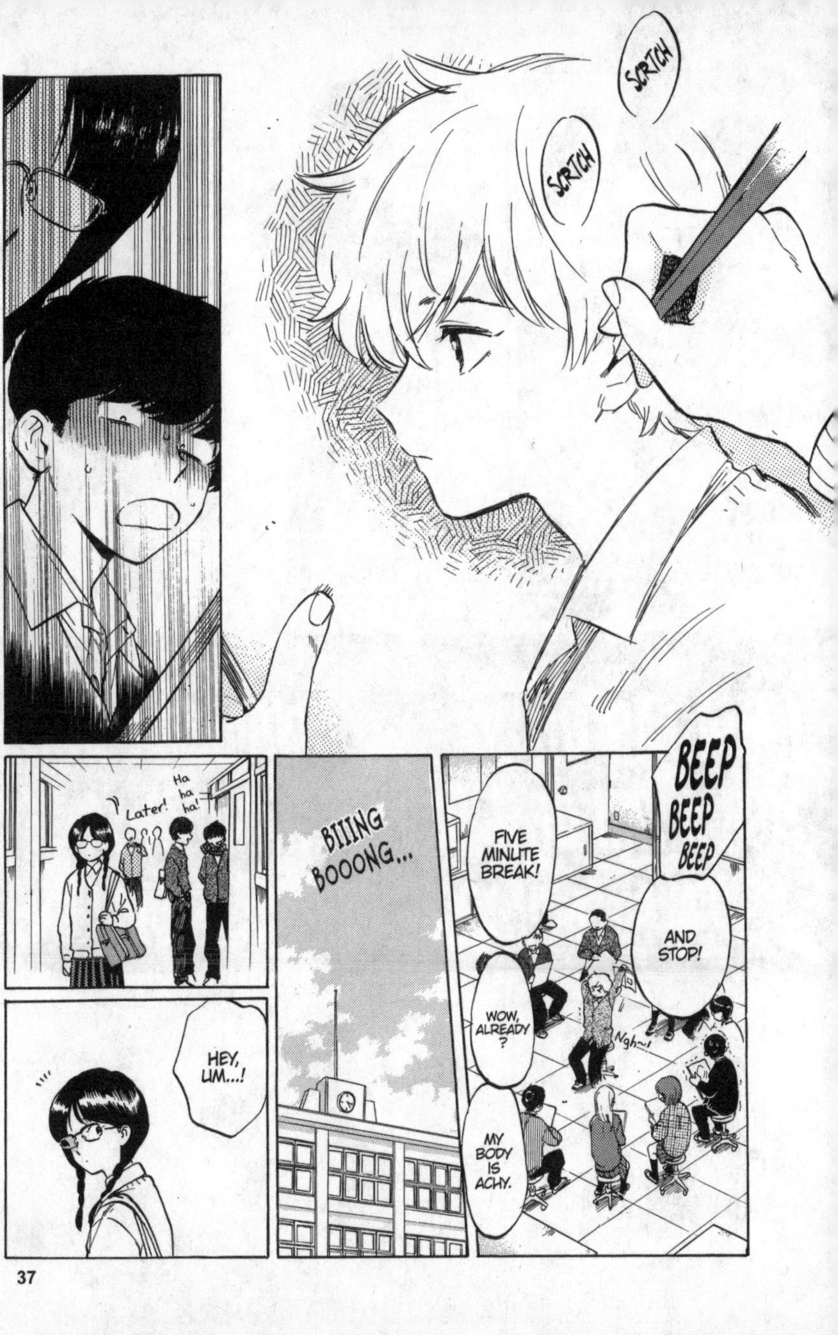
SCRTCH
SCRTCH
BEEP BEEP BEEP
AND STOP!
FIVE MINUTE BREAK!
Ngh~!
WOW, ALREADY?
MY BODY IS ACHY.
BIIING BOOONG...
Ha ha ha!
Later!
HEY, UM...!

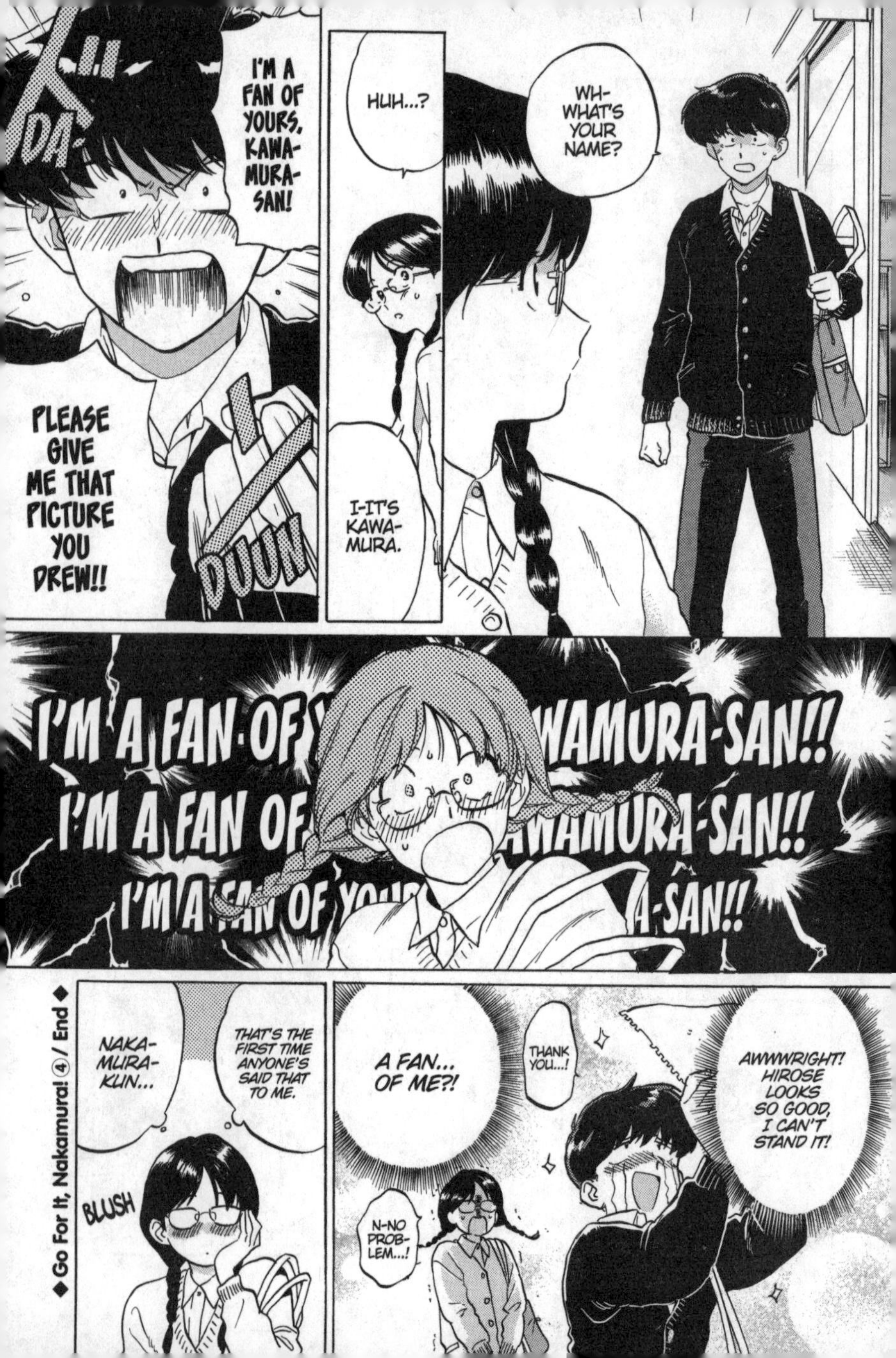
WH-WHAT'S YOUR NAME?
HUH...?
I-IT'S KAWAMURA.
DA-
I'M A FAN OF YOURS, KAWAMURA-SAN!
PLEASE GIVE ME THAT PICTURE YOU DREW!!
DUUN
I'M A FAN OF Y WAMURA-SAN!!
I'M A FAN OF AWAMURA-SAN!!
I'M A FAN OF YOU A-SAN!!
AWWWRIGHT! HIROSE LOOKS SO GOOD, I CAN'T STAND IT!
THANK YOU...!
A FAN... OF ME?!
N-NO PROBLEM...!
THAT'S THE FIRST TIME ANYONE'S SAID THAT TO ME.
NAKAMURA-KUN...
BLUSH

◆Go For It, Nakamura! 4 / End◆

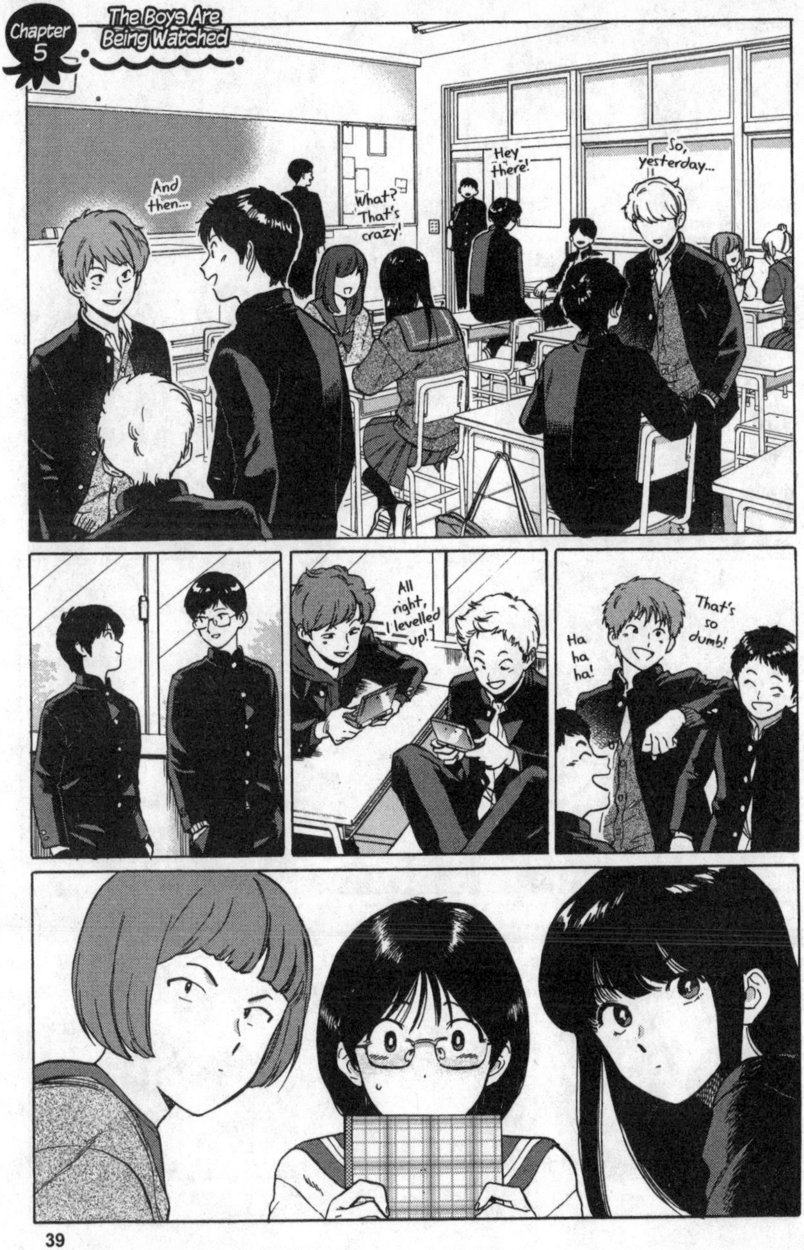
Chapter 5
The Boys Are Being Watched
So, yesterday...
Hey there!
What? That's crazy!
And then...
That's so dumb!
Ha ha ha!
All right, I levelled up!

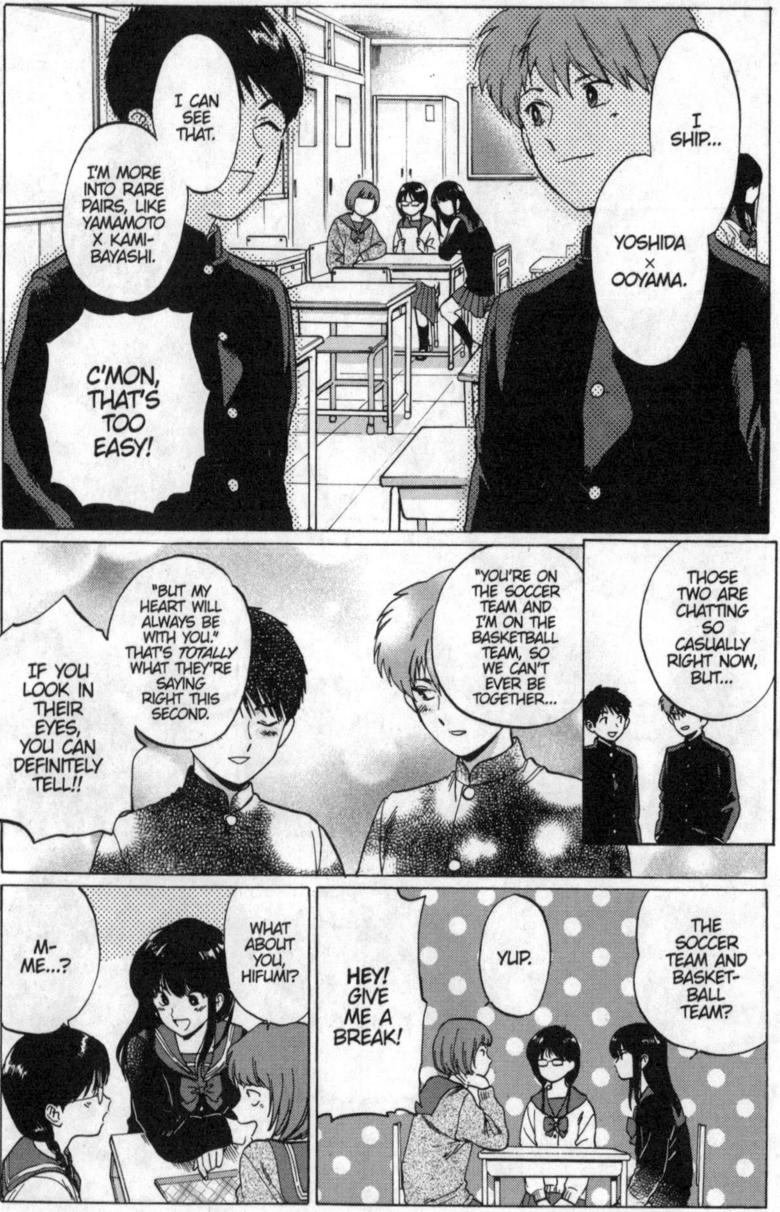
I SHIP...
YOSHIDA × OOYAMA.
I CAN SEE THAT.
I'M MORE INTO RARE PAIRS, LIKE YAMAMOTO X KAMI-BAYASHI.
C'MON, THAT'S TOO EASY!
THOSE TWO ARE CHATTING SO CASUALLY RIGHT NOW, BUT...
"YOU'RE ON THE SOCCER TEAM AND I'M ON THE BASKETBALL TEAM, SO WE CAN'T EVER BE TOGETHER...
"BUT MY HEART WILL ALWAYS BE WITH YOU." THAT'S *TOTALLY* WHAT THEY'RE SAYING RIGHT THIS SECOND.
IF YOU LOOK IN THEIR EYES, YOU CAN DEFINITELY TELL!!
THE SOCCER TEAM AND BASKET-BALL TEAM?
YUP.
HEY! GIVE ME A BREAK!
WHAT ABOUT YOU, HIFUMI?
M-ME...?

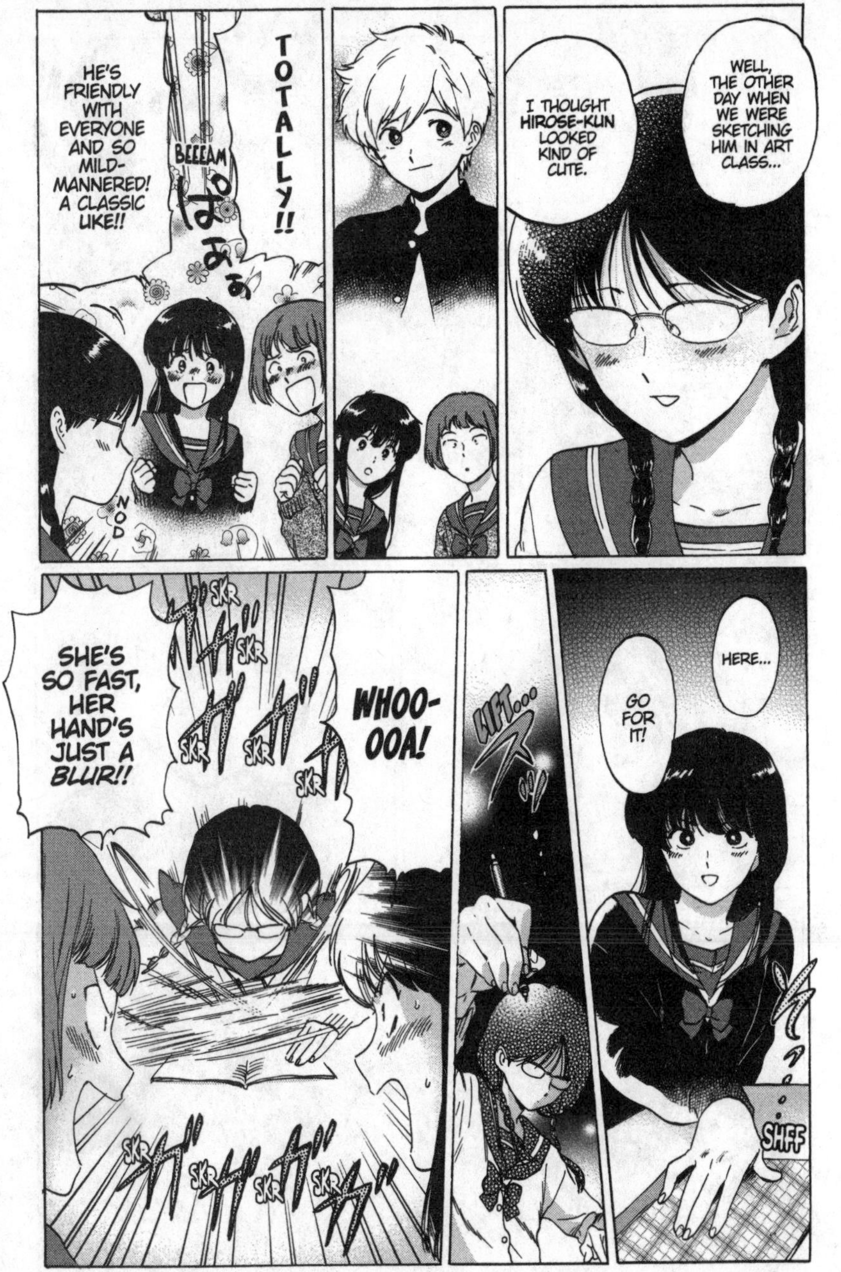
WELL, THE OTHER DAY WHEN WE WERE SKETCHING HIM IN ART CLASS...
I THOUGHT HIROSE-KUN LOOKED KIND OF CUTE.
TOTALLY!!
BEEEAM
HE'S FRIENDLY WITH EVERYONE AND SO MILD-MANNERED! A CLASSIC UKE!!
NOD
HERE...
GO FOR IT!
SHFF
LIFT...
WHOO-OOA!
SKR
SKR
SHE'S SO FAST, HER HAND'S JUST A BLUR!!
SKR
SKR
SKR
SKR
SKR
SKR
SKR

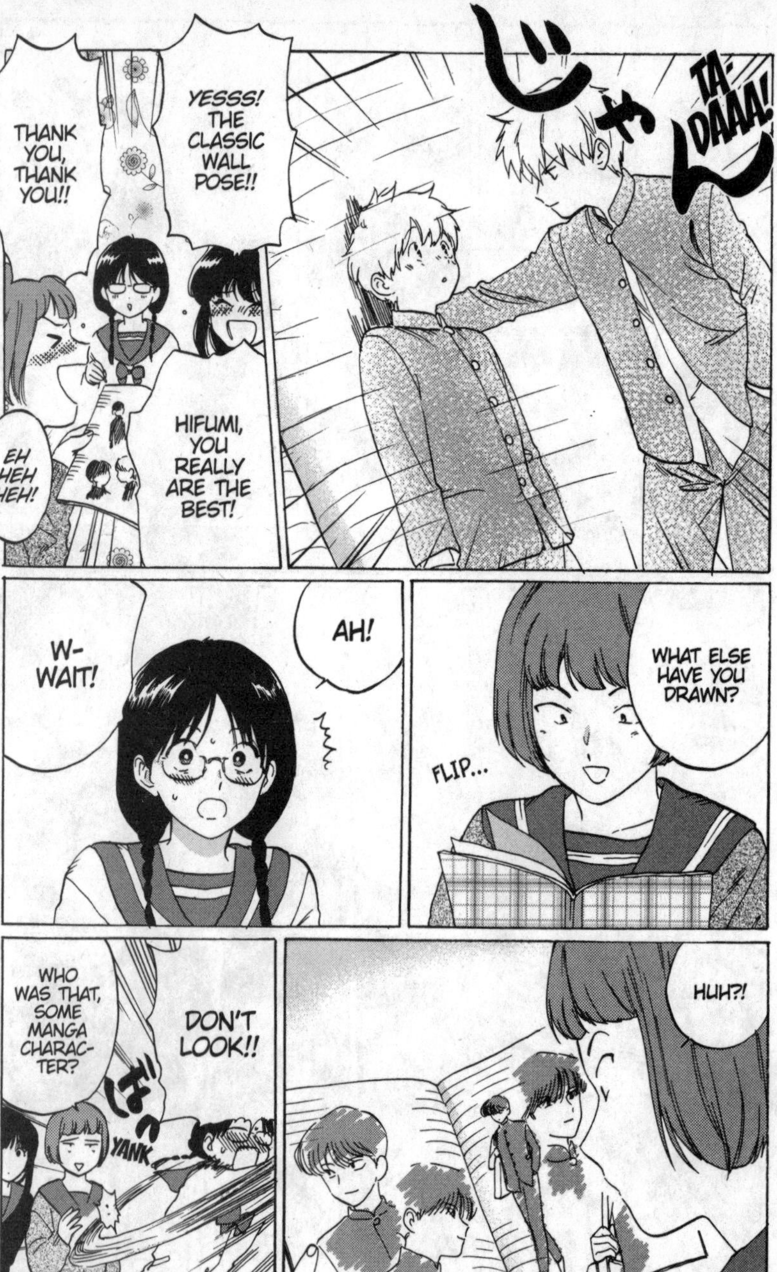
じゃん
TA-DAAA!
YESSS! THE CLASSIC WALL POSE!!
THANK YOU, THANK YOU!!
HIFUMI, YOU REALLY ARE THE BEST!
EH HEH HEH!
WHAT ELSE HAVE YOU DRAWN?
FLIP...
AH!
W-WAIT!
HUH?!
DON'T LOOK!!
WHO WAS THAT, SOME MANGA CHARACTER?
ぱっ
YANK

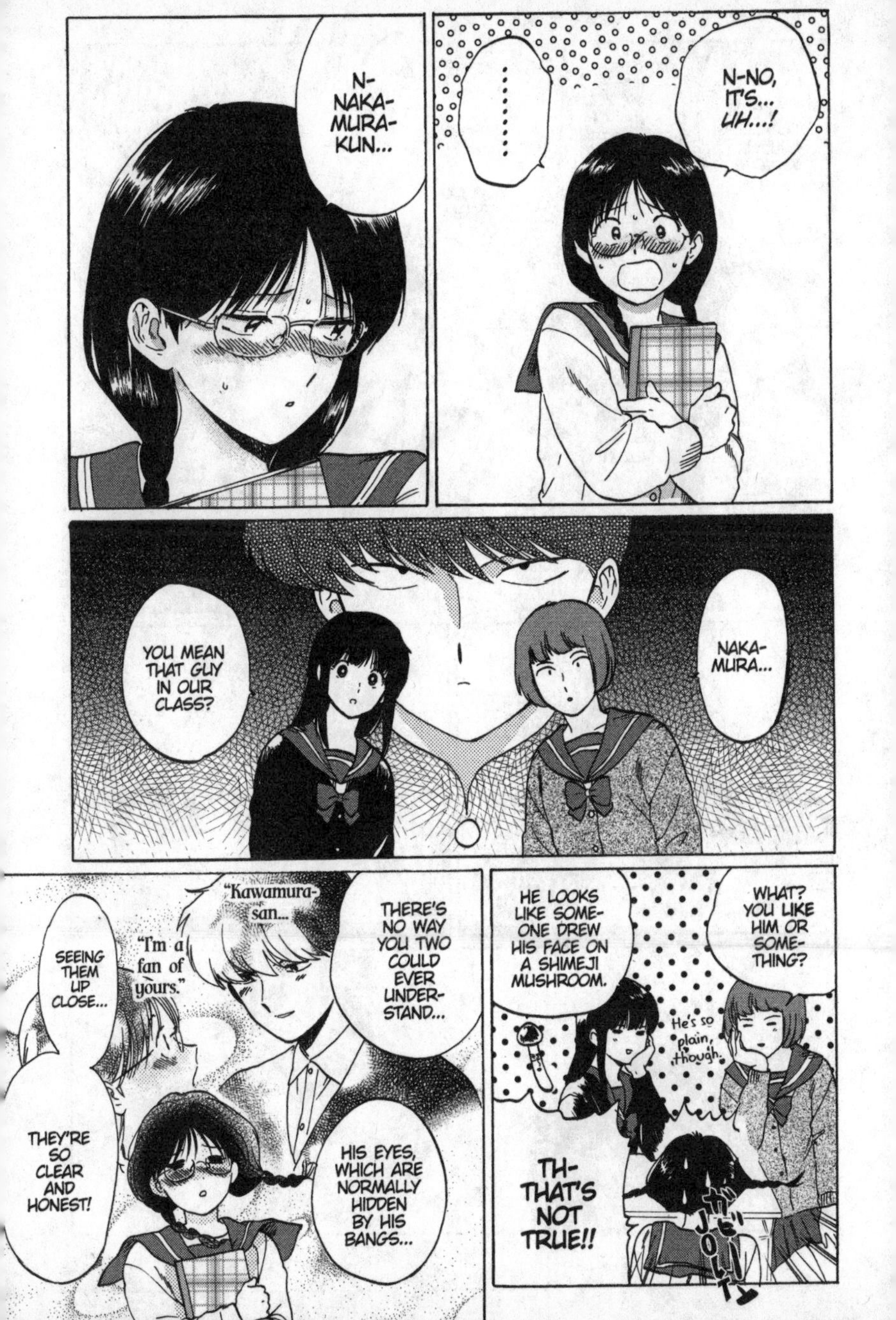

N-NO, IT'S... UH...!
......
N-NAKAMURA-KUN...
NAKAMURA...
YOU MEAN THAT GUY IN OUR CLASS?
WHAT? YOU LIKE HIM OR SOMETHING?
HE LOOKS LIKE SOMEONE DREW HIS FACE ON A SHIMEJI MUSHROOM.
He's so plain, though.
TH-THAT'S NOT TRUE!!
JOLT
THERE'S NO WAY YOU TWO COULD EVER UNDERSTAND...
"Kawamura-san...
"I'm a fan of yours."
SEEING THEM UP CLOSE...
HIS EYES, WHICH ARE NORMALLY HIDDEN BY HIS BANGS...
THEY'RE SO CLEAR AND HONEST!

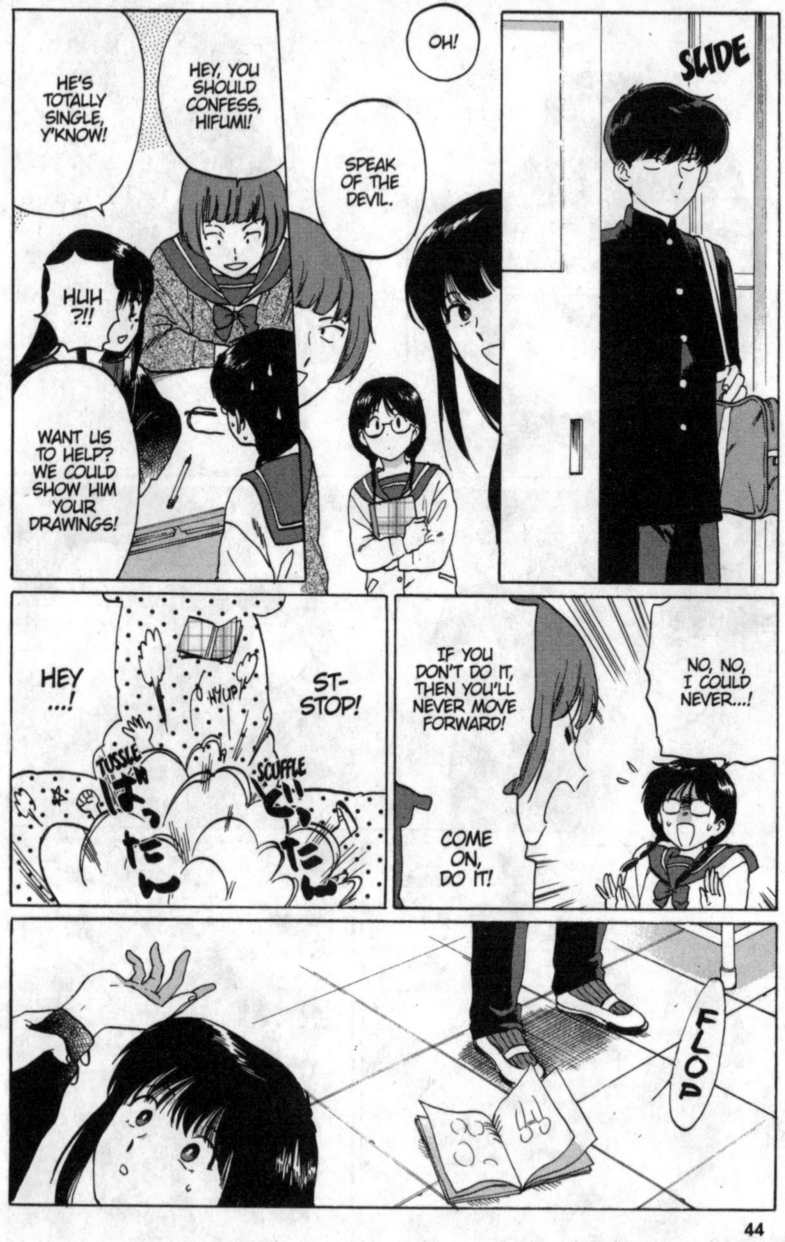
SLIDE
OH!
SPEAK OF THE DEVIL.
HEY, YOU SHOULD CONFESS, HIFUMI!
HE'S TOTALLY SINGLE, Y'KNOW!
HUH ?!!
WANT US TO HELP? WE COULD SHOW HIM YOUR DRAWINGS!
NO, NO, I COULD NEVER...!
IF YOU DON'T DO IT, THEN YOU'LL NEVER MOVE FORWARD!
COME ON, DO IT!
ST- STOP!
HY'UP
SCUFFLE
TUSSLE
HEY ...!
FLOP

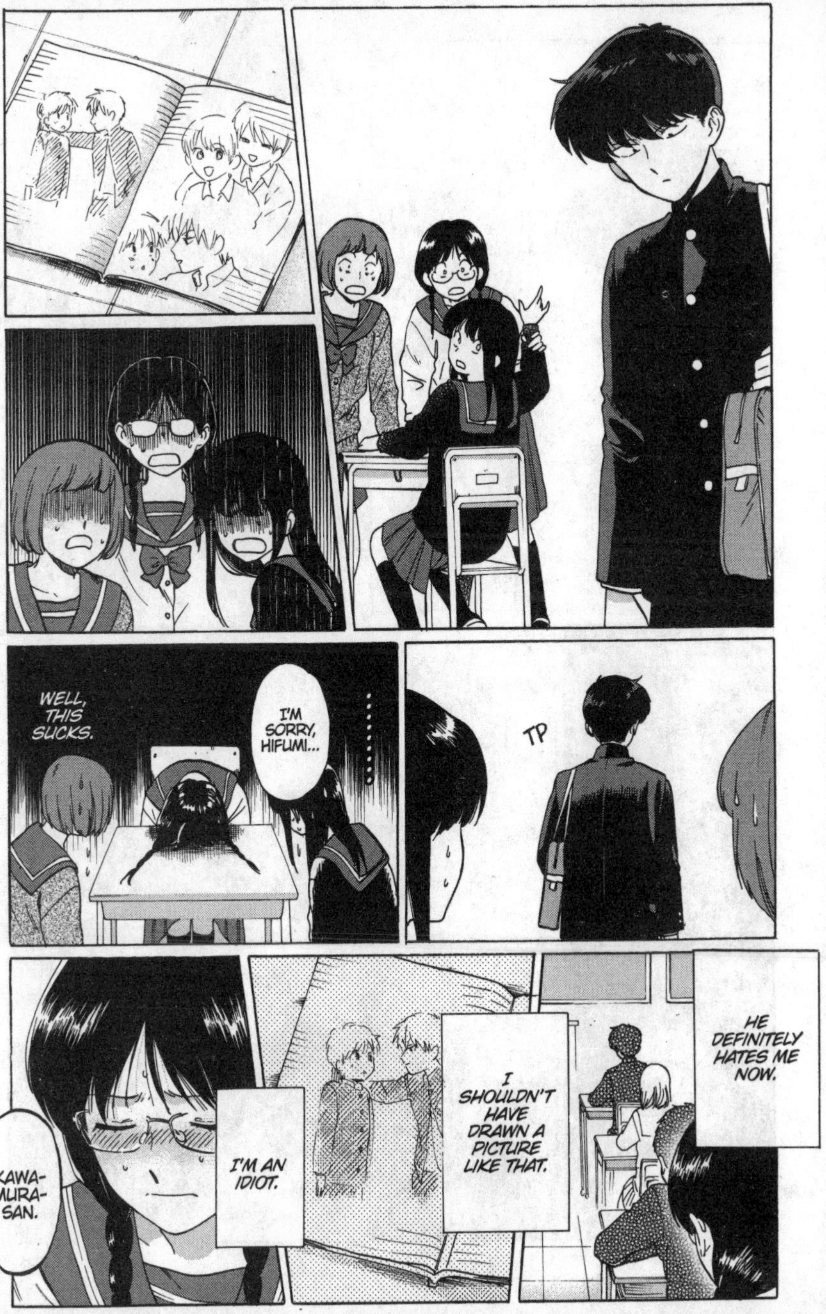
TP
I'M SORRY, HIFUMI...
WELL, THIS SUCKS.
HE DEFINITELY HATES ME NOW.
I SHOULDN'T HAVE DRAWN A PICTURE LIKE THAT.
I'M AN IDIOT.
KAWAMURA-SAN.

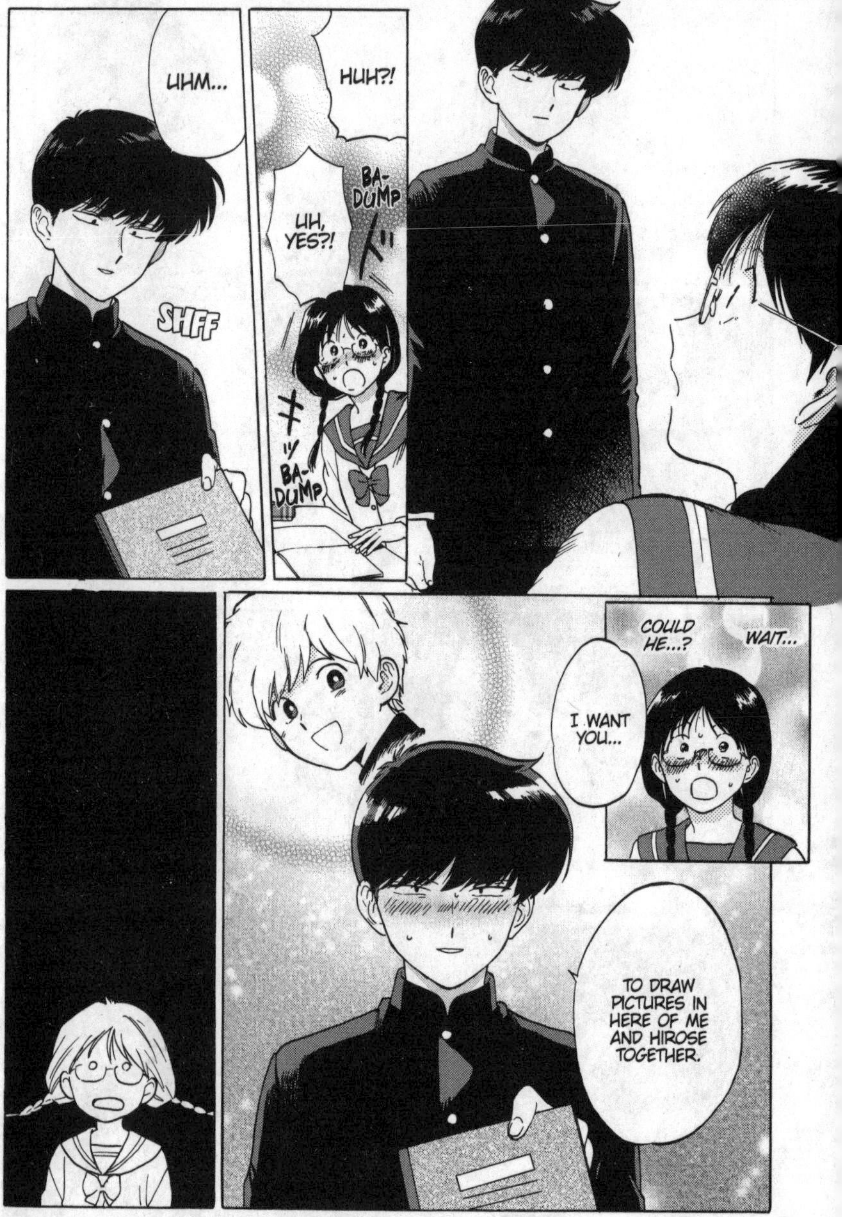
HUH?!
BA-DUMP
UH, YES?!
BA-DUMP
UHM...
SHFF
WAIT...
COULD HE...?
I WANT YOU...
TO DRAW PICTURES IN HERE OF ME AND HIROSE TOGETHER.

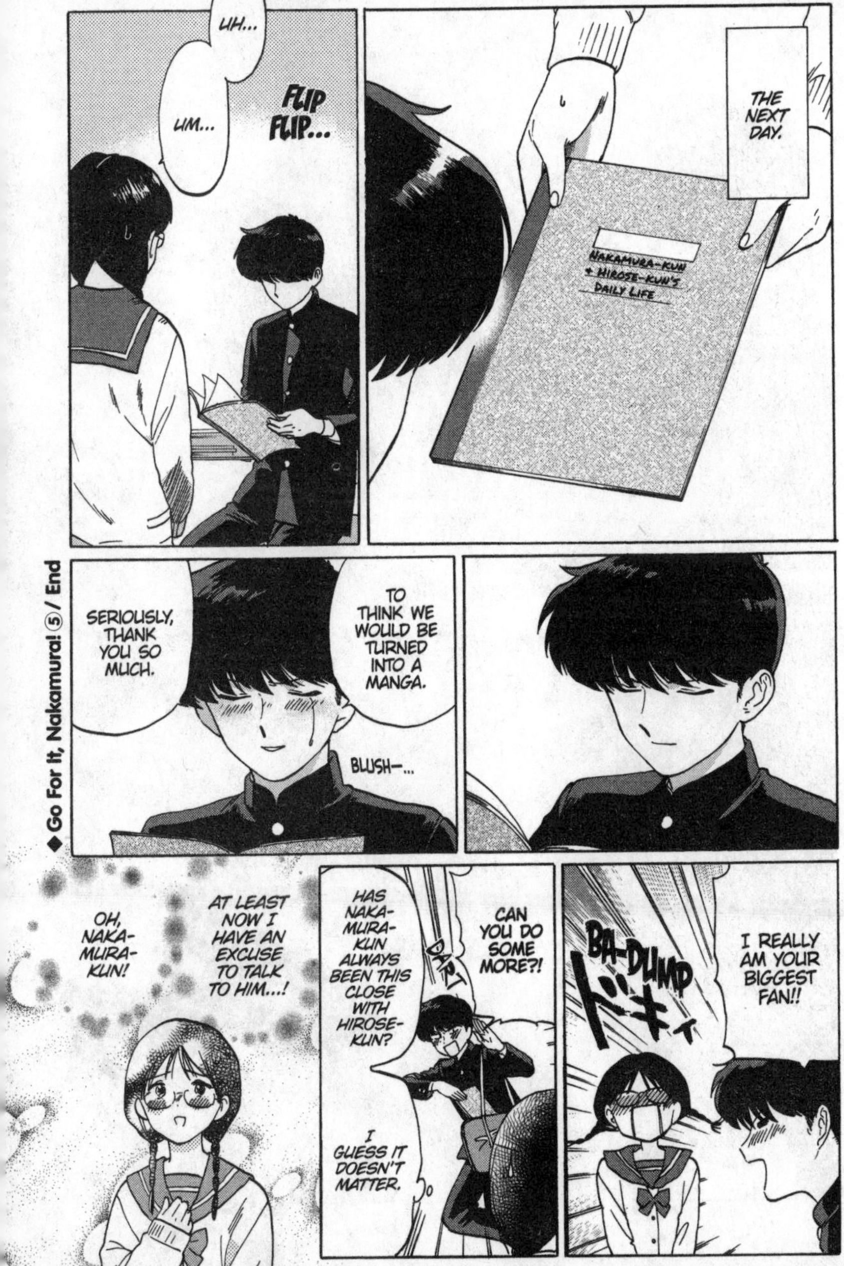
THE NEXT DAY.
NAKAMURA-KUN + HIROSE-KUN'S DAILY LIFE
FLIP FLIP...
UH...
UM...
TO THINK WE WOULD BE TURNED INTO A MANGA.
SERIOUSLY, THANK YOU SO MUCH.
BLUSH—...
I REALLY AM YOUR BIGGEST FAN!!
BA-DUMP
CAN YOU DO SOME MORE?!
HAS NAKA-MURA-KUN ALWAYS BEEN THIS CLOSE WITH HIROSE-KUN?
DART
I GUESS IT DOESN'T MATTER.
AT LEAST NOW I HAVE AN EXCUSE TO TALK TO HIM...!
OH, NAKA-MURA-KUN!

◆Go For It, Nakamura!! ⑤ / End

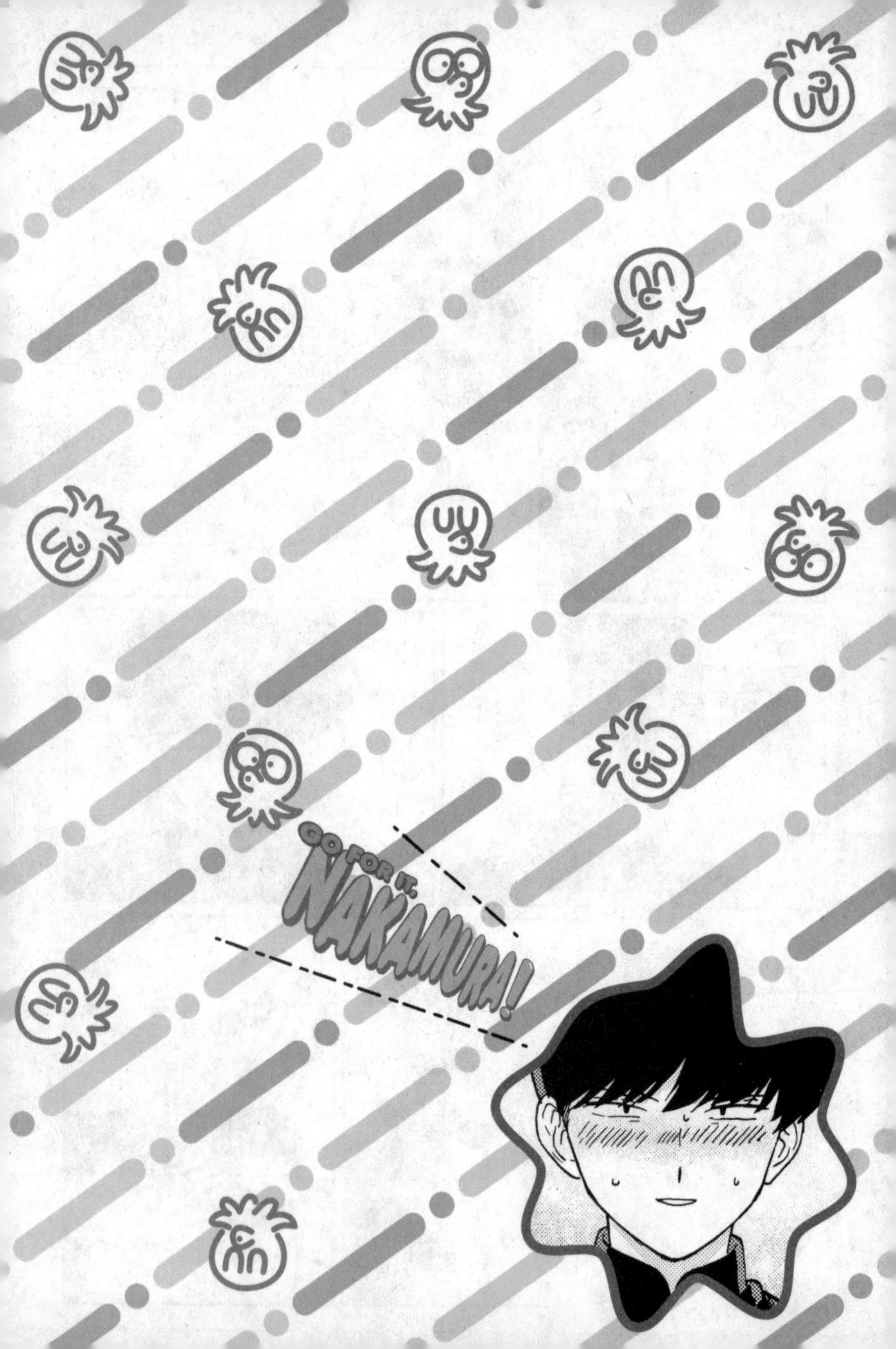
GO FOR IT, NAKAMURA!

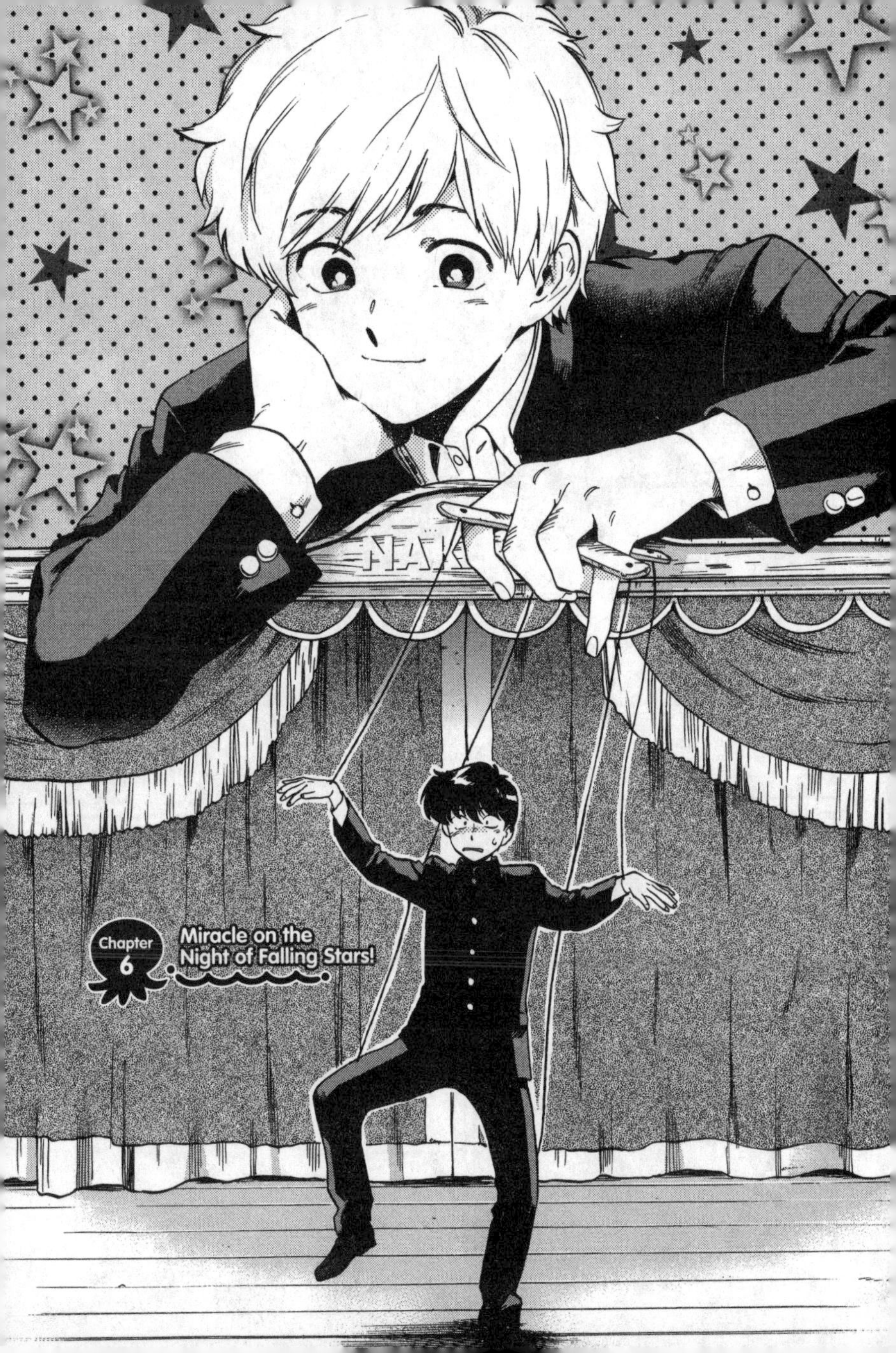
NAK
Chapter 6
Miracle on the Night of Falling Stars!

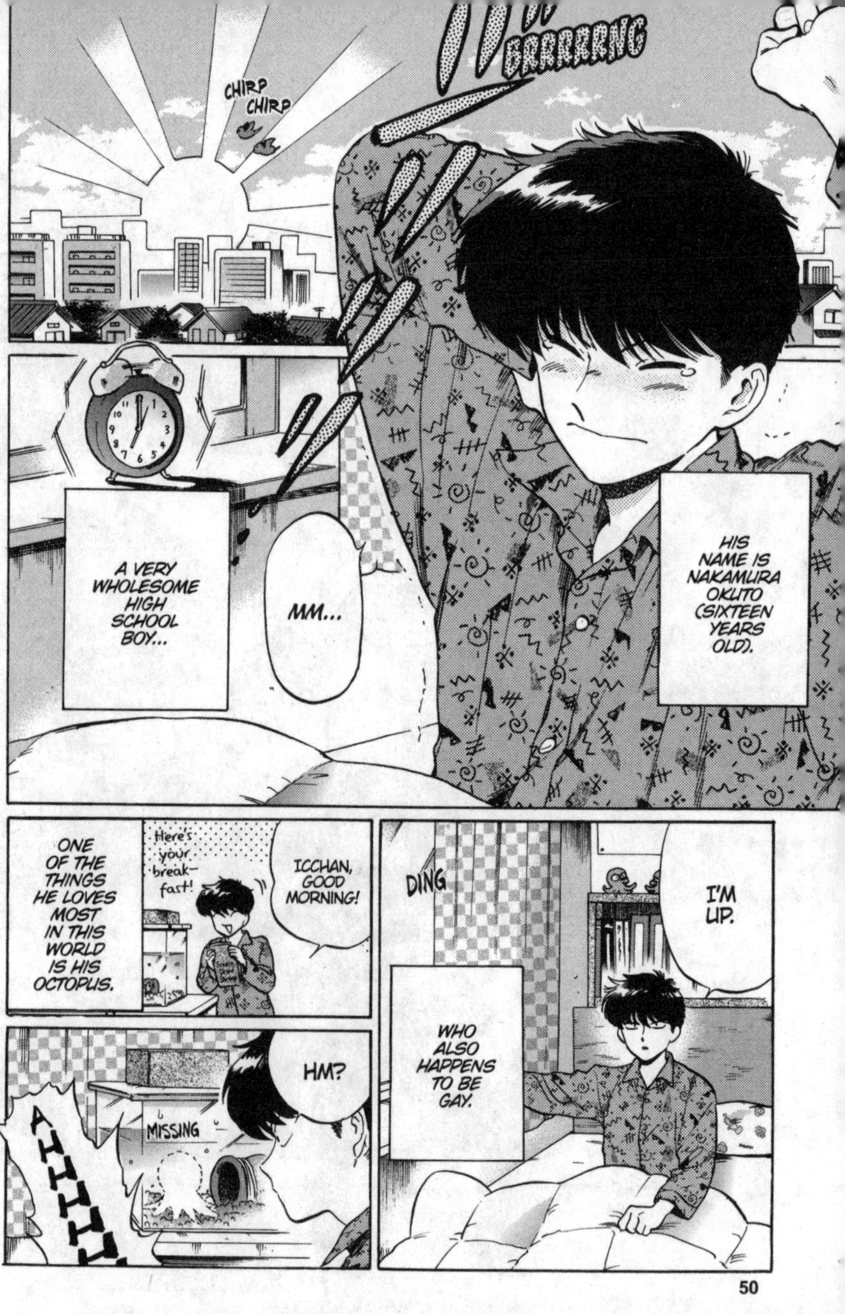
BRRRRRNG
CHIRP CHIRP
HIS NAME IS NAKAMURA OKUTO (SIXTEEN YEARS OLD).
MM...
A VERY WHOLESOME HIGH SCHOOL BOY...
DING
I'M UP.
WHO ALSO HAPPENS TO BE GAY.
ICCHAN, GOOD MORNING!
Here's your breakfast!
ONE OF THE THINGS HE LOVES MOST IN THIS WORLD IS HIS OCTOPUS.
HM?
MISSING
AHHHHH

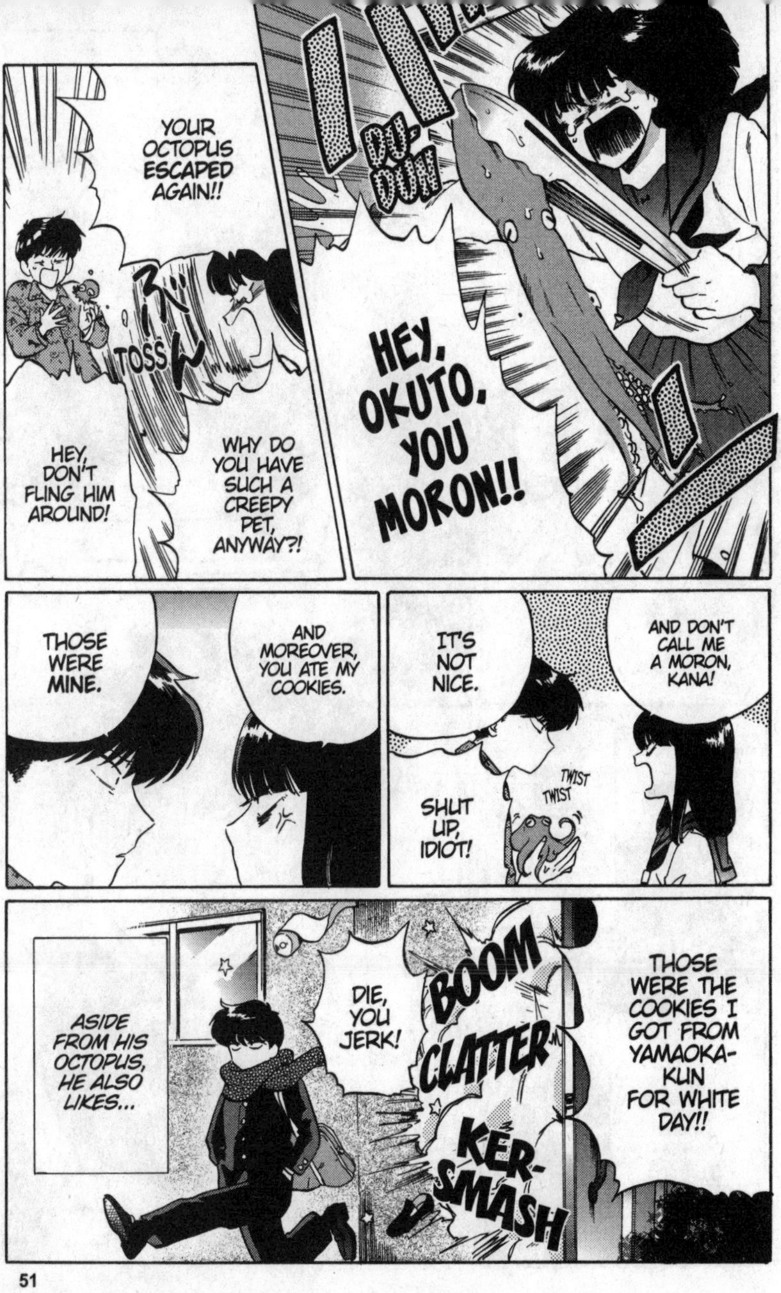
DU-DUN
HEY, OKUTO, YOU MORON!!
YOUR OCTOPUS ESCAPED AGAIN!!
TOSS
WHY DO YOU HAVE SUCH A CREEPY PET, ANYWAY?!
HEY, DON'T FLING HIM AROUND!
AND DON'T CALL ME A MORON, KANA!
IT'S NOT NICE.
TWIST TWIST
SHUT UP, IDIOT!
AND MOREOVER, YOU ATE MY COOKIES.
THOSE WERE MINE.
THOSE WERE THE COOKIES I GOT FROM YAMAOKA-KUN FOR WHITE DAY!!
BOOM
CLATTER
KER-SMASH
DIE, YOU JERK!
ASIDE FROM HIS OCTOPUS, HE ALSO LIKES...

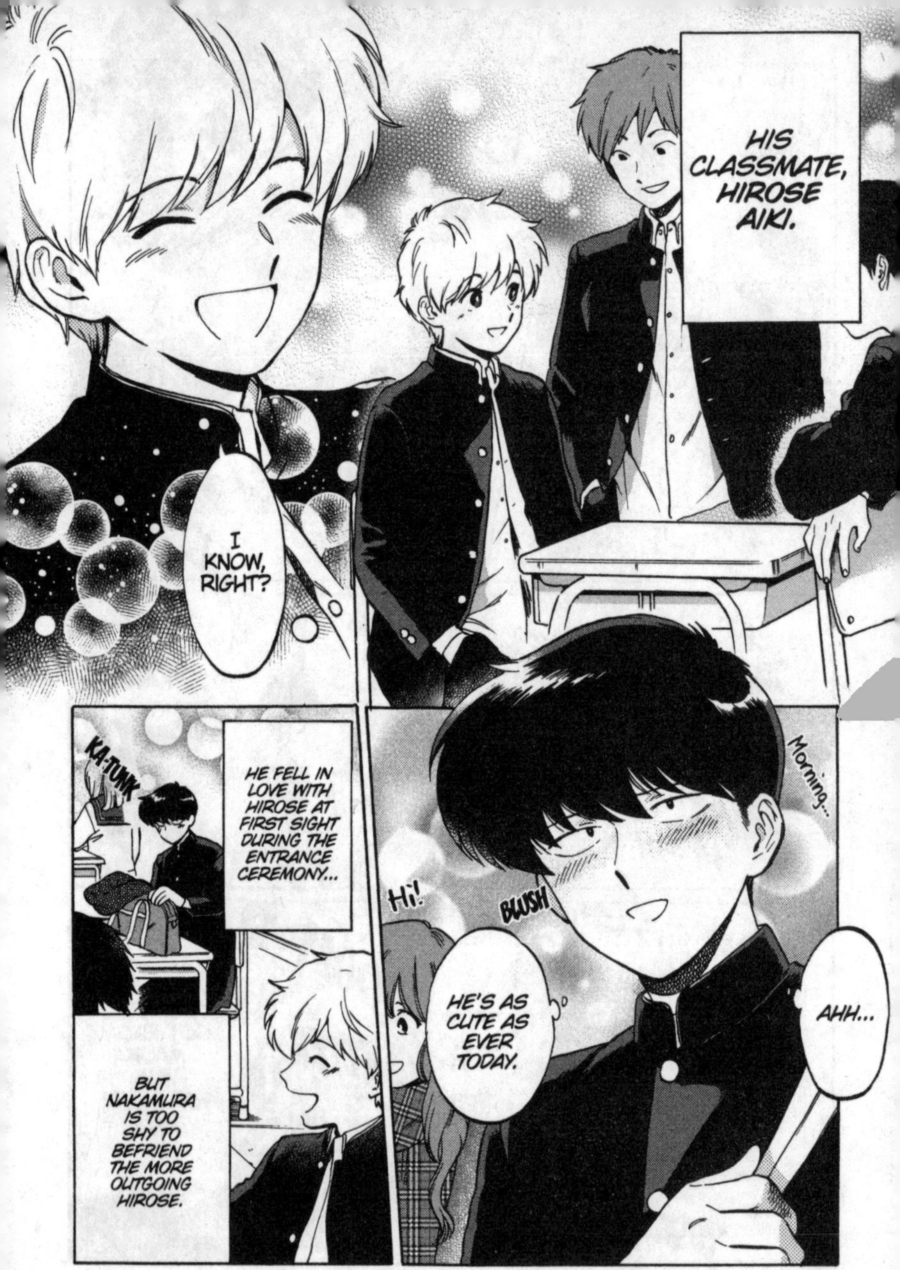
HIS CLASSMATE, HIROSE AIKI.
I KNOW, RIGHT?
Morning...
AHH...
BLUSH
Hi!
HE'S AS CUTE AS EVER TODAY.
KA-TUNK
HE FELL IN LOVE WITH HIROSE AT FIRST SIGHT DURING THE ENTRANCE CEREMONY...
BUT NAKAMURA IS TOO SHY TO BEFRIEND THE MORE OUTGOING HIROSE.

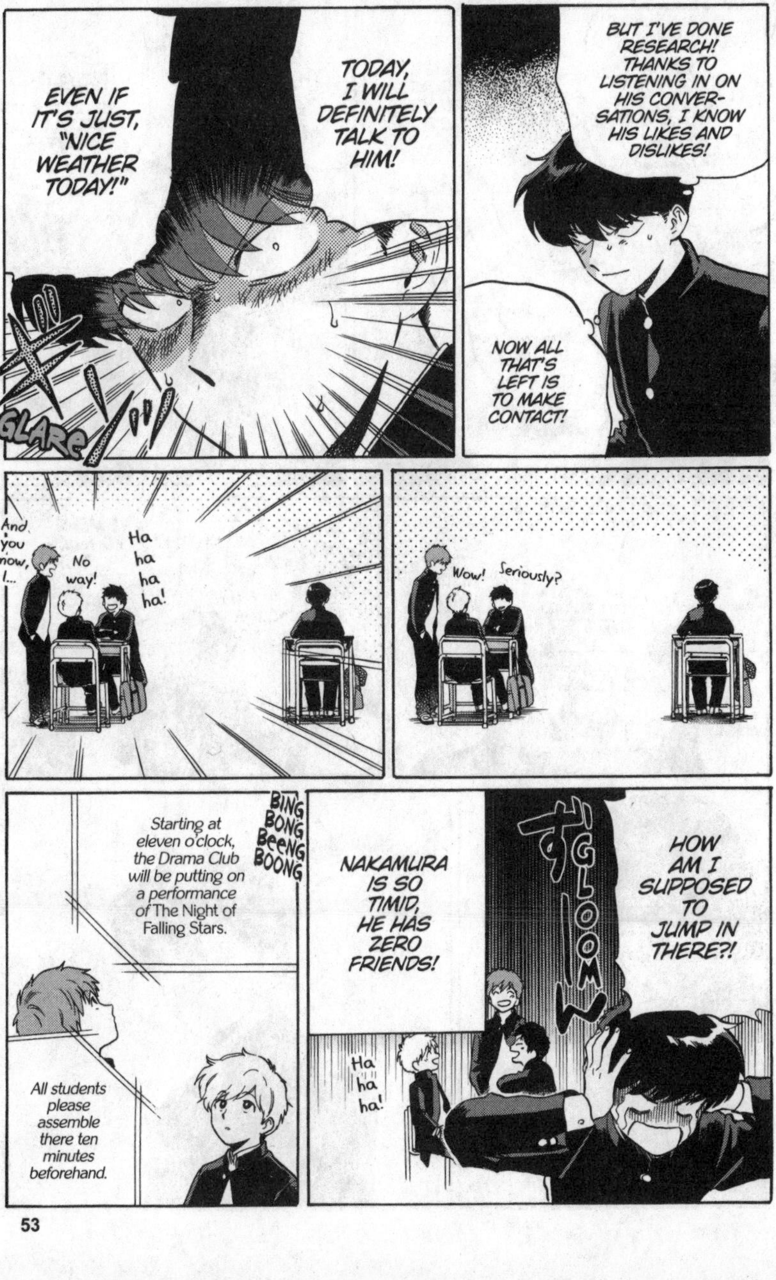
BUT I'VE DONE RESEARCH! THANKS TO LISTENING IN ON HIS CONVER- SATIONS, I KNOW HIS LIKES AND DISLIKES!
NOW ALL THAT'S LEFT IS TO MAKE CONTACT!
TODAY, I WILL DEFINITELY TALK TO HIM!
EVEN IF IT'S JUST, "NICE WEATHER TODAY!"
GLARE
Wow!
Seriously?
Ha ha ha ha!
No way!
And you know, I...
HOW AM I SUPPOSED TO JUMP IN THERE?!
GLOOM
NAKAMURA IS SO TIMID, HE HAS ZERO FRIENDS!
Ha ha ha!
BING BONG BEENG BOONG
Starting at eleven o'clock, the Drama Club will be putting on a performance of The Night of Falling Stars.
All students please assemble there ten minutes beforehand.

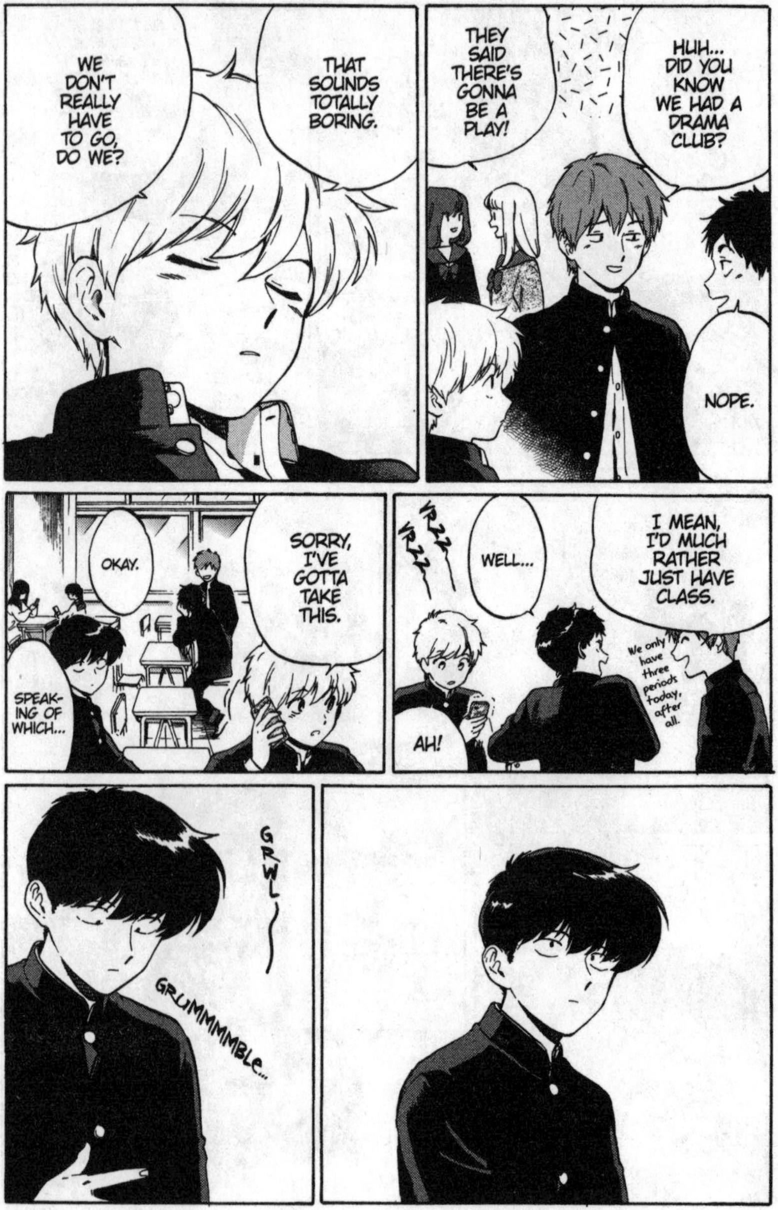
HUH... DID YOU KNOW WE HAD A DRAMA CLUB?
THEY SAID THERE'S GONNA BE A PLAY!
NOPE.
THAT SOUNDS TOTALLY BORING.
WE DON'T REALLY HAVE TO GO, DO WE?
I MEAN, I'D MUCH RATHER JUST HAVE CLASS.
We only have three periods today, after all.
WELL...
VRZZ VRZZ
AH!
SORRY, I'VE GOTTA TAKE THIS.
OKAY.
SPEAK-ING OF WHICH...
GRWL
GRUMMMMBLe...

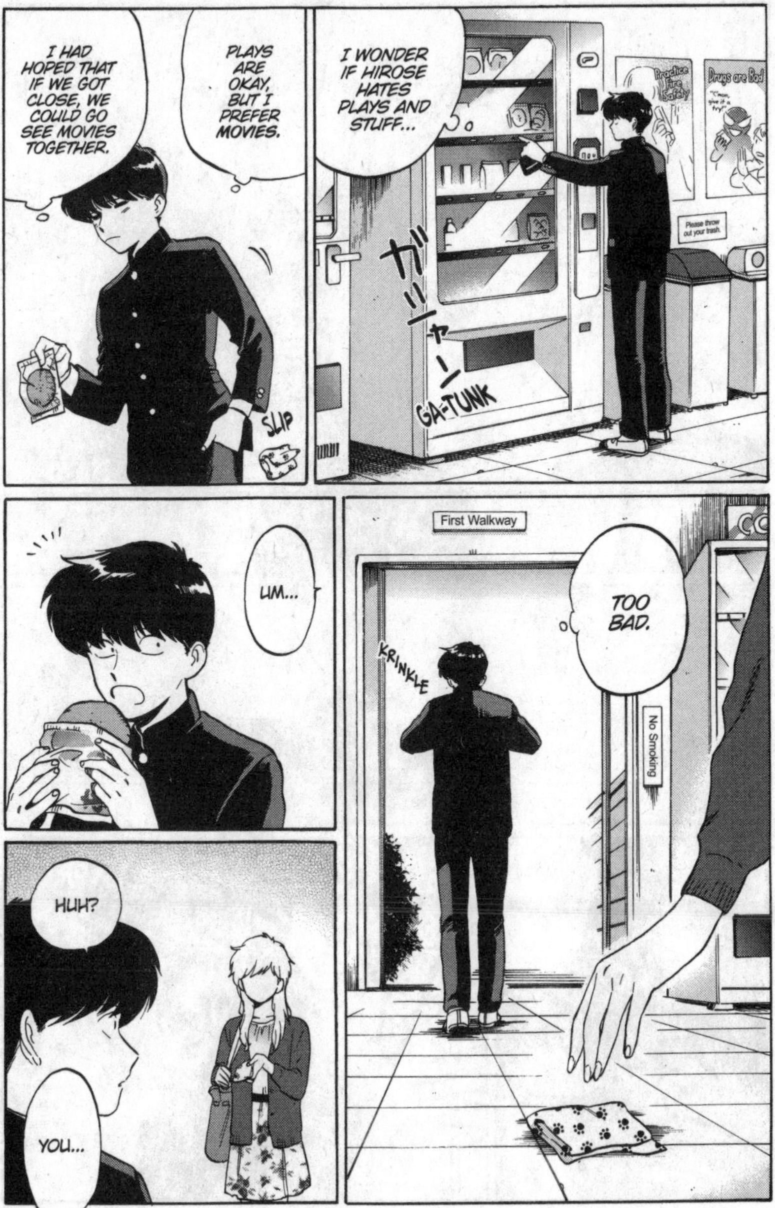
Drugs are Bad
"C'mon, give it a try!"
Practice Fire Safety
Please throw out your trash.
I WONDER IF HIROSE HATES PLAYS AND STUFF...
ガシャーン
GA-TUNK
PLAYS ARE OKAY, BUT I PREFER MOVIES.
I HAD HOPED THAT IF WE GOT CLOSE, WE COULD GO SEE MOVIES TOGETHER.
SLIP
First Walkway
TOO BAD.
No Smoking
KRINKLE
UM...
HUH?
YOU...

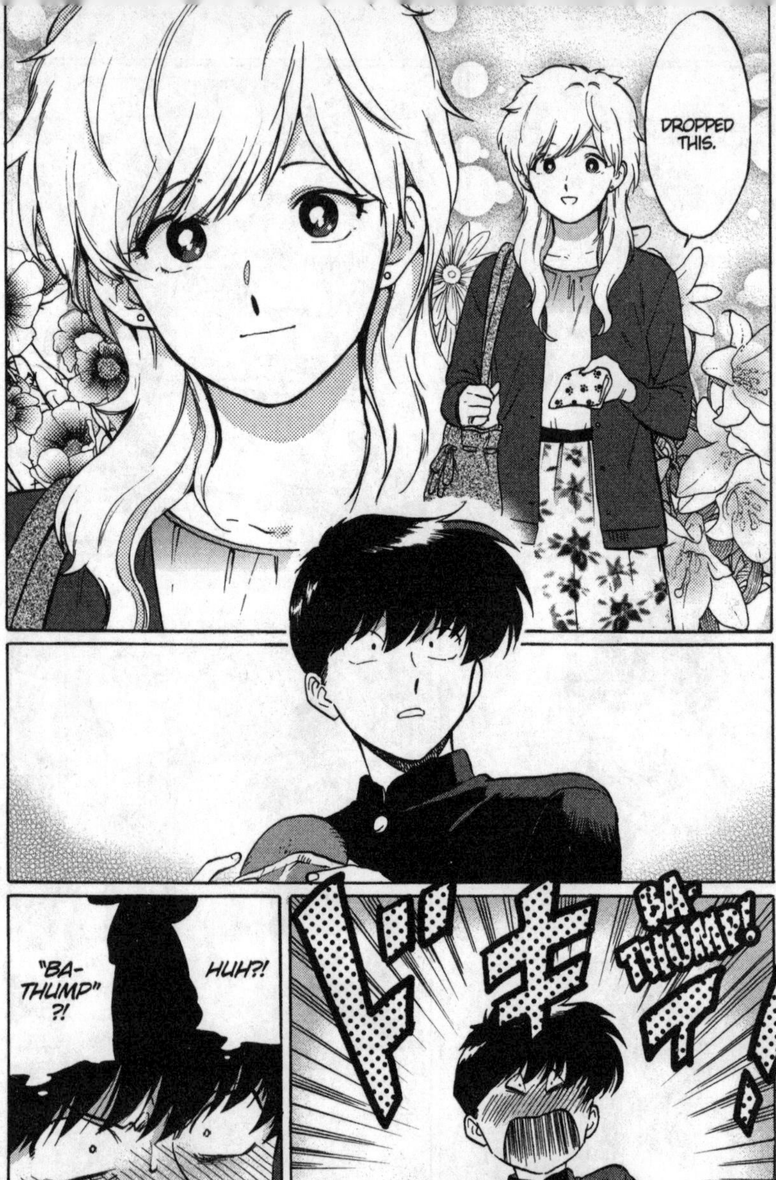
DROPPED THIS.
BA-THUMP!
ドキィ!!
HUH?!
"BA-THUMP"?!

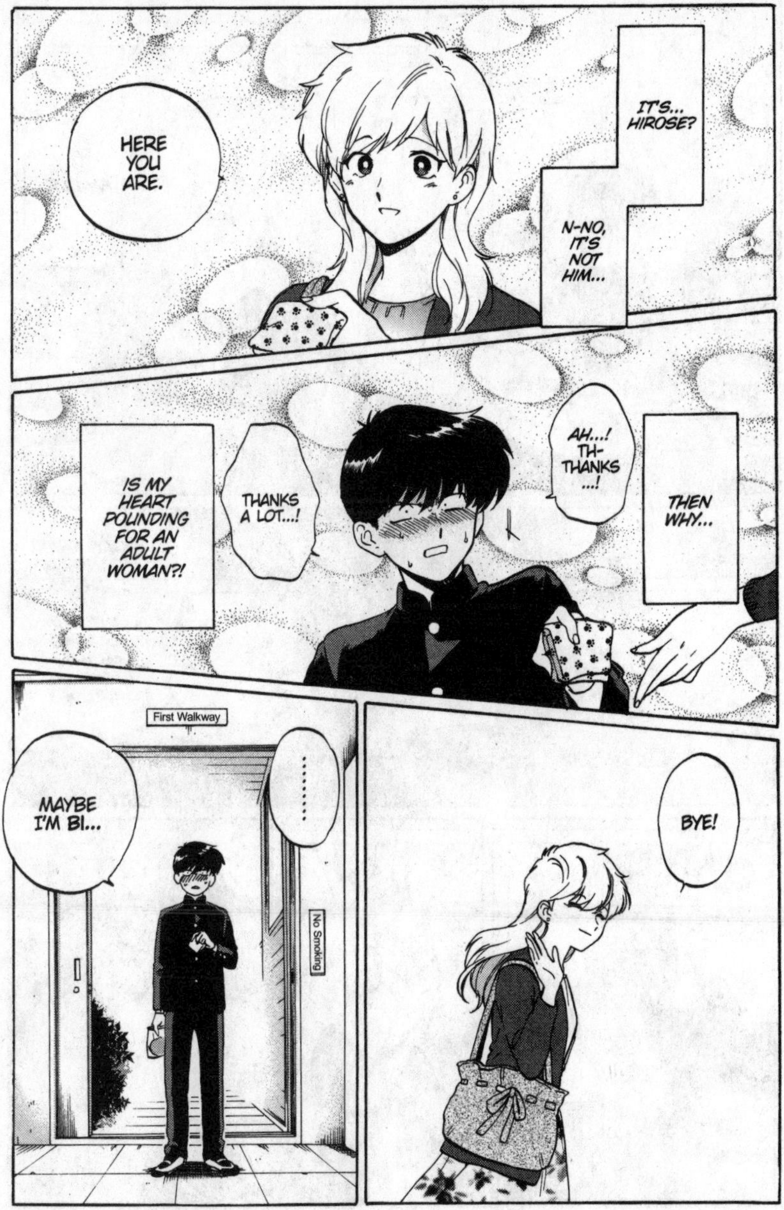
IT'S... HIROSE?
N-NO, IT'S NOT HIM...
HERE YOU ARE.
THEN WHY...
AH...! TH-THANKS ...!
THANKS A LOT...!
IS MY HEART POUNDING FOR AN ADULT WOMAN?!
BYE!
First Walkway
......
MAYBE I'M BI...
No Smoking

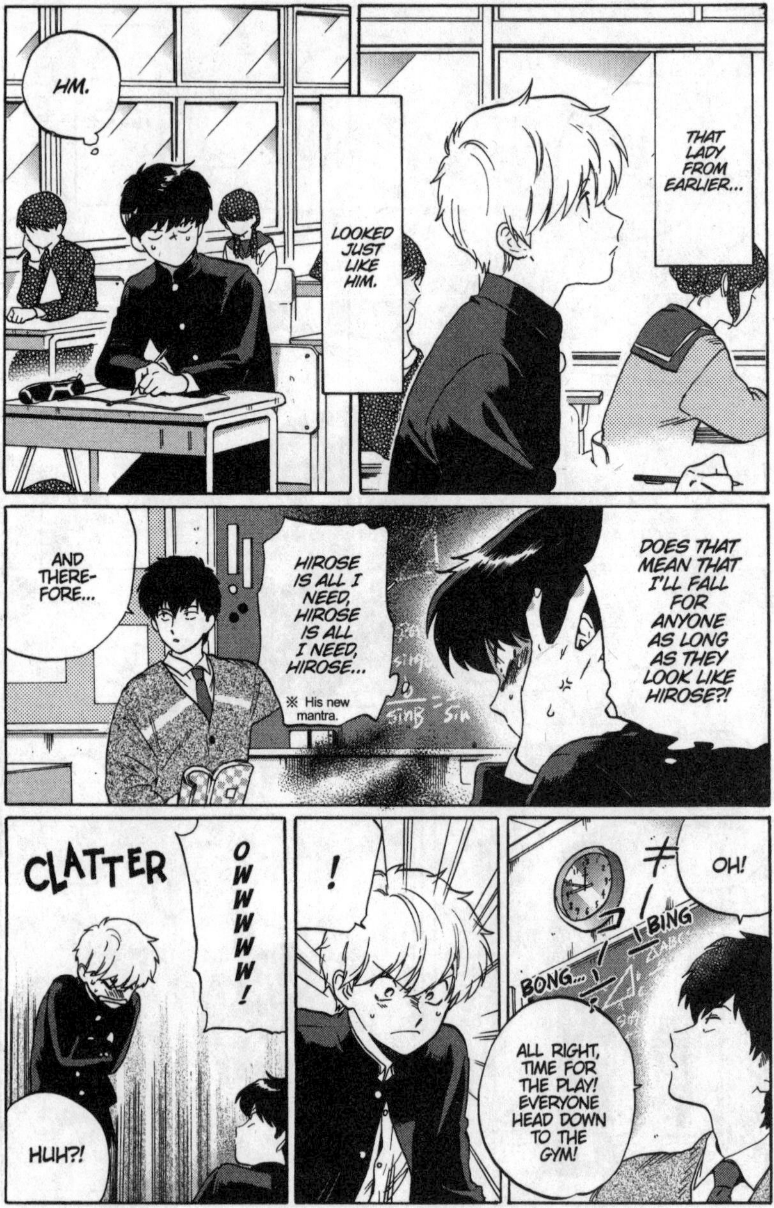

THAT LADY FROM EARLIER...
LOOKED JUST LIKE HIM.
HM.
DOES THAT MEAN THAT I'LL FALL FOR ANYONE AS LONG AS THEY LOOK LIKE HIROSE?!
HIROSE IS ALL I NEED, HIROSE IS ALL I NEED, HIROSE...
※ His new mantra.
AND THEREFORE...
OH!
BING
BONG...
ALL RIGHT, TIME FOR THE PLAY! EVERYONE HEAD DOWN TO THE GYM!
!
OWWWWWW!
CLATTER
HUH?!

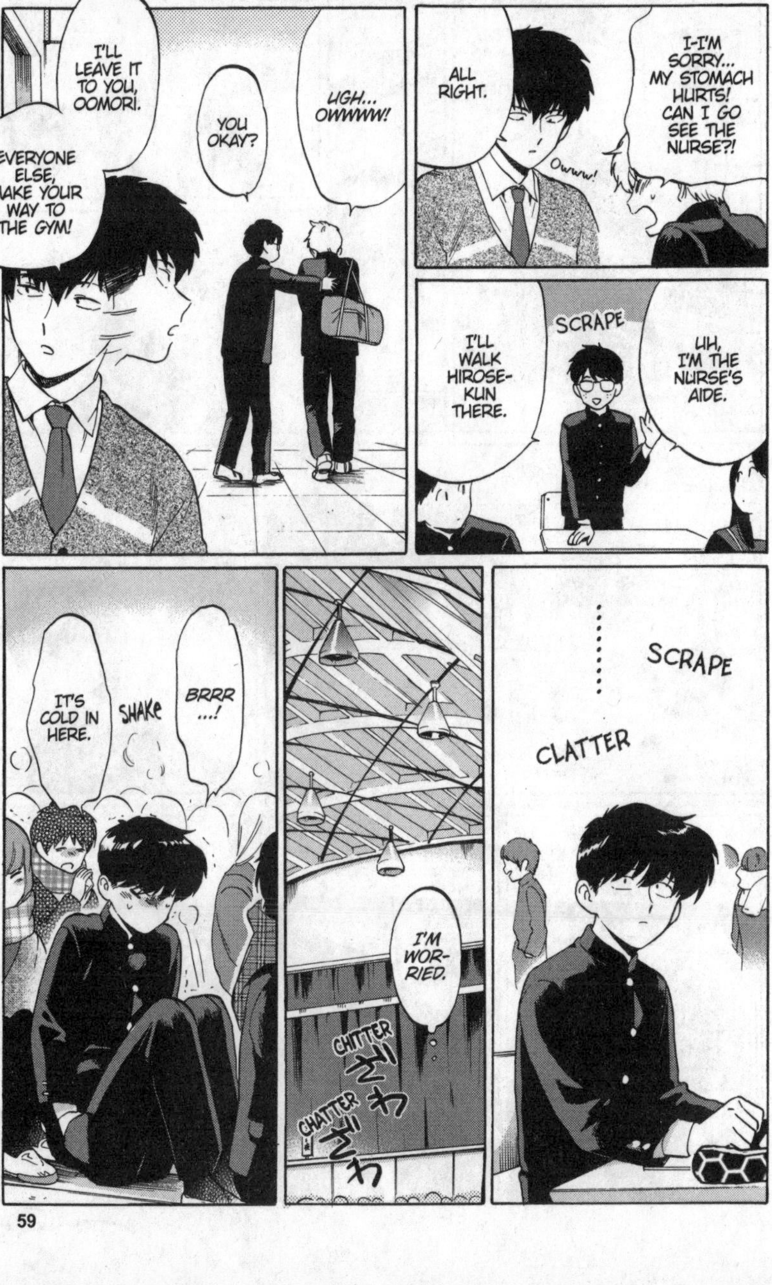
I-I'M SORRY... MY STOMACH HURTS! CAN I GO SEE THE NURSE?!
Owww!
ALL RIGHT.
UH, I'M THE NURSE'S AIDE.
SCRAPE
I'LL WALK HIROSE-KUN THERE.
UGH... OWWWW!
YOU OKAY?
I'LL LEAVE IT TO YOU, OOMORI.
EVERYONE ELSE, MAKE YOUR WAY TO THE GYM!
SCRAPE
......
CLATTER
I'M WOR-RIED.
CHITTER ざわ
CHATTER ざわ
BRRR ...!
SHAKE
IT'S COLD IN HERE.

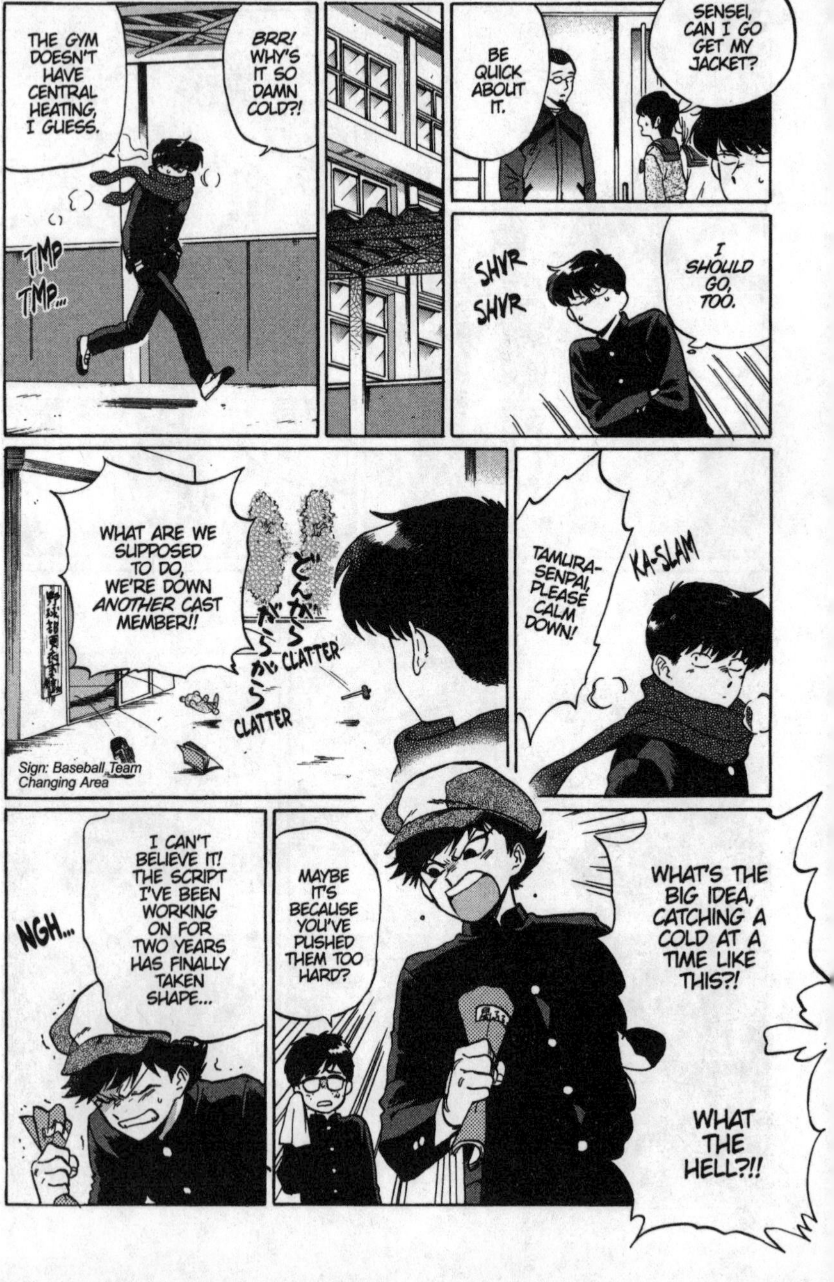
SENSEI, CAN I GO GET MY JACKET?
BE QUICK ABOUT IT.
I SHOULD GO, TOO.
SHVR SHVR
BRR! WHY'S IT SO DAMN COLD?!
THE GYM DOESN'T HAVE CENTRAL HEATING, I GUESS.
TMP TMP...
KA-SLAM
TAMURA-SENPAI, PLEASE CALM DOWN!
どんがらがらがら
CLATTER
CLATTER
WHAT ARE WE SUPPOSED TO DO, WE'RE DOWN *ANOTHER CAST* MEMBER!!
Sign: Baseball Team Changing Area
WHAT'S THE BIG IDEA, CATCHING A COLD AT A TIME LIKE THIS?!
WHAT THE HELL?!!
MAYBE IT'S BECAUSE YOU'VE PUSHED THEM TOO HARD?
I CAN'T BELIEVE IT! THE SCRIPT I'VE BEEN WORKING ON FOR TWO YEARS HAS FINALLY TAKEN SHAPE...
NGH...

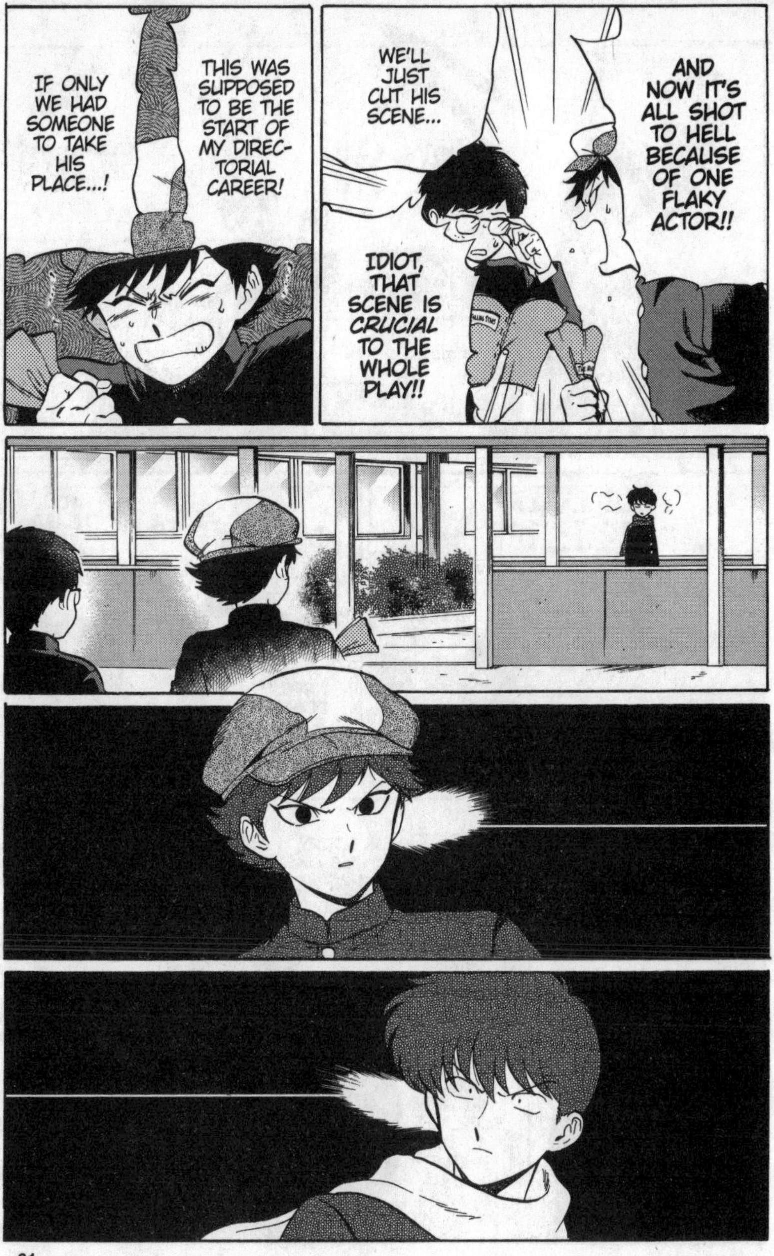
AND NOW IT'S ALL SHOT TO HELL BECAUSE OF ONE FLAKY ACTOR!!
WE'LL JUST CUT HIS SCENE...
IDIOT, THAT SCENE IS CRUCIAL TO THE WHOLE PLAY!!
THIS WAS SUPPOSED TO BE THE START OF MY DIRECTORIAL CAREER!
IF ONLY WE HAD SOMEONE TO TAKE HIS PLACE...!

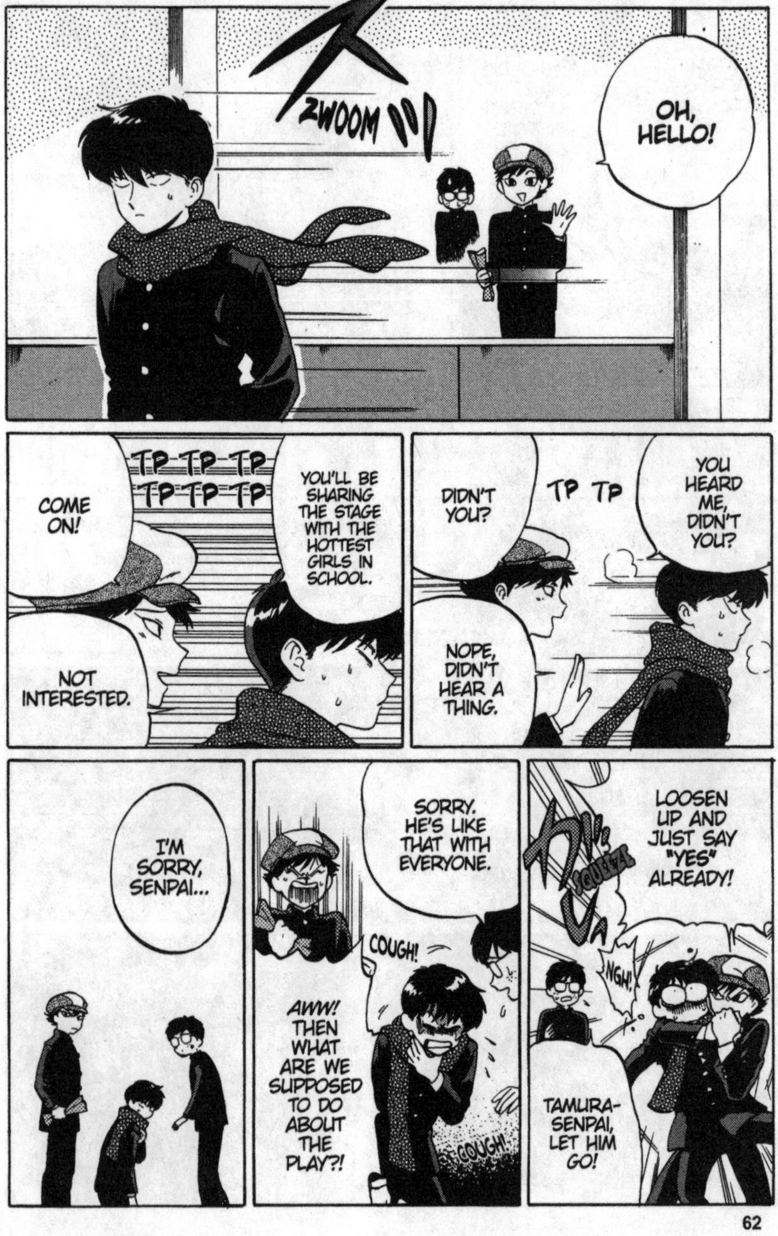
ZWOOM
OH, HELLO!
YOU HEARD ME, DIDN'T YOU?
TP TP
DIDN'T YOU?
NOPE, DIDN'T HEAR A THING.
YOU'LL BE SHARING THE STAGE WITH THE HOTTEST GIRLS IN SCHOOL.
TP TP TP TP TP TP
COME ON!
NOT INTERESTED.
LOOSEN UP AND JUST SAY "YES" ALREADY!
NGH!
TAMURA-SENPAI, LET HIM GO!
SORRY. HE'S LIKE THAT WITH EVERYONE.
COUGH!
AWW! THEN WHAT ARE WE SUPPOSED TO DO ABOUT THE PLAY?!
COUGH!
I'M SORRY, SENPAI...

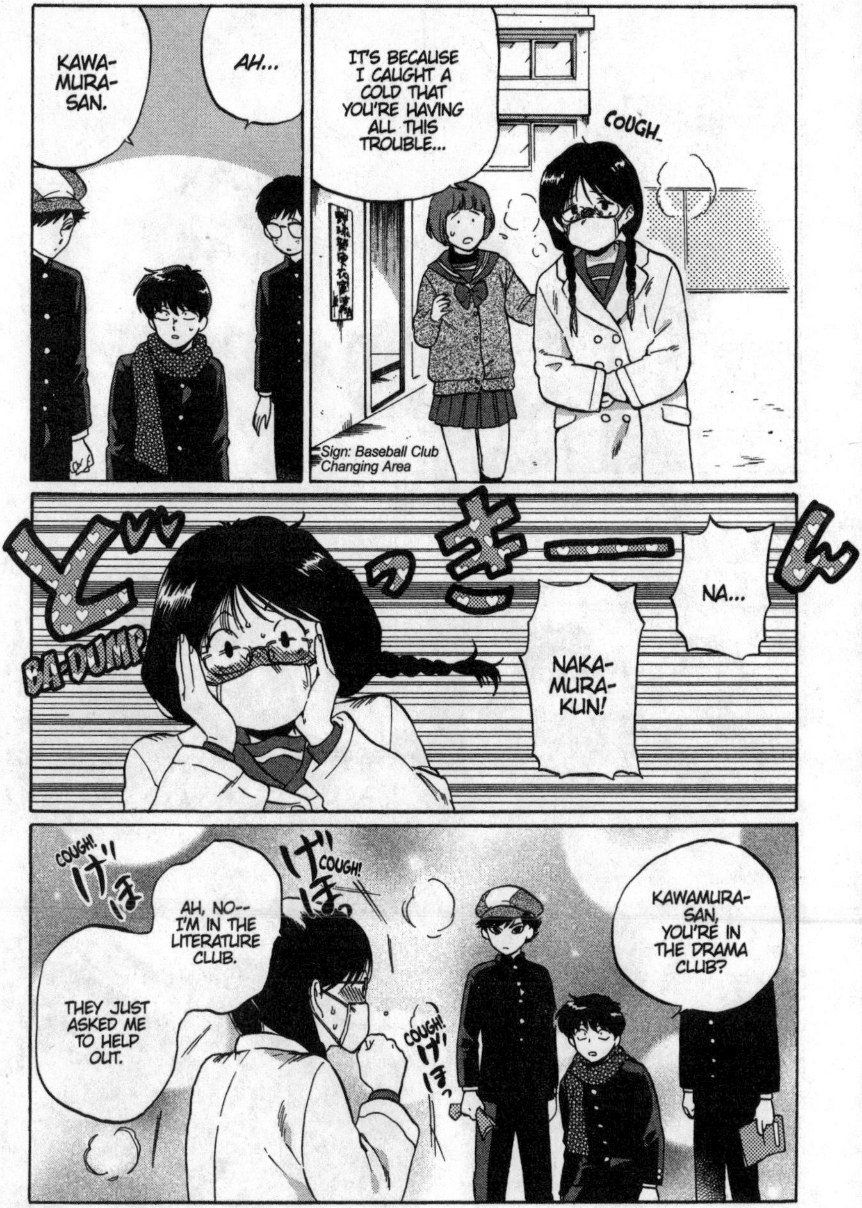
IT'S BECAUSE I CAUGHT A COLD THAT YOU'RE HAVING ALL THIS TROUBLE...
COUGH
Sign: Baseball Club Changing Area
AH...
KAWA-MURA-SAN.
どっきーん
BA-DUMP
NA...
NAKA-MURA-KUN!
KAWAMURA-SAN, YOU'RE IN THE DRAMA CLUB?
COUGH! げほっ
COUGH! げほっ
AH, NO-- I'M IN THE LITERATURE CLUB.
COUGH! げほ
THEY JUST ASKED ME TO HELP OUT.

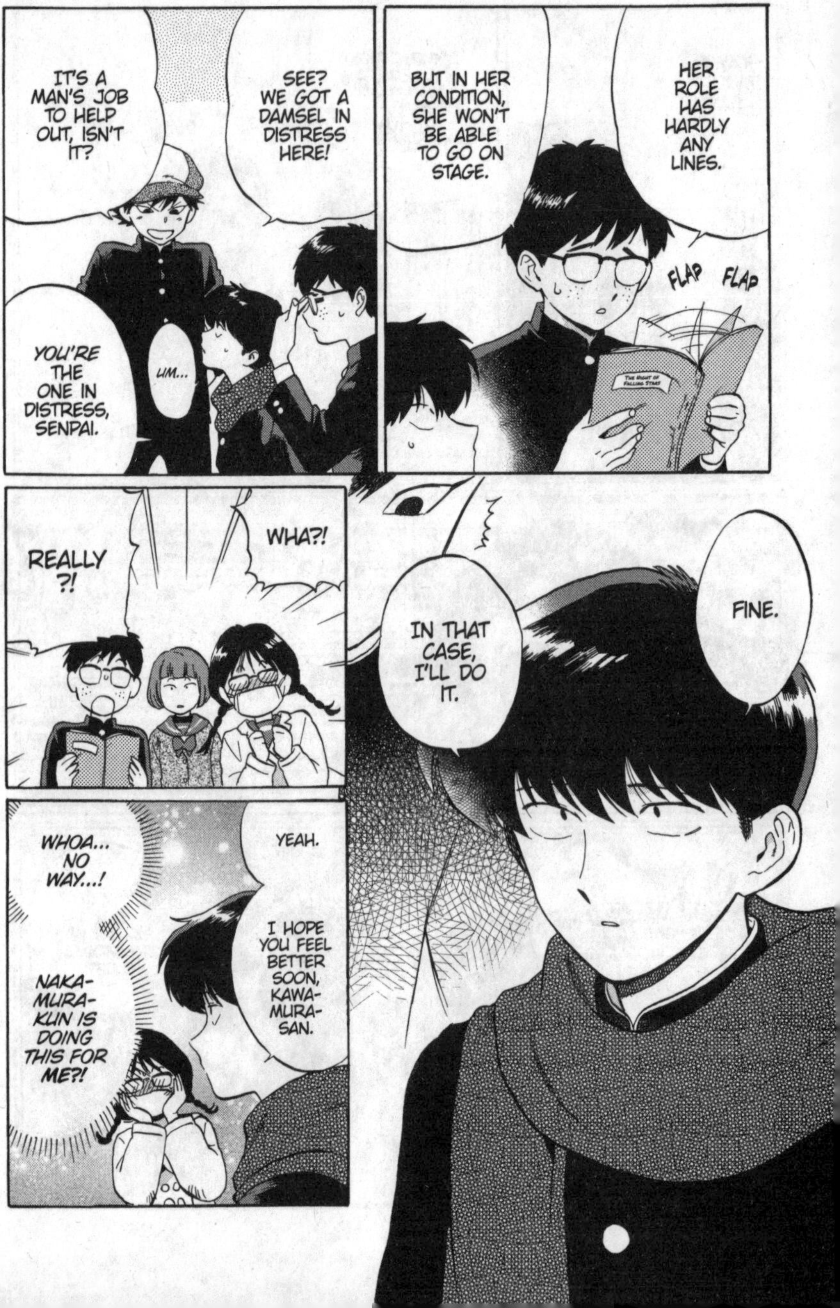
HER ROLE HAS HARDLY ANY LINES.
BUT IN HER CONDITION, SHE WON'T BE ABLE TO GO ON STAGE.
FLAP
FLAP
THE NIGHT OF FALLING STARS
SEE? WE GOT A DAMSEL IN DISTRESS HERE!
IT'S A MAN'S JOB TO HELP OUT, ISN'T IT?
UM...
YOU'RE THE ONE IN DISTRESS, SENPAI.
FINE.
IN THAT CASE, I'LL DO IT.
WHA?!
REALLY ?!
YEAH.
I HOPE YOU FEEL BETTER SOON, KAWA-MURA-SAN.
WHOA... NO WAY...!
NAKA-MURA-KUN IS DOING THIS FOR ME?!

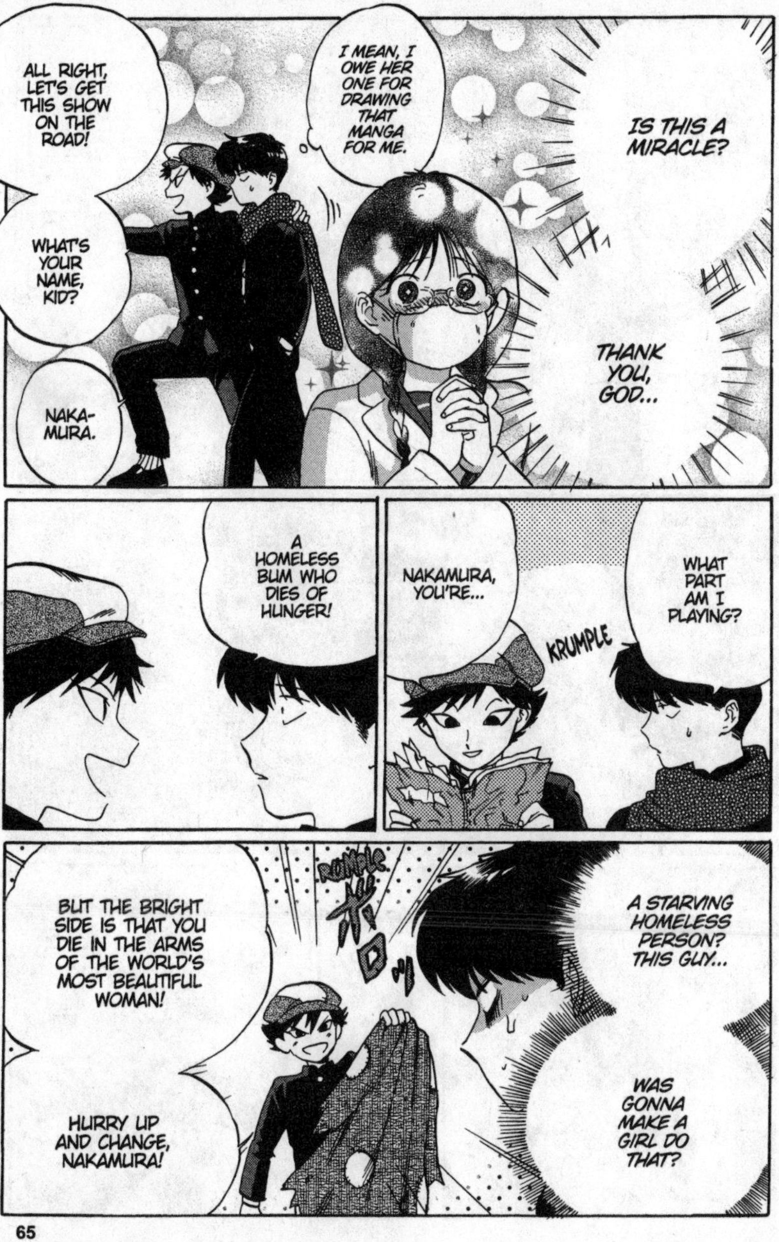
IS THIS A MIRACLE?
THANK YOU, GOD...
I MEAN, I OWE HER ONE FOR DRAWING THAT MANGA FOR ME.
ALL RIGHT, LET'S GET THIS SHOW ON THE ROAD!
WHAT'S YOUR NAME, KID?
NAKA-MURA.
WHAT PART AM I PLAYING?
KRUMPLE
NAKAMURA, YOU'RE...
A HOMELESS BUM WHO DIES OF HUNGER!
A STARVING HOMELESS PERSON? THIS GUY...
WAS GONNA MAKE A GIRL DO THAT?
RUMPLE
BUT THE BRIGHT SIDE IS THAT YOU DIE IN THE ARMS OF THE WORLD'S MOST BEAUTIFUL WOMAN!
HURRY UP AND CHANGE, NAKAMURA!

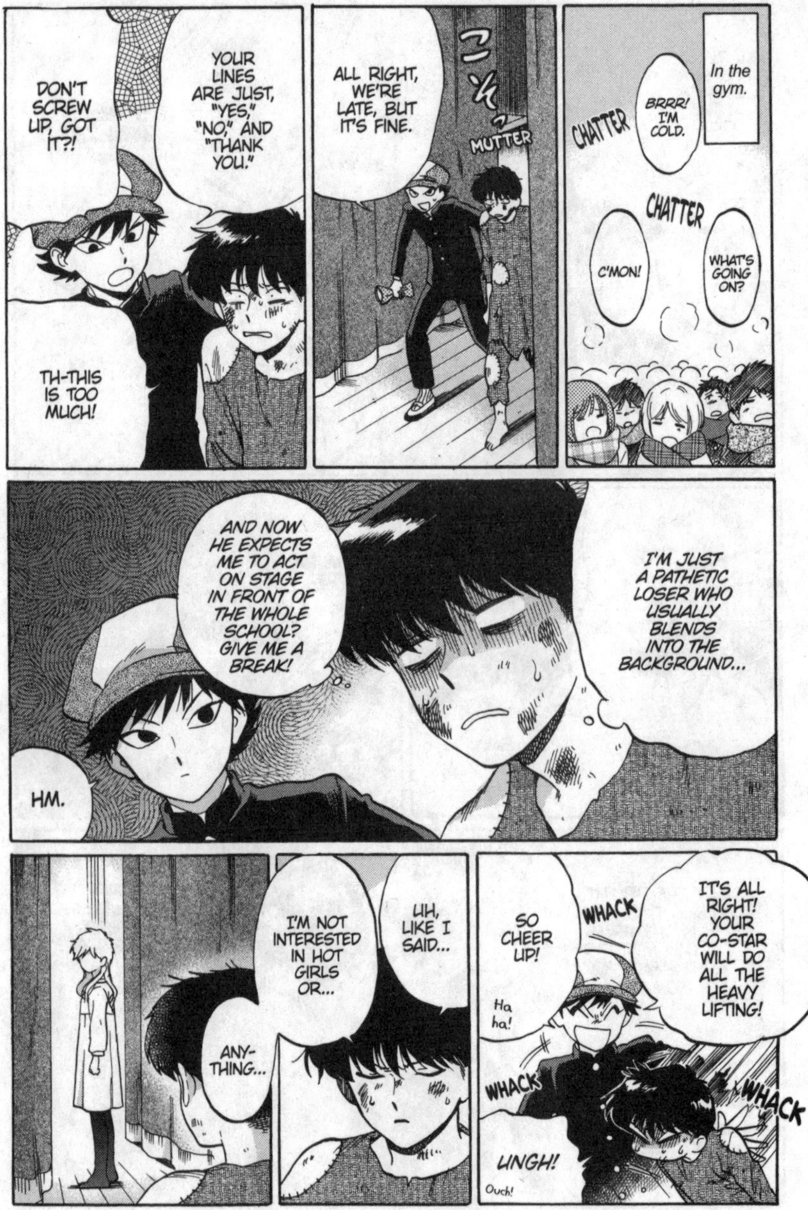

In the gym.
BRRR! I'M COLD.
CHATTER
CHATTER
WHAT'S GOING ON?
C'MON!
ALL RIGHT, WE'RE LATE, BUT IT'S FINE.
MUTTER
YOUR LINES ARE JUST, "YES," "NO," AND "THANK YOU."
DON'T SCREW UP, GOT IT?!
TH-THIS IS TOO MUCH!
I'M JUST A PATHETIC LOSER WHO USUALLY BLENDS INTO THE BACKGROUND...
AND NOW HE EXPECTS ME TO ACT ON STAGE IN FRONT OF THE WHOLE SCHOOL? GIVE ME A BREAK!
HM.
IT'S ALL RIGHT! YOUR CO-STAR WILL DO ALL THE HEAVY LIFTING!
WHACK
SO CHEER UP!
Ha ha!
WHACK
WHACK
UNGH!
Ouch!
UH, LIKE I SAID...
I'M NOT INTERESTED IN HOT GIRLS OR...
ANY-THING...

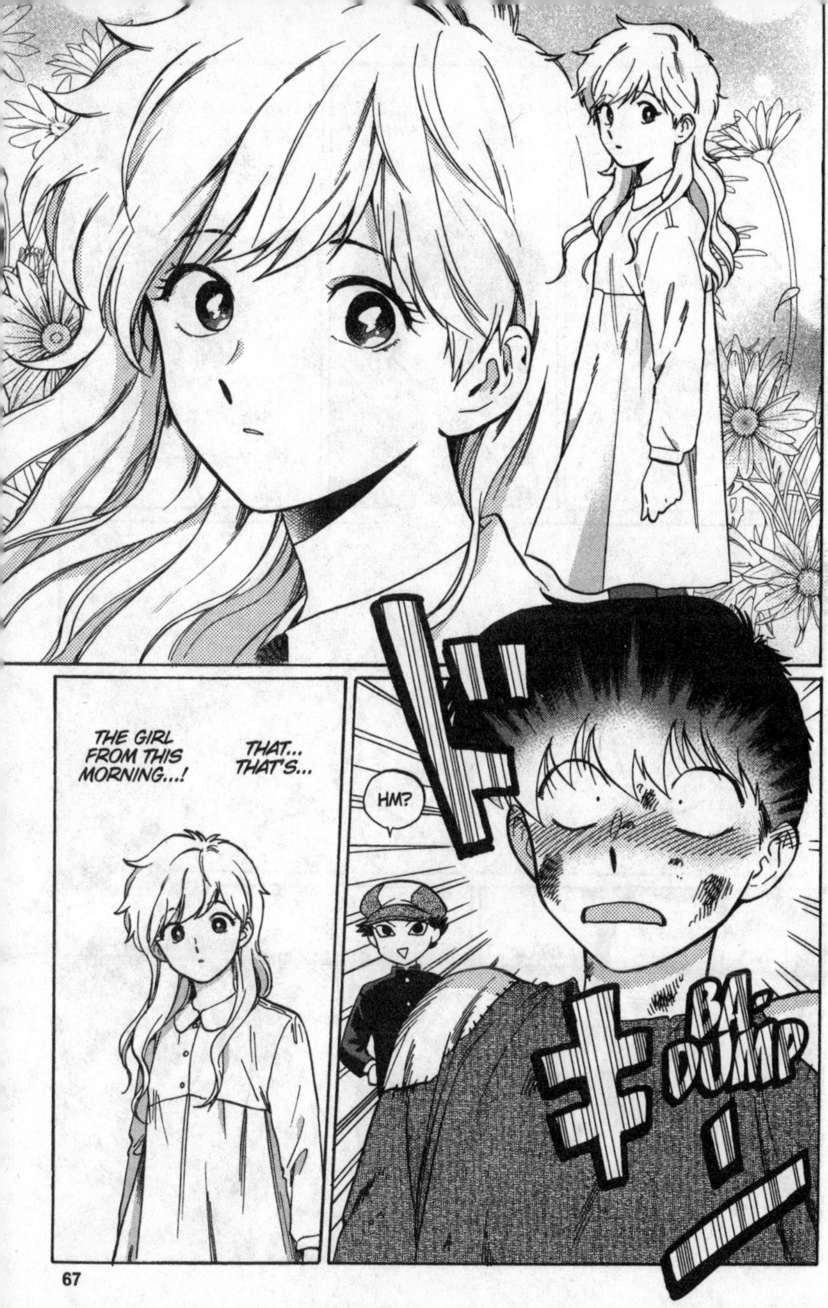
HM?
BA-DUMP
THAT... THAT'S...
THE GIRL FROM THIS MORNING...!

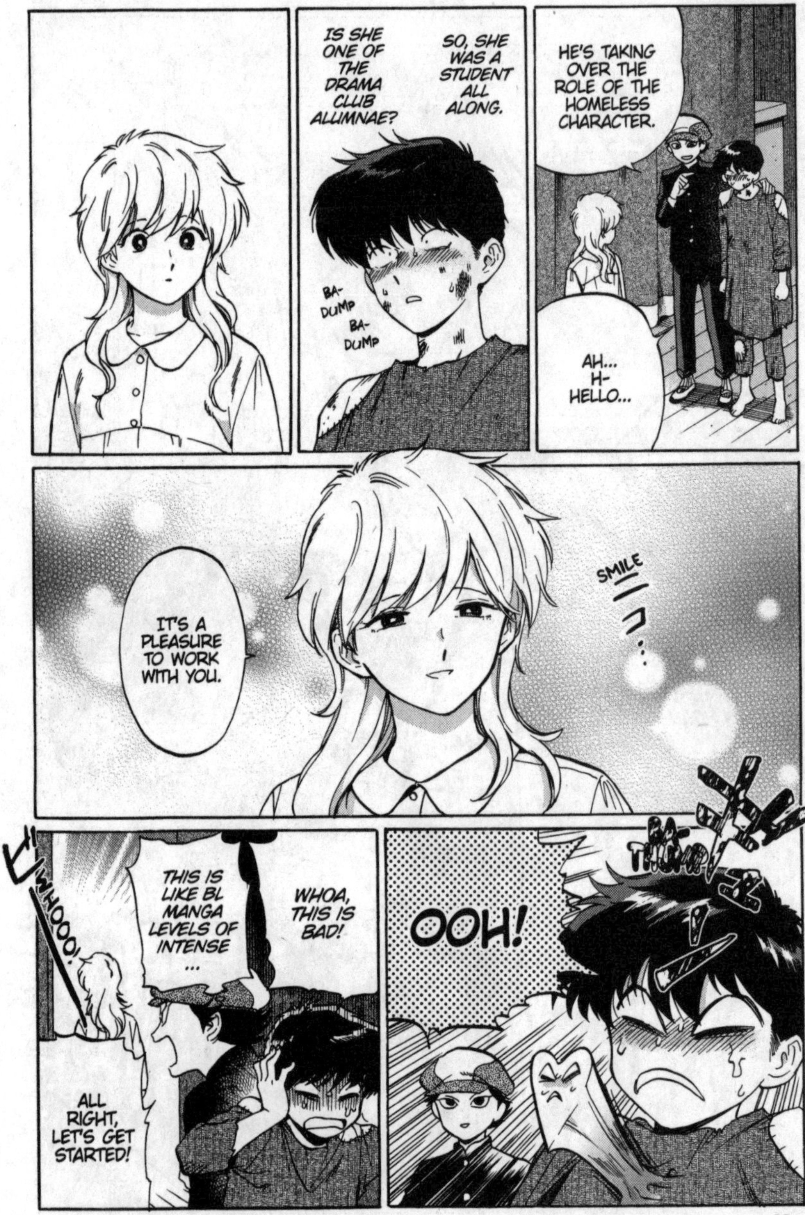
HE'S TAKING OVER THE ROLE OF THE HOMELESS CHARACTER.
AH... H-HELLO...
SO, SHE WAS A STUDENT ALL ALONG.
IS SHE ONE OF THE DRAMA CLUB ALUMNAE?
BA-DUMP BA-DUMP
SMILE
IT'S A PLEASURE TO WORK WITH YOU.
BA-THUMP
OOH!
WHOA, THIS IS BAD!
THIS IS LIKE BL MANGA LEVELS OF INTENSE ...
WHOOO!
ALL RIGHT, LET'S GET STARTED!

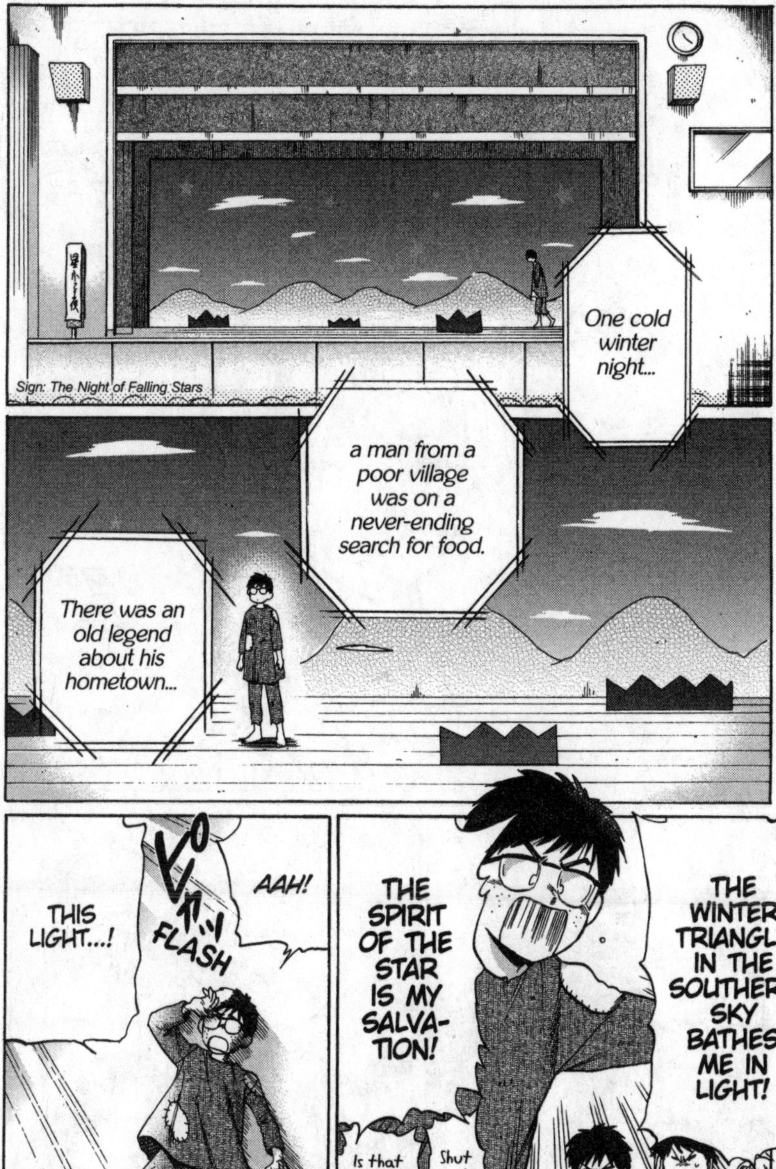
Sign: The Night of Falling Stars
One cold winter night...
a man from a poor village was on a never-ending search for food.
There was an old legend about his hometown...
THE WINTER TRIANGLE IN THE SOUTHERN SKY BATHES ME IN LIGHT!
THE SPIRIT OF THE STAR IS MY SALVATION!
Shut up!
Is that Oomori?!
AAH!
FLASH
THIS LIGHT...!

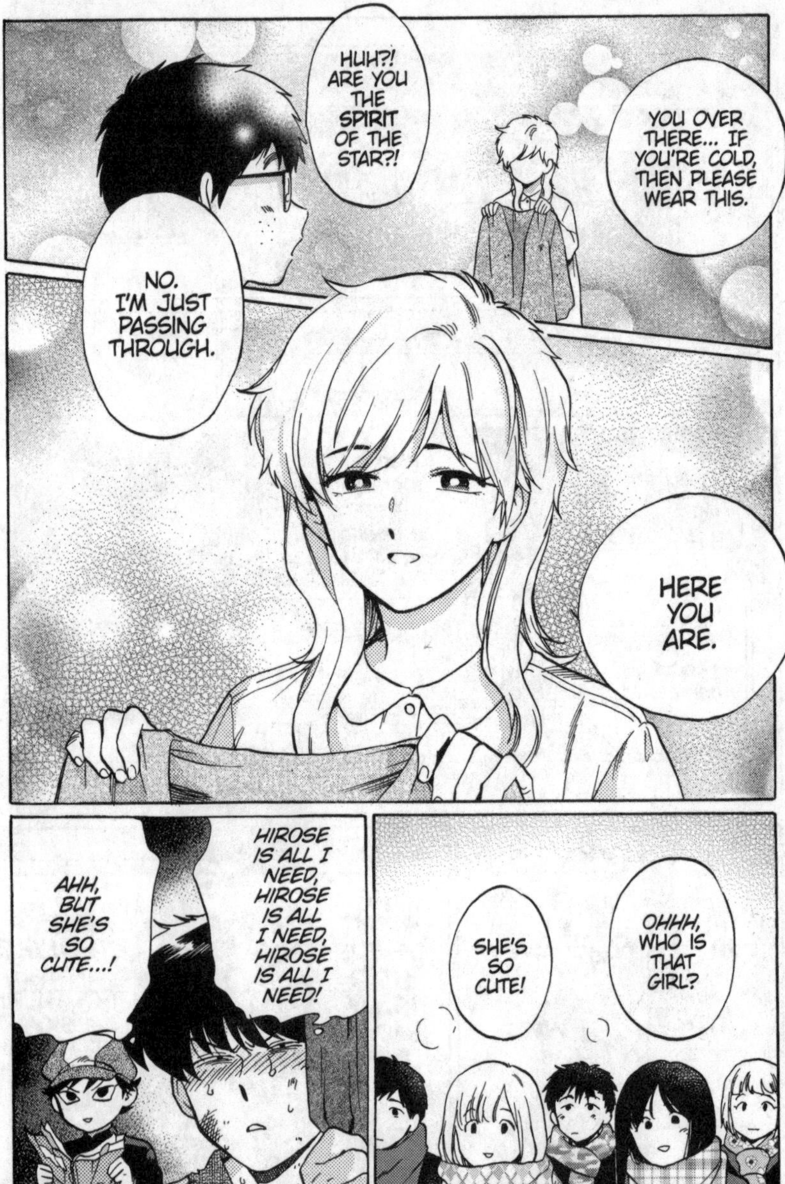
YOU OVER THERE... IF YOU'RE COLD, THEN PLEASE WEAR THIS.
HUH?! ARE YOU THE SPIRIT OF THE STAR?!
NO. I'M JUST PASSING THROUGH.
HERE YOU ARE.
OHHH, WHO IS THAT GIRL?
SHE'S SO CUTE!
HIROSE IS ALL I NEED, HIROSE IS ALL I NEED, HIROSE IS ALL I NEED!
AHH, BUT SHE'S SO CUTE...!

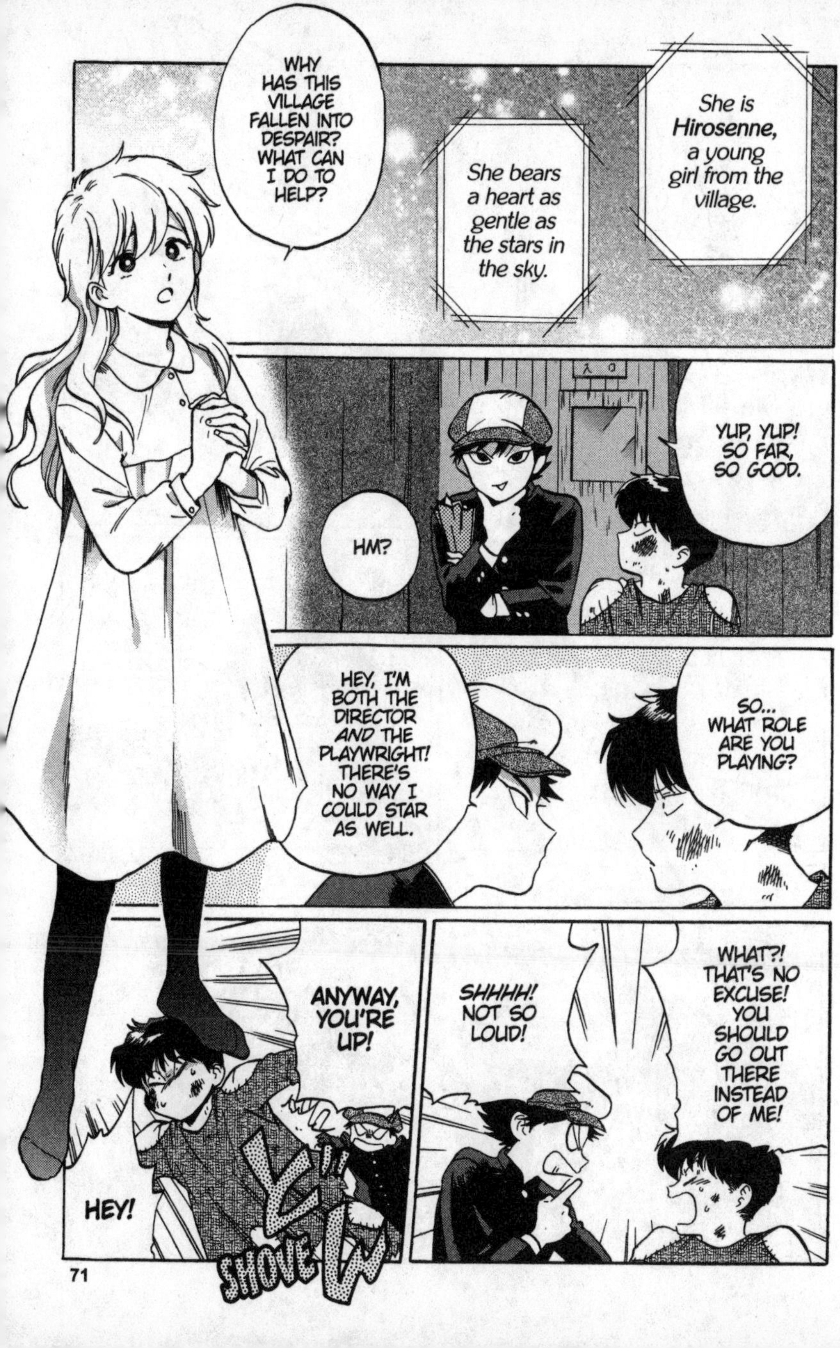
She is Hirosenne, a young girl from the village.
She bears a heart as gentle as the stars in the sky.
WHY HAS THIS VILLAGE FALLEN INTO DESPAIR? WHAT CAN I DO TO HELP?
YUP, YUP! SO FAR, SO GOOD.
HM?
SO... WHAT ROLE ARE YOU PLAYING?
HEY, I'M BOTH THE DIRECTOR *AND* THE PLAYWRIGHT! THERE'S NO WAY I COULD STAR AS WELL.
WHAT?! THAT'S NO EXCUSE! YOU SHOULD GO OUT THERE INSTEAD OF ME!
SHHHH! NOT SO LOUD!
ANYWAY, YOU'RE UP!
HEY!
SHOVE

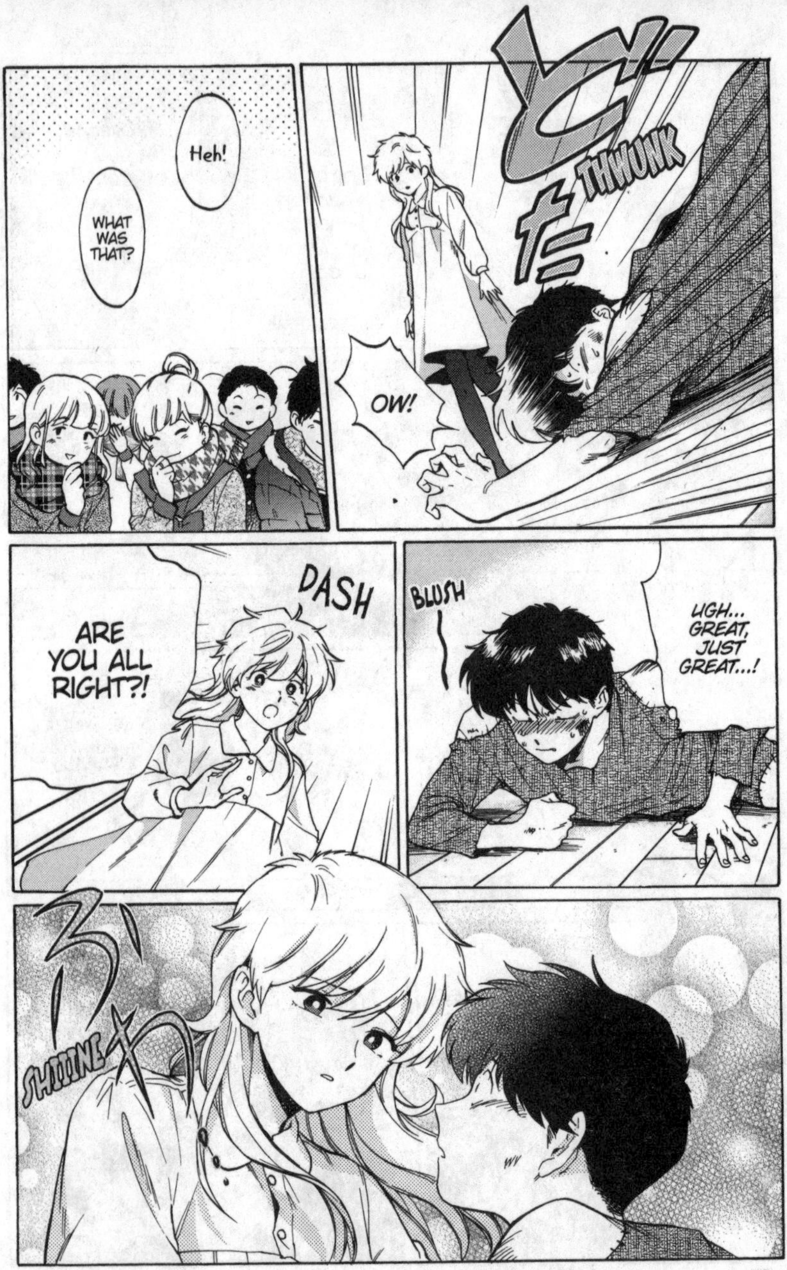
THWUNK
OW!
Heh!
WHAT WAS THAT?
UGH... GREAT, JUST GREAT...!
BLUSH
DASH
ARE YOU ALL RIGHT?!
SHIIINE

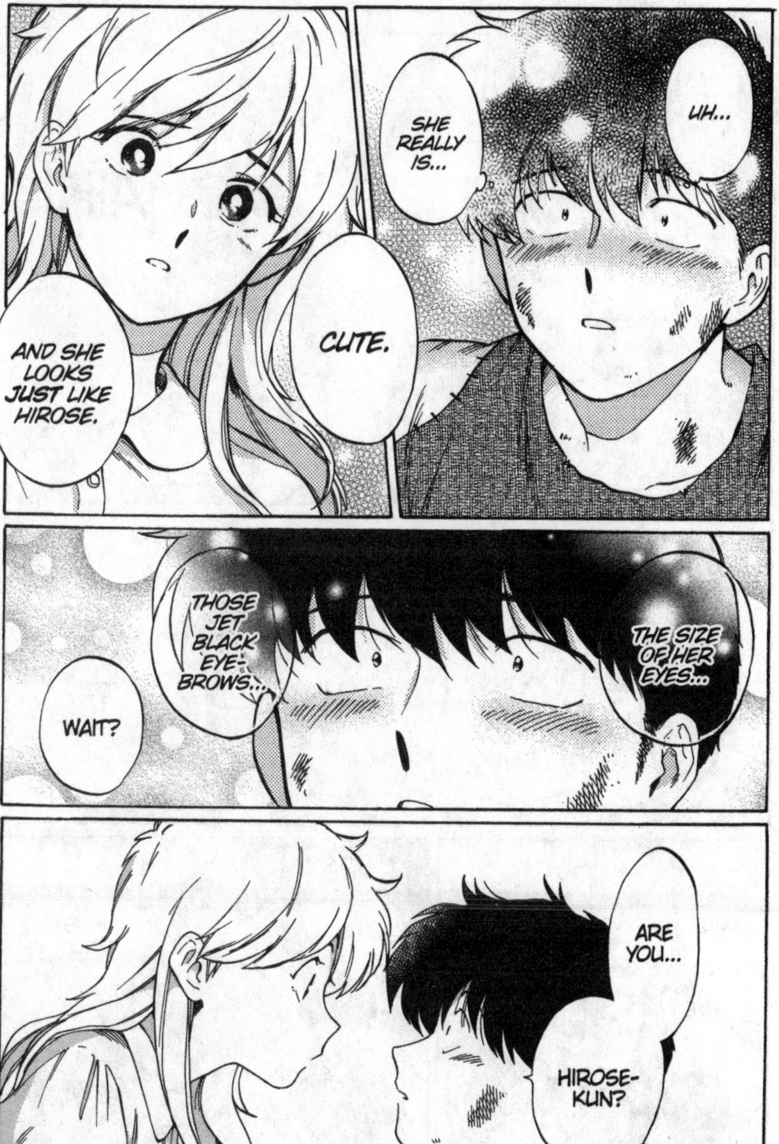
UH...
SHE REALLY IS...
CUTE.
AND SHE LOOKS JUST LIKE HIROSE.
THE SIZE OF HER EYES...
THOSE JET BLACK EYE-BROWS...
WAIT?
ARE YOU...
HIROSE-KUN?

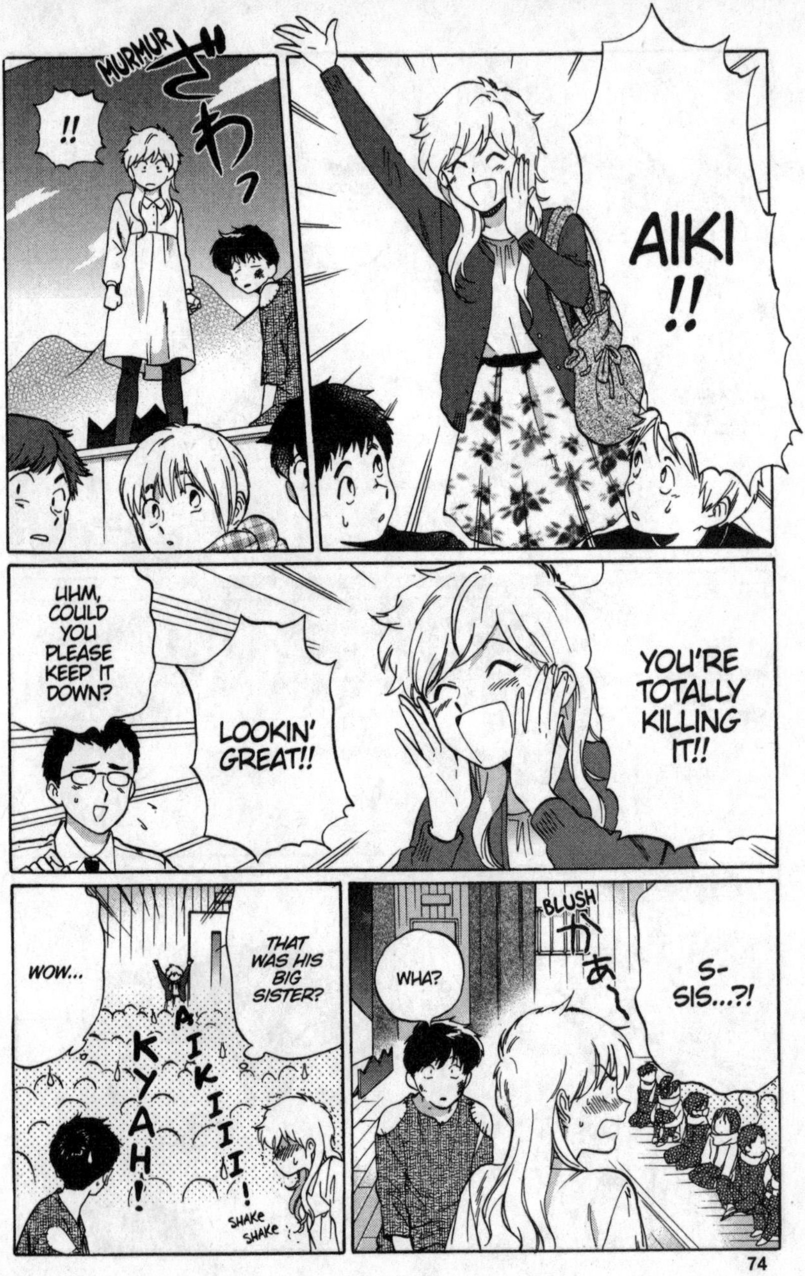
AIKI !!
MURMUR
ざわっ
!!
YOU'RE TOTALLY KILLING IT!!
LOOKIN' GREAT!!
UHM, COULD YOU PLEASE KEEP IT DOWN?
S- SIS...?!
BLUSH
かあ~
WHA?
THAT WAS HIS BIG SISTER?
WOW...
AIKIIII!
KYAH!
SHAKE SHAKE

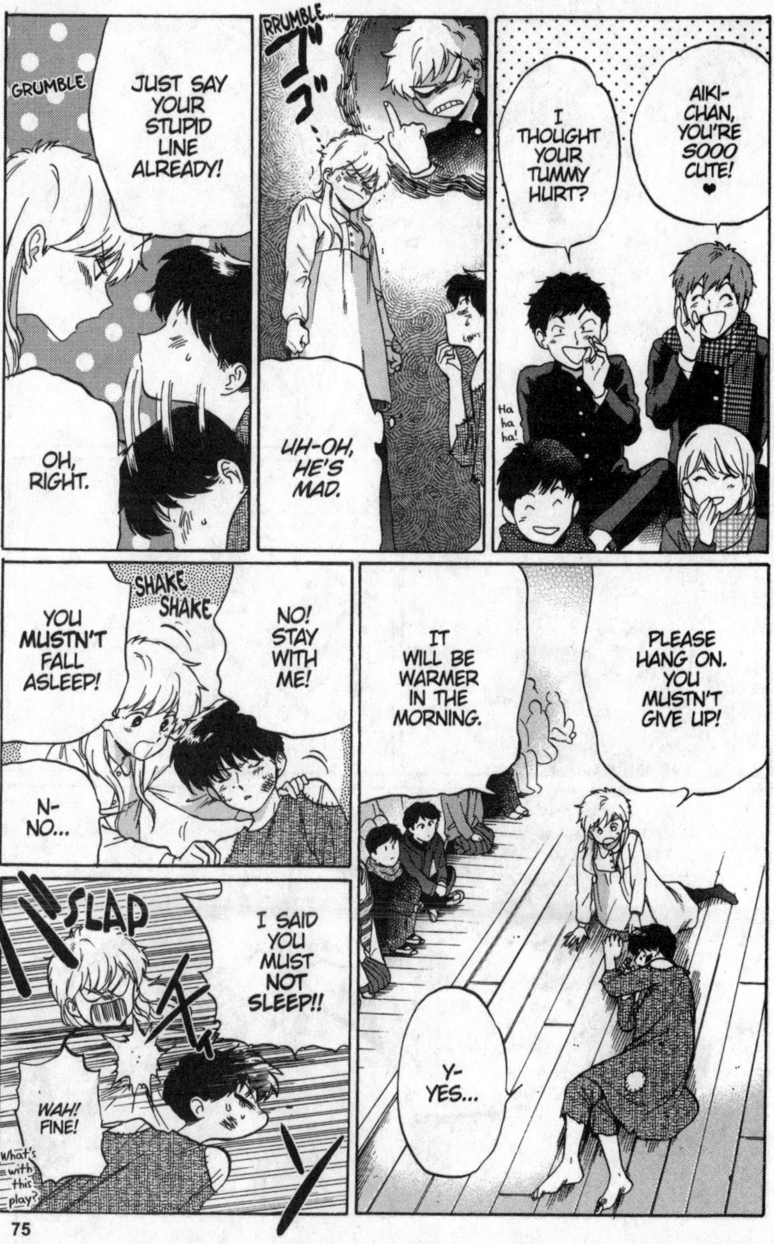

AIKI-CHAN, YOU'RE SOOO CUTE! ❤
I THOUGHT YOUR TUMMY HURT?
Ha ha ha!
RRUMBLE...
UH-OH, HE'S MAD.
GRUMBLE
JUST SAY YOUR STUPID LINE ALREADY!
OH, RIGHT.
PLEASE HANG ON. YOU MUSTN'T GIVE UP!
IT WILL BE WARMER IN THE MORNING.
Y-YES...
NO! STAY WITH ME!
SHAKE SHAKE
YOU MUSTN'T FALL ASLEEP!
N-NO...
I SAID YOU MUST NOT SLEEP!!
SLAP
WAH! FINE!
What's with this play?

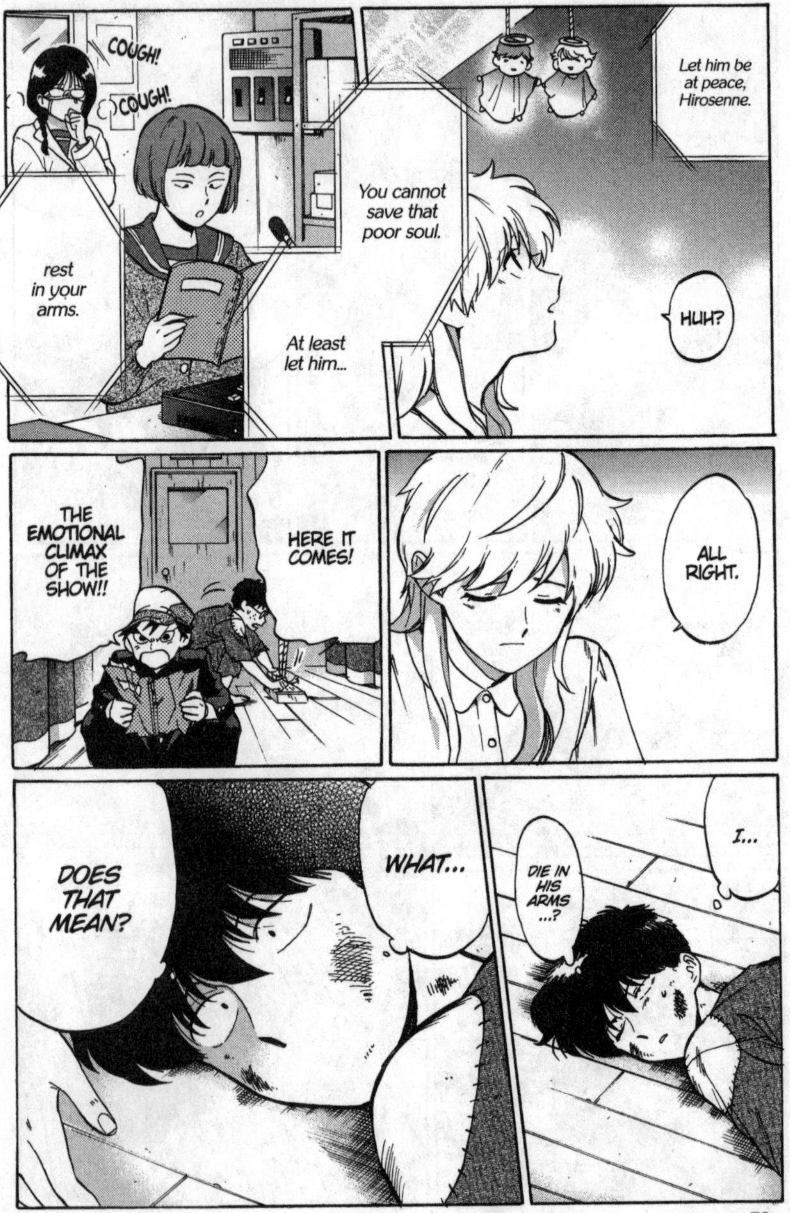
Let him be at peace, Hirosenne.
HUH?
You cannot save that poor soul.
At least let him...
COUGH!
COUGH!
rest in your arms.
ALL RIGHT.
HERE IT COMES!
THE EMOTIONAL CLIMAX OF THE SHOW!!
I...
DIE IN HIS ARMS ...?
WHAT...
DOES THAT MEAN?

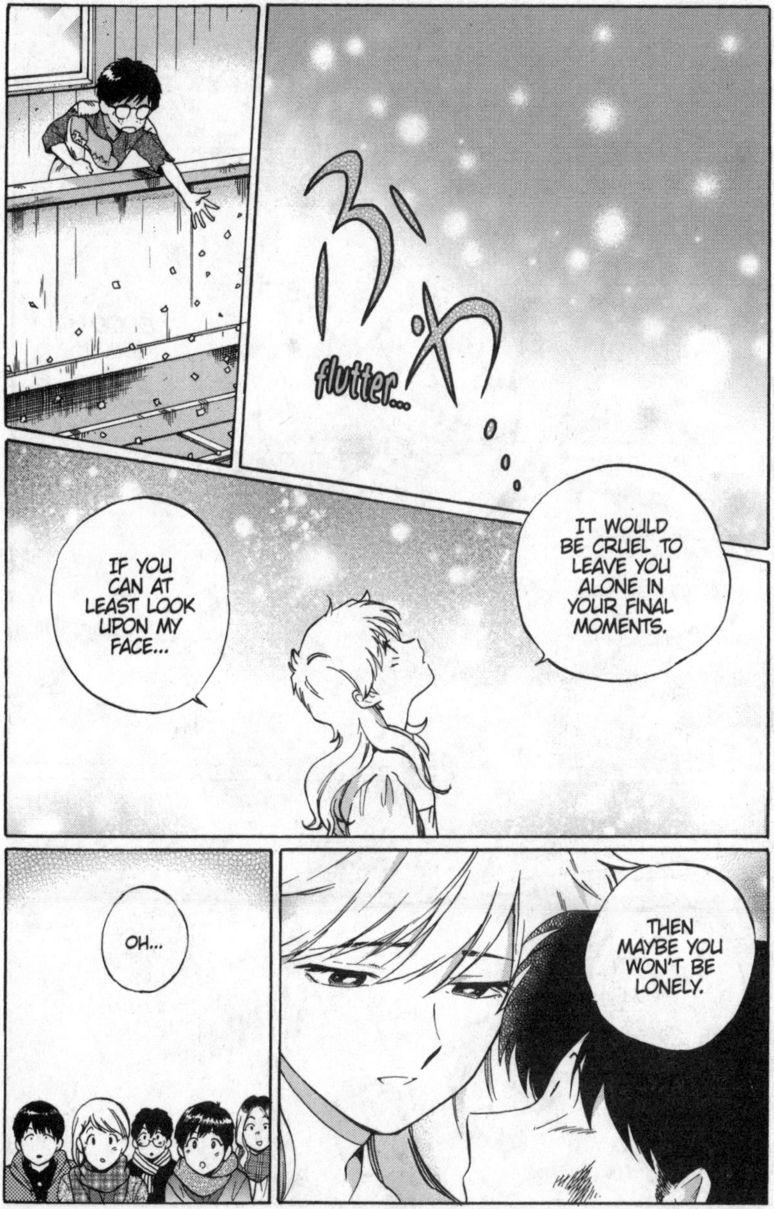
ふわ
flutter...
IT WOULD BE CRUEL TO LEAVE YOU ALONE IN YOUR FINAL MOMENTS.
IF YOU CAN AT LEAST LOOK UPON MY FACE...
THEN MAYBE YOU WON'T BE LONELY.
OH...

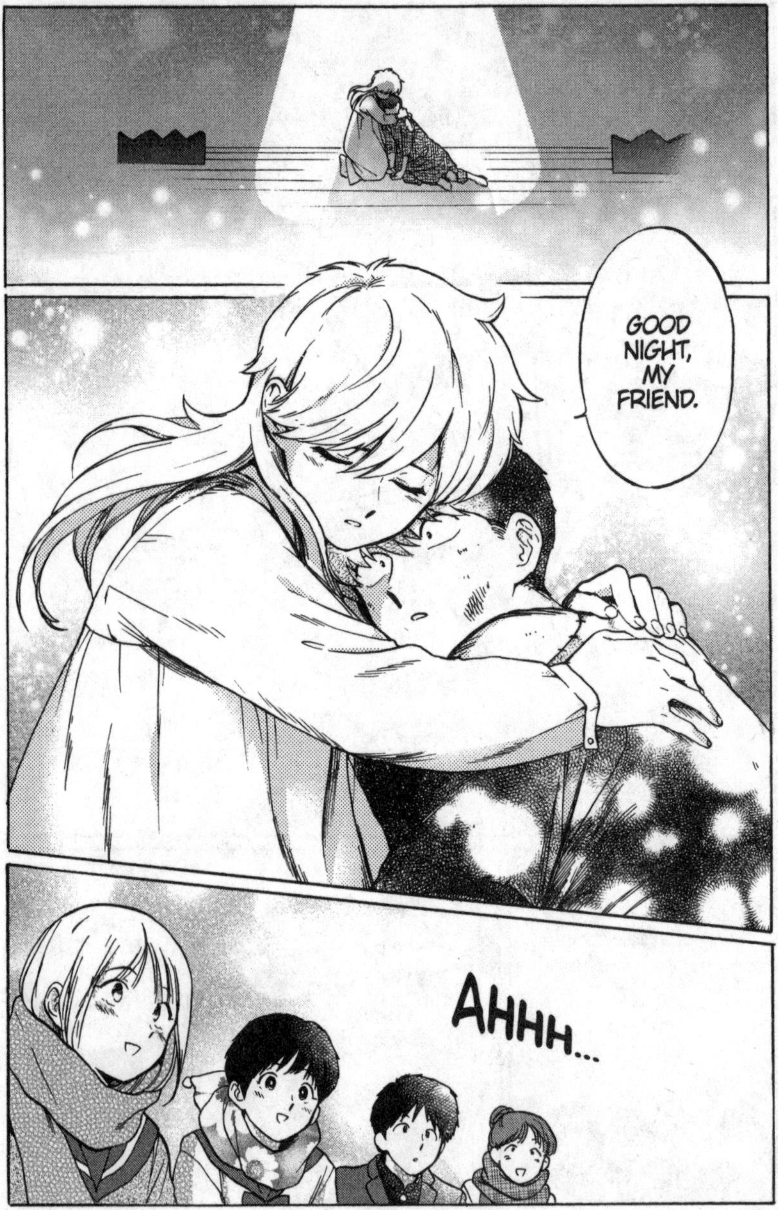
GOOD NIGHT, MY FRIEND.
AHHH...

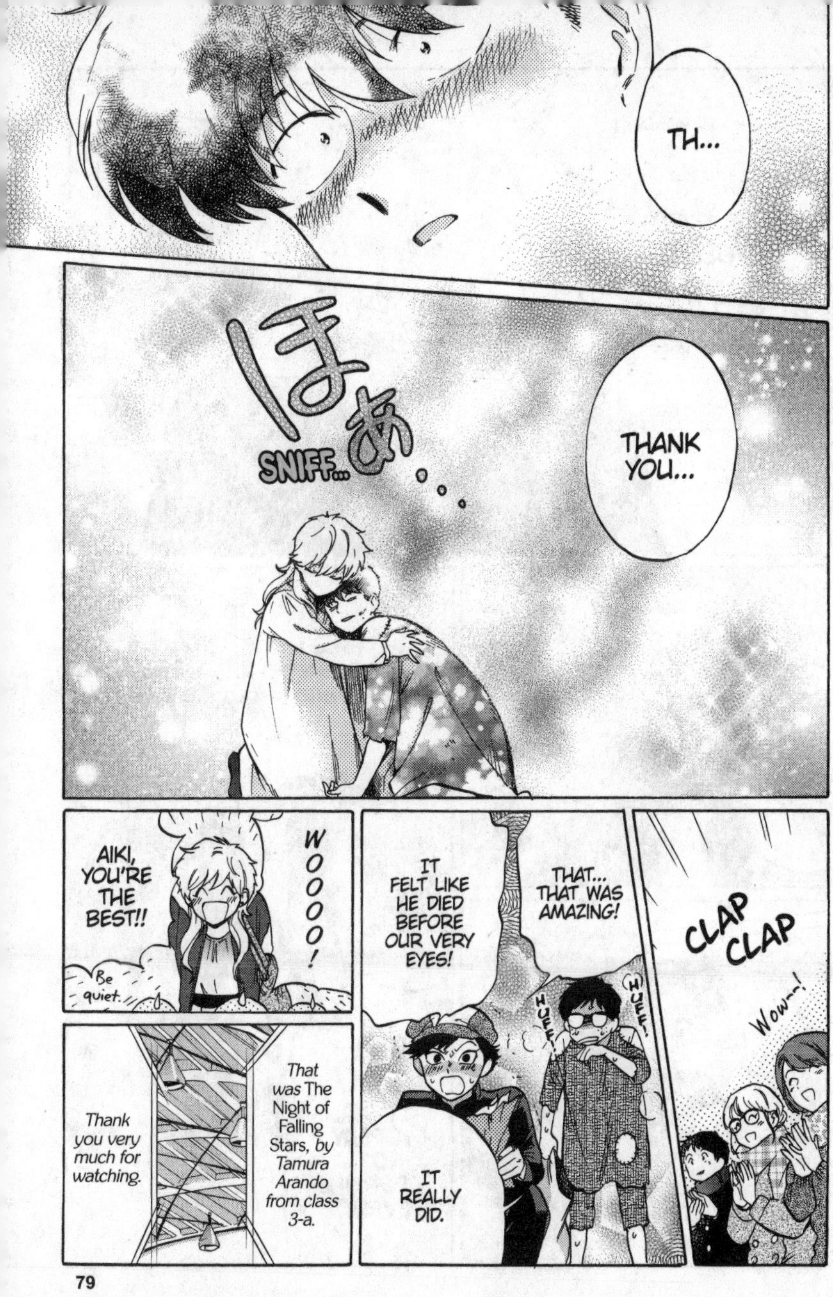
TH...
THANK YOU...
ほぁ
SNIFF...
CLAP CLAP
Wow--!
THAT... THAT WAS AMAZING!
IT FELT LIKE HE DIED BEFORE OUR VERY EYES!
HUFF HUFF
IT REALLY DID.
WOOOOO!
AIKI, YOU'RE THE BEST!!
Be quiet.
That was The Night of Falling Stars, by Tamura Arando from class 3-a.
Thank you very much for watching.

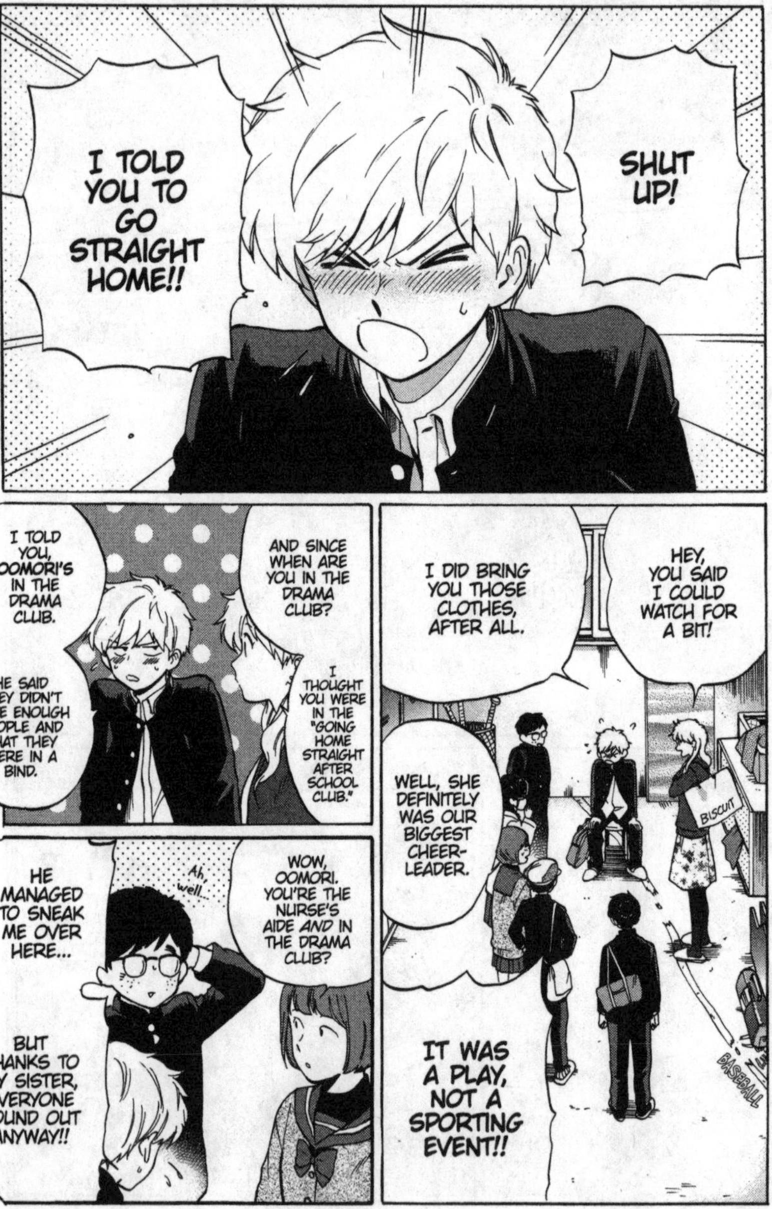
SHUT UP!
I TOLD YOU TO GO STRAIGHT HOME!!
HEY, YOU SAID I COULD WATCH FOR A BIT!
I DID BRING YOU THOSE CLOTHES, AFTER ALL.
WELL, SHE DEFINITELY WAS OUR BIGGEST CHEER-LEADER.
BISCUIT
BASEBALL
IT WAS A PLAY, NOT A SPORTING EVENT!!
AND SINCE WHEN ARE YOU IN THE DRAMA CLUB?
I THOUGHT YOU WERE IN THE "GOING HOME STRAIGHT AFTER SCHOOL CLUB."
I TOLD YOU, OOMORI'S IN THE DRAMA CLUB.
HE SAID THEY DIDN'T HAVE ENOUGH PEOPLE AND THAT THEY WERE IN A BIND.
WOW, OOMORI. YOU'RE THE NURSE'S AIDE *AND* IN THE DRAMA CLUB?
Ah, well...
HE MANAGED TO SNEAK ME OVER HERE...
BUT THANKS TO MY SISTER, EVERYONE FOUND OUT ANYWAY!!

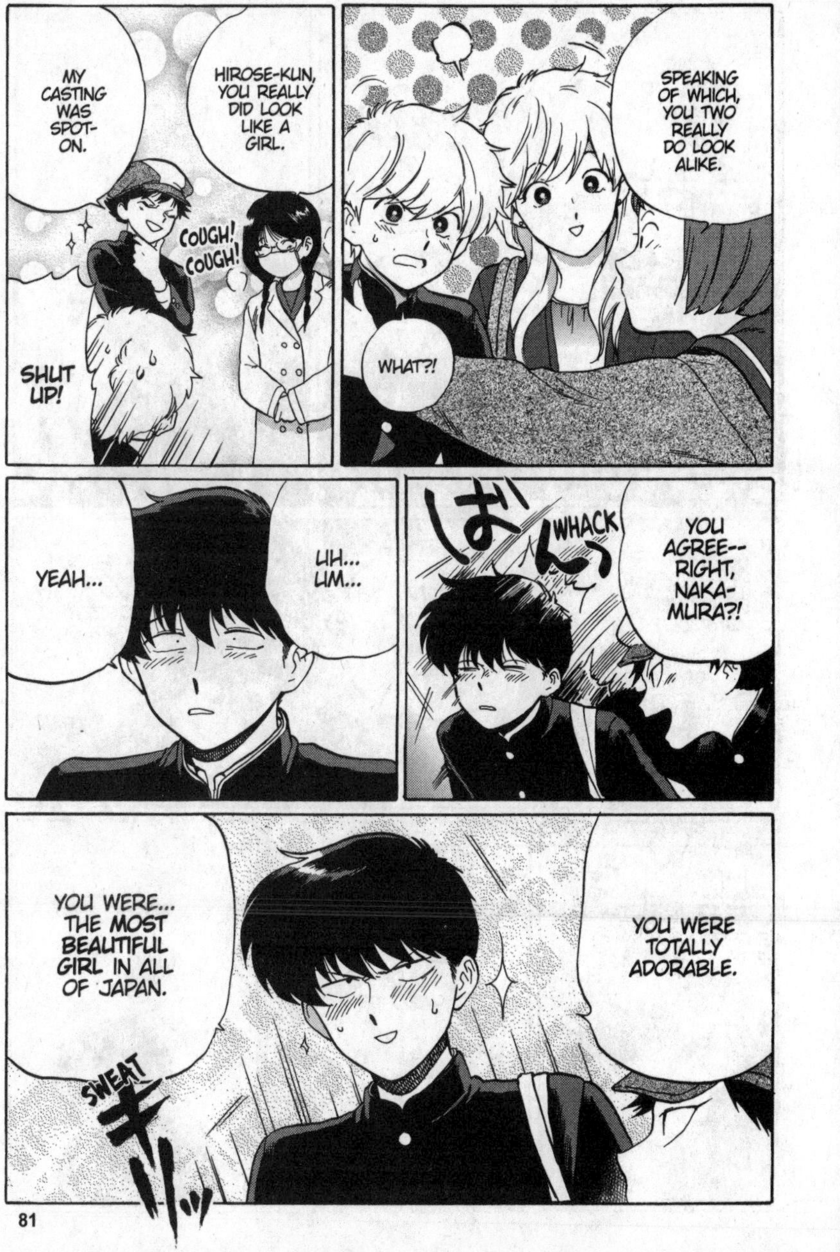
SPEAKING OF WHICH, YOU TWO REALLY DO LOOK ALIKE.
WHAT?!
HIROSE-KUN, YOU REALLY DID LOOK LIKE A GIRL.
MY CASTING WAS SPOT-ON.
COUGH! COUGH!
SHUT UP!
WHACK
YOU AGREE--RIGHT, NAKAMURA?!
UH... UM...
YEAH...
YOU WERE TOTALLY ADORABLE.
YOU WERE... THE MOST BEAUTIFUL GIRL IN ALL OF JAPAN.
SWEAT

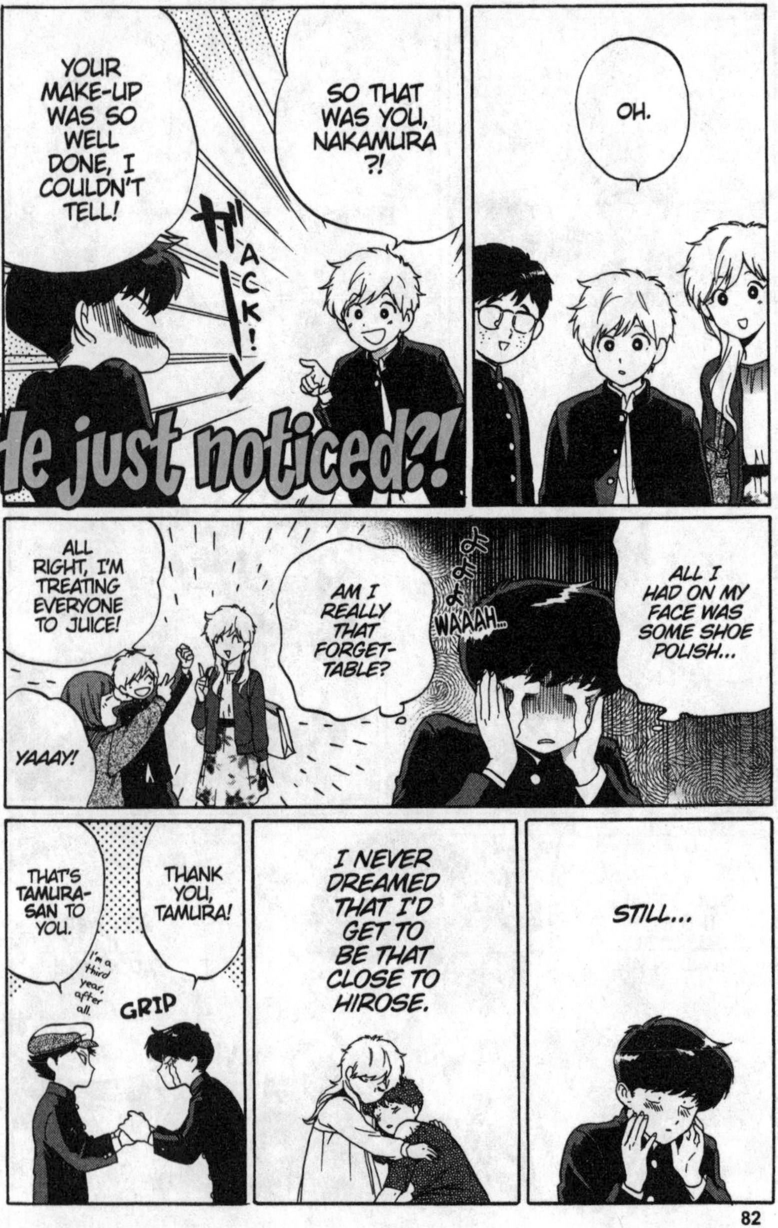
OH.
SO THAT WAS YOU, NAKAMURA?!
YOUR MAKE-UP WAS SO WELL DONE, I COULDN'T TELL!
HACK!
He just noticed?!
ALL I HAD ON MY FACE WAS SOME SHOE POLISH...
WAAAH...
AM I REALLY THAT FORGET-TABLE?
ALL RIGHT, I'M TREATING EVERYONE TO JUICE!
YAAAY!
STILL...
I NEVER DREAMED THAT I'D GET TO BE THAT CLOSE TO HIROSE.
THANK YOU, TAMURA!
THAT'S TAMURA-SAN TO YOU.
I'm a third year, after all.
GRIP

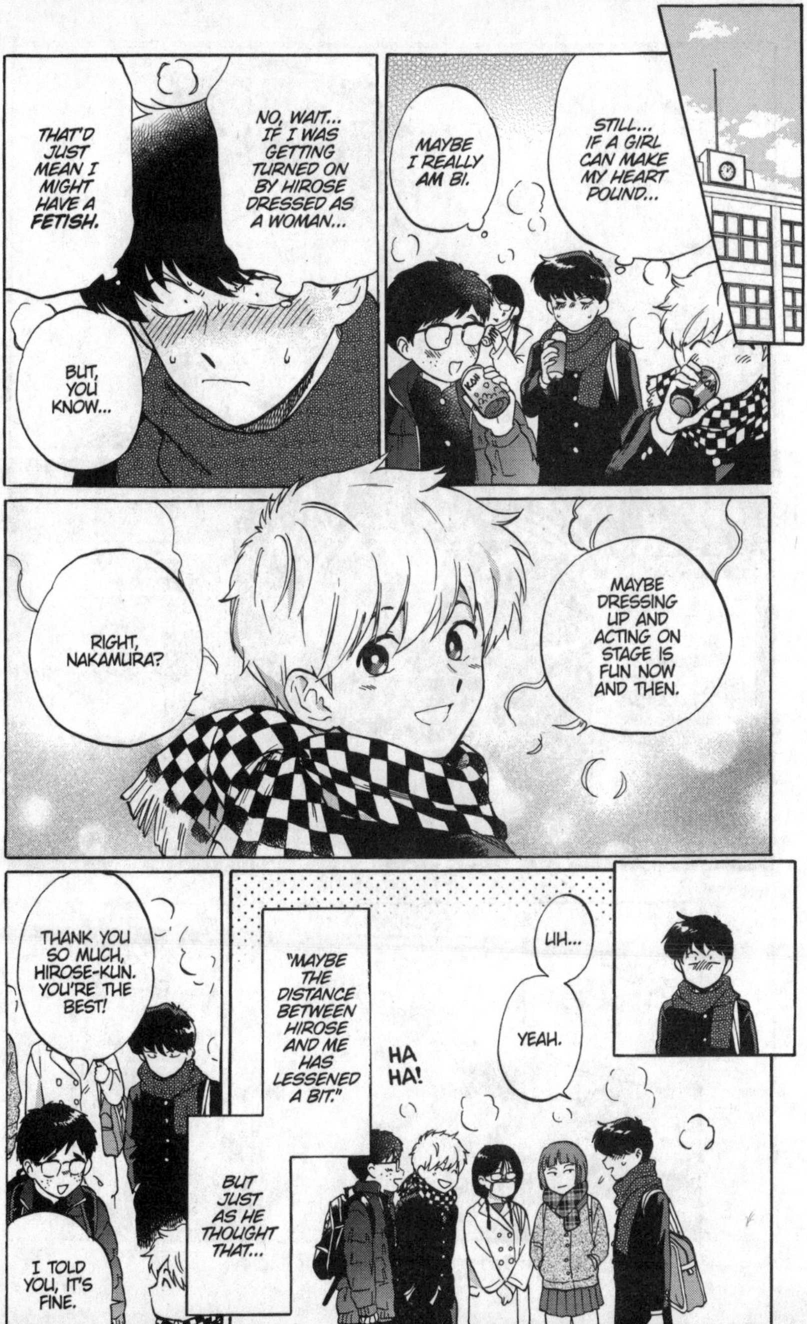
STILL... IF A GIRL CAN MAKE MY HEART POUND...
MAYBE I REALLY AM BI.
NO, WAIT... IF I WAS GETTING TURNED ON BY HIROSE DRESSED AS A WOMAN...
THAT'D JUST MEAN I MIGHT HAVE A FETISH.
BUT, YOU KNOW...
MAYBE DRESSING UP AND ACTING ON STAGE IS FUN NOW AND THEN.
RIGHT, NAKAMURA?
UH...
YEAH.
HA HA!
"MAYBE THE DISTANCE BETWEEN HIROSE AND ME HAS LESSENED A BIT."
BUT JUST AS HE THOUGHT THAT...
THANK YOU SO MUCH, HIROSE-KUN. YOU'RE THE BEST!
I TOLD YOU, IT'S FINE.

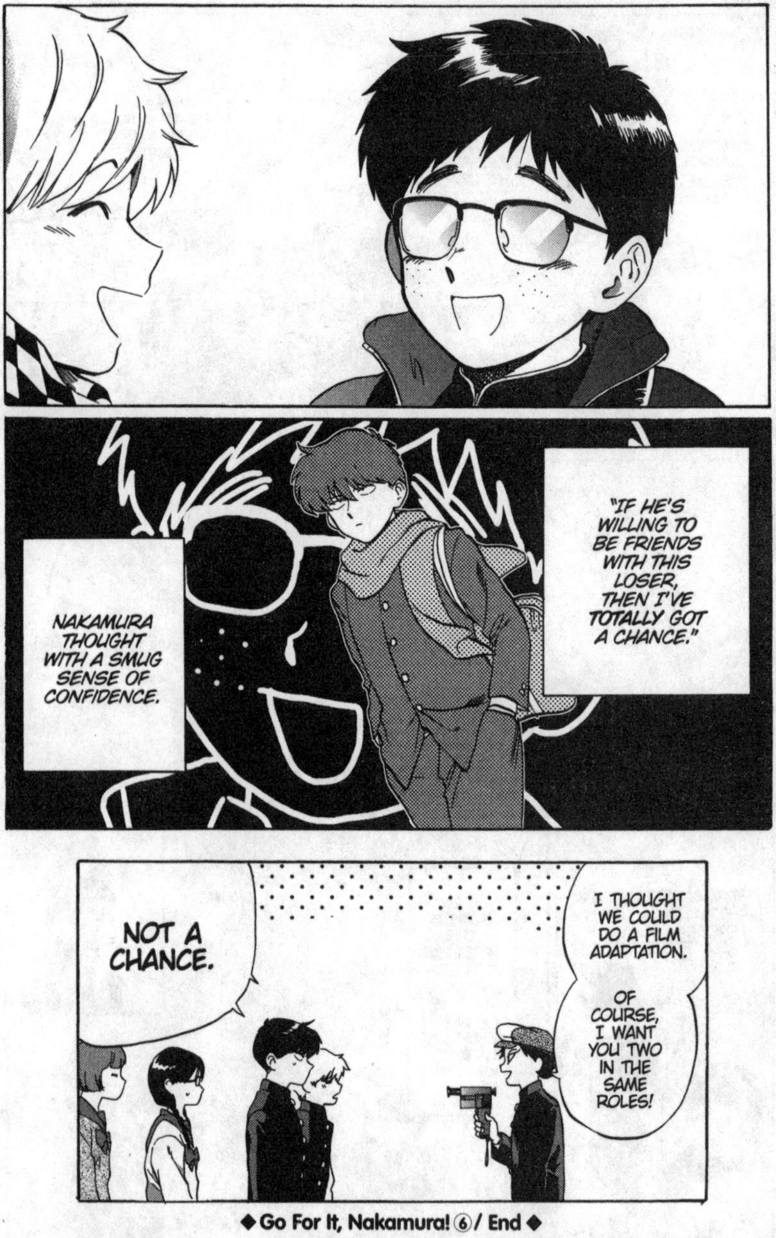
"IF HE'S WILLING TO BE FRIENDS WITH THIS LOSER, THEN I'VE TOTALLY GOT A CHANCE."
NAKAMURA THOUGHT WITH A SMUG SENSE OF CONFIDENCE.
I THOUGHT WE COULD DO A FILM ADAPTATION.
OF COURSE, I WANT YOU TWO IN THE SAME ROLES!
NOT A CHANCE.

◆Go For It, Nakamura! ⑥ / End◆

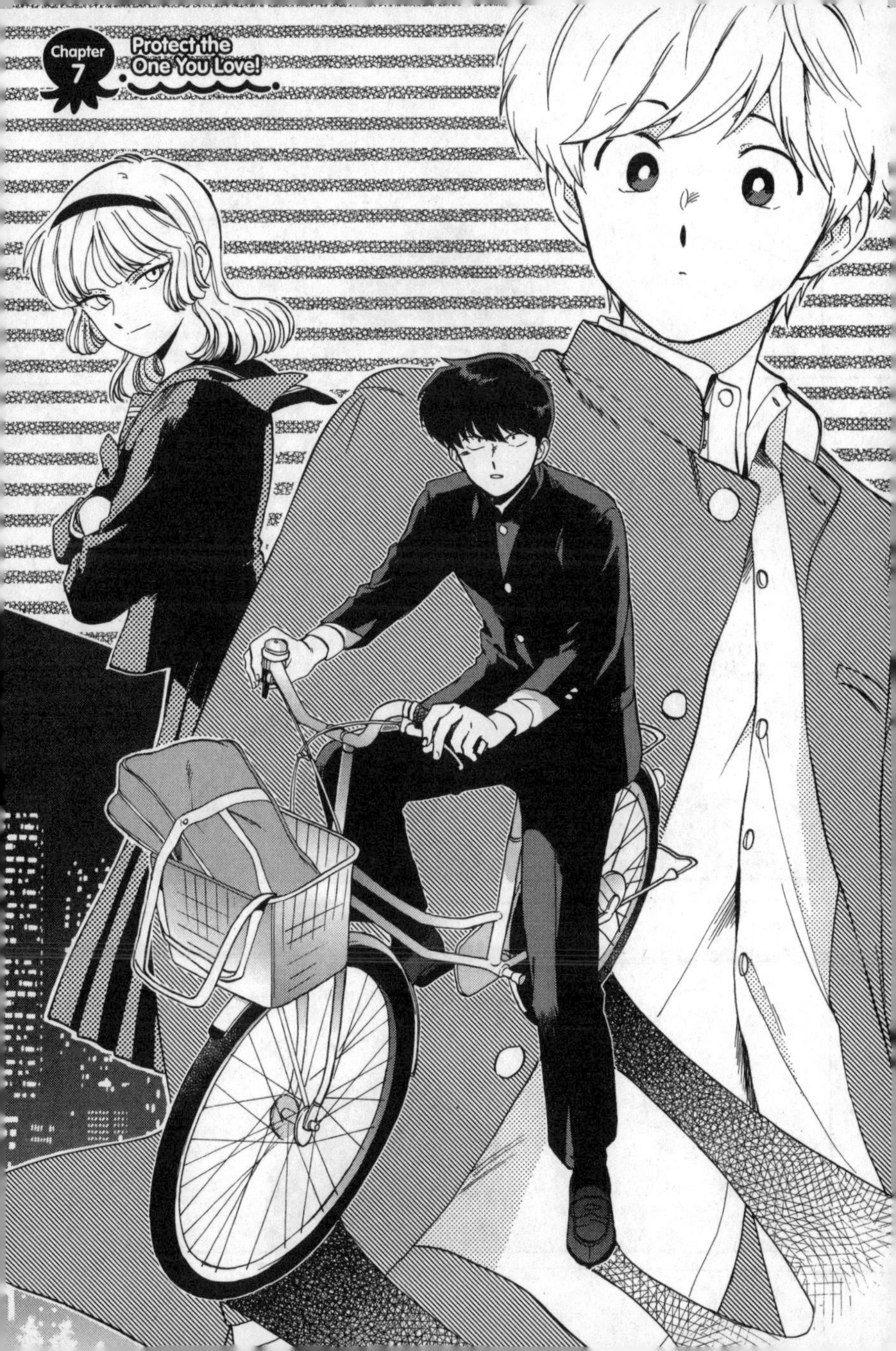
Chapter 7
Protect the One You Love!

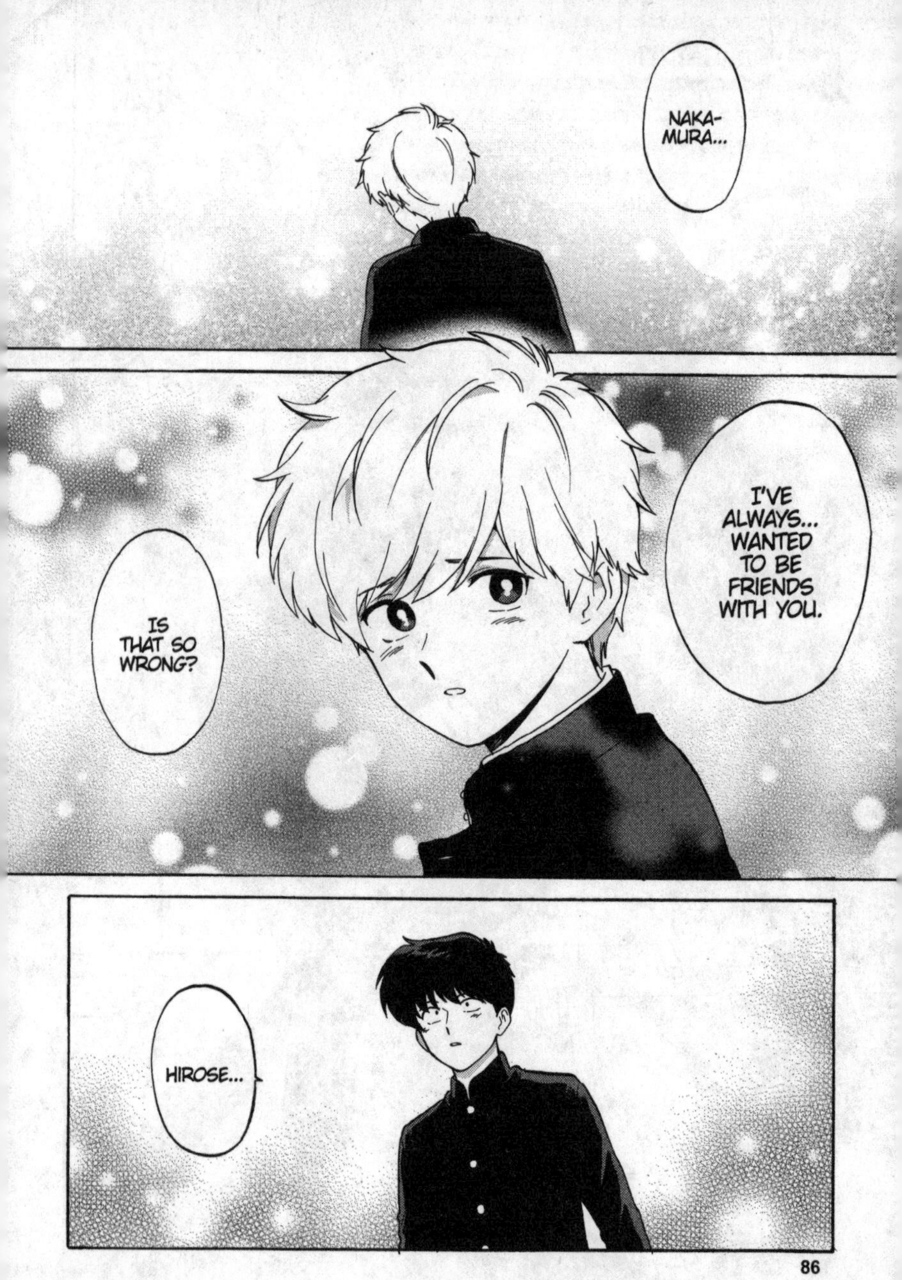
NAKA-MURA...
I'VE ALWAYS... WANTED TO BE FRIENDS WITH YOU.
IS THAT SO WRONG?
HIROSE...

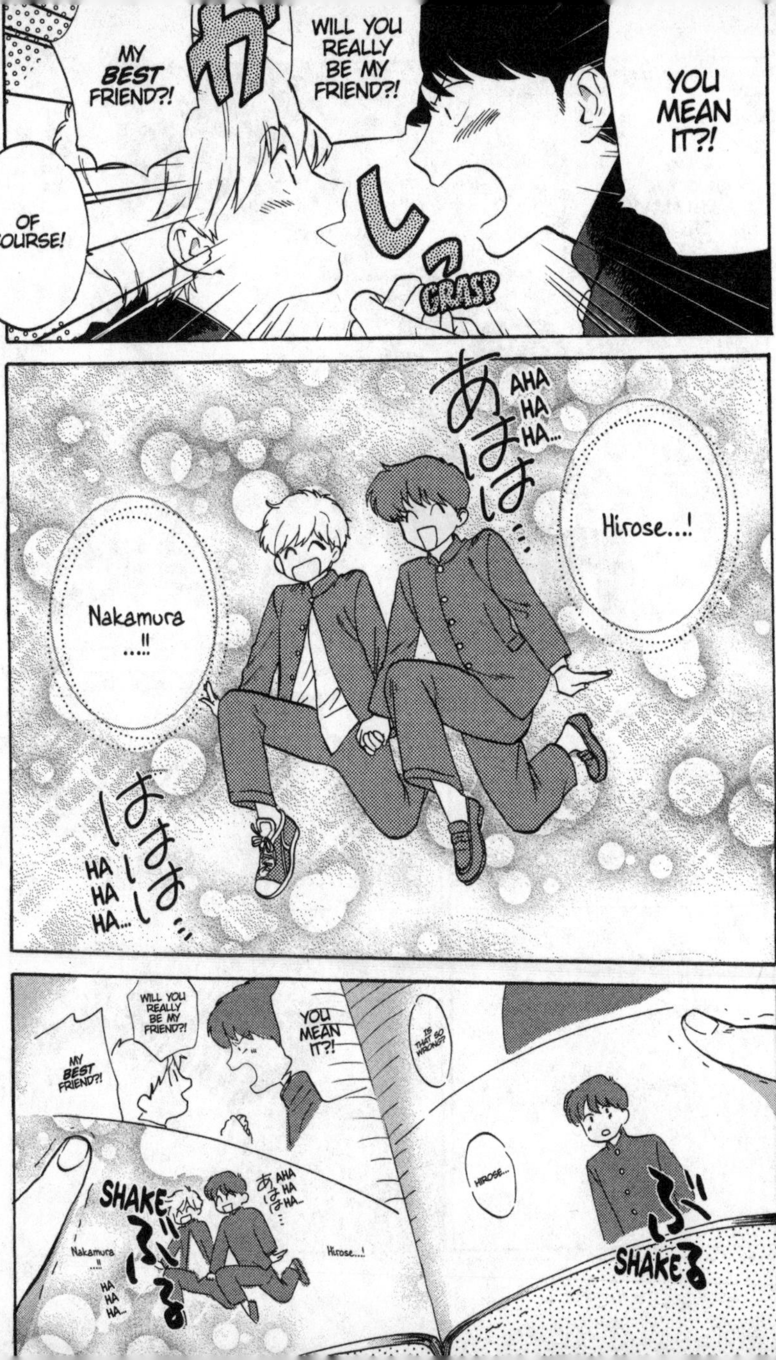
YOU MEAN IT?!
WILL YOU REALLY BE MY FRIEND?!
MY BEST FRIEND?!
OF COURSE!
GRASP
AHA HA HA...
Hirose...!
Nakamura ...!!
HA HA HA...
SHAKE
HIROSE...
IS THAT SO WRONG?
YOU MEAN IT?!
WILL YOU REALLY BE MY FRIEND?!
MY BEST FRIEND?!
AHA HA HA...
Hirose...!
SHAKE
Nakamura ...!!
HA HA HA...

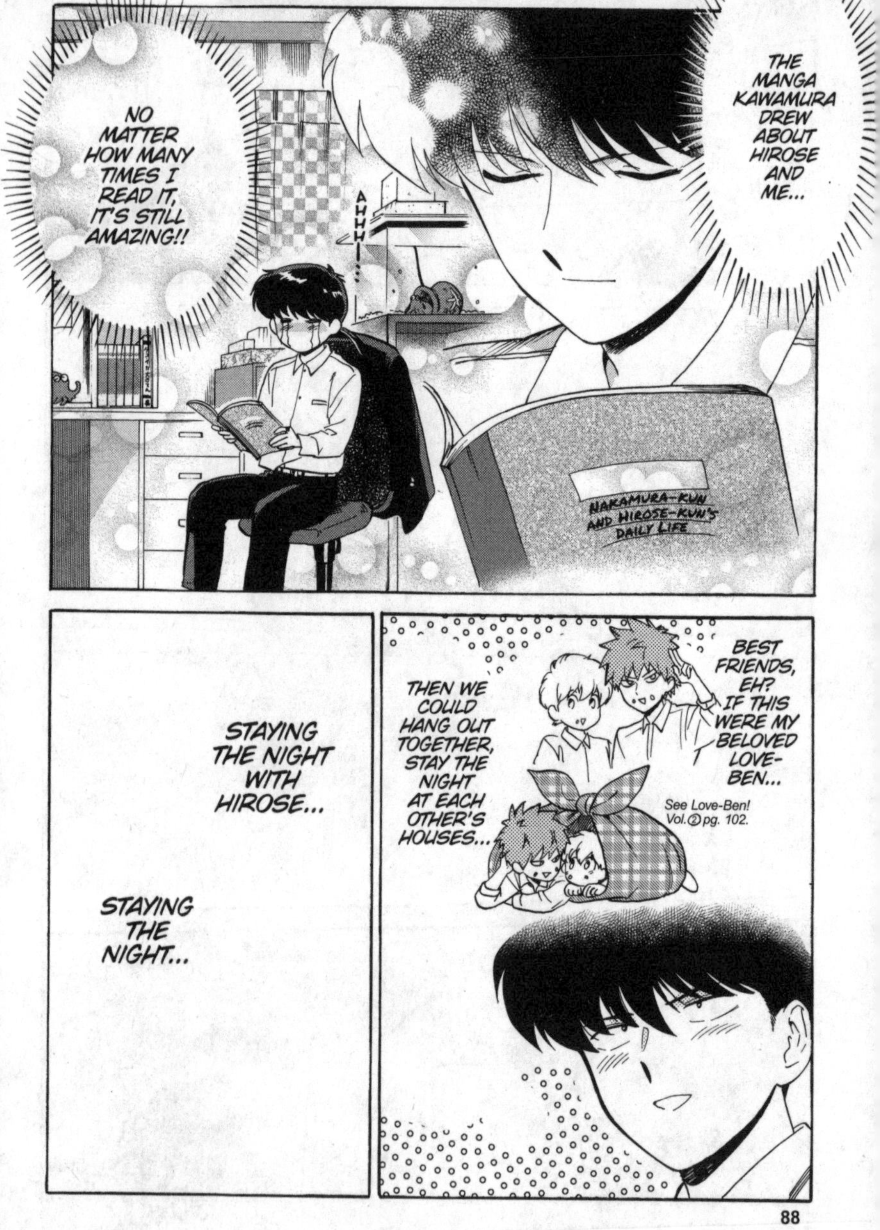
THE MANGA KAWAMURA DREW ABOUT HIROSE AND ME...
NO MATTER HOW MANY TIMES I READ IT, IT'S STILL AMAZING!!
AHHH!!
NAKAMURA-KUN AND HIROSE-KUN'S DAILY LIFE
BEST FRIENDS, EH? IF THIS WERE MY BELOVED LOVE-BEN...
See Love-Ben! Vol.② pg. 102.
THEN WE COULD HANG OUT TOGETHER, STAY THE NIGHT AT EACH OTHER'S HOUSES...
STAYING THE NIGHT WITH HIROSE...
STAYING THE NIGHT...

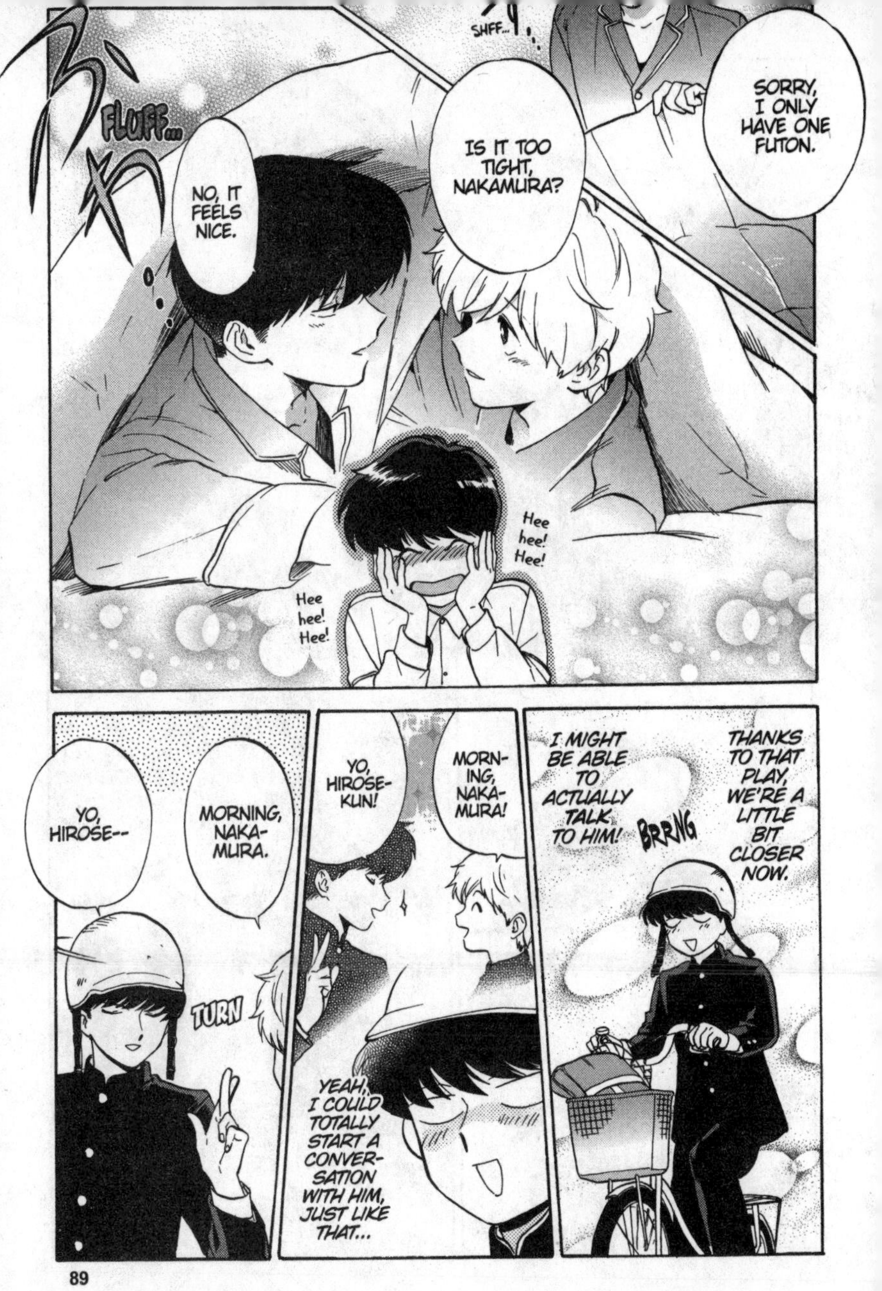
SHFF...
SORRY, I ONLY HAVE ONE FUTON.
IS IT TOO TIGHT, NAKAMURA?
NO, IT FEELS NICE.
FLUFF...
Hee hee! Hee!
Hee hee! Hee!
THANKS TO THAT PLAY, WE'RE A LITTLE BIT CLOSER NOW.
BRRNG
I MIGHT BE ABLE TO ACTUALLY TALK TO HIM!
MORNING, NAKAMURA!
YO, HIROSE-KUN!
YEAH, I COULD TOTALLY START A CONVERSATION WITH HIM, JUST LIKE THAT...
MORNING, NAKAMURA.
YO, HIROSE--
TURN

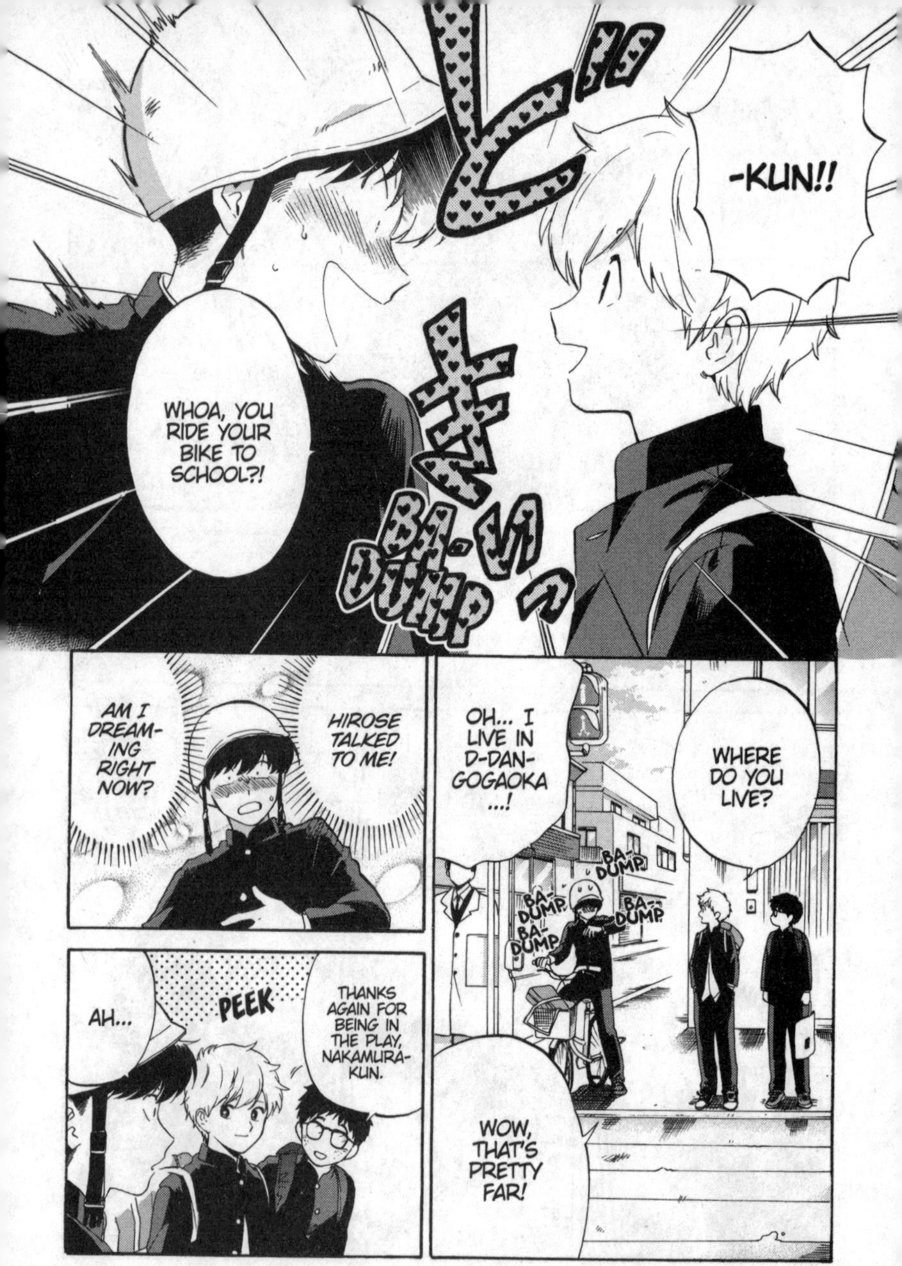
-KUN!!
BA-DUMP
WHOA, YOU RIDE YOUR BIKE TO SCHOOL?!
WHERE DO YOU LIVE?
BA-DUMP
BA-DUMP
BA-DUMP
BA-DUMP
OH... I LIVE IN D-DAN-GOGAOKA ...!
WOW, THAT'S PRETTY FAR!
HIROSE TALKED TO ME!
AM I DREAMING RIGHT NOW?
THANKS AGAIN FOR BEING IN THE PLAY, NAKAMURA-KUN.
PEEK
AH...

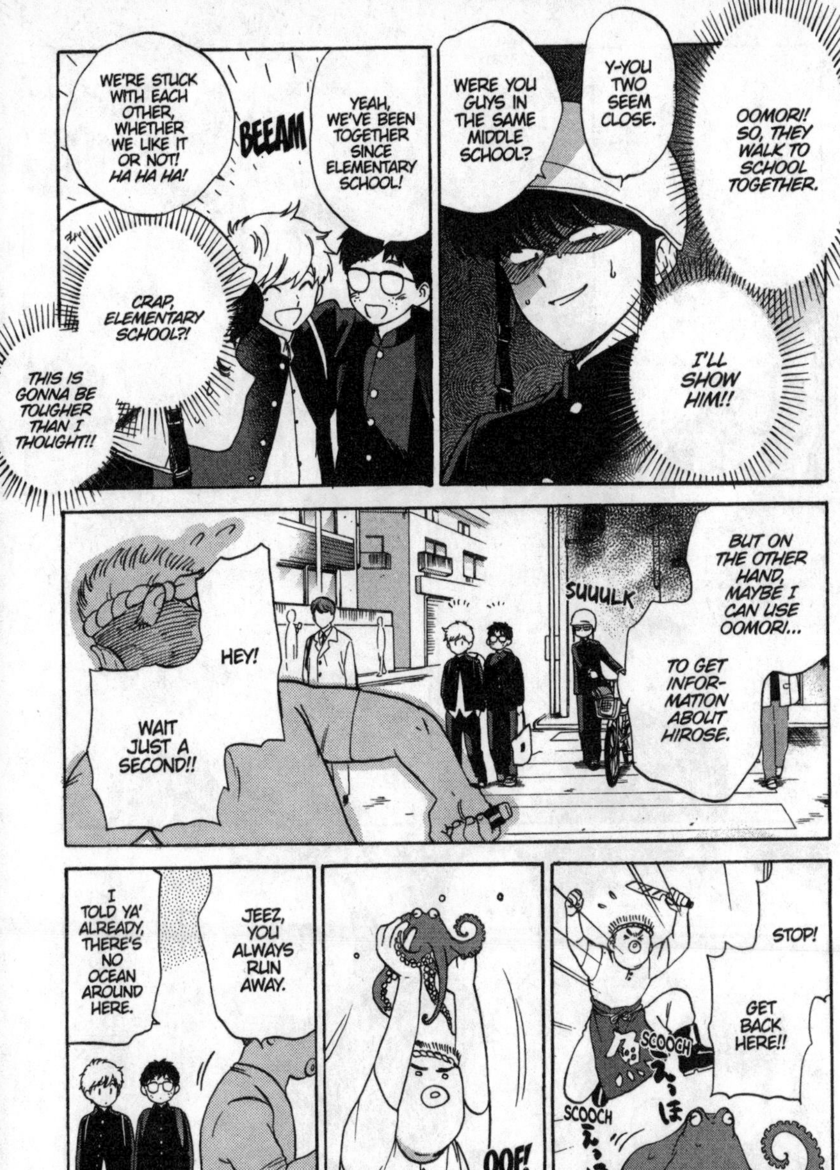
OOMORI! SO, THEY WALK TO SCHOOL TOGETHER.
Y-YOU TWO SEEM CLOSE.
WERE YOU GUYS IN THE SAME MIDDLE SCHOOL?
I'LL SHOW HIM!!
YEAH, WE'VE BEEN TOGETHER SINCE ELEMENTARY SCHOOL!
BEEAM
WE'RE STUCK WITH EACH OTHER, WHETHER WE LIKE IT OR NOT! HA HA HA!
CRAP, ELEMENTARY SCHOOL?!
THIS IS GONNA BE TOUGHER THAN I THOUGHT!!
BUT ON THE OTHER HAND, MAYBE I CAN USE OOMORI...
TO GET INFORMATION ABOUT HIROSE.
SUUULK
HEY!
WAIT JUST A SECOND!!
STOP!
GET BACK HERE!!
SCOOCH
SCOOCH
OOF!
JEEZ, YOU ALWAYS RUN AWAY.
I TOLD YA' ALREADY, THERE'S NO OCEAN AROUND HERE.

Apron: Fish

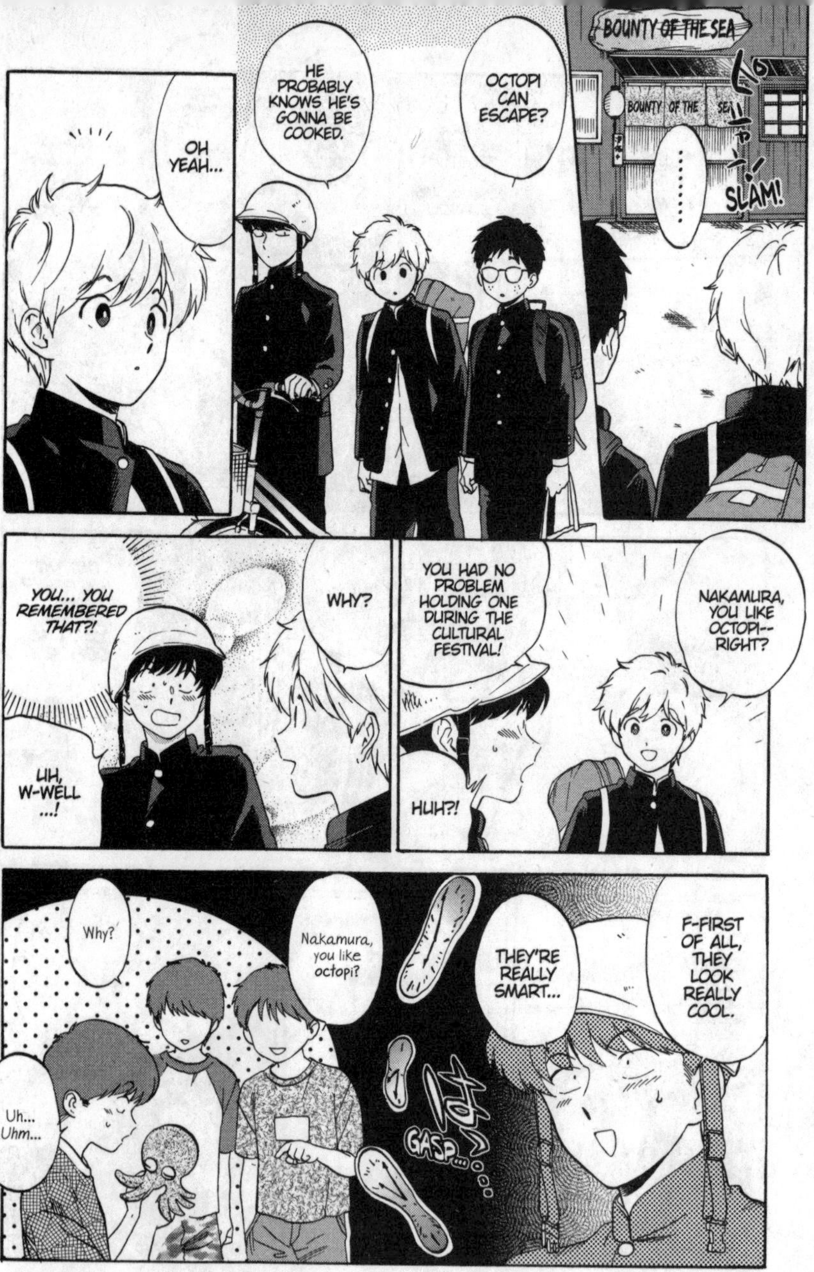
BOUNTY OF THE SEA
BOUNTY OF THE SEA
SLAM!
......
OCTOPI CAN ESCAPE?
HE PROBABLY KNOWS HE'S GONNA BE COOKED.
OH YEAH...
NAKAMURA, YOU LIKE OCTOPI--RIGHT?
YOU HAD NO PROBLEM HOLDING ONE DURING THE CULTURAL FESTIVAL!
HUH?!
WHY?
YOU... YOU REMEMBERED THAT?!
UH, W-WELL ...!
F-FIRST OF ALL, THEY LOOK REALLY COOL.
THEY'RE REALLY SMART...
GASP...
Nakamura, you like octopi?
Why?
Uh... Uhm...

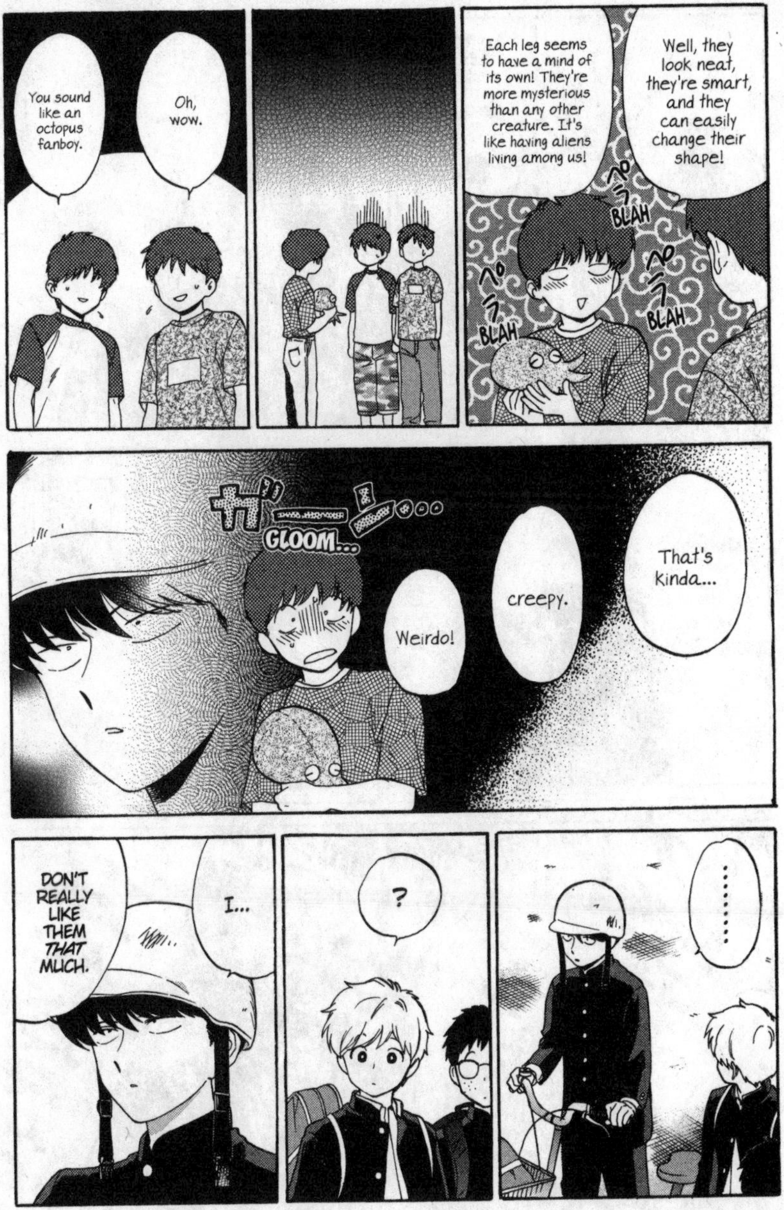
Well, they look neat, they're smart, and they can easily change their shape!
Each leg seems to have a mind of its own! They're more mysterious than any other creature. It's like having aliens living among us!
BLAH
BLAH
BLAH
Oh, wow.
You sound like an octopus fanboy.
That's kinda...
creepy.
Weirdo!
GLOOM...
......
?
I...
DON'T REALLY LIKE THEM *THAT* MUCH.

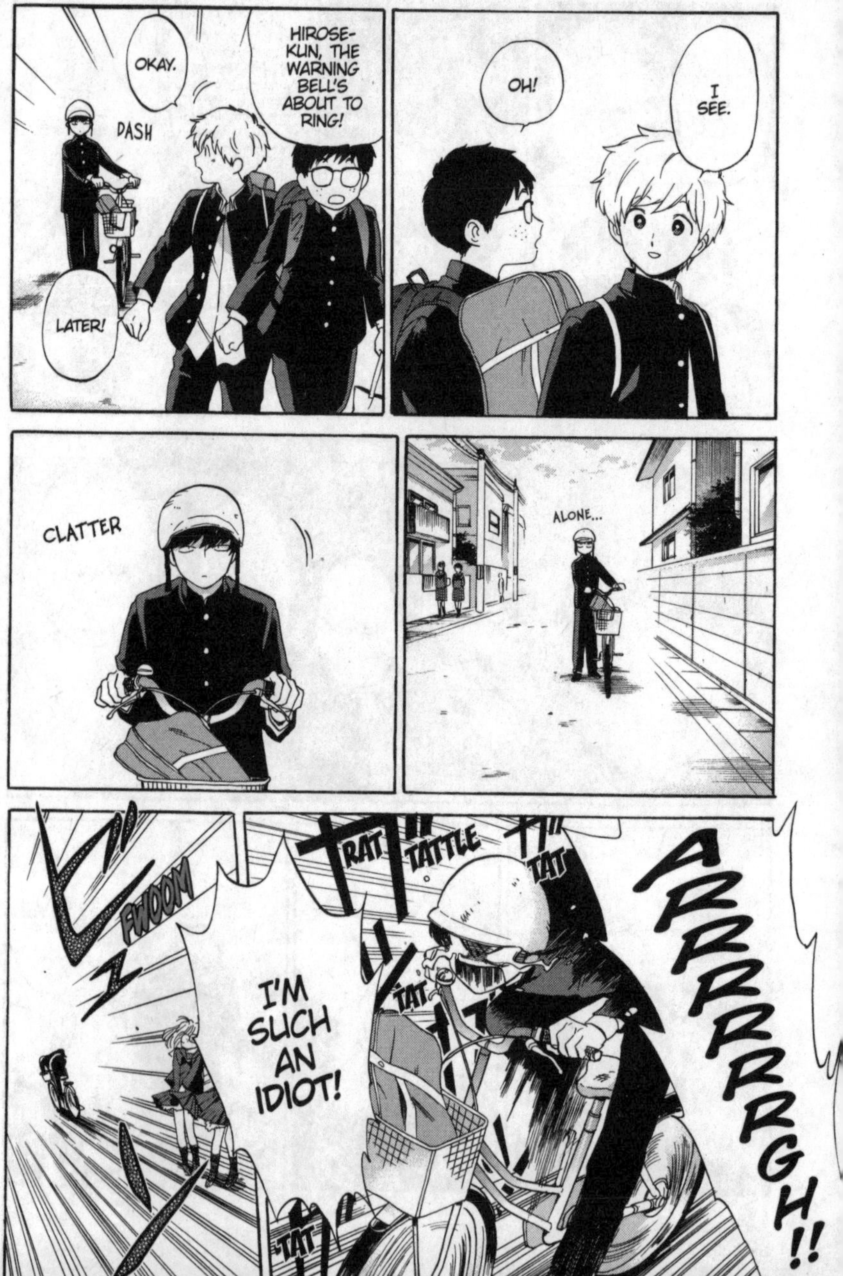
I SEE.
OH!
HIROSE-KUN, THE WARNING BELL'S ABOUT TO RING!
OKAY.
DASH
LATER!
ALONE...
CLATTER
ARRRRRRGH!!
TAT
TATTLE
RAT
FWOOM
I'M SUCH AN IDIOT!
TAT
TAT

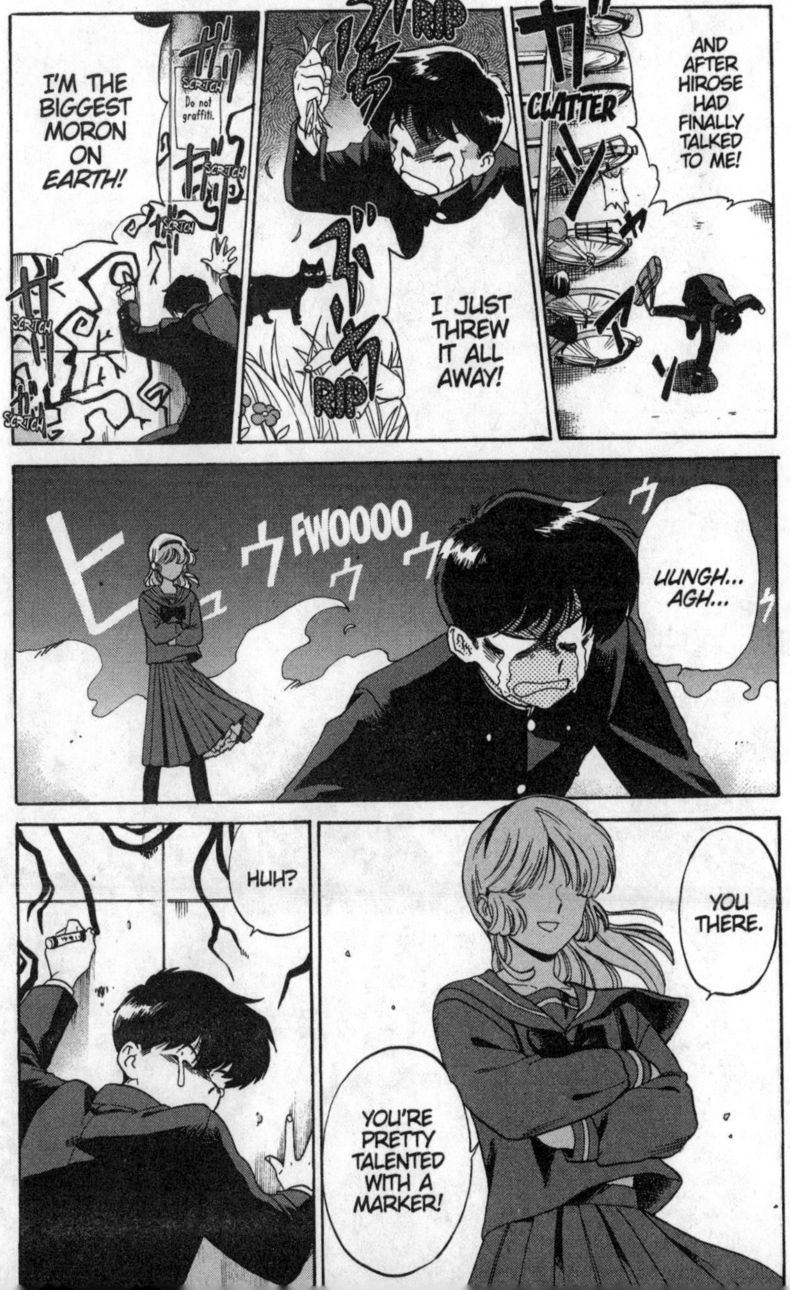
AND AFTER HIROSE HAD FINALLY TALKED TO ME!
CLATTER
RIP
I JUST THREW IT ALL AWAY!
RIP
I'M THE BIGGEST MORON ON EARTH!
SCRTCH
Do not graffiti.
SCRTCH
SCRTCH
SCRTCH
SCRTCH
UUNGH... AGH...
FWOOOO
YOU THERE.
YOU'RE PRETTY TALENTED WITH A MARKER!
HUH?

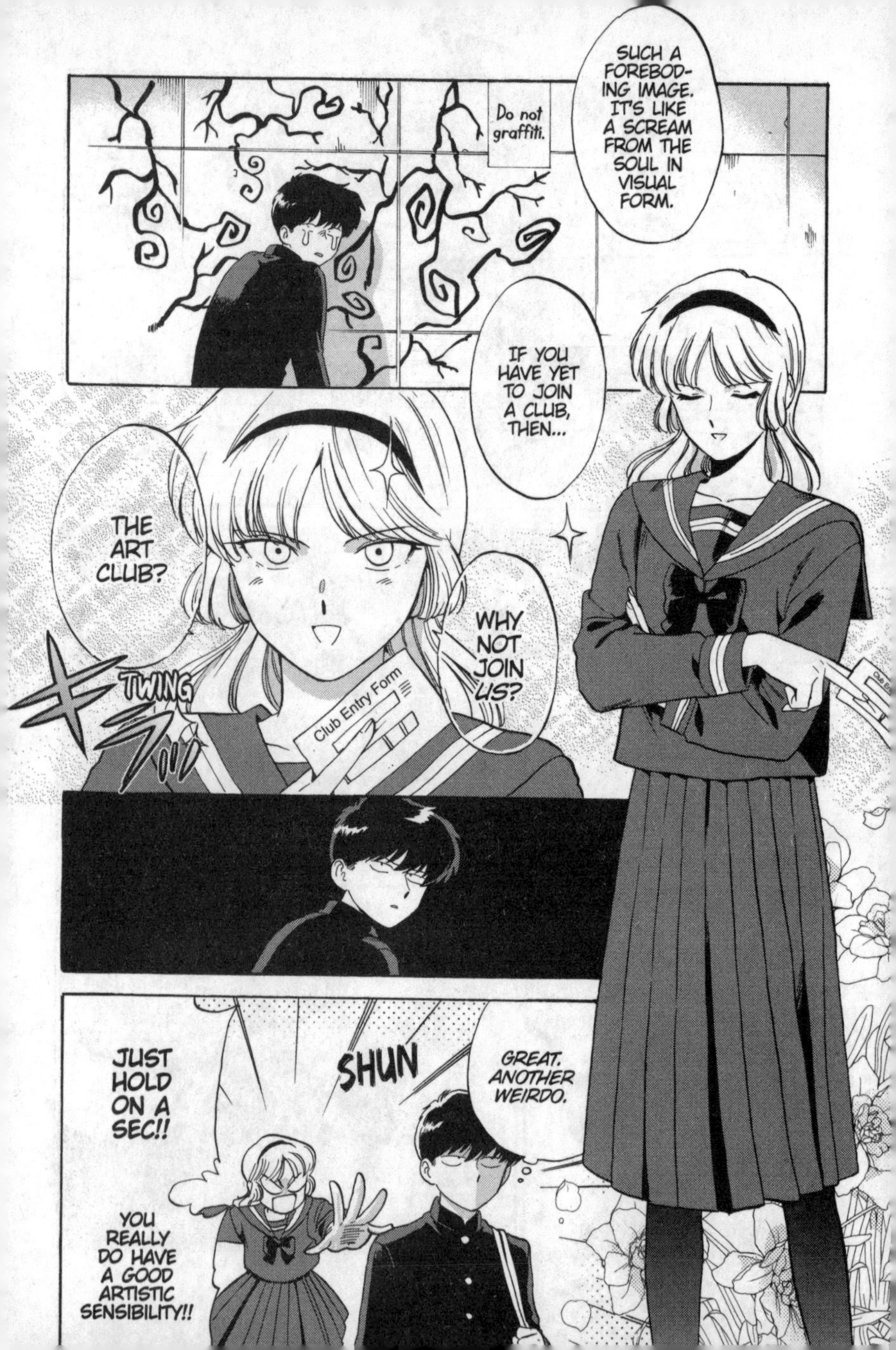
SUCH A FOREBODING IMAGE. IT'S LIKE A SCREAM FROM THE SOUL IN VISUAL FORM.
Do not graffiti.
IF YOU HAVE YET TO JOIN A CLUB, THEN...
WHY NOT JOIN US?
Club Entry Form
THE ART CLUB?
TWING
GREAT. ANOTHER WEIRDO.
SHUN
JUST HOLD ON A SEC!!
YOU REALLY DO HAVE A GOOD ARTISTIC SENSIBILITY!!

すた
TP
OUR CLUB ONLY WANTS THE MOST TALENTED PEOPLE.
SHE'S FOLLOWING ME?!
WE'RE LOOKING FOR GIFTED ARTISTS LIKE YOU!
JUST GIVE IT A TRY!
EVEN IF YOU COULD JUST PARTICIPATE IN THE COMPETITION FOR US!
I, CLUB PRESIDENT AOKIYAMA REIKO, AM BEGGING YOU!
SO, UM...
I'M REALLY NOT INTERESTED.
I'M SORRY, BUT PLEASE JUST DROP IT.
HMPH! I SEE. TOO BAD.
THERE'S AN OLD LEGEND ABOUT THIS ART CONTEST...
IT'S SAID THAT THE THING FEATURED IN YOUR ARTWORK WILL BECOME REALITY.
ARE YOU SURE YOU WON'T TAKE PART?
FREEZE

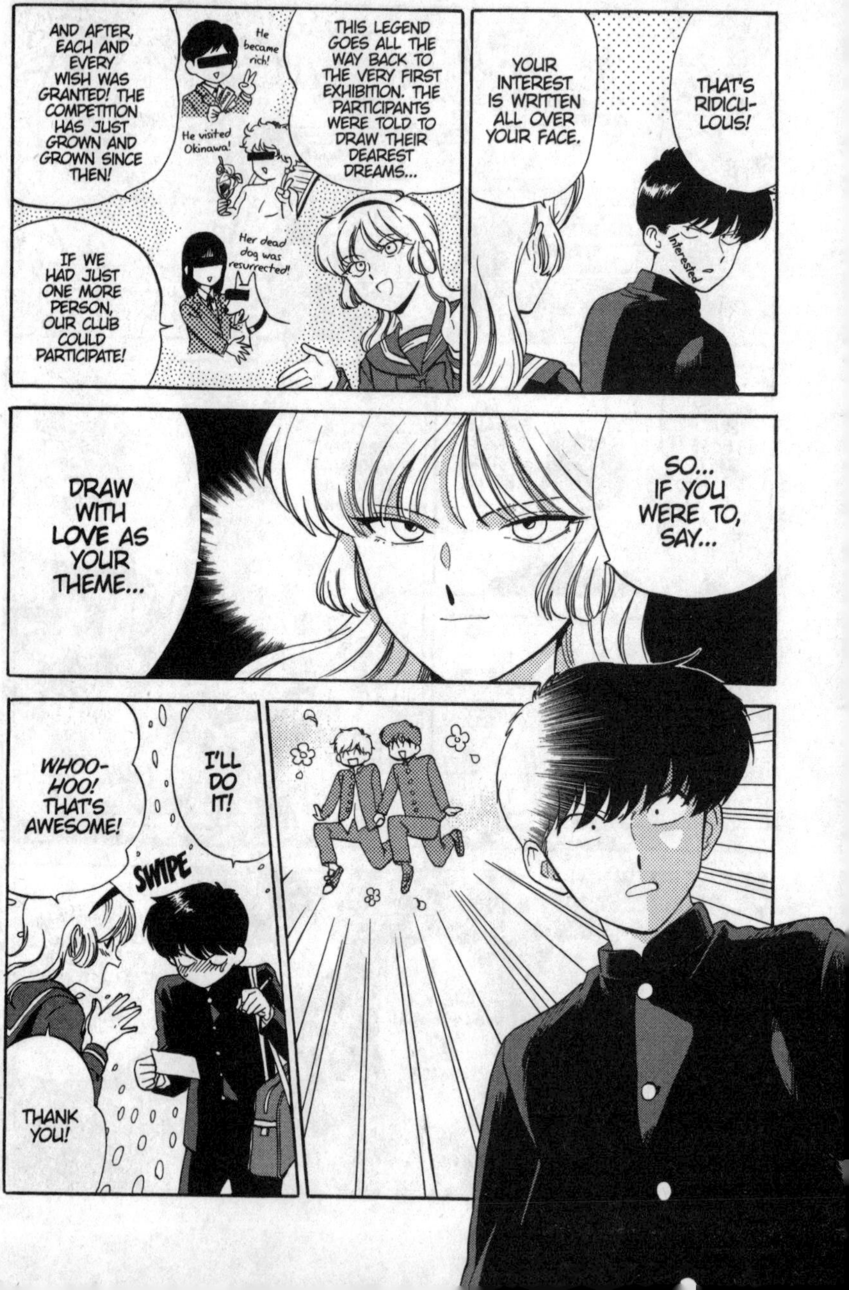
THAT'S RIDICU-LOUS!
Interested
YOUR INTEREST IS WRITTEN ALL OVER YOUR FACE.
THIS LEGEND GOES ALL THE WAY BACK TO THE VERY FIRST EXHIBITION. THE PARTICIPANTS WERE TOLD TO DRAW THEIR DEAREST DREAMS...
He became rich!
AND AFTER, EACH AND EVERY WISH WAS GRANTED! THE COMPETITION HAS JUST GROWN AND GROWN SINCE THEN!
He visited Okinawa!
Her dead dog was resurrected!
IF WE HAD JUST ONE MORE PERSON, OUR CLUB COULD PARTICIPATE!
SO... IF YOU WERE TO, SAY...
DRAW WITH LOVE AS YOUR THEME...
I'LL DO IT!
WHOO-HOO! THAT'S AWESOME!
SWIPE
THANK YOU!

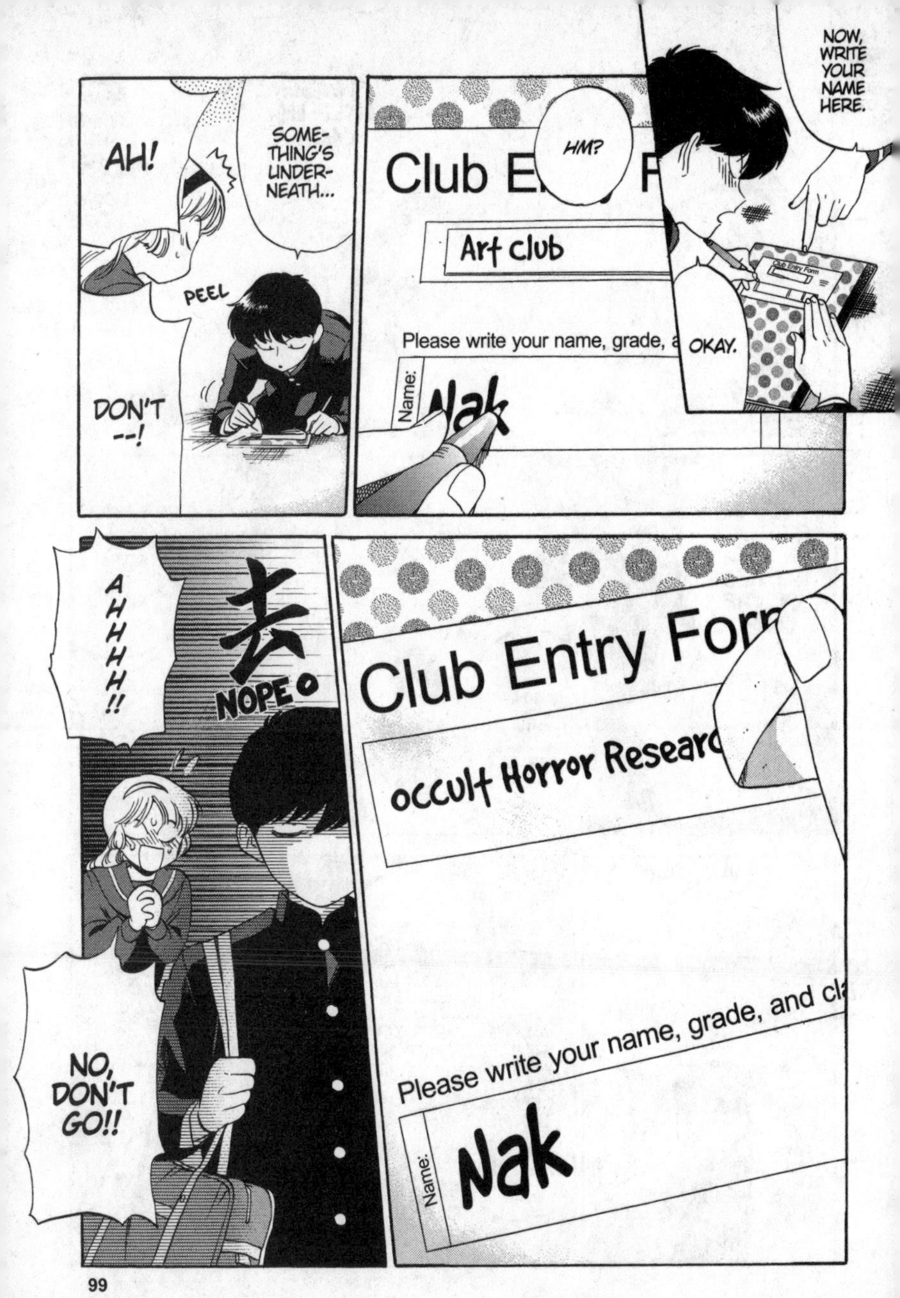
NOW, WRITE YOUR NAME HERE.
Club Entry Form
OKAY.
HM?
Club E
Art club
Please write your name, grade, a
Name:
Nak
SOME-THING'S UNDER-NEATH...
AH!
PEEL
DON'T --!
Club Entry Forr
Occult Horror Researc
Please write your name, grade, and cl
Name:
Nak
AHHHHH!!
NOPE
NO, DON'T GO!!

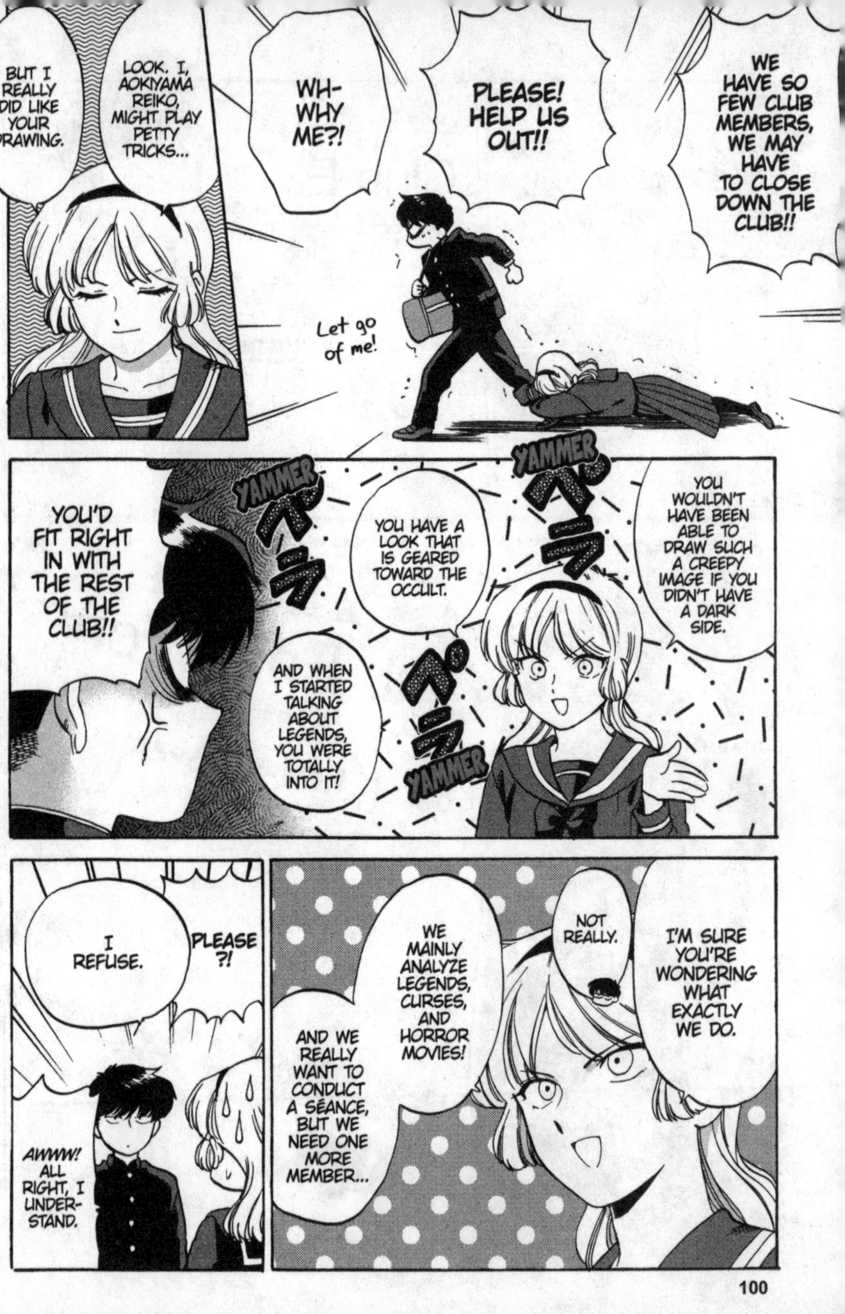
WE HAVE SO FEW CLUB MEMBERS, WE MAY HAVE TO CLOSE DOWN THE CLUB!!
PLEASE! HELP US OUT!!
WH- WHY ME?!
Let go of me!
LOOK. I, AOKIYAMA REIKO, MIGHT PLAY PETTY TRICKS...
BUT I REALLY DID LIKE YOUR DRAWING.
YOU WOULDN'T HAVE BEEN ABLE TO DRAW SUCH A CREEPY IMAGE IF YOU DIDN'T HAVE A DARK SIDE.
YAMMER
YOU HAVE A LOOK THAT IS GEARED TOWARD THE OCCULT.
YAMMER
AND WHEN I STARTED TALKING ABOUT LEGENDS, YOU WERE TOTALLY INTO IT!
YAMMER
YOU'D FIT RIGHT IN WITH THE REST OF THE CLUB!!
I'M SURE YOU'RE WONDERING WHAT EXACTLY WE DO.
NOT REALLY.
WE MAINLY ANALYZE LEGENDS, CURSES, AND HORROR MOVIES!
AND WE REALLY WANT TO CONDUCT A SÉANCE, BUT WE NEED ONE MORE MEMBER...
PLEASE ?!
I REFUSE.
AWWW! ALL RIGHT, I UNDERSTAND.

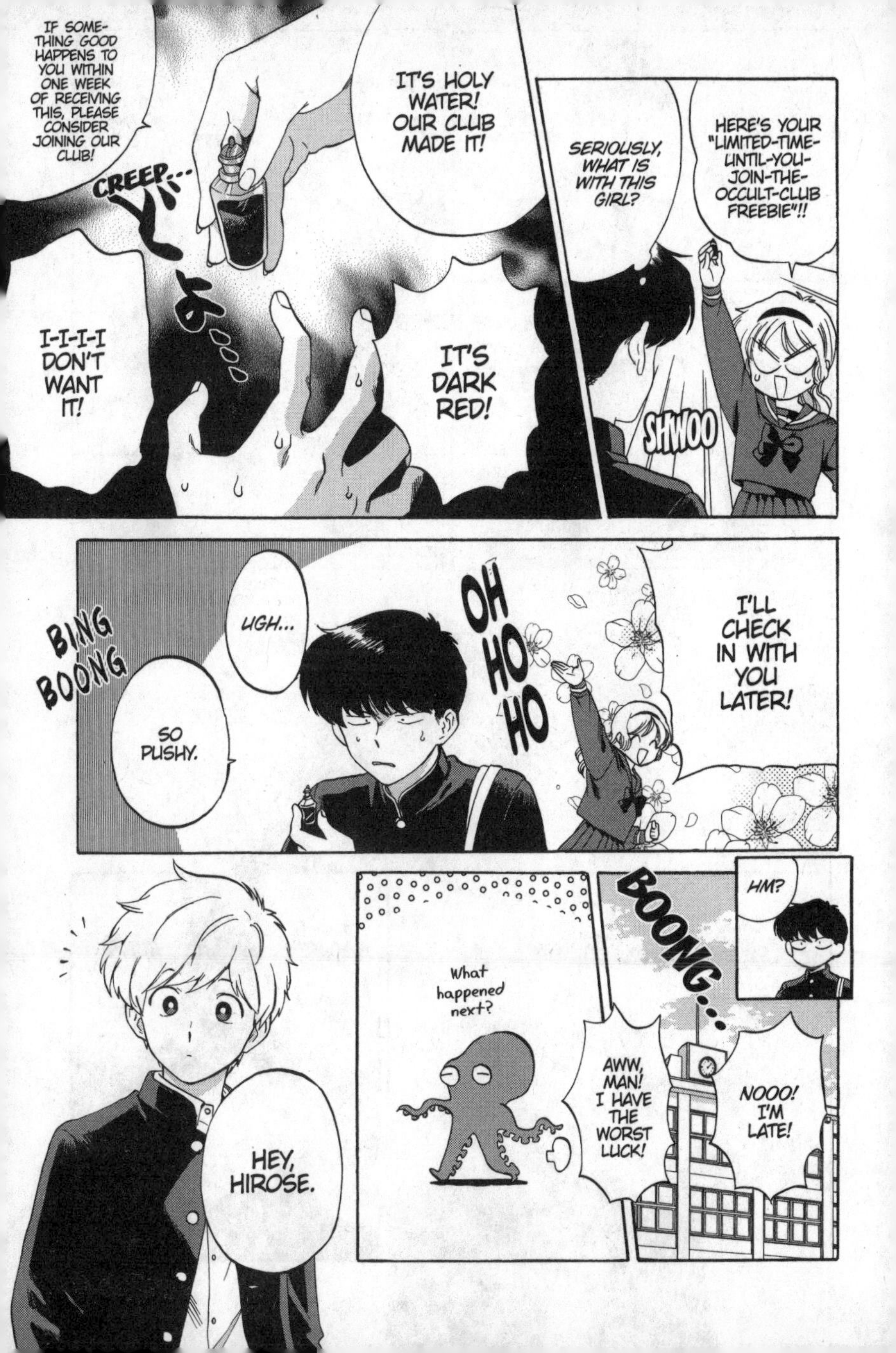
HERE'S YOUR "LIMITED-TIME-UNTIL-YOU-JOIN-THE-OCCULT-CLUB FREEBIE"!!
SERIOUSLY, WHAT IS WITH THIS GIRL?
SHWOO
IT'S HOLY WATER! OUR CLUB MADE IT!
IF SOMETHING GOOD HAPPENS TO YOU WITHIN ONE WEEK OF RECEIVING THIS, PLEASE CONSIDER JOINING OUR CLUB!
CREEP...
IT'S DARK RED!
I-I-I-I DON'T WANT IT!
I'LL CHECK IN WITH YOU LATER!
OH HO HO HO
UGH...
SO PUSHY.
BING BOONG
HM?
BOOONG...
NOOO! I'M LATE!
AWW, MAN! I HAVE THE WORST LUCK!
What happened next?
HEY, HIROSE.

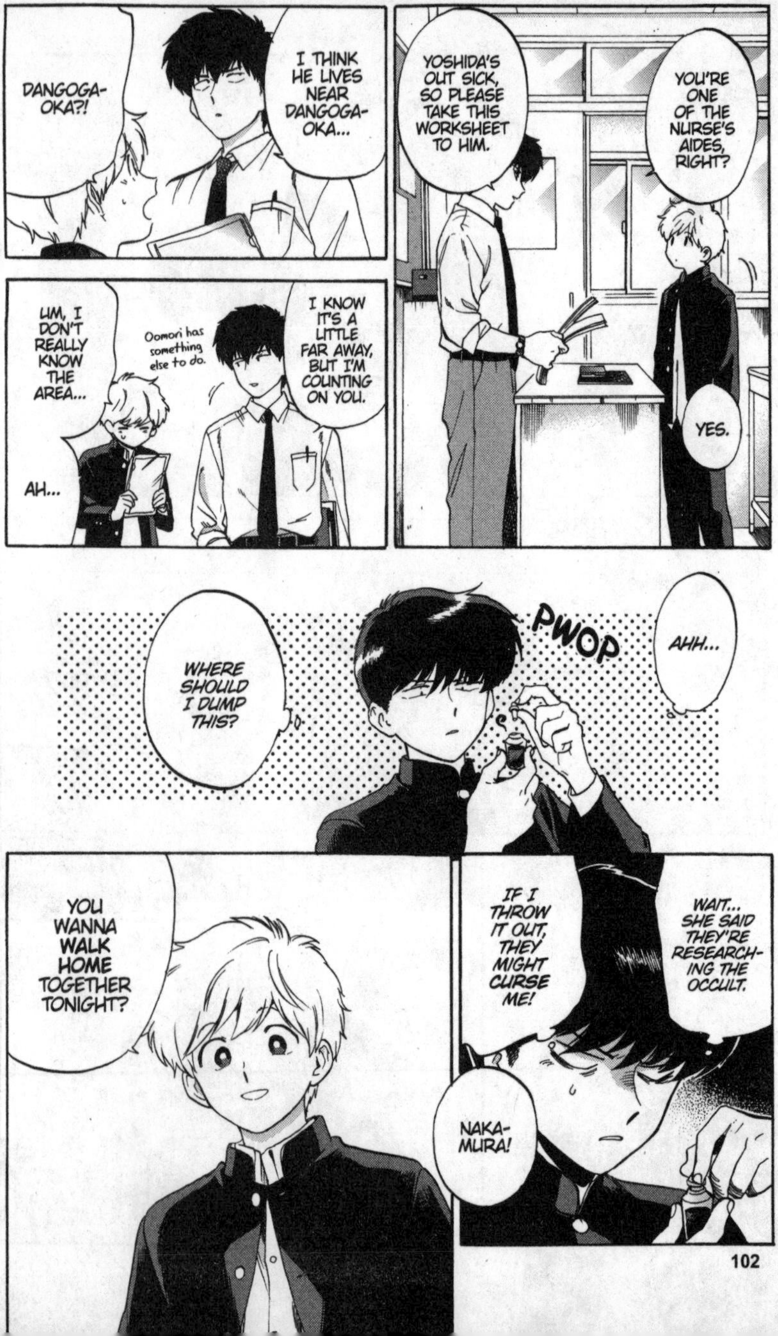
YOU'RE ONE OF THE NURSE'S AIDES, RIGHT?
YOSHIDA'S OUT SICK, SO PLEASE TAKE THIS WORKSHEET TO HIM.
YES.
I THINK HE LIVES NEAR DANGOGA-OKA...
DANGOGA-OKA?!
I KNOW IT'S A LITTLE FAR AWAY, BUT I'M COUNTING ON YOU.
Oomori has something else to do.
UM, I DON'T REALLY KNOW THE AREA...
AH...
AHH...
PWOP
WHERE SHOULD I DUMP THIS?
WAIT... SHE SAID THEY'RE RESEARCHING THE OCCULT.
IF I THROW IT OUT, THEY MIGHT CURSE ME!
NAKAMURA!
YOU WANNA WALK HOME TOGETHER TONIGHT?

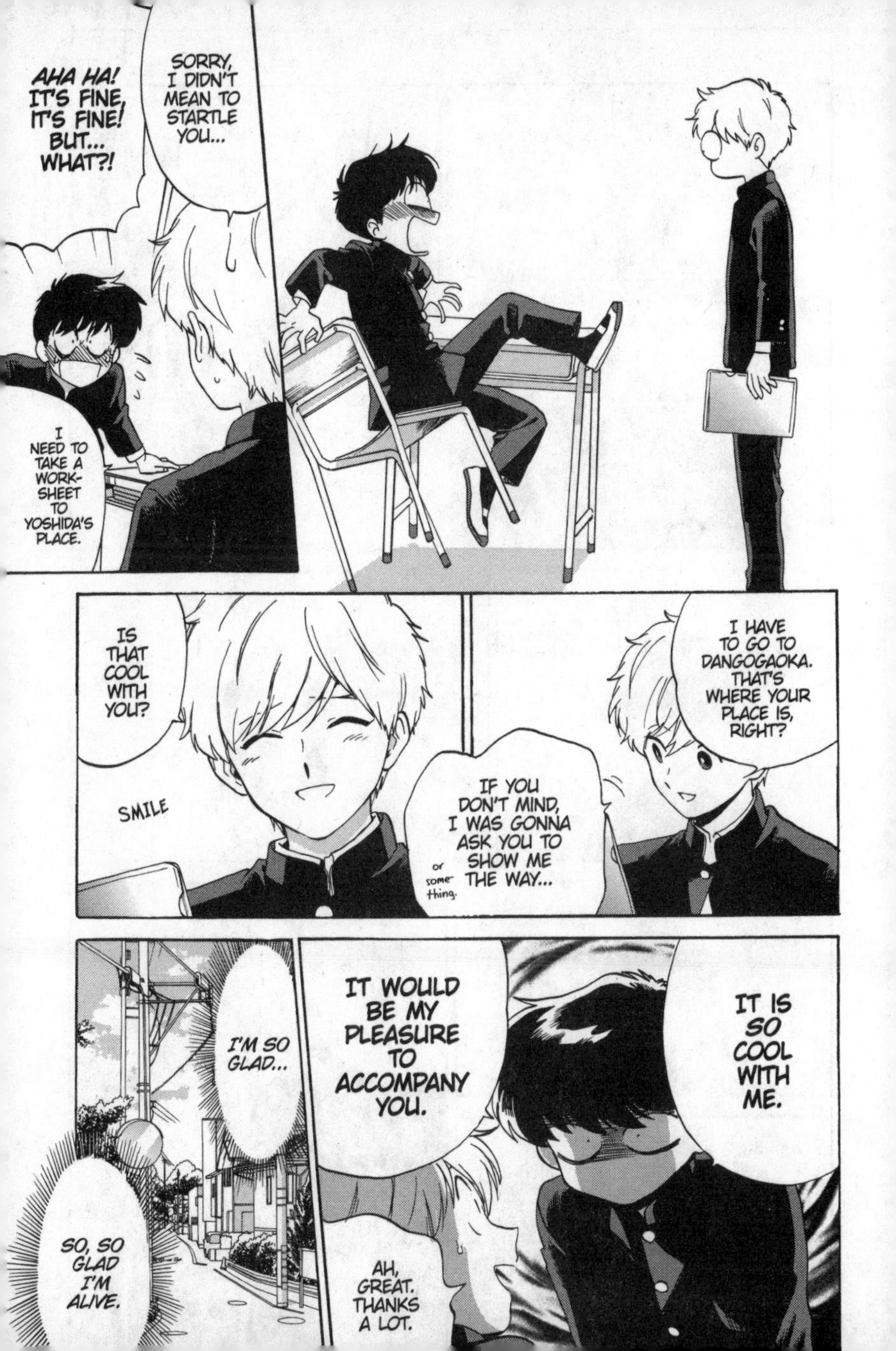
SORRY, I DIDN'T MEAN TO STARTLE YOU...
AHA HA! IT'S FINE, IT'S FINE! BUT... WHAT?!
I NEED TO TAKE A WORKSHEET TO YOSHIDA'S PLACE.
I HAVE TO GO TO DANGOGAOKA. THAT'S WHERE YOUR PLACE IS, RIGHT?
IF YOU DON'T MIND, I WAS GONNA ASK YOU TO SHOW ME THE WAY...
or something.
IS THAT COOL WITH YOU?
SMILE
IT IS SO COOL WITH ME.
IT WOULD BE MY PLEASURE TO ACCOMPANY YOU.
AH, GREAT. THANKS A LOT.
I'M SO GLAD...
SO, SO GLAD I'M ALIVE.

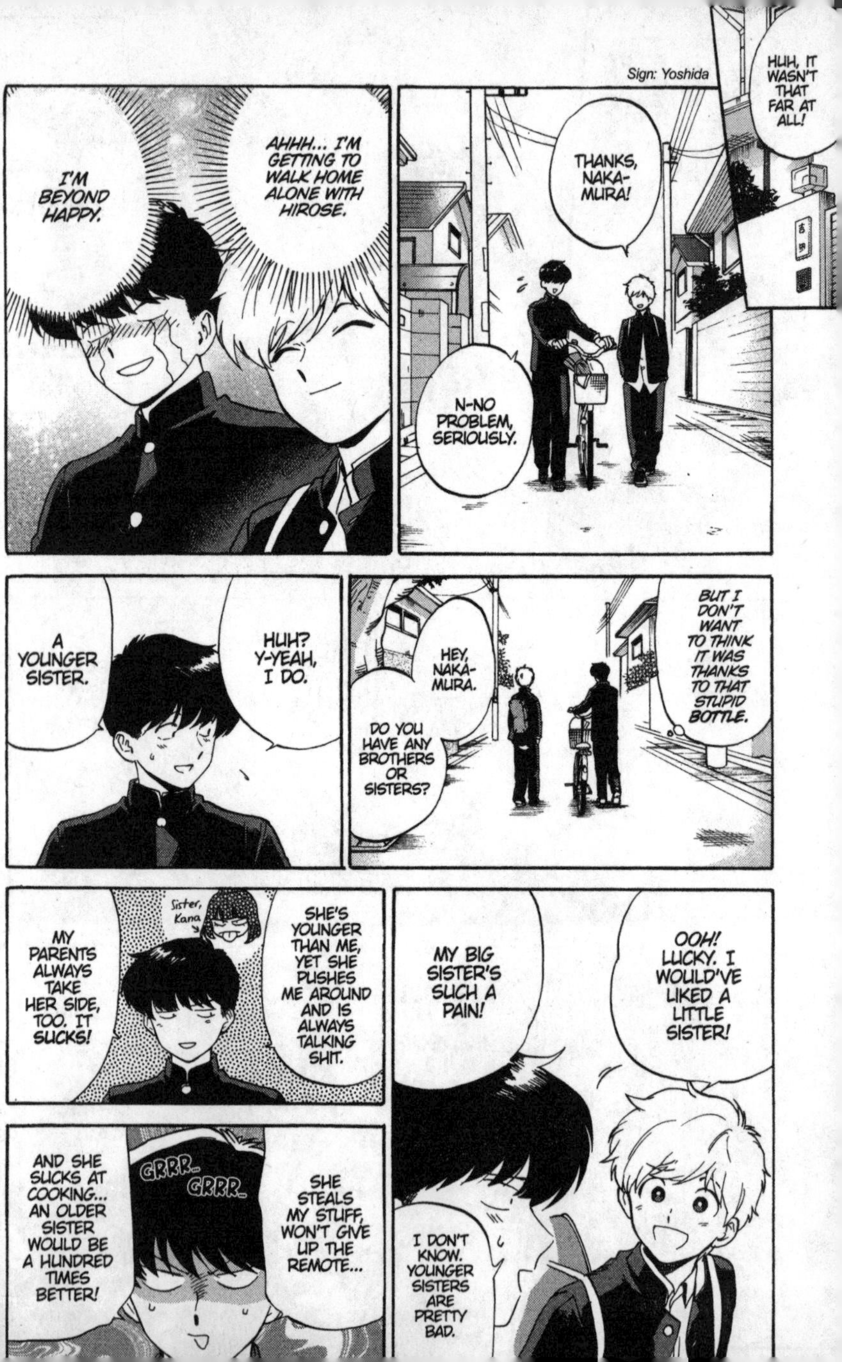
Sign: Yoshida
HUH, IT WASN'T THAT FAR AT ALL!
THANKS, NAKAMURA!
N-NO PROBLEM, SERIOUSLY.
AHHH... I'M GETTING TO WALK HOME ALONE WITH HIROSE.
I'M BEYOND HAPPY.
BUT I DON'T WANT TO THINK IT WAS THANKS TO THAT STUPID BOTTLE.
HEY, NAKAMURA.
DO YOU HAVE ANY BROTHERS OR SISTERS?
HUH? Y-YEAH, I DO.
A YOUNGER SISTER.
OOH! LUCKY. I WOULD'VE LIKED A LITTLE SISTER!
MY BIG SISTER'S SUCH A PAIN!
I DON'T KNOW. YOUNGER SISTERS ARE PRETTY BAD.
SHE'S YOUNGER THAN ME, YET SHE PUSHES ME AROUND AND IS ALWAYS TALKING SHIT.
Sister, Kana
MY PARENTS ALWAYS TAKE HER SIDE, TOO. IT SUCKS!
SHE STEALS MY STUFF, WON'T GIVE UP THE REMOTE...
GRRR.. GRRR..
AND SHE SUCKS AT COOKING... AN OLDER SISTER WOULD BE A HUNDRED TIMES BETTER!

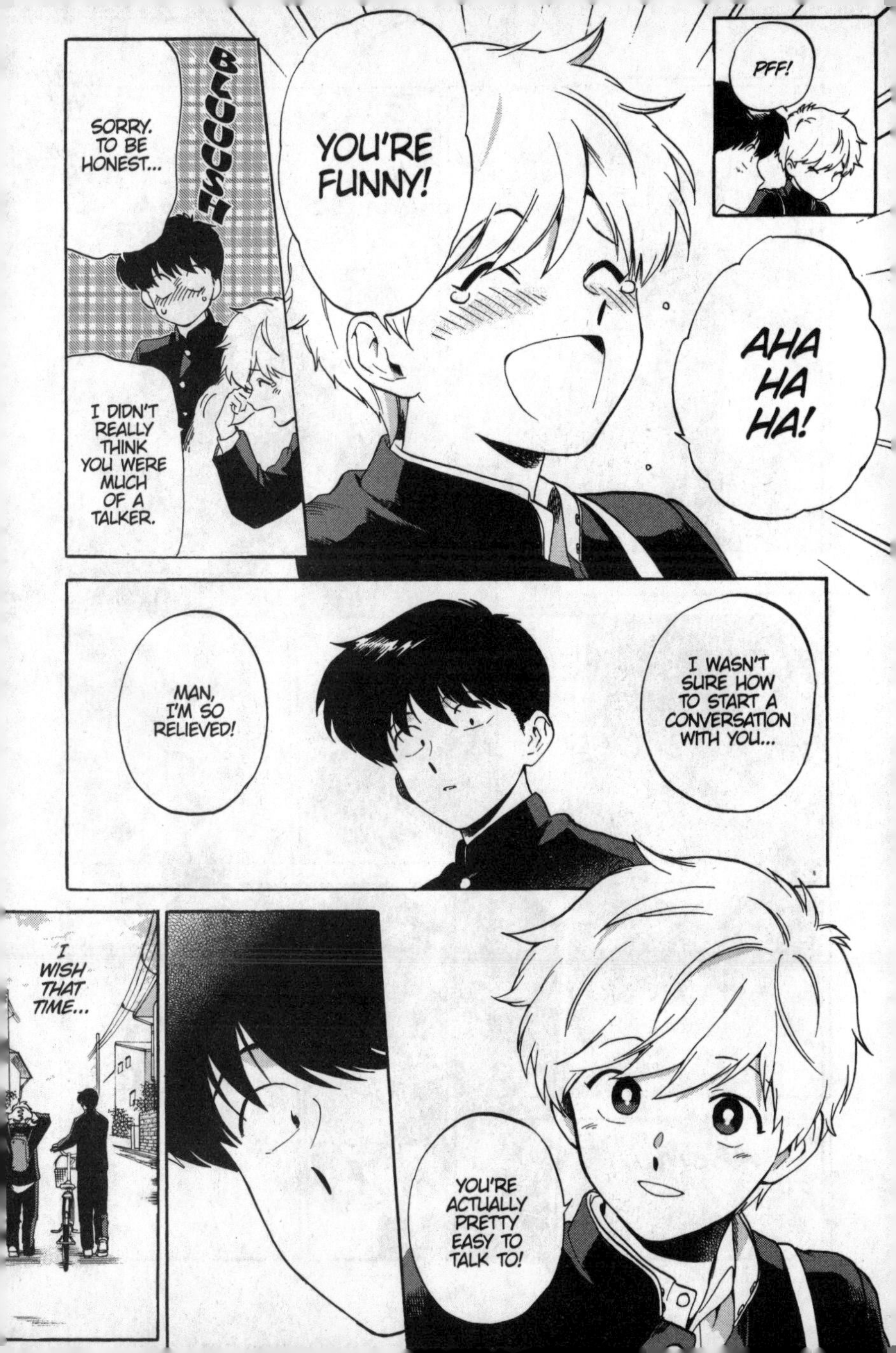
PFF!
AHA HA HA!
YOU'RE FUNNY!
BLUUUSH!
SORRY. TO BE HONEST...
I DIDN'T REALLY THINK YOU WERE MUCH OF A TALKER.
I WASN'T SURE HOW TO START A CONVERSATION WITH YOU...
MAN, I'M SO RELIEVED!
YOU'RE ACTUALLY PRETTY EASY TO TALK TO!
I WISH THAT TIME...

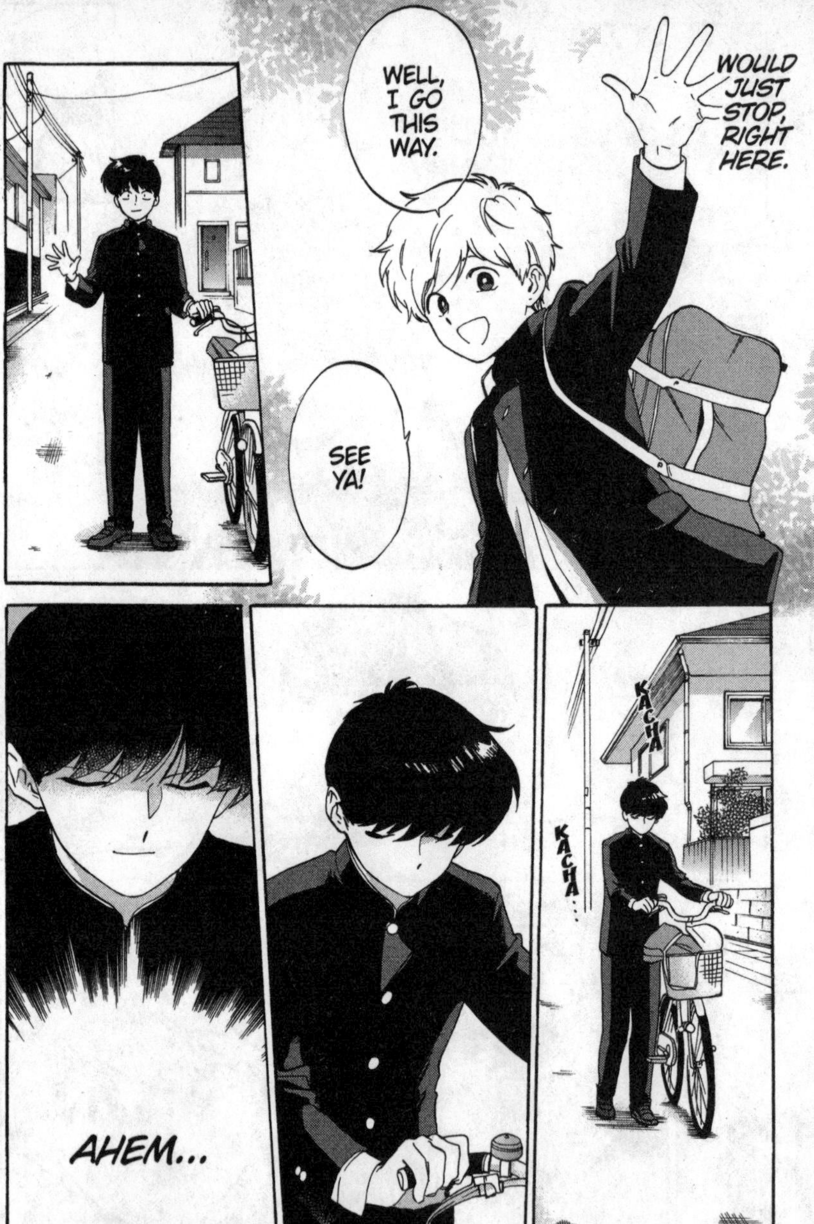
WOULD JUST STOP, RIGHT HERE.
WELL, I GO THIS WAY.
SEE YA!
KACHA
KACHA...
AHEM...

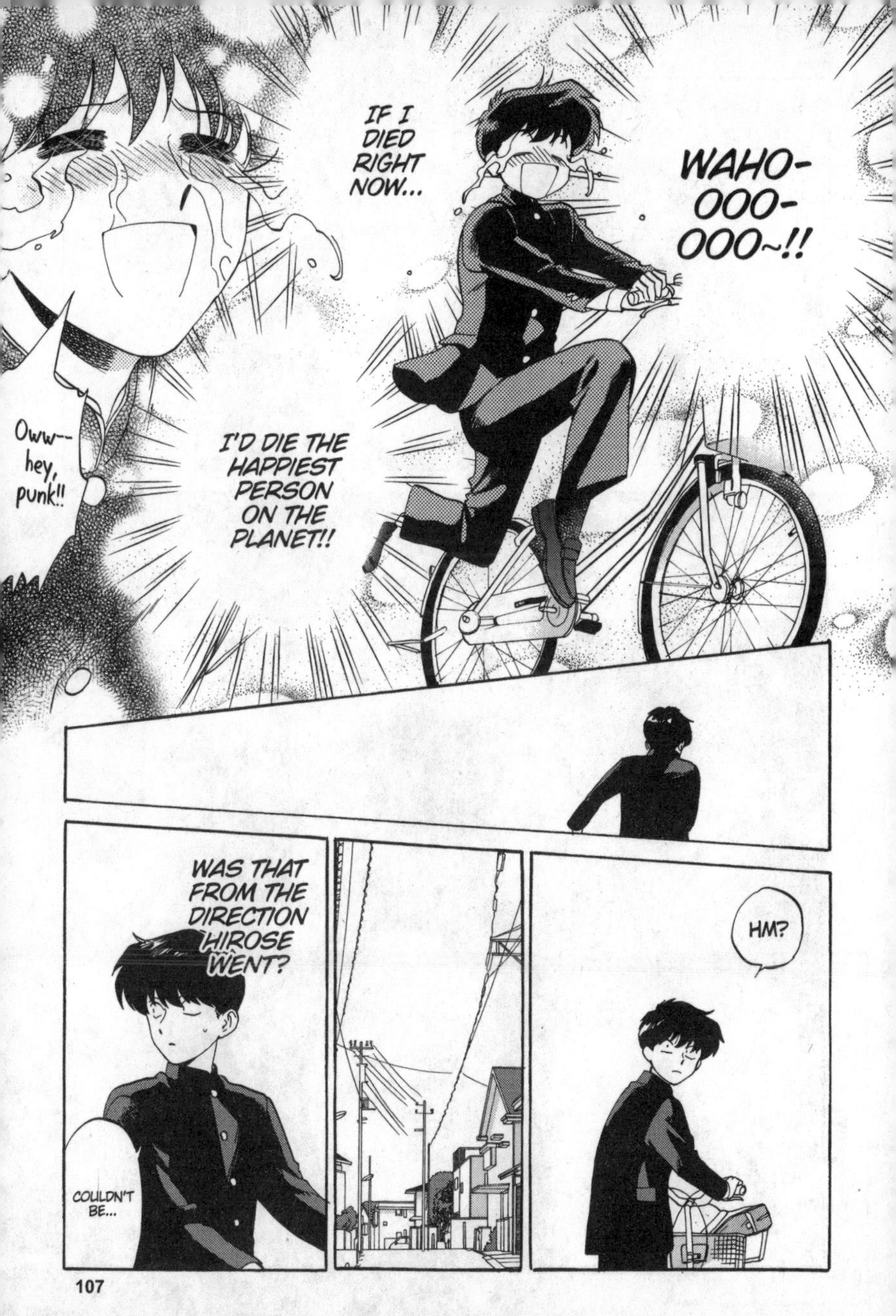
WAHO-OOO-OOO~!!
IF I DIED RIGHT NOW...
I'D DIE THE HAPPIEST PERSON ON THE PLANET!!
Oww-- hey, punk!!
HM?
WAS THAT FROM THE DIRECTION HIROSE WENT?
COULDN'T BE...

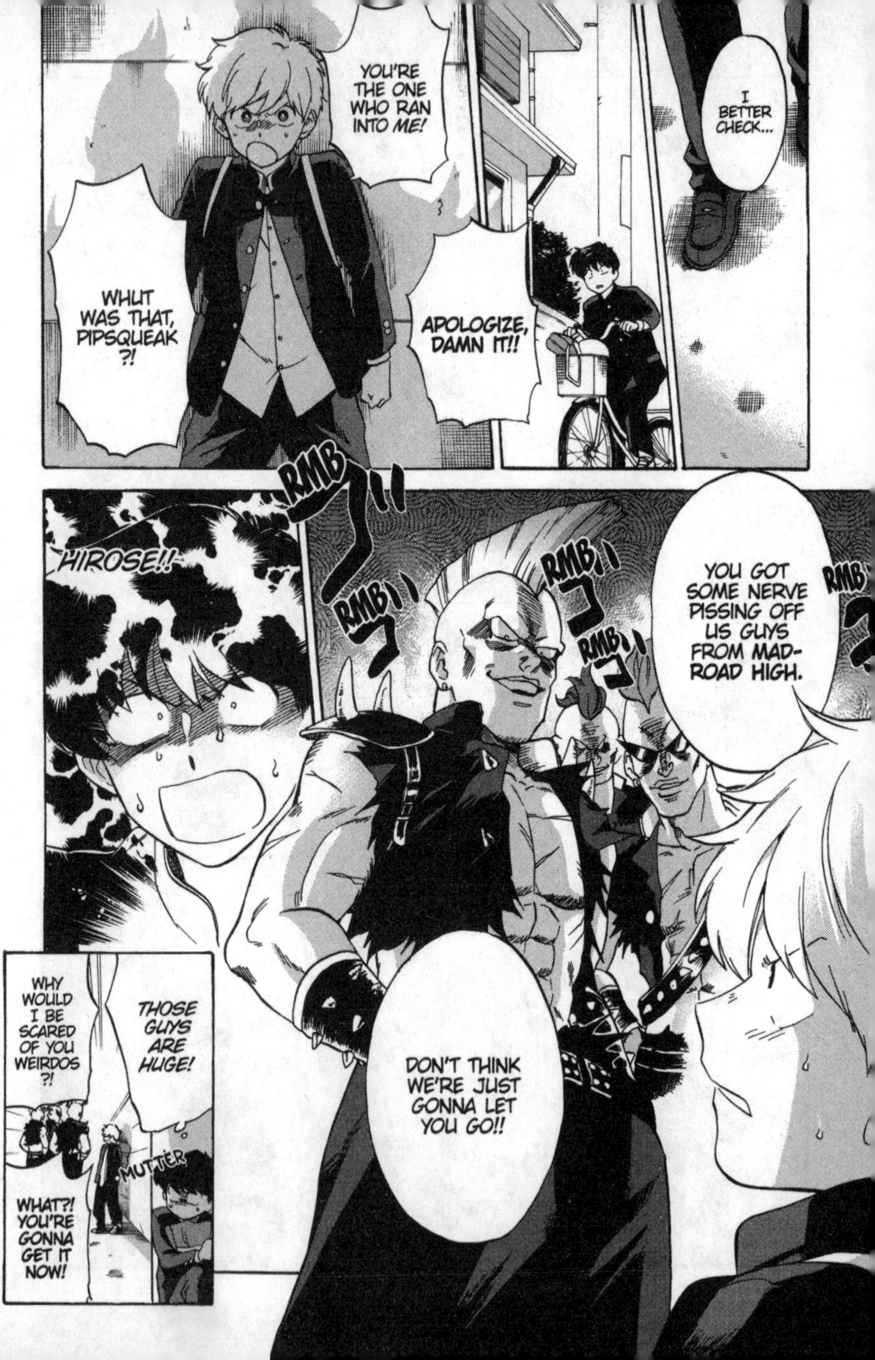
I BETTER CHECK...
YOU'RE THE ONE WHO RAN INTO ME!
APOLOGIZE, DAMN IT!!
WHUT WAS THAT, PIPSQUEAK?!
RMB
RMB
RMB
RMB
RMB
YOU GOT SOME NERVE PISSING OFF US GUYS FROM MAD-ROAD HIGH.
DON'T THINK WE'RE JUST GONNA LET YOU GO!!
HIROSE!!
THOSE GUYS ARE HUGE!
WHY WOULD I BE SCARED OF YOU WEIRDOS?!
MUTTER
WHAT?! YOU'RE GONNA GET IT NOW!

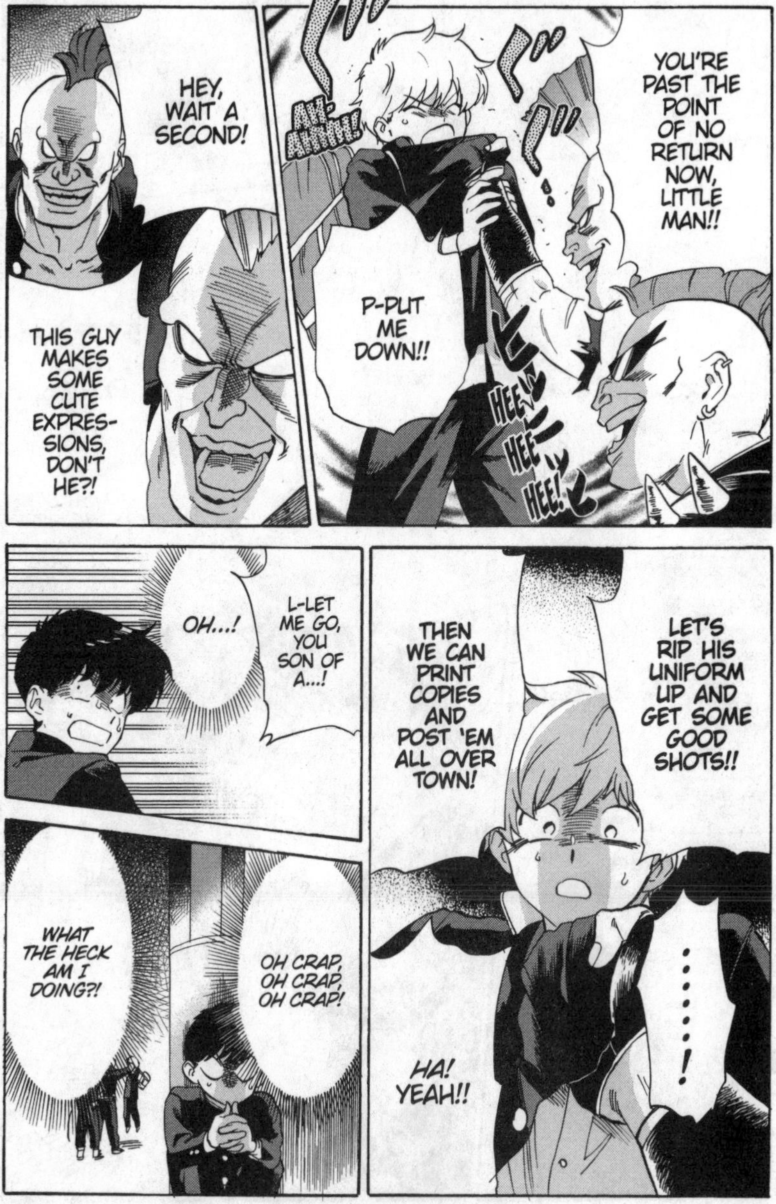
YOU'RE PAST THE POINT OF NO RETURN NOW, LITTLE MAN!!
AH- AHHH!
P-PUT ME DOWN!!
HEE HEE HEE!
HEY, WAIT A SECOND!
THIS GUY MAKES SOME CUTE EXPRES-SIONS, DON'T HE?!
LET'S RIP HIS UNIFORM UP AND GET SOME GOOD SHOTS!!
THEN WE CAN PRINT COPIES AND POST 'EM ALL OVER TOWN!
HA! YEAH!!
......!
L-LET ME GO, YOU SON OF A...!
OH...!
OH CRAP, OH CRAP, OH CRAP!
WHAT THE HECK AM I DOING?!

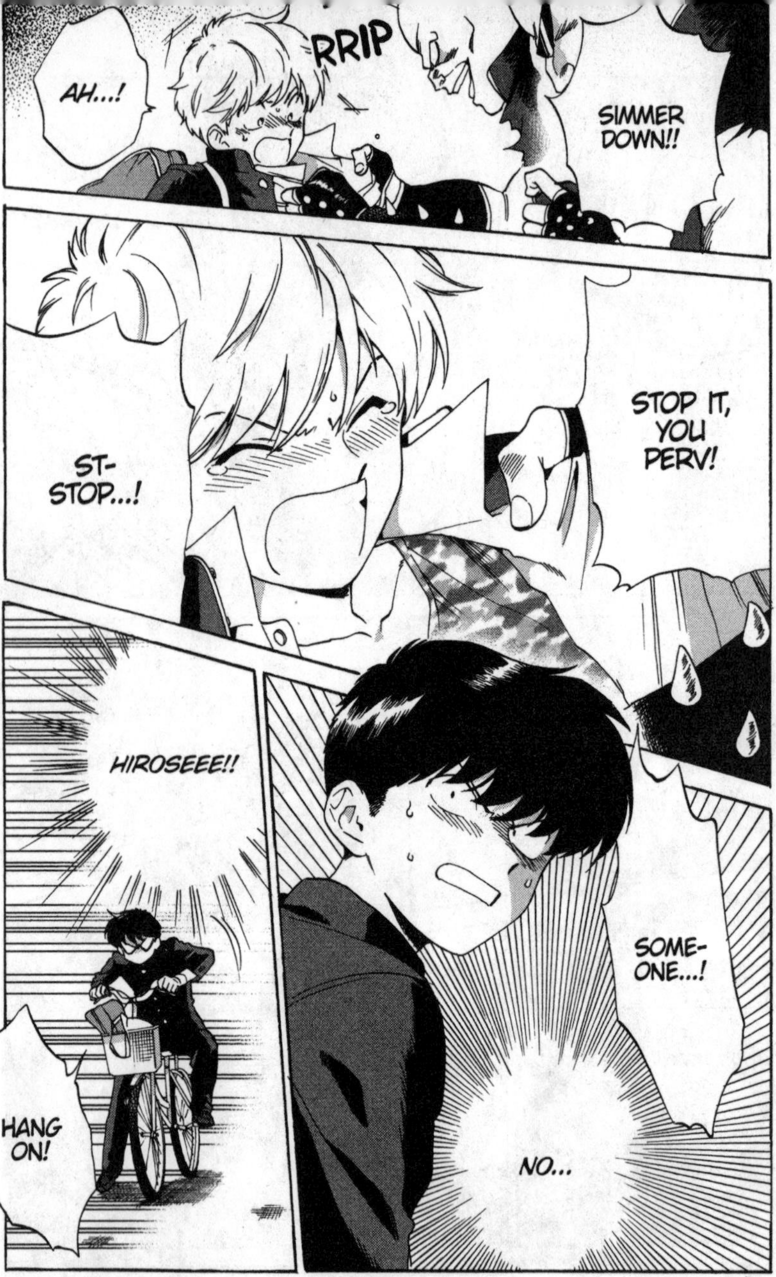
SIMMER DOWN!!
RRIP
AH...!
STOP IT, YOU PERV!
ST- STOP...!
SOME- ONE...!
NO...
HIROSEEE!!
HANG ON!

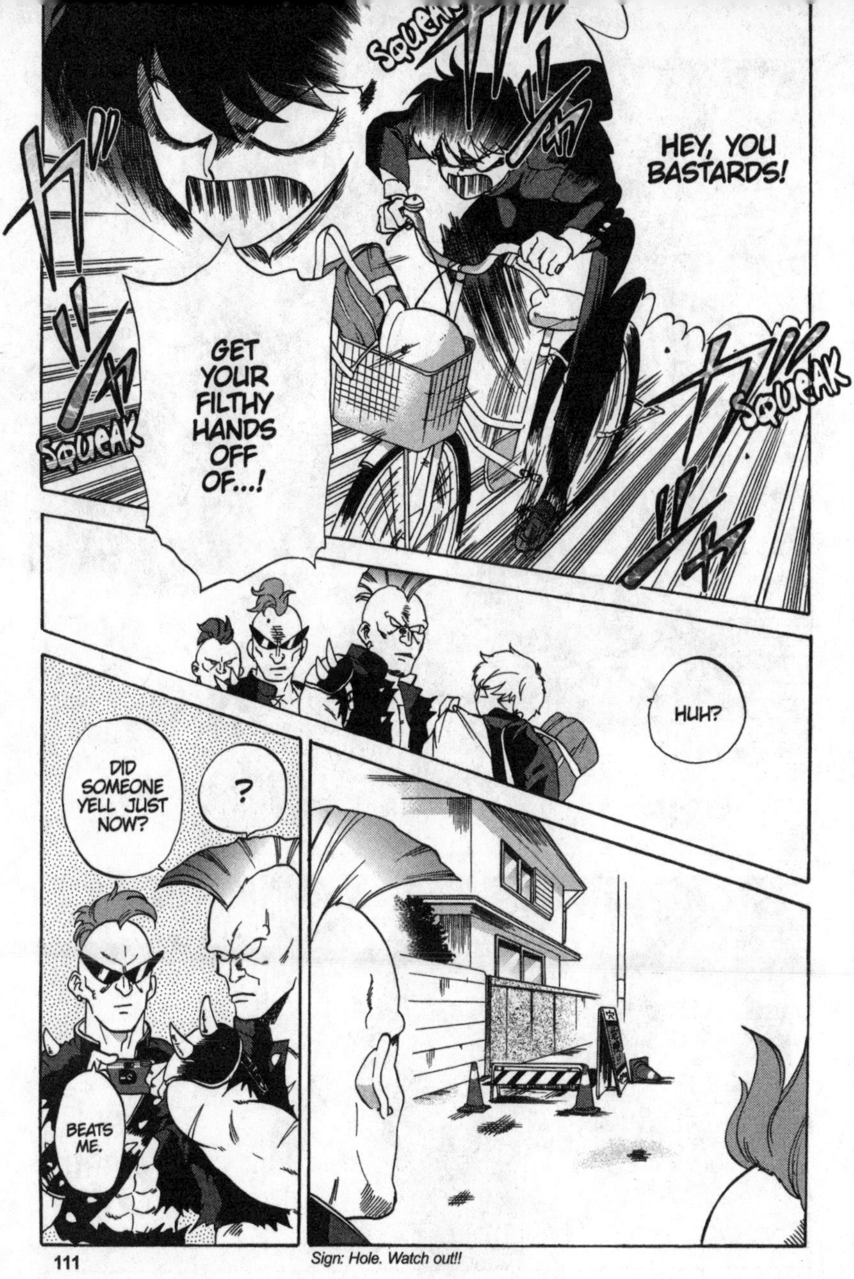
SQUEAK
HEY, YOU BASTARDS!
GET YOUR FILTHY HANDS OFF OF...!
SQUEAK
SQUEAK
HUH?
?
DID SOMEONE YELL JUST NOW?
BEATS ME.

Sign: Hole. Watch out!!

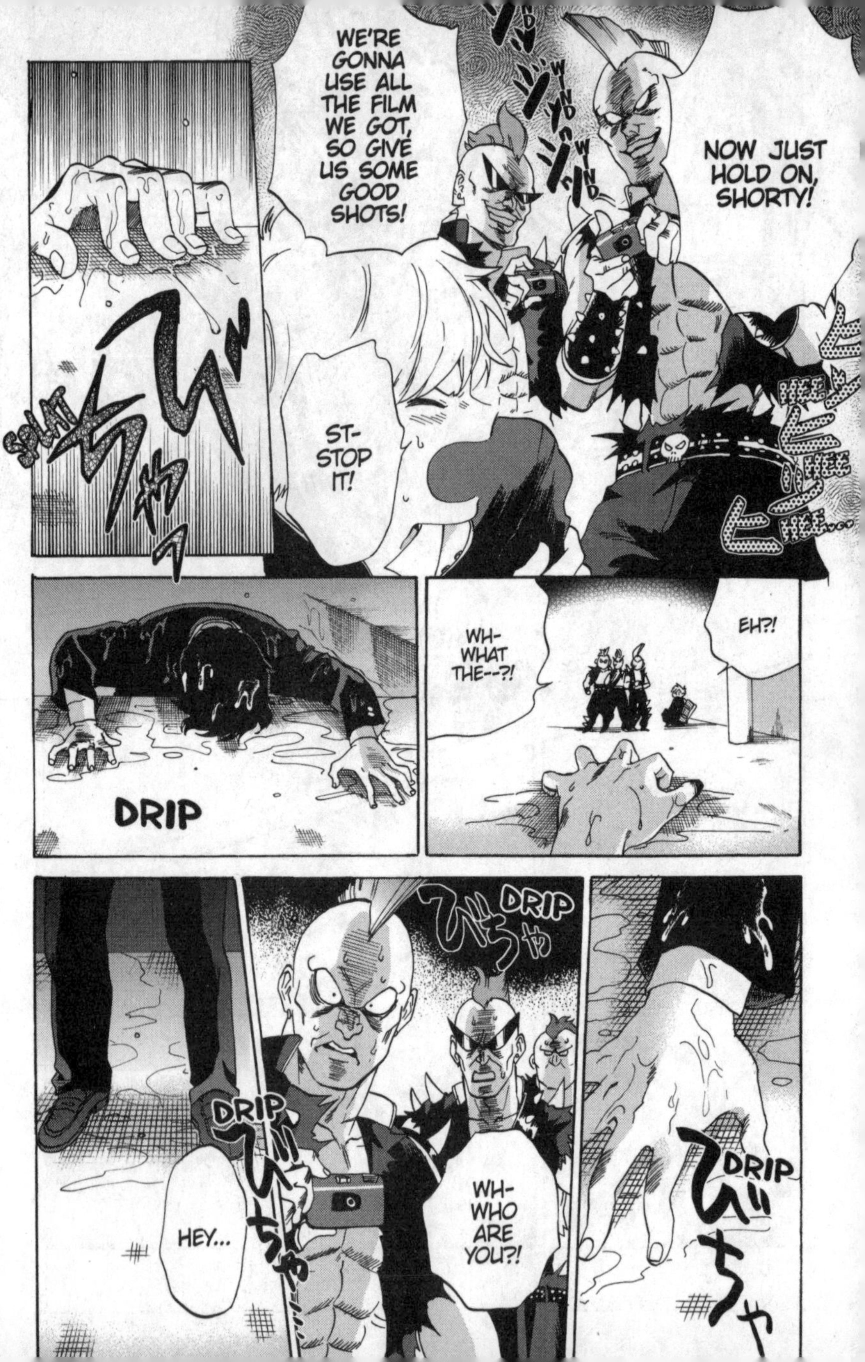

NOW JUST HOLD ON, SHORTY!
WIND WIND WIND
WE'RE GONNA USE ALL THE FILM WE GOT, SO GIVE US SOME GOOD SHOTS!
HEE HEE HEE...
ST- STOP IT!
SPLAT
EH?!
WH- WHAT THE--?!
DRIP
DRIP
DRIP
WH- WHO ARE YOU?!
DRIP
HEY...

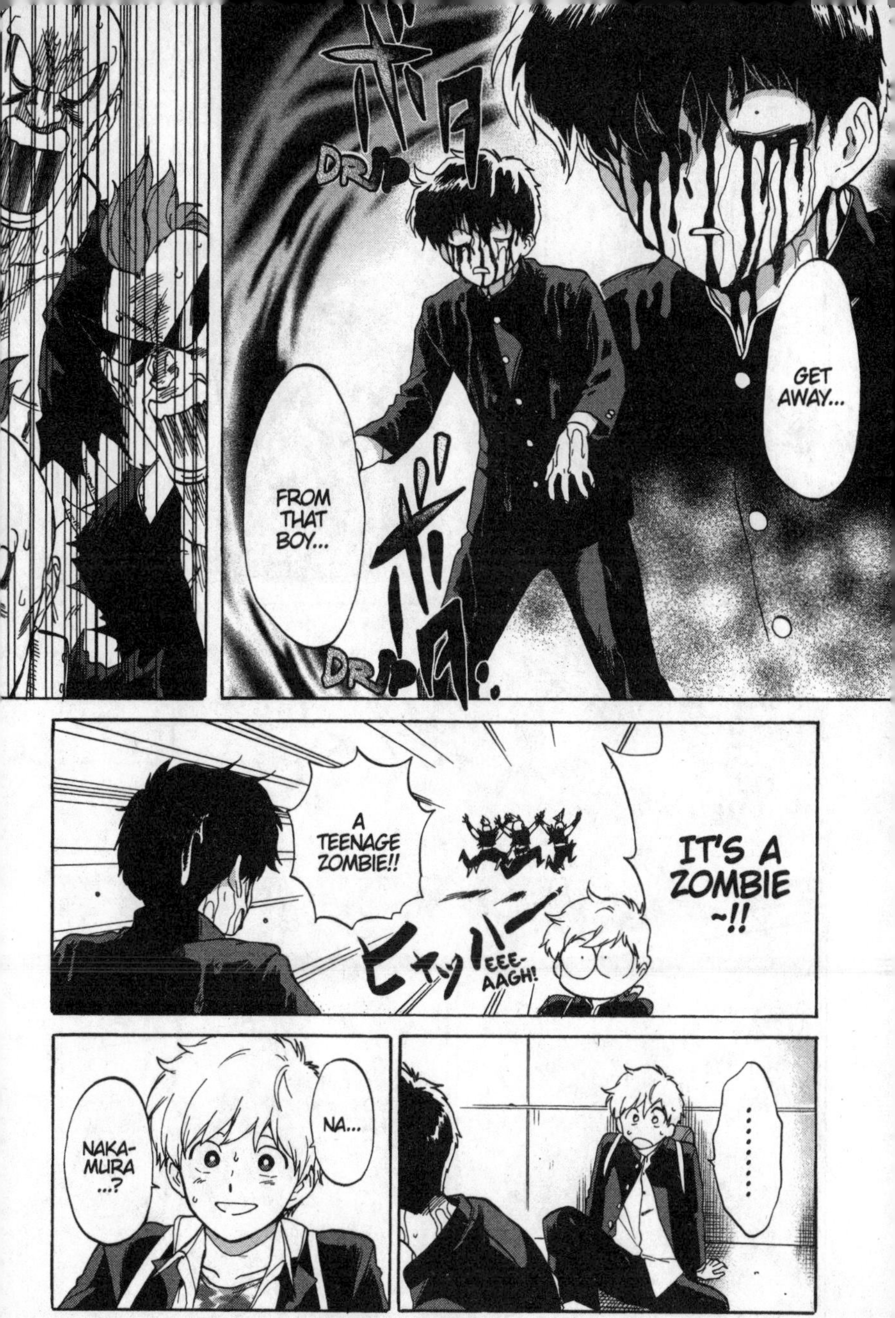

GET AWAY...
DRIP
FROM THAT BOY...
DRIP
IT'S A ZOMBIE ~!!
A TEENAGE ZOMBIE!!
EEE-AAGH!
......
NA...
NAKA-MURA ...?

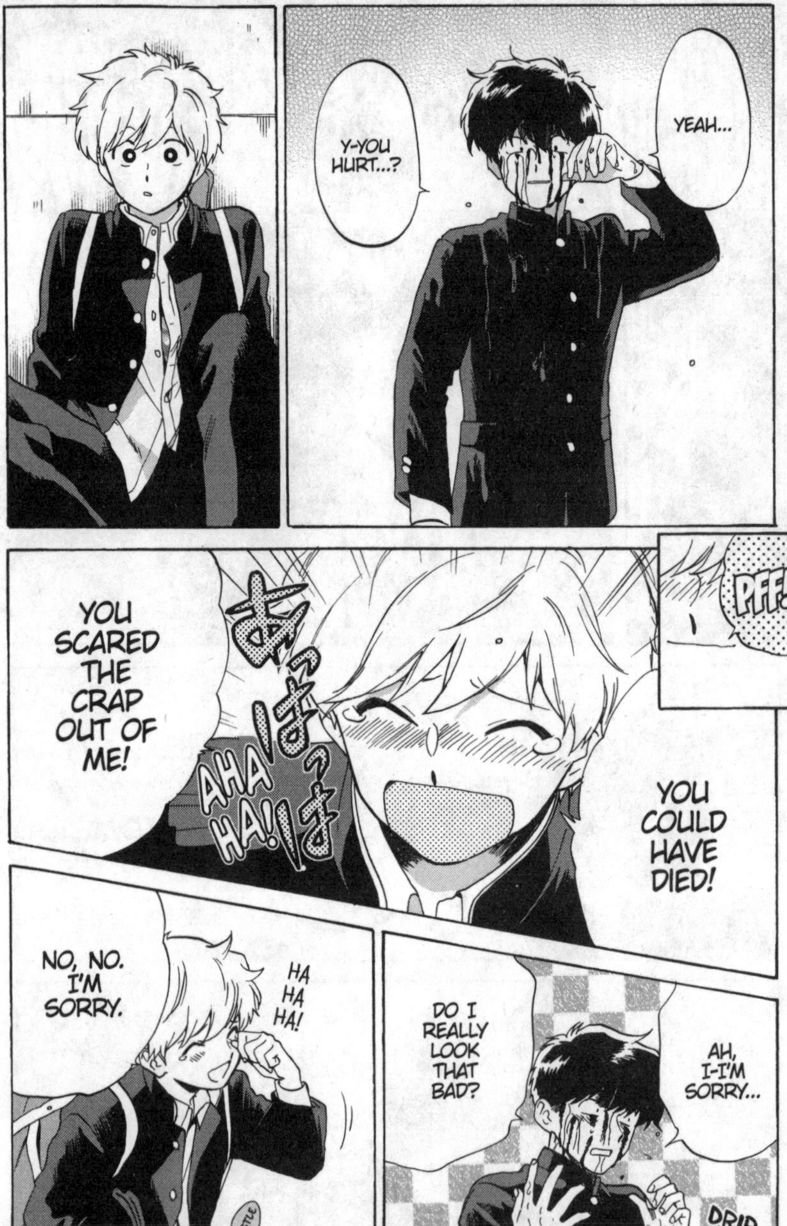
YEAH...
Y-YOU HURT...?
PFF!
あっはっはっ
AHA HA!!
YOU SCARED THE CRAP OUT OF ME!
YOU COULD HAVE DIED!
AH, I-I'M SORRY...
DO I REALLY LOOK THAT BAD?
DRIP
HA HA HA!
NO, NO. I'M SORRY.
RUSTLE

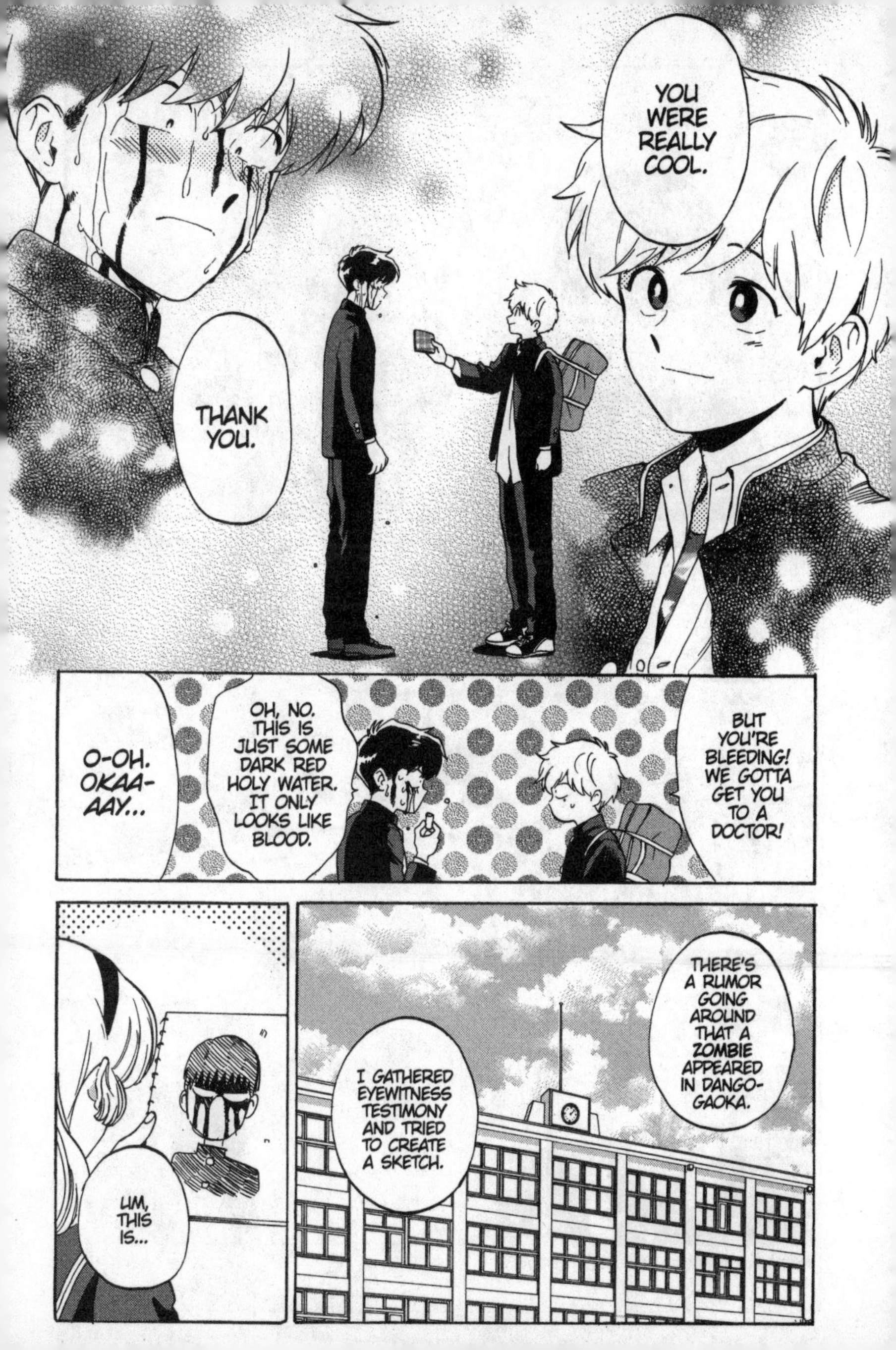
YOU WERE REALLY COOL.
THANK YOU.
BUT YOU'RE BLEEDING! WE GOTTA GET YOU TO A DOCTOR!
OH, NO. THIS IS JUST SOME DARK RED HOLY WATER. IT ONLY LOOKS LIKE BLOOD.
O-OH. OKAAA-AAY...
THERE'S A RUMOR GOING AROUND THAT A ZOMBIE APPEARED IN DANGO-GAOKA.
I GATHERED EYEWITNESS TESTIMONY AND TRIED TO CREATE A SKETCH.
UM, THIS IS...

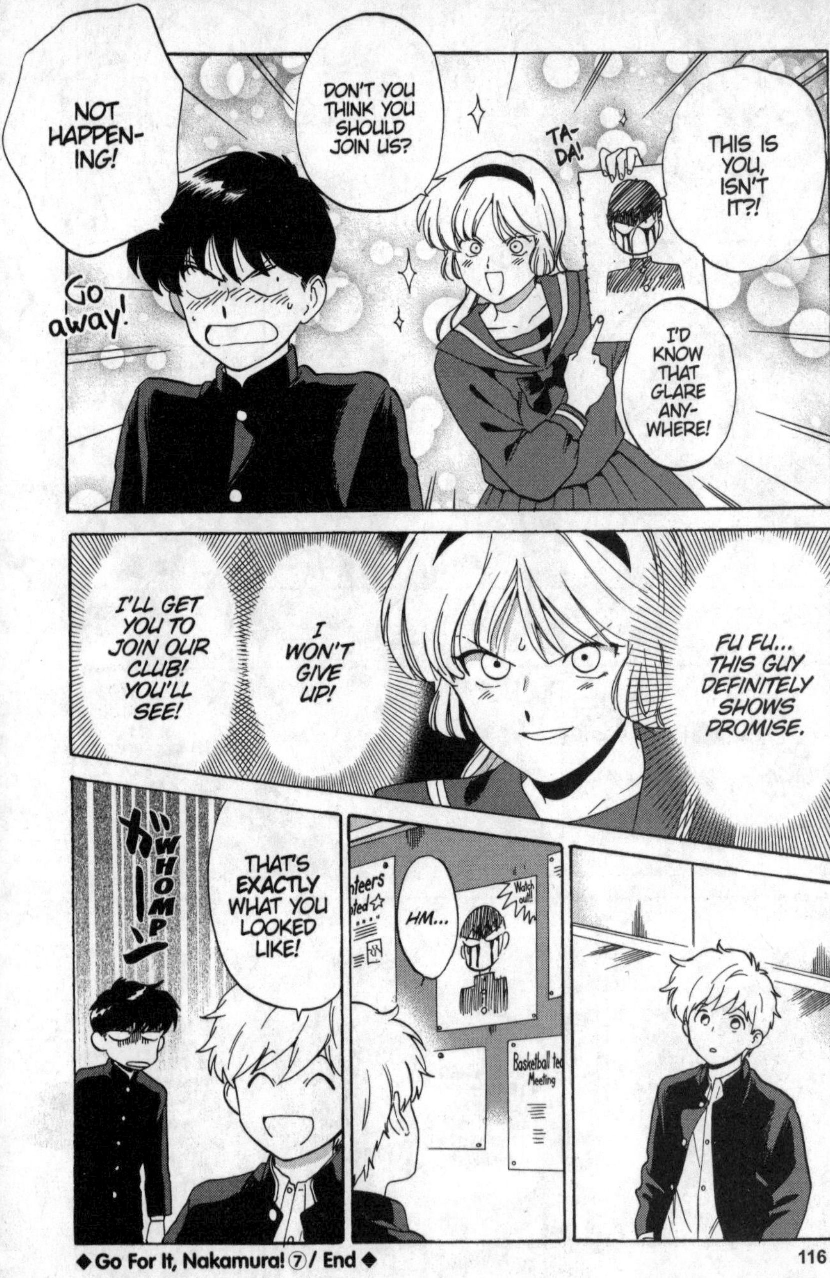
THIS IS YOU, ISN'T IT?!
TA-DA!
I'D KNOW THAT GLARE ANYWHERE!
DON'T YOU THINK YOU SHOULD JOIN US?
NOT HAPPENING!
Go away!
FU FU... THIS GUY DEFINITELY SHOWS PROMISE.
I WON'T GIVE UP!
I'LL GET YOU TO JOIN OUR CLUB! YOU'LL SEE!
Watch out!!
HM...
THAT'S EXACTLY WHAT YOU LOOKED LIKE!
WHOMP

◆Go For It, Nakamura! ⑦ / End◆

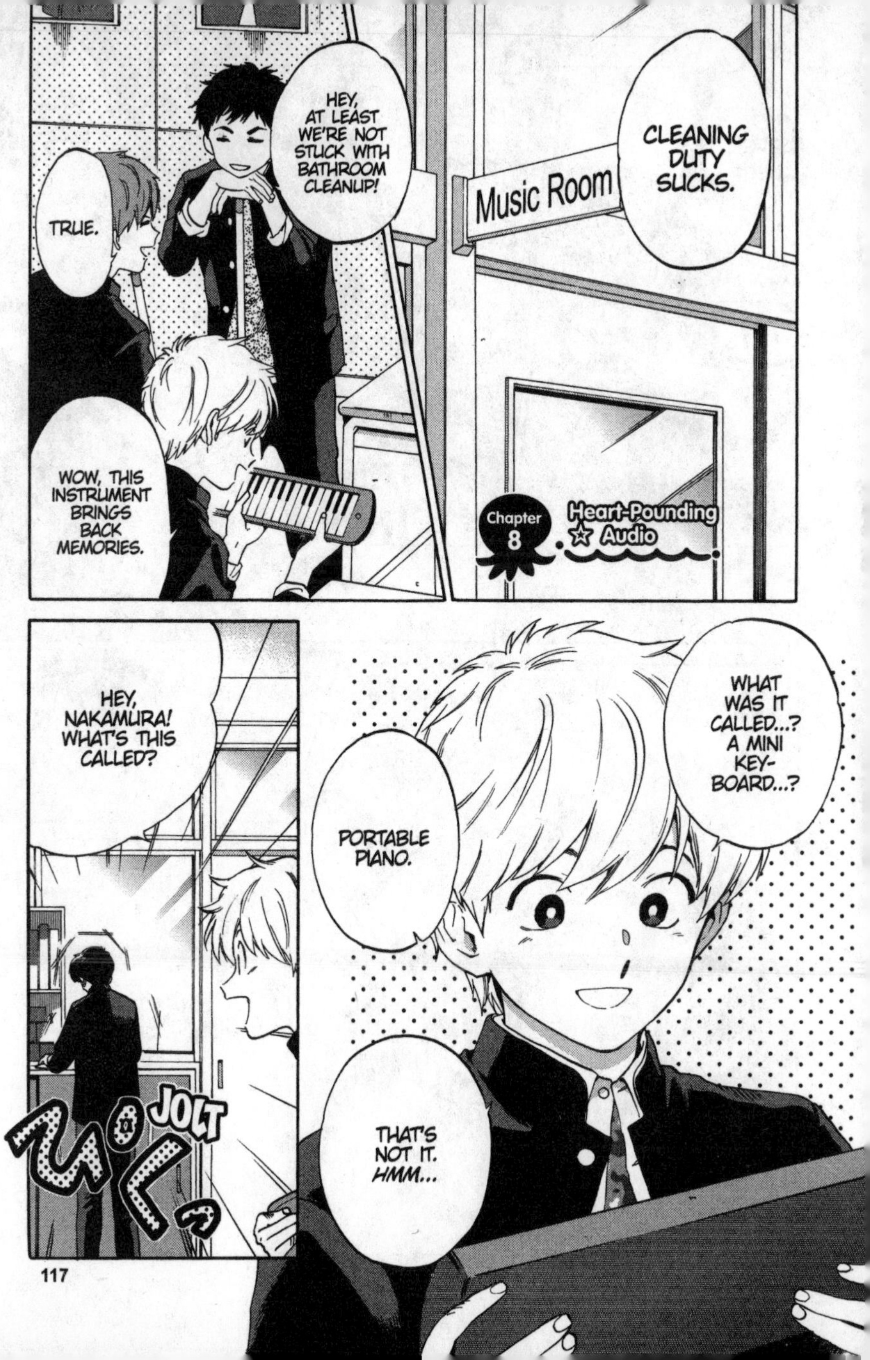
Music Room
CLEANING DUTY SUCKS.
Chapter 8
Heart-Pounding ☆ Audio
HEY, AT LEAST WE'RE NOT STUCK WITH BATHROOM CLEANUP!
TRUE.
WOW, THIS INSTRUMENT BRINGS BACK MEMORIES.
WHAT WAS IT CALLED...? A MINI KEY-BOARD...?
PORTABLE PIANO.
THAT'S NOT IT. *HMM...*
HEY, NAKAMURA! WHAT'S THIS CALLED?
JOLT

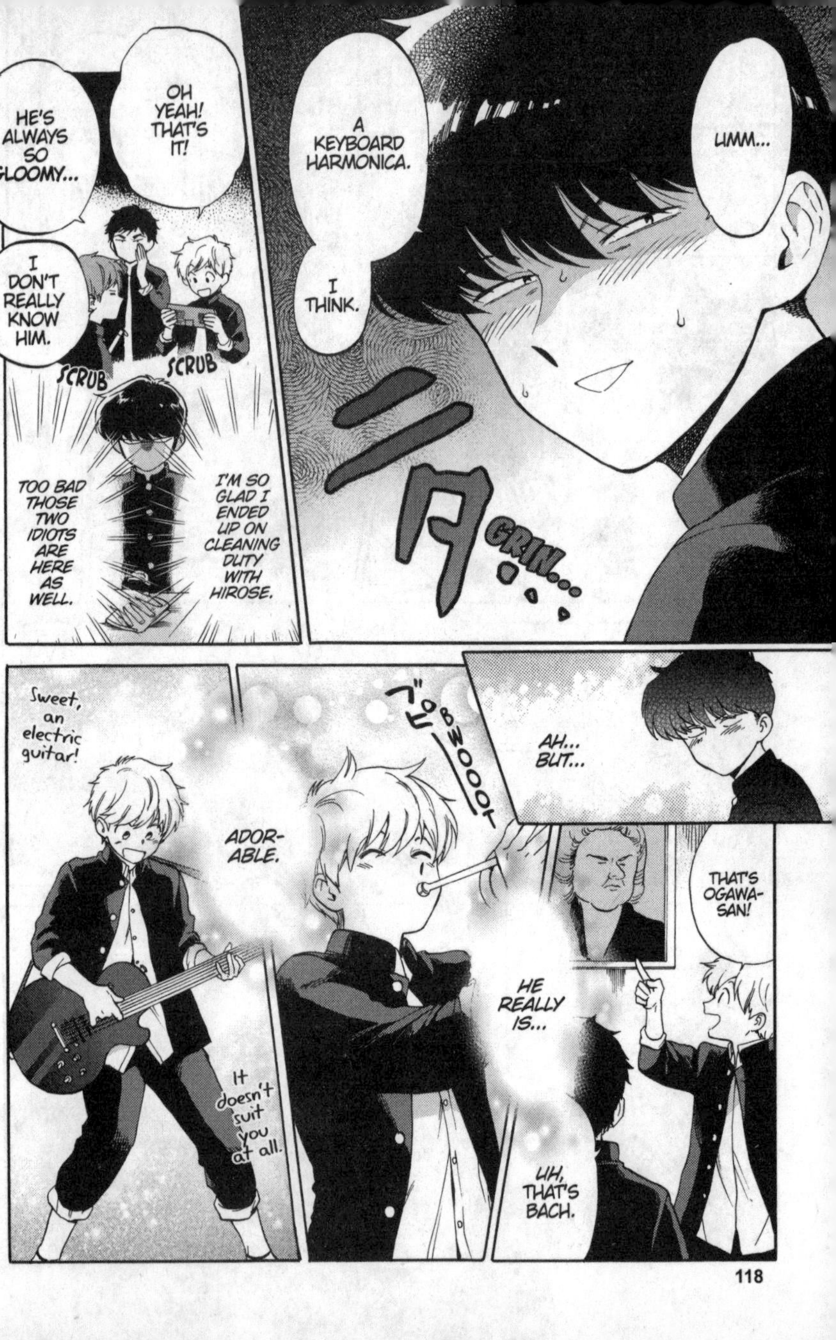
UMM...
A KEYBOARD HARMONICA.
I THINK.
ニタ
GRIN...
OH YEAH! THAT'S IT!
HE'S ALWAYS SO GLOOMY...
I DON'T REALLY KNOW HIM.
SCRUB
SCRUB
I'M SO GLAD I ENDED UP ON CLEANING DUTY WITH HIROSE.
TOO BAD THOSE TWO IDIOTS ARE HERE AS WELL.
AH... BUT...
THAT'S OGAWA-SAN!
HE REALLY IS...
UH, THAT'S BACH.
ブピ
BWOOOT
ADORABLE.
Sweet, an electric guitar!
It doesn't suit you at all.

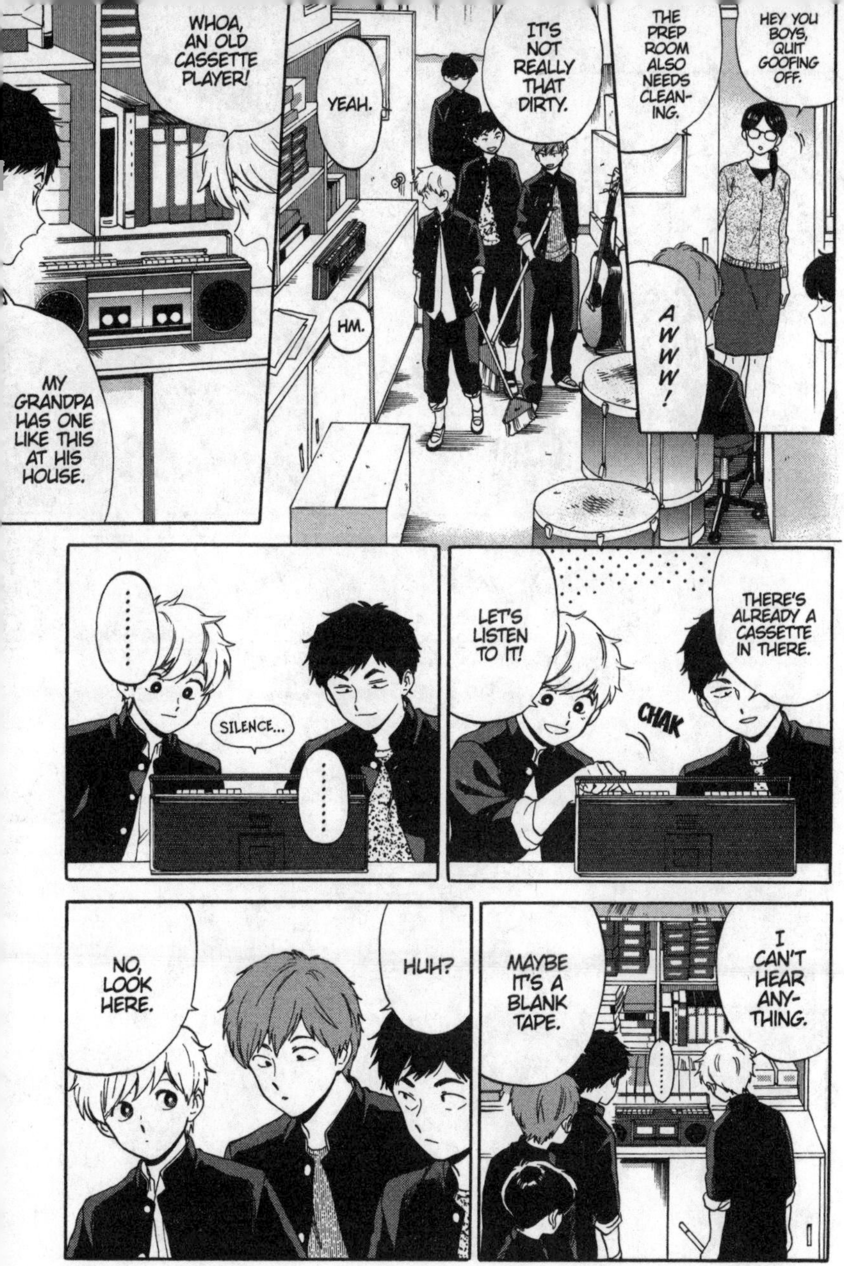
HEY YOU BOYS, QUIT GOOFING OFF.
THE PREP ROOM ALSO NEEDS CLEANING.
AWWW!
IT'S NOT REALLY THAT DIRTY.
YEAH.
HM.
WHOA, AN OLD CASSETTE PLAYER!
MY GRANDPA HAS ONE LIKE THIS AT HIS HOUSE.
THERE'S ALREADY A CASSETTE IN THERE.
LET'S LISTEN TO IT!
CHAK
......
SILENCE...
......
I CAN'T HEAR ANYTHING.
MAYBE IT'S A BLANK TAPE.
......
HUH?
NO, LOOK HERE.

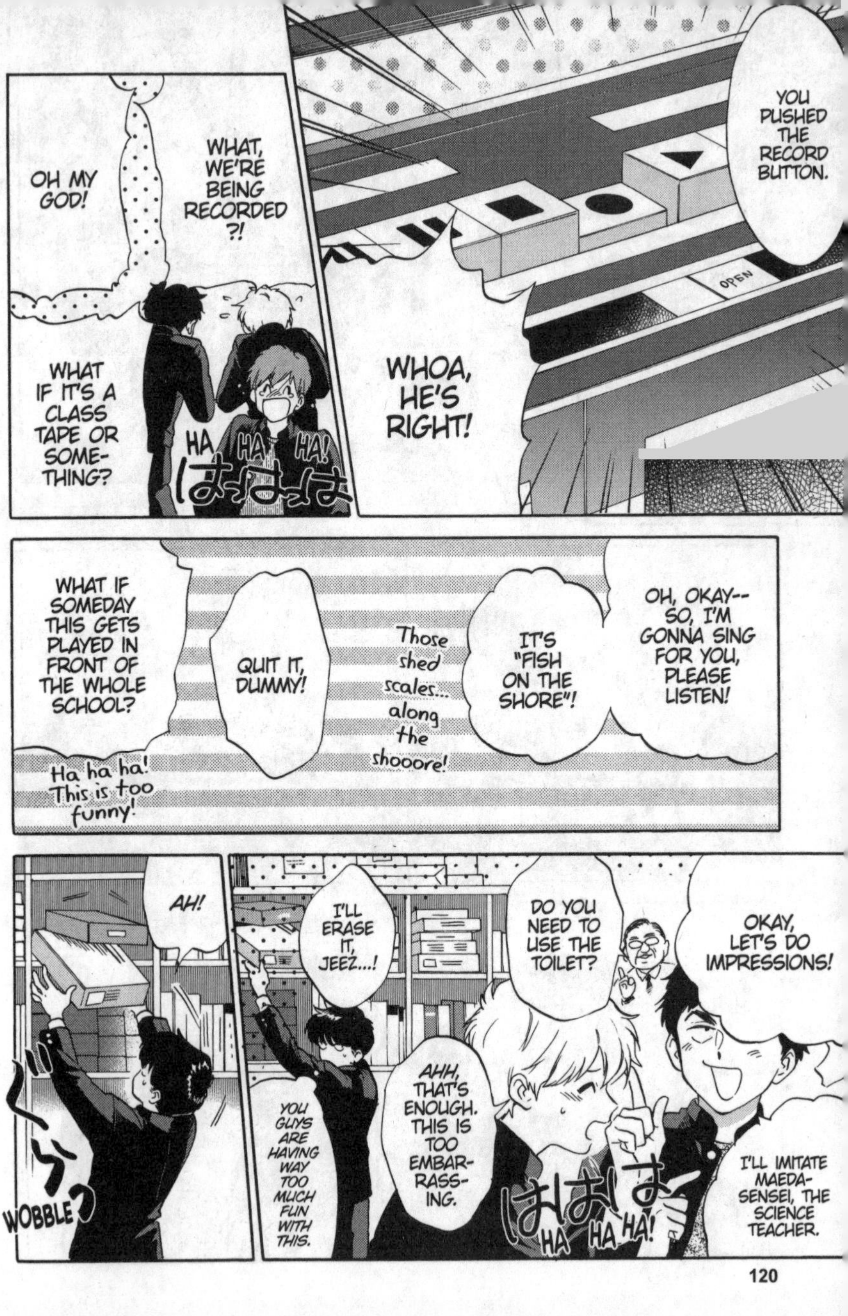
YOU PUSHED THE RECORD BUTTON.
OPEN
WHOA, HE'S RIGHT!
WHAT, WE'RE BEING RECORDED ?!
OH MY GOD!
WHAT IF IT'S A CLASS TAPE OR SOME-THING?
HA HA HA!
はははは
OH, OKAY-- SO, I'M GONNA SING FOR YOU, PLEASE LISTEN!
IT'S "FISH ON THE SHORE"!
Those shed scales... along the shooore!
QUIT IT, DUMMY!
WHAT IF SOMEDAY THIS GETS PLAYED IN FRONT OF THE WHOLE SCHOOL?
Ha ha ha! This is too funny!
OKAY, LET'S DO IMPRESSIONS!
I'LL IMITATE MAEDA-SENSEI, THE SCIENCE TEACHER.
DO YOU NEED TO USE THE TOILET?
ははは
HA HA HA!
AHH, THAT'S ENOUGH. THIS IS TOO EMBAR-RASS-ING.
YOU GUYS ARE HAVING WAY TOO MUCH FUN WITH THIS.
I'LL ERASE IT, JEEZ...!
AH!
ぐらっ
WOBBLE

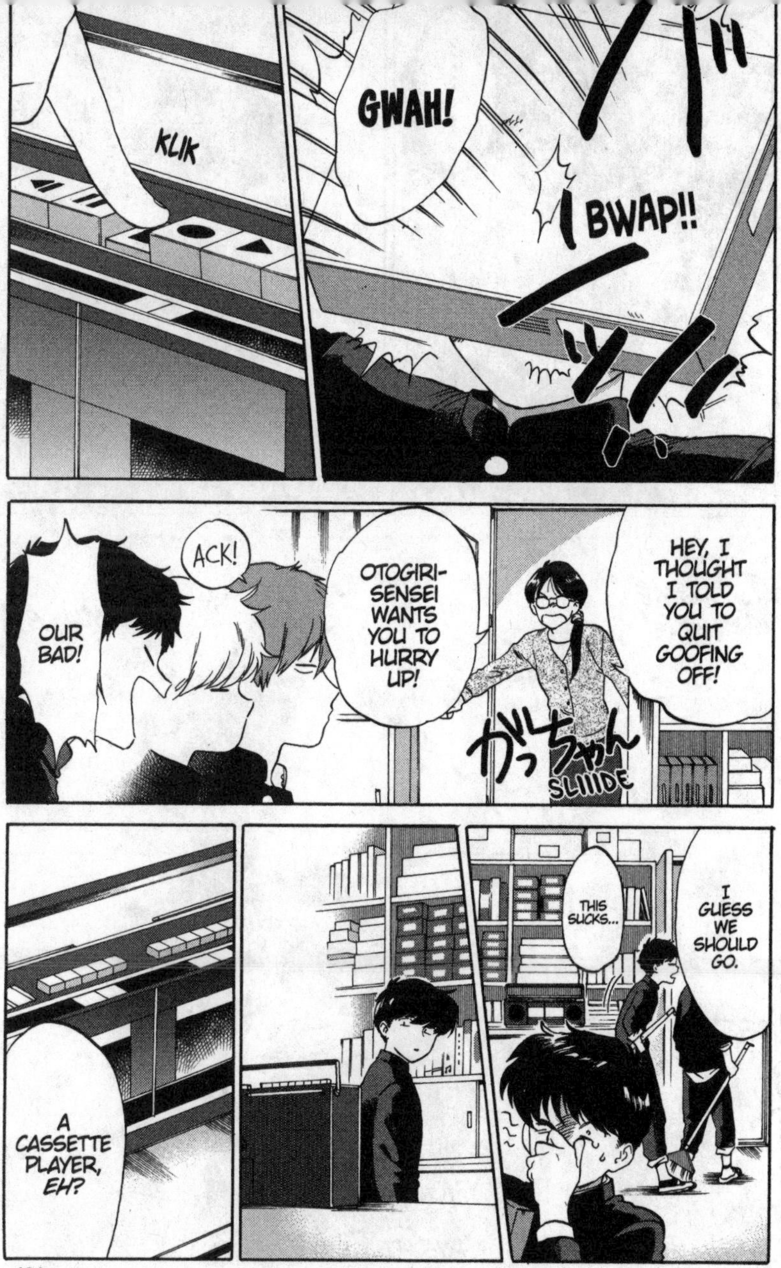
GWAH!
BWAP!!
KLIK
HEY, I THOUGHT I TOLD YOU TO QUIT GOOFING OFF!
がっちゃん
SLIIIDE
OTOGIRI-SENSEI WANTS YOU TO HURRY UP!
ACK!
OUR BAD!
I GUESS WE SHOULD GO.
THIS SUCKS...
A CASSETTE PLAYER, EH?

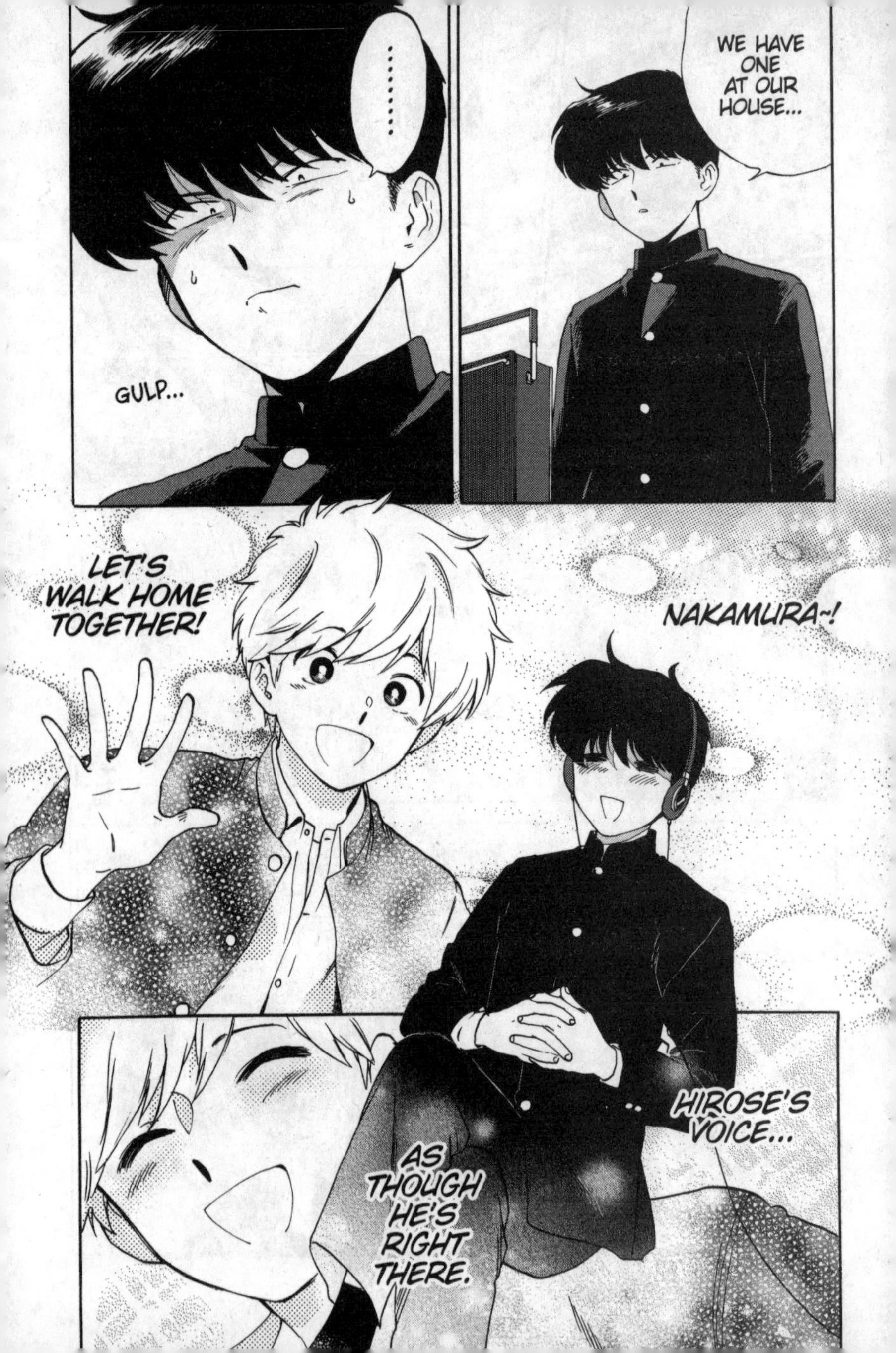
WE HAVE ONE AT OUR HOUSE...
......
GULP...
NAKAMURA~!
LET'S WALK HOME TOGETHER!
HIROSE'S VOICE...
AS THOUGH HE'S RIGHT THERE.

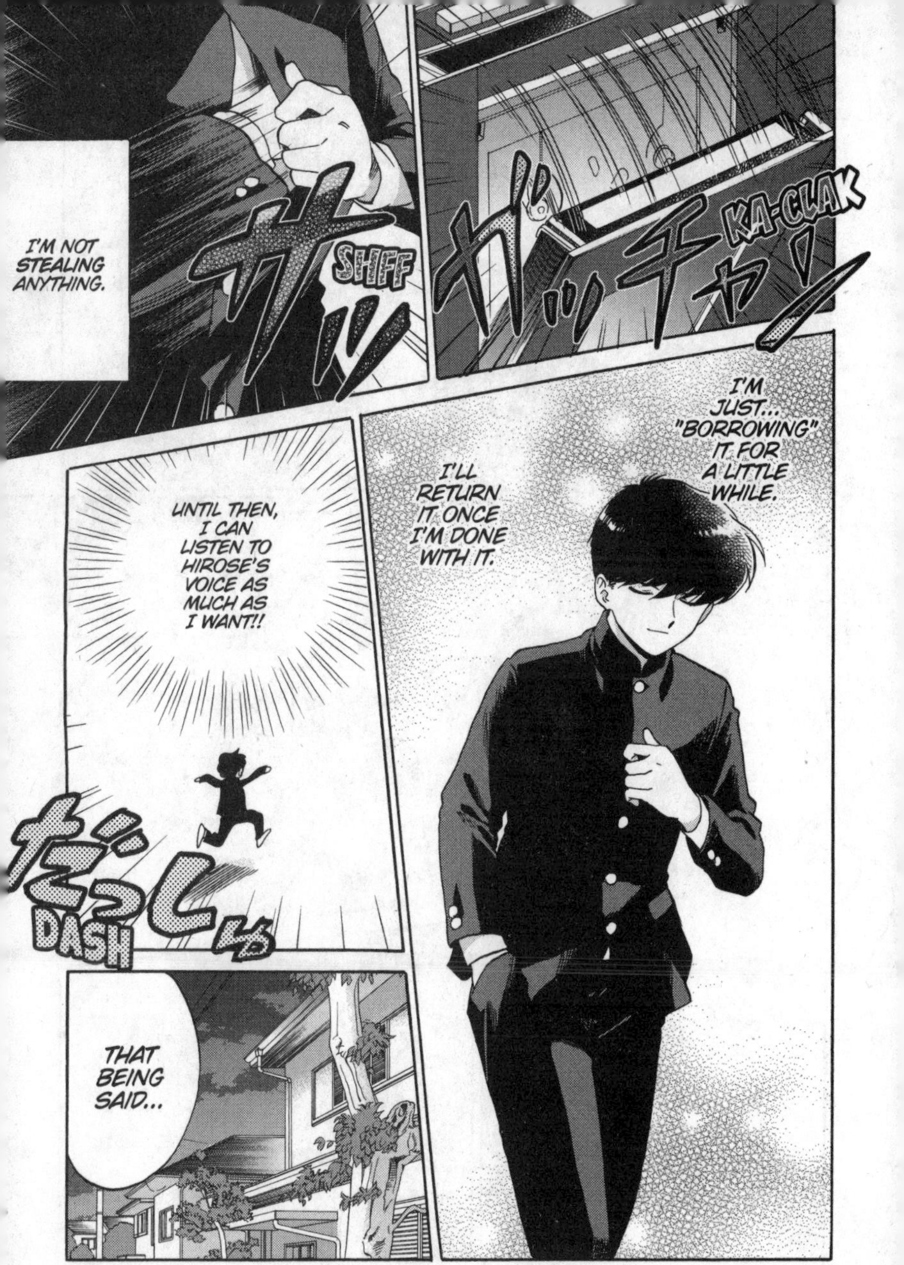
ガッチャン
KA-CLAK
ザッ
SHFF
I'M NOT STEALING ANYTHING.
I'M JUST... "BORROWING" IT FOR A LITTLE WHILE.
I'LL RETURN IT ONCE I'M DONE WITH IT.
UNTIL THEN, I CAN LISTEN TO HIROSE'S VOICE AS MUCH AS I WANT!!
だっしゅ
DASH
THAT BEING SAID...

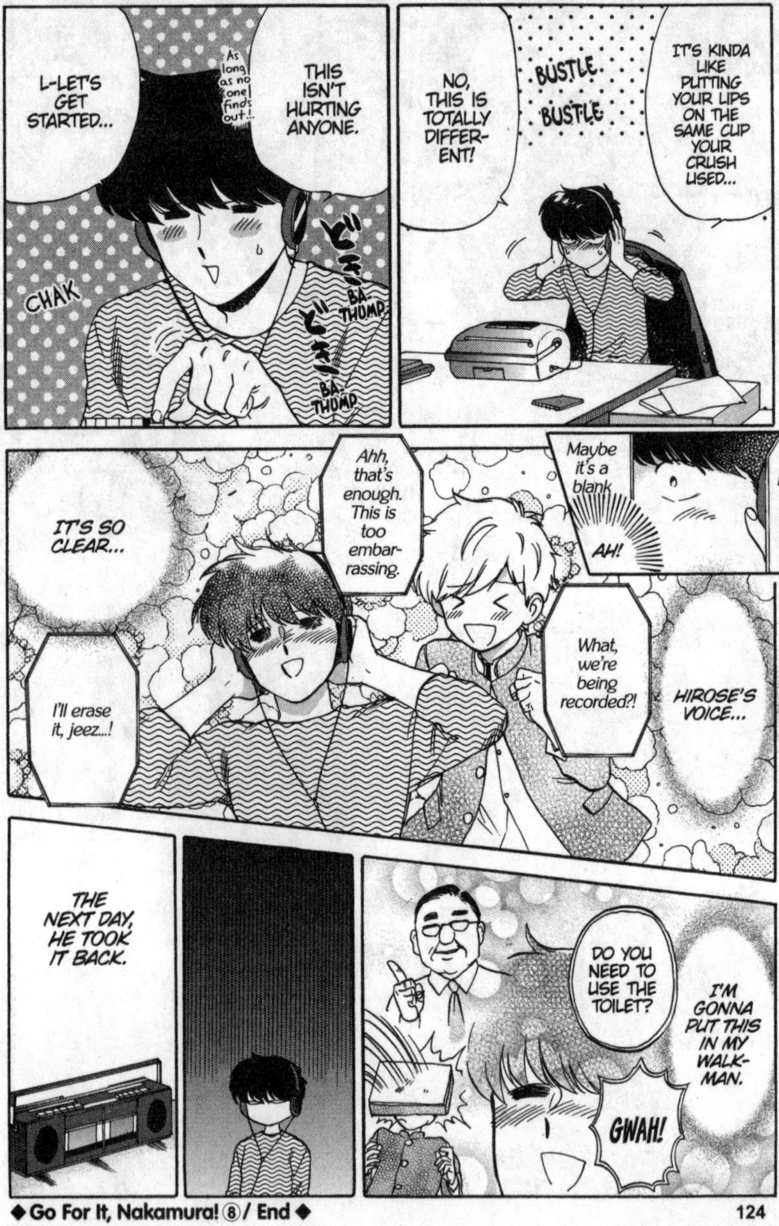
IT'S KINDA LIKE PUTTING YOUR LIPS ON THE SAME CUP YOUR CRUSH USED...
BUSTLE
BUSTLE
NO, THIS IS TOTALLY DIFFER-ENT!
THIS ISN'T HURTING ANYONE.
As long as no one finds out...
L-LET'S GET STARTED...
BA-THUMP
BA-THUMP
CHAK
I can't hear any-thing.
Maybe it's a blank
AH!
HIROSE'S VOICE...
What, we're being recorded?!
Ahh, that's enough. This is too embar-rassing.
IT'S SO CLEAR...
I'll erase it, jeez...!
I'M GONNA PUT THIS IN MY WALK-MAN.
DO YOU NEED TO USE THE TOILET?
GWAH!
THE NEXT DAY, HE TOOK IT BACK.

Chapter 9 The Tragedy of G

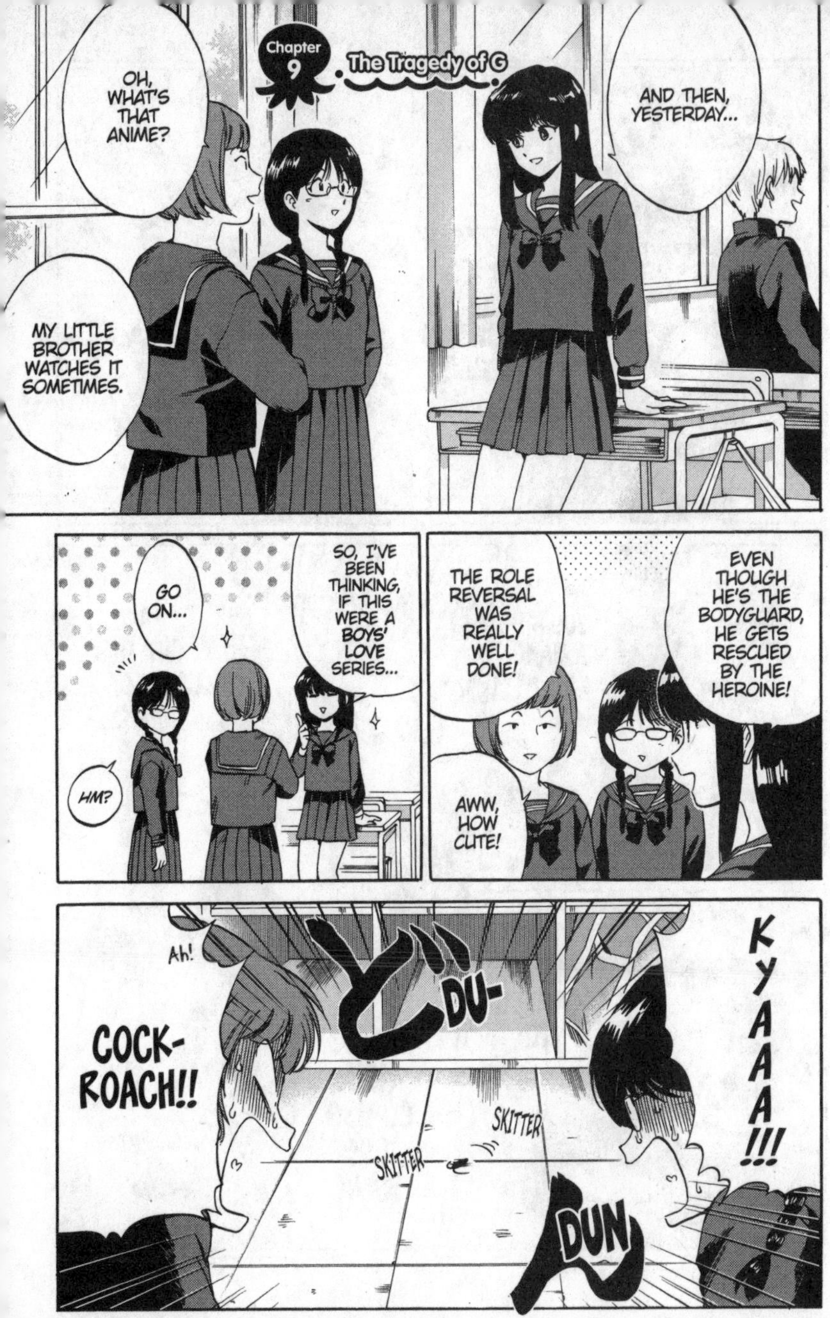

AND THEN, YESTERDAY...
OH, WHAT'S THAT ANIME?
MY LITTLE BROTHER WATCHES IT SOMETIMES.
EVEN THOUGH HE'S THE BODYGUARD, HE GETS RESCUED BY THE HEROINE!
THE ROLE REVERSAL WAS REALLY WELL DONE!
AWW, HOW CUTE!
SO, I'VE BEEN THINKING, IF THIS WERE A BOYS' LOVE SERIES...
GO ON...
HM?
KYAAAA!!!
DU-
Ah!
COCK-ROACH!!
SKITTER
SKITTER
DUN

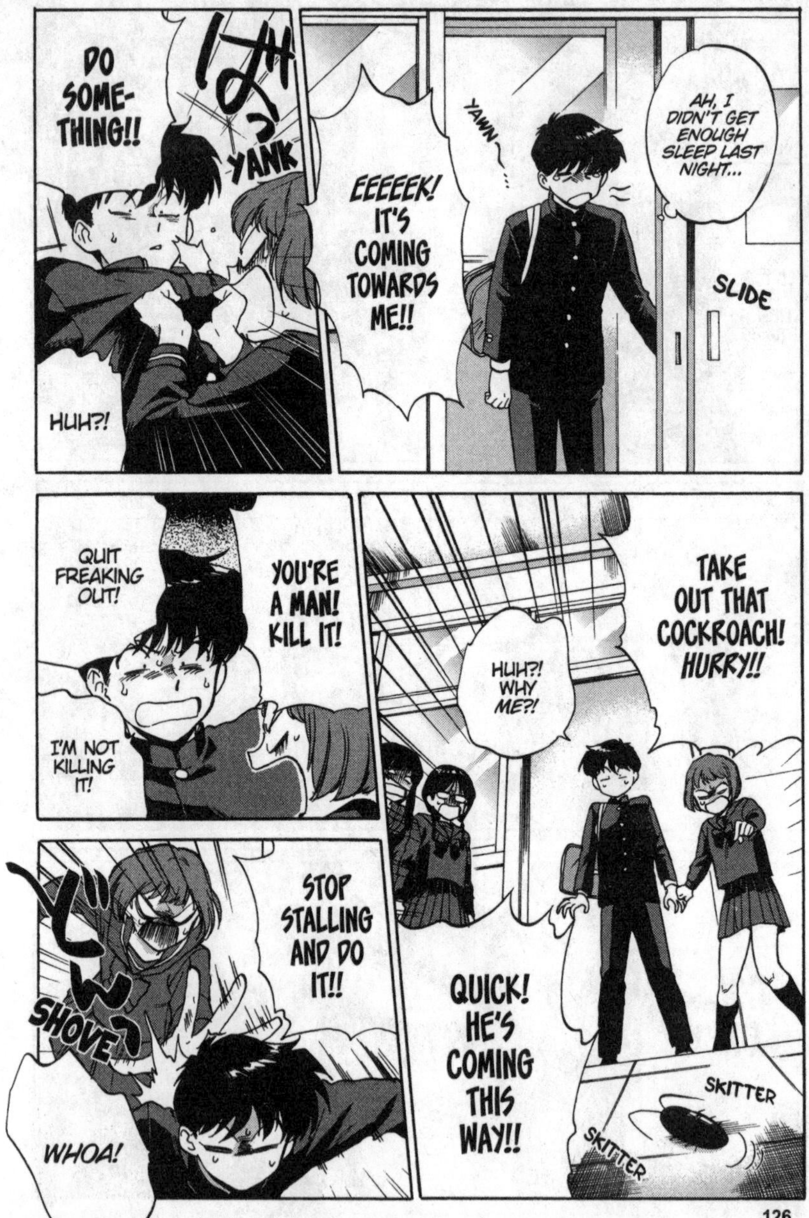
AH, I DIDN'T GET ENOUGH SLEEP LAST NIGHT...
YAWN...
SLIDE
EEEEEK! IT'S COMING TOWARDS ME!!
ばっ
YANK
DO SOME-THING!!
HUH?!
TAKE OUT THAT COCKROACH! HURRY!!
HUH?! WHY ME?!
QUICK! HE'S COMING THIS WAY!!
SKITTER
SKITTER
YOU'RE A MAN! KILL IT!
QUIT FREAKING OUT!
I'M NOT KILLING IT!
STOP STALLING AND DO IT!!
SHOVE
WHOA!

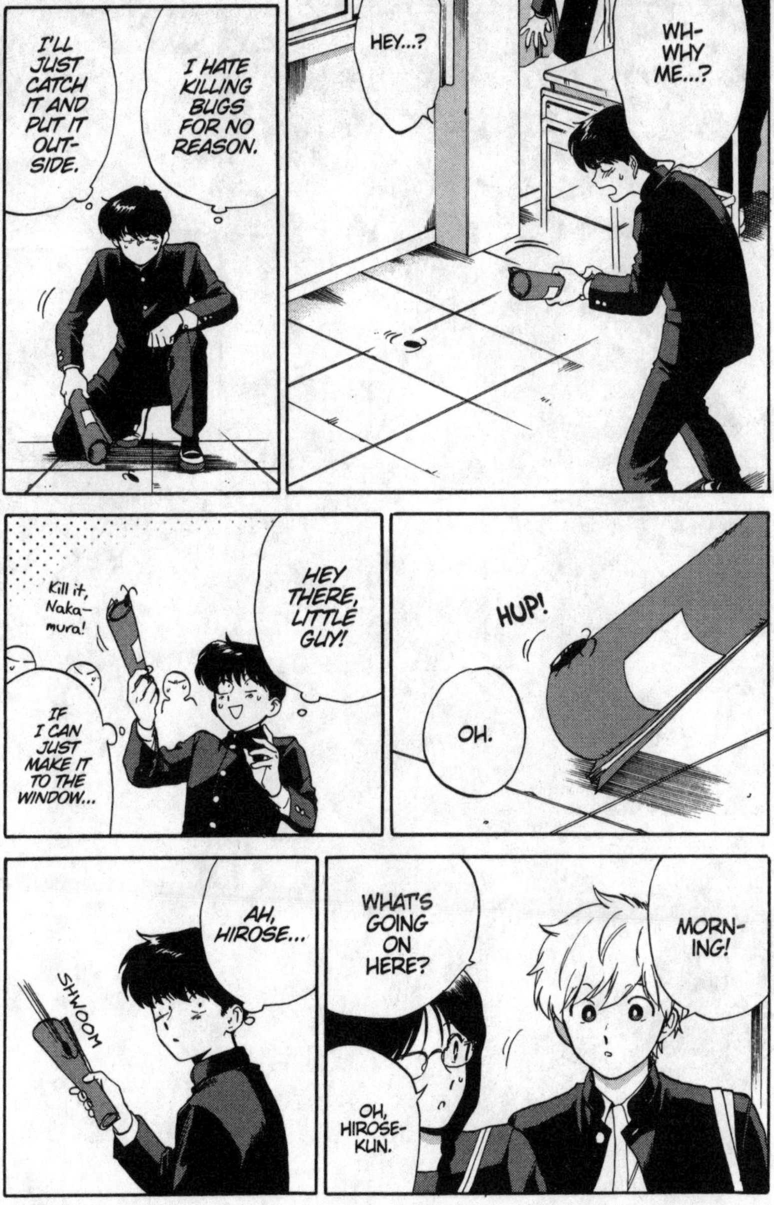
WH- WHY ME...?
HEY...?
I HATE KILLING BUGS FOR NO REASON.
I'LL JUST CATCH IT AND PUT IT OUT-SIDE.
HUP!
OH.
HEY THERE, LITTLE GUY!
Kill it, Naka-mura!
IF I CAN JUST MAKE IT TO THE WINDOW...
MORN-ING!
WHAT'S GOING ON HERE?
OH, HIROSE-KUN.
AH, HIROSE...
SHWOOM

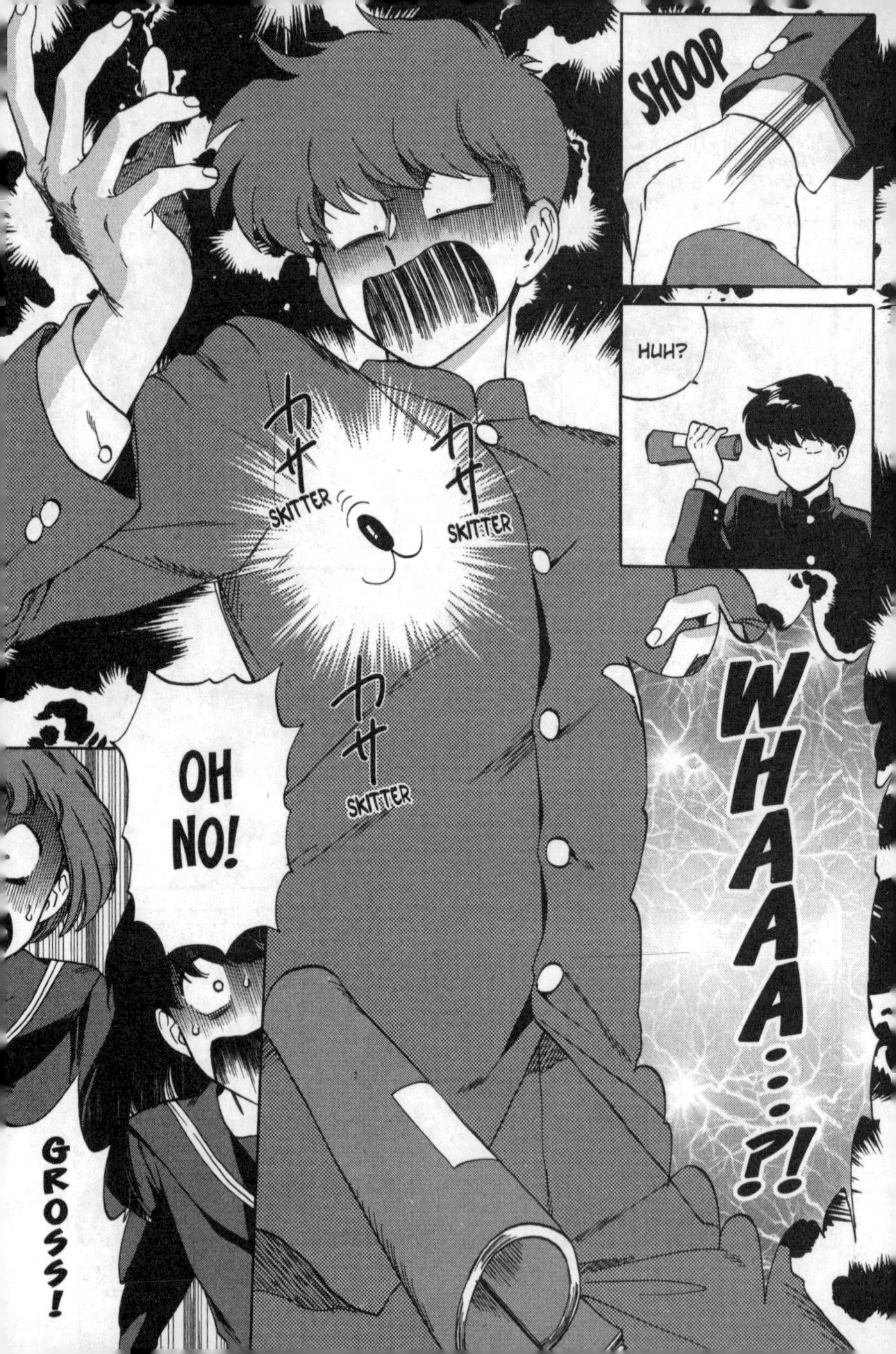
SHOOP
HUH?
WHAAA...?!
カサ SKITTER
カサ SKITTER
カサ SKITTER
OH NO!
GROSS!

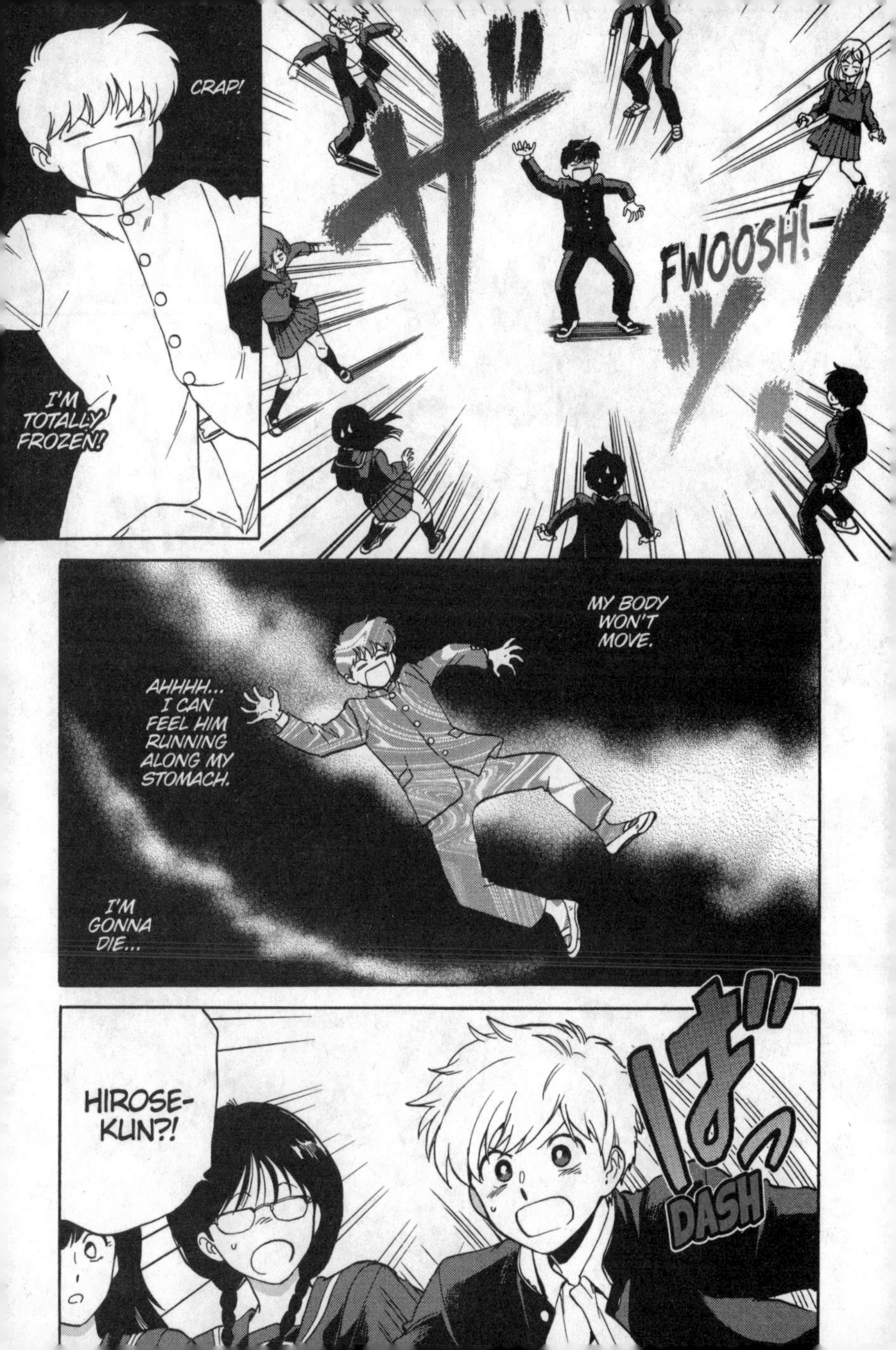
FWOOSH!
CRAP!
I'M TOTALLY FROZEN!
MY BODY WON'T MOVE.
AHHHH... I CAN FEEL HIM RUNNING ALONG MY STOMACH.
I'M GONNA DIE...
DASH
HIROSE-KUN?!

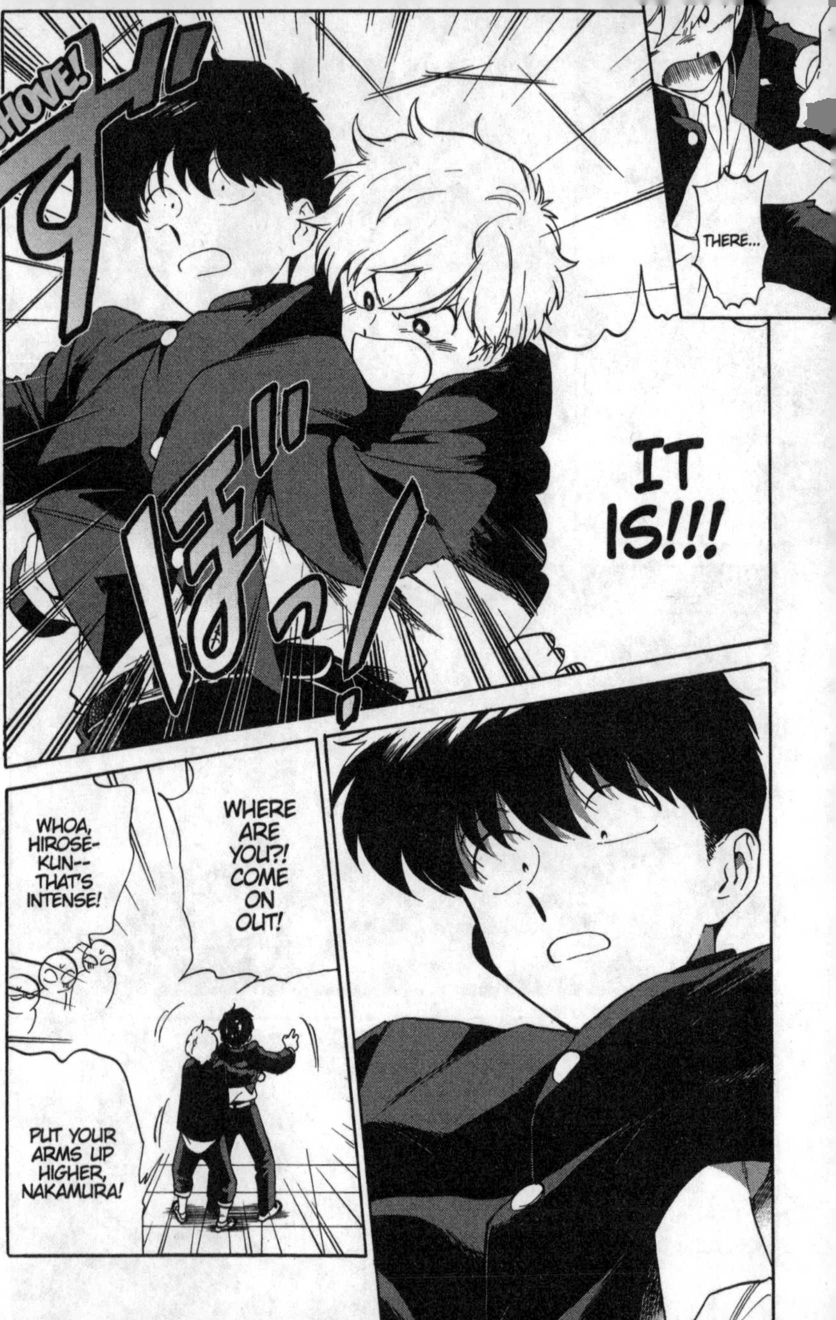
THERE...
SHOVE!
ぼっ!
IT IS!!!
WHERE ARE YOU?! COME ON OUT!
WHOA, HIROSE-KUN--THAT'S INTENSE!
PUT YOUR ARMS UP HIGHER, NAKAMURA!

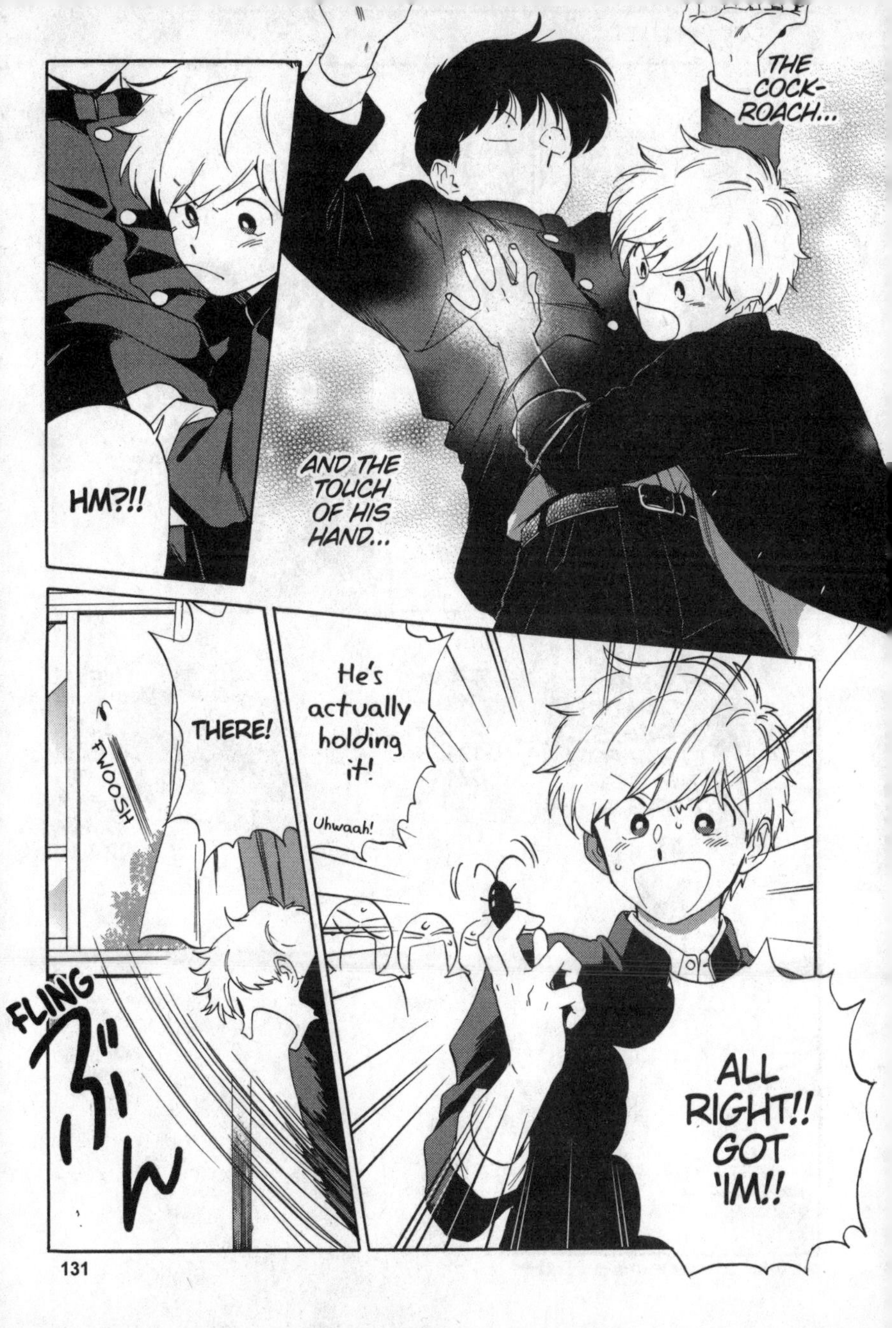
THE COCK-ROACH...
AND THE TOUCH OF HIS HAND...
HM?!!
He's actually holding it!
Uhwaah!
ALL RIGHT!! GOT 'IM!!
THERE!
FWOOSH
FLING
ぶーん

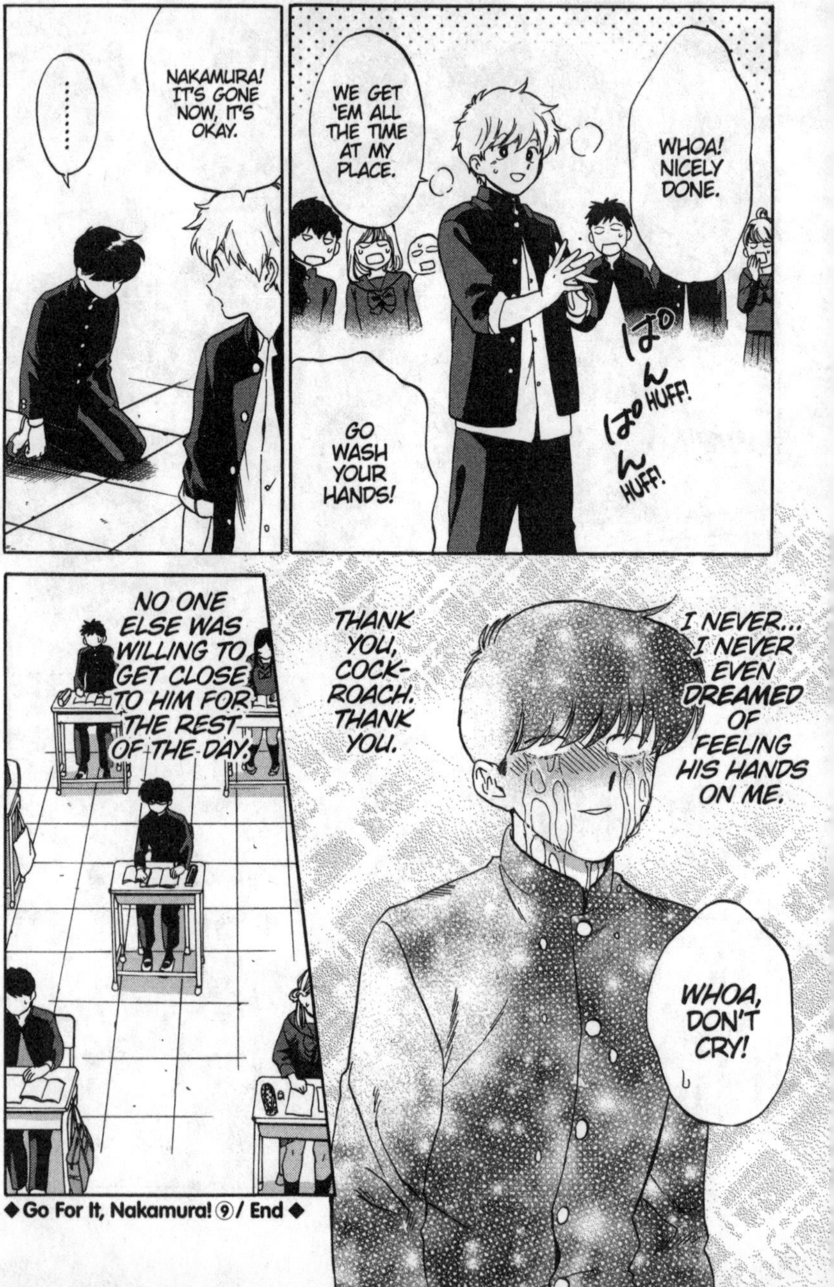
WHOA! NICELY DONE.
WE GET 'EM ALL THE TIME AT MY PLACE.
ぱん HUFF!
ぱん HUFF!
GO WASH YOUR HANDS!
NAKAMURA! IT'S GONE NOW, IT'S OKAY.
……
I NEVER… I NEVER EVEN DREAMED OF FEELING HIS HANDS ON ME.
THANK YOU, COCKROACH. THANK YOU.
WHOA, DON'T CRY!
NO ONE ELSE WAS WILLING TO GET CLOSE TO HIM FOR THE REST OF THE DAY.

◆ Go For It, Nakamura! ⑨ / End ◆

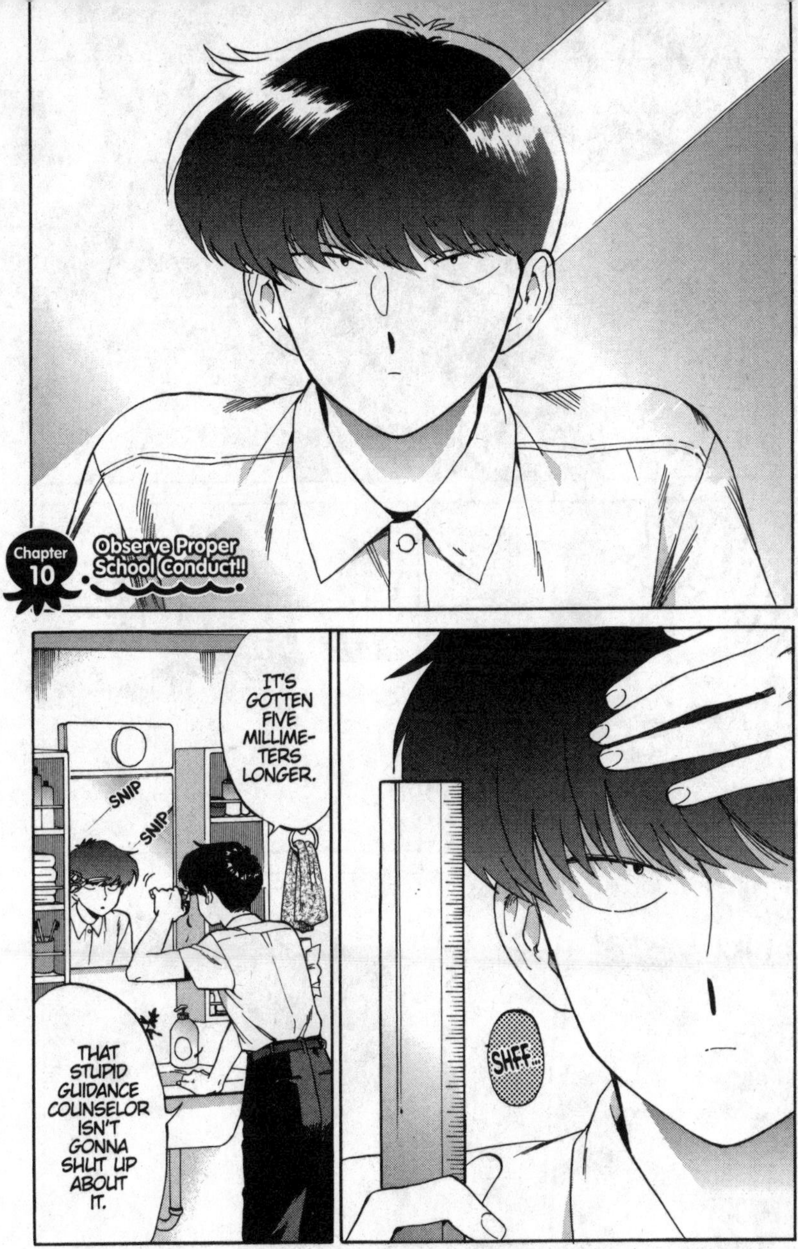
Chapter 10
Observe Proper School Conduct!!
SHFF...
IT'S GOTTEN FIVE MILLIMETERS LONGER.
SNIP
SNIP
THAT STUPID GUIDANCE COUNSELOR ISN'T GONNA SHUT UP ABOUT IT.

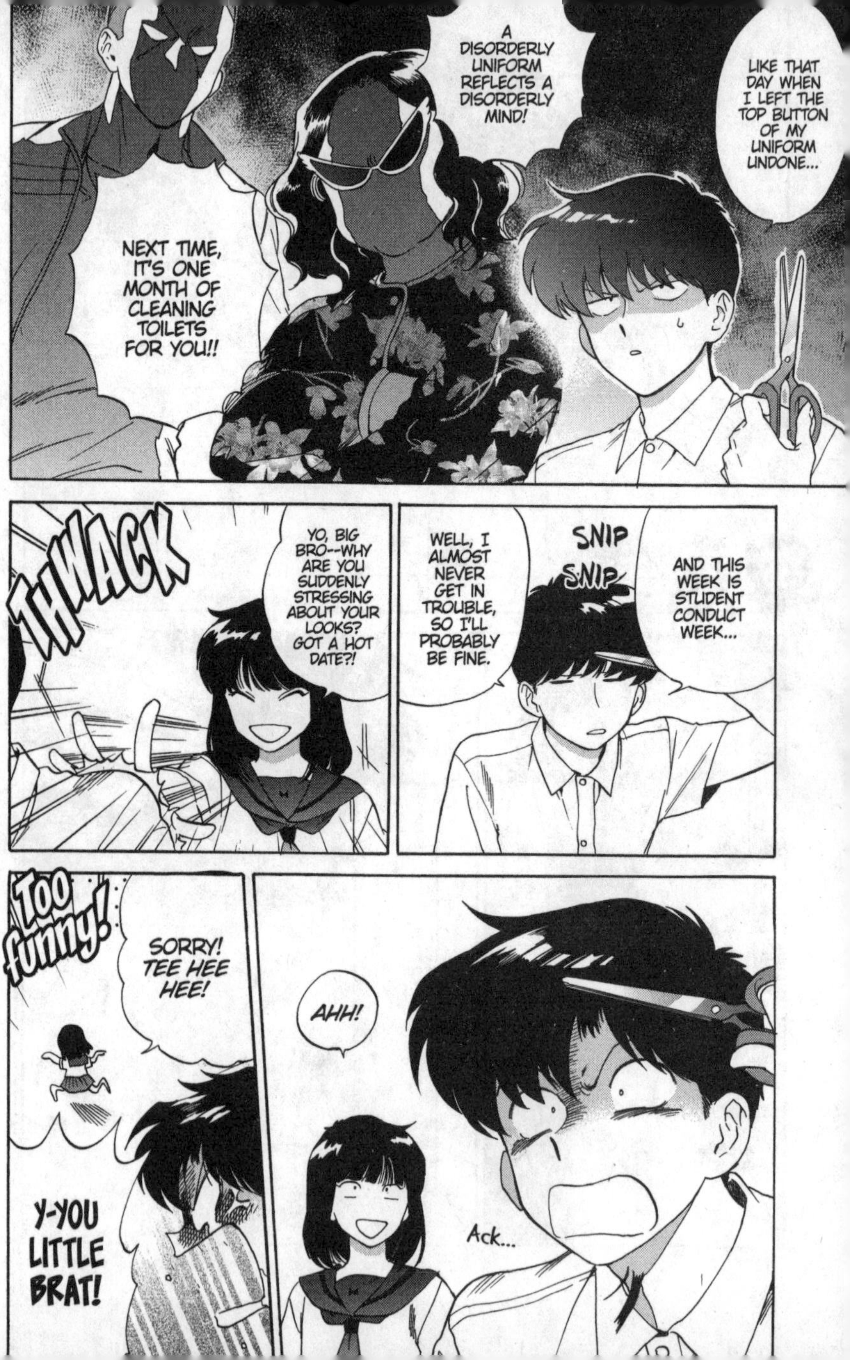
LIKE THAT DAY WHEN I LEFT THE TOP BUTTON OF MY UNIFORM UNDONE...
A DISORDERLY UNIFORM REFLECTS A DISORDERLY MIND!
NEXT TIME, IT'S ONE MONTH OF CLEANING TOILETS FOR YOU!!
AND THIS WEEK IS STUDENT CONDUCT WEEK...
SNIP SNIP
WELL, I ALMOST NEVER GET IN TROUBLE, SO I'LL PROBABLY BE FINE.
YO, BIG BRO--WHY ARE YOU SUDDENLY STRESSING ABOUT YOUR LOOKS? GOT A HOT DATE?!
THWACK
AHH!
Ack...
Too funny!
SORRY! TEE HEE HEE!
Y-YOU LITTLE BRAT!

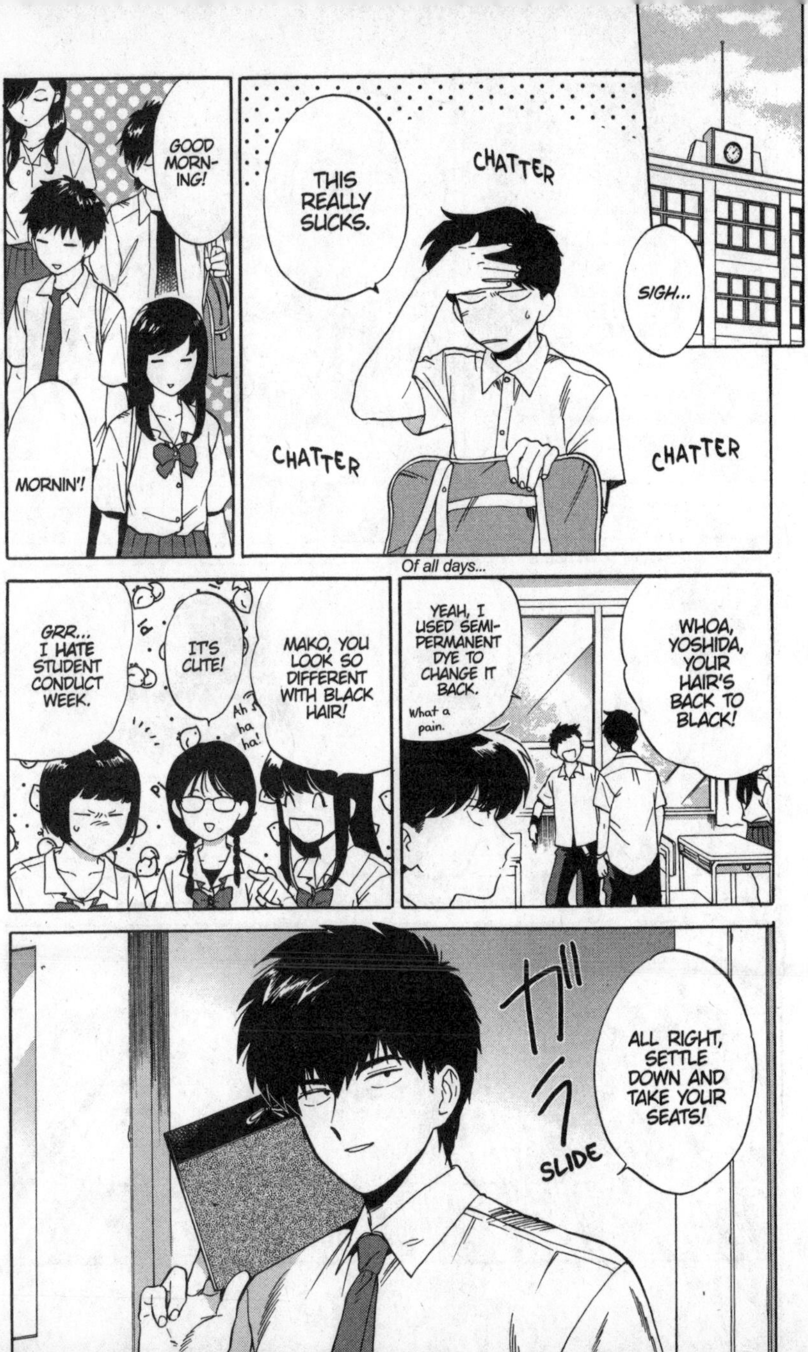
SIGH...
THIS REALLY SUCKS.
CHATTER
CHATTER
CHATTER
Of all days...
GOOD MORNING!
MORNIN'!
WHOA, YOSHIDA, YOUR HAIR'S BACK TO BLACK!
YEAH, I USED SEMI-PERMANENT DYE TO CHANGE IT BACK.
What a pain.
MAKO, YOU LOOK SO DIFFERENT WITH BLACK HAIR!
Ah ha ha!
IT'S CUTE!
GRR... I HATE STUDENT CONDUCT WEEK.
ガラ
SLIDE
ALL RIGHT, SETTLE DOWN AND TAKE YOUR SEATS!

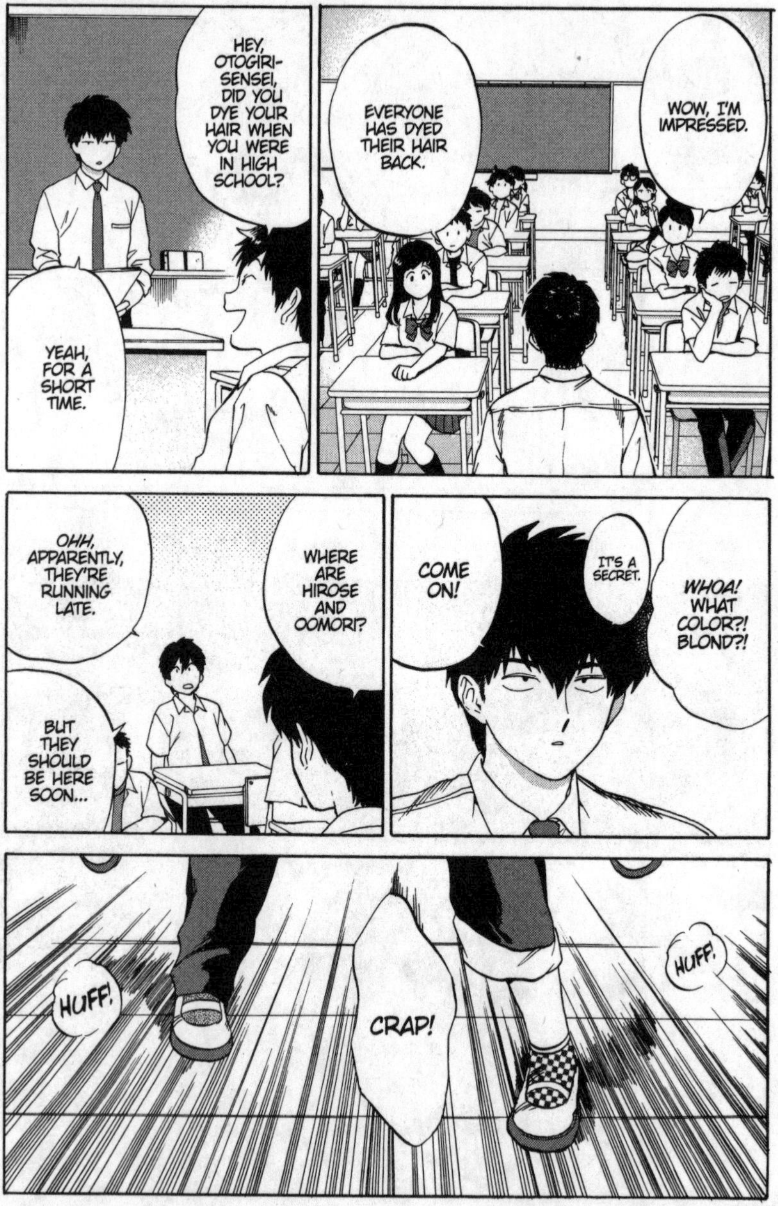
WOW, I'M IMPRESSED.
EVERYONE HAS DYED THEIR HAIR BACK.
HEY, OTOGIRI-SENSEI, DID YOU DYE YOUR HAIR WHEN YOU WERE IN HIGH SCHOOL?
YEAH, FOR A SHORT TIME.
WHOA! WHAT COLOR?! BLOND?!
IT'S A SECRET.
COME ON!
WHERE ARE HIROSE AND OOMORI?
OHH, APPARENTLY, THEY'RE RUNNING LATE.
BUT THEY SHOULD BE HERE SOON...
HUFF!
CRAP!
HUFF!

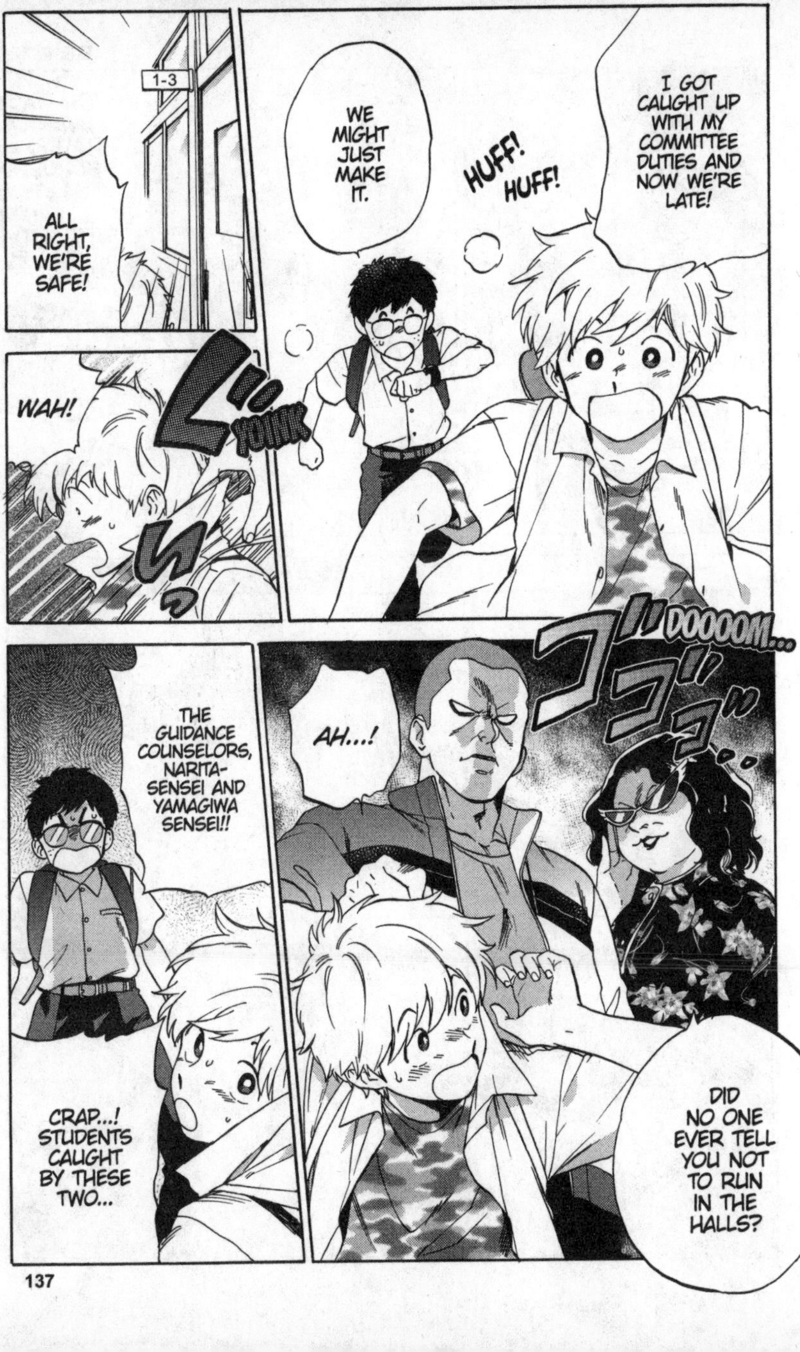
I GOT CAUGHT UP WITH MY COMMITTEE DUTIES AND NOW WE'RE LATE!
HUFF! HUFF!
WE MIGHT JUST MAKE IT.
ALL RIGHT, WE'RE SAFE!
YOINK
WAH!
DOOOOM...
AH...!
DID NO ONE EVER TELL YOU NOT TO RUN IN THE HALLS?
THE GUIDANCE COUNSELORS, NARITA-SENSEI AND YAMAGIWA SENSEI!!
CRAP...! STUDENTS CAUGHT BY THESE TWO...

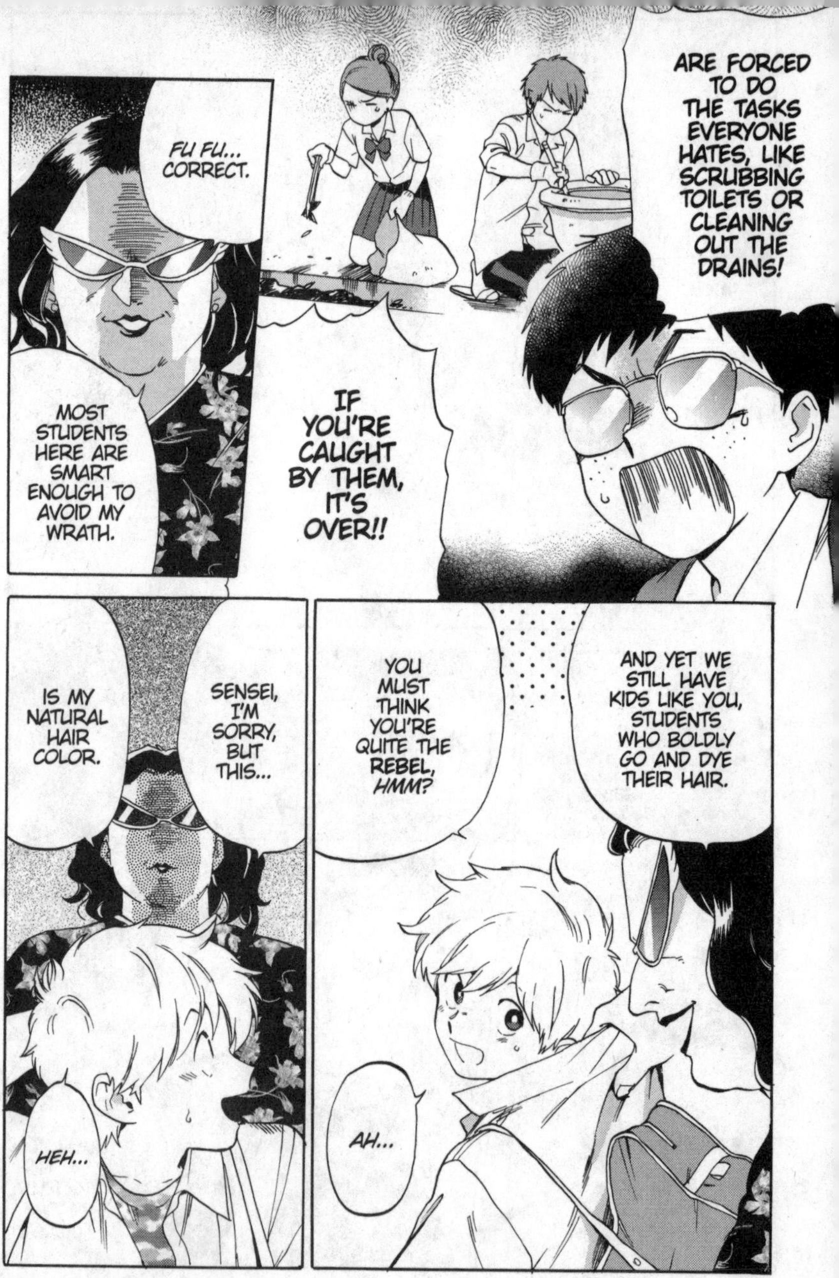
ARE FORCED TO DO THE TASKS EVERYONE HATES, LIKE SCRUBBING TOILETS OR CLEANING OUT THE DRAINS!
IF YOU'RE CAUGHT BY THEM, IT'S OVER!!
FU FU... CORRECT.
MOST STUDENTS HERE ARE SMART ENOUGH TO AVOID MY WRATH.
AND YET WE STILL HAVE KIDS LIKE YOU, STUDENTS WHO BOLDLY GO AND DYE THEIR HAIR.
YOU MUST THINK YOU'RE QUITE THE REBEL, HMM?
AH...
SENSEI, I'M SORRY, BUT THIS...
IS MY NATURAL HAIR COLOR.
HEH...

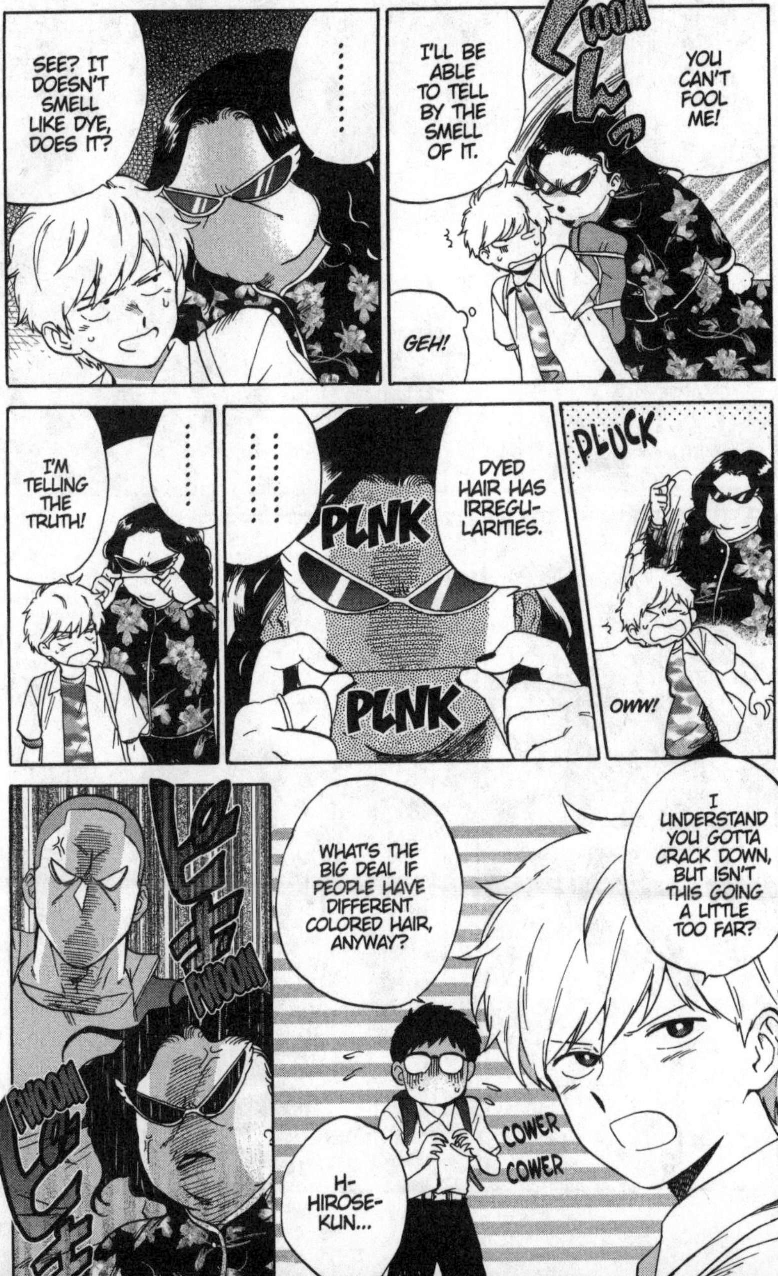
YOU CAN'T FOOL ME!
LOOM
I'LL BE ABLE TO TELL BY THE SMELL OF IT.
GEH!
......
SEE? IT DOESN'T SMELL LIKE DYE, DOES IT?
PLUCK
OWW!
DYED HAIR HAS IRREGU-LARITIES.
......
PLNK
PLNK
......
I'M TELLING THE TRUTH!
I UNDERSTAND YOU GOTTA CRACK DOWN, BUT ISN'T THIS GOING A LITTLE TOO FAR?
WHAT'S THE BIG DEAL IF PEOPLE HAVE DIFFERENT COLORED HAIR, ANYWAY?
COWER
COWER
H-HIROSE-KUN...
FWOOM
FWOOM

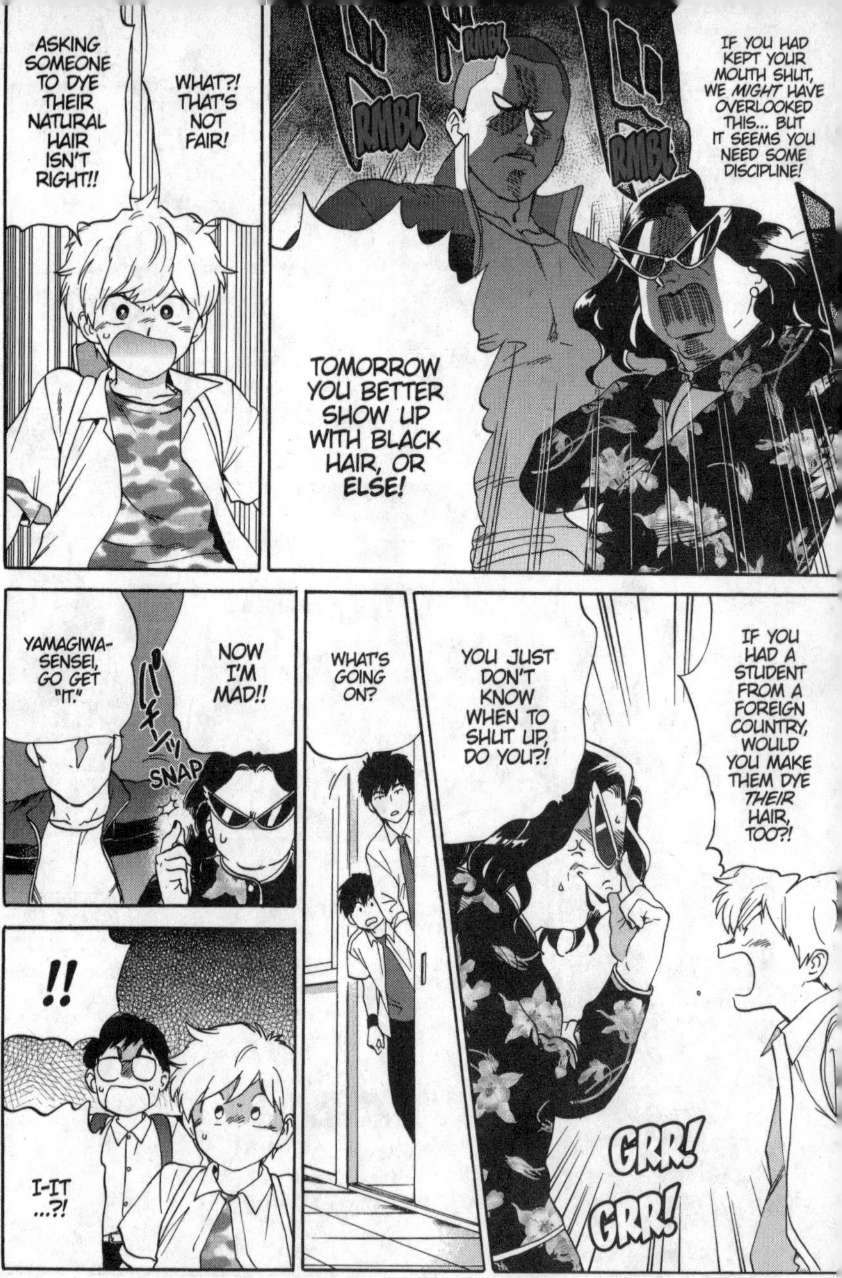

RMBL
RMBL
RMBL
RMBL
IF YOU HAD KEPT YOUR MOUTH SHUT, WE *MIGHT* HAVE OVERLOOKED THIS... BUT IT SEEMS YOU NEED SOME DISCIPLINE!
TOMORROW YOU BETTER SHOW UP WITH BLACK HAIR, OR ELSE!
WHAT?! THAT'S NOT FAIR!
ASKING SOMEONE TO DYE THEIR NATURAL HAIR ISN'T RIGHT!!
IF YOU HAD A STUDENT FROM A FOREIGN COUNTRY, WOULD YOU MAKE THEM DYE *THEIR* HAIR, TOO?!
YOU JUST DON'T KNOW WHEN TO SHUT UP, DO YOU?!
GRR!
GRR!
WHAT'S GOING ON?
NOW I'M MAD!!
YAMAGIWA-SENSEI, GO GET "IT."
SNAP
!!
I-IT ...?!

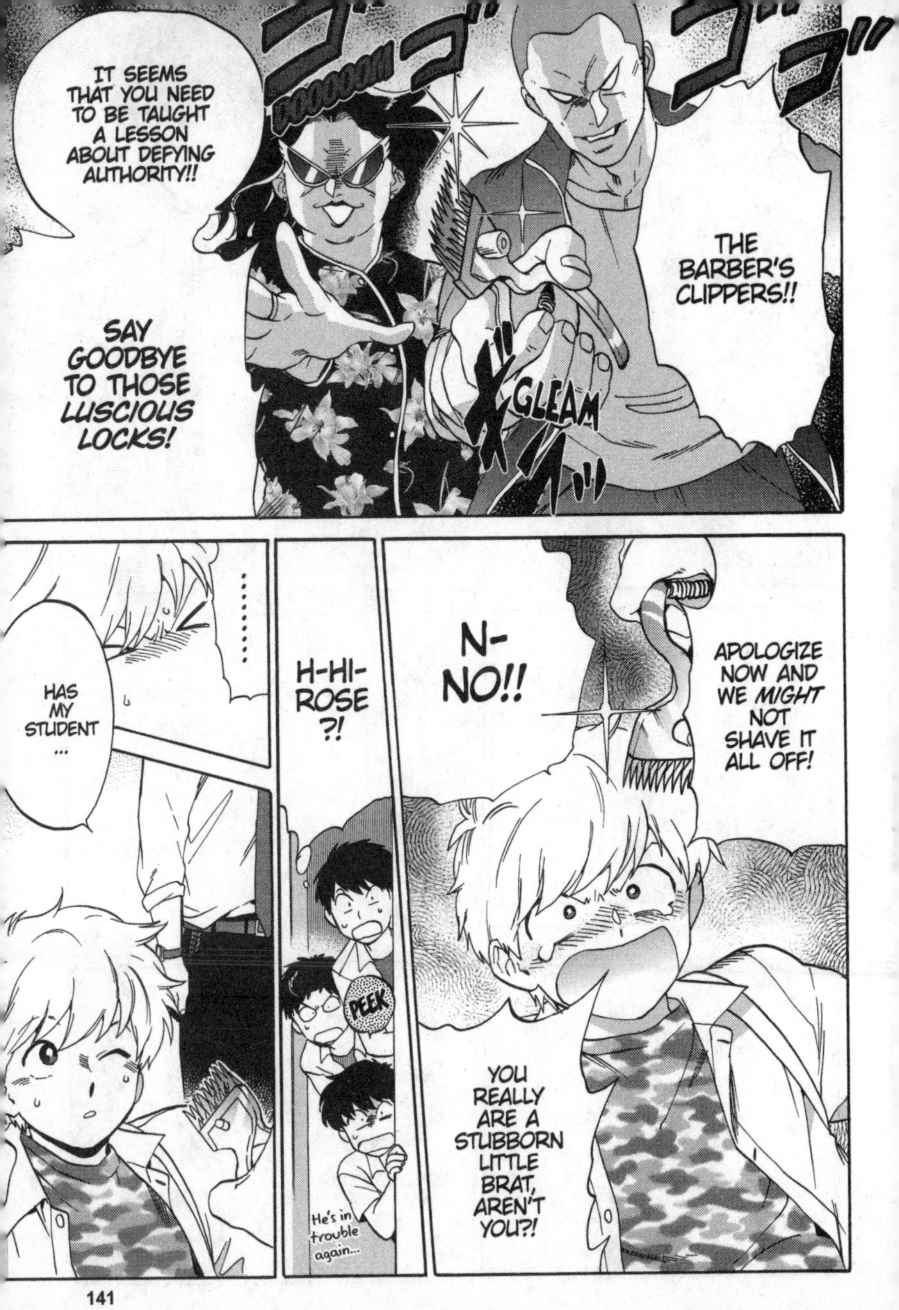
DOOOOOM
IT SEEMS THAT YOU NEED TO BE TAUGHT A LESSON ABOUT DEFYING AUTHORITY!!
THE BARBER'S CLIPPERS!!
GLEAM
SAY GOODBYE TO THOSE *LUSCIOUS* LOCKS!
APOLOGIZE NOW AND WE *MIGHT* NOT SHAVE IT ALL OFF!
N-NO!!
YOU REALLY ARE A STUBBORN LITTLE BRAT, AREN'T YOU?!
H-HI-ROSE?!
PEEK
He's in trouble again...
......
HAS MY STUDENT ...

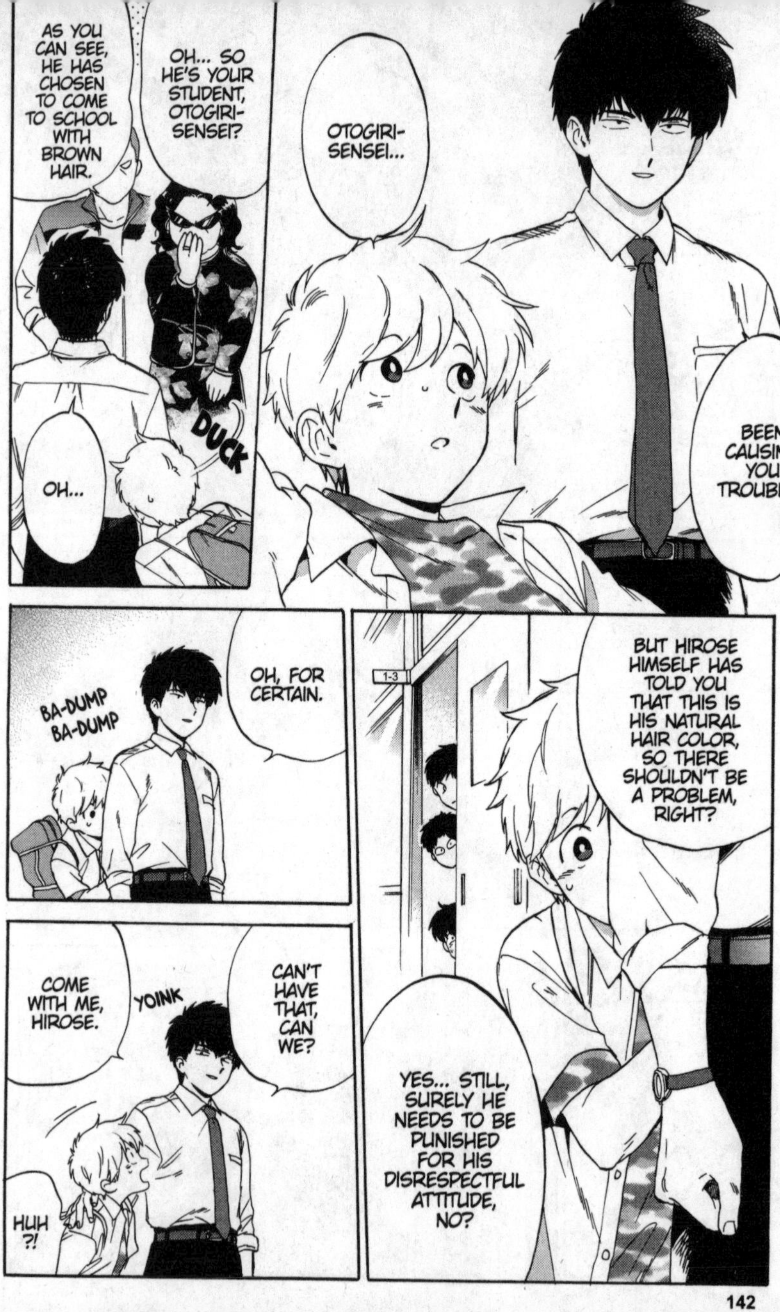
OTOGIRI-SENSEI...
BEEN CAUSING YOU TROUBLE?
OH... SO HE'S YOUR STUDENT, OTOGIRI-SENSEI?
AS YOU CAN SEE, HE HAS CHOSEN TO COME TO SCHOOL WITH BROWN HAIR.
DUCK
OH...
BUT HIROSE HIMSELF HAS TOLD YOU THAT THIS IS HIS NATURAL HAIR COLOR, SO THERE SHOULDN'T BE A PROBLEM, RIGHT?
1-3
YES... STILL, SURELY HE NEEDS TO BE PUNISHED FOR HIS DISRESPECTFUL ATTITUDE, NO?
OH, FOR CERTAIN.
BA-DUMP BA-DUMP
CAN'T HAVE THAT, CAN WE?
COME WITH ME, HIROSE.
YOINK
HUH ?!

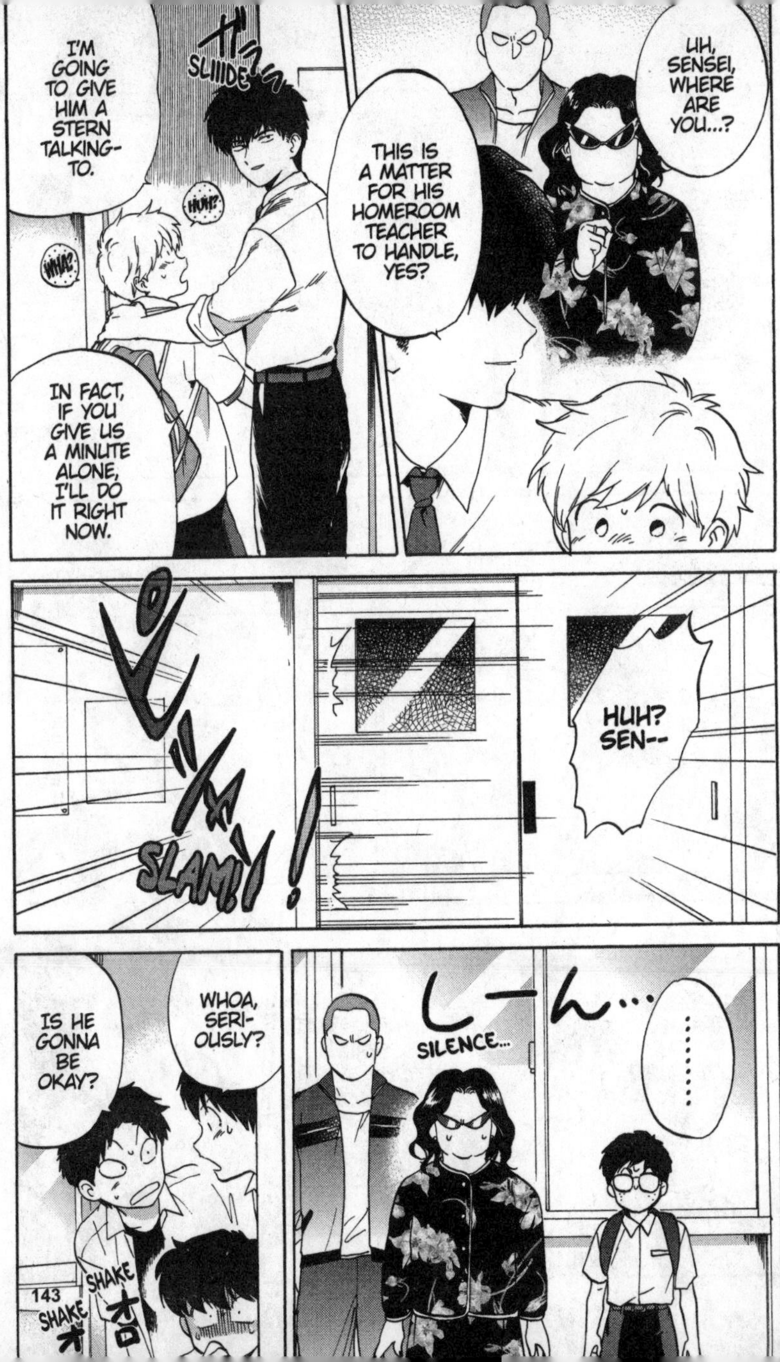
UH, SENSEI, WHERE ARE YOU...?
THIS IS A MATTER FOR HIS HOMEROOM TEACHER TO HANDLE, YES?
SLIIIDE
I'M GOING TO GIVE HIM A STERN TALKING-TO.
HUH?
WHA?
IN FACT, IF YOU GIVE US A MINUTE ALONE, I'LL DO IT RIGHT NOW.
HUH? SEN--
SLAM!
SILENCE...
......
WHOA, SERIOUSLY?
IS HE GONNA BE OKAY?
SHAKE
SHAKE

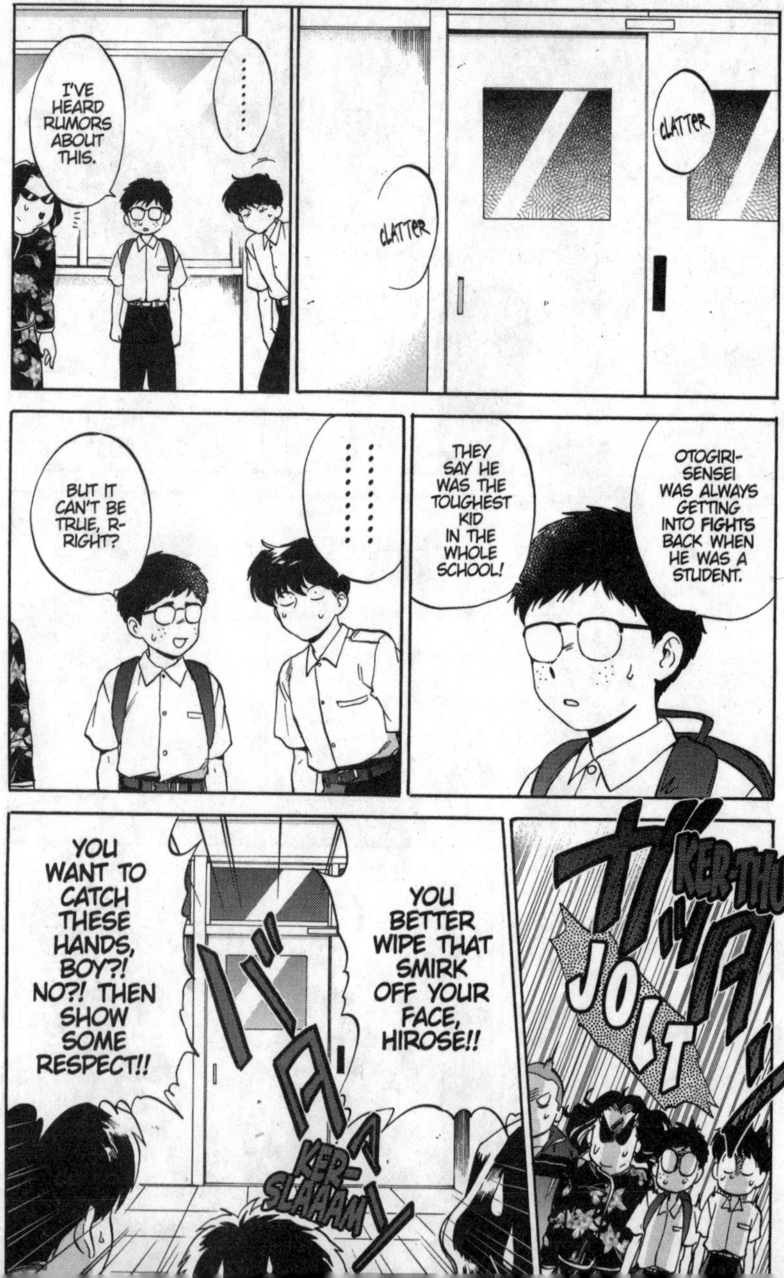
CLATTER
CLATTER
......
I'VE HEARD RUMORS ABOUT THIS.
OTOGIRI-SENSEI WAS ALWAYS GETTING INTO FIGHTS BACK WHEN HE WAS A STUDENT.
THEY SAY HE WAS THE TOUGHEST KID IN THE WHOLE SCHOOL!
......
BUT IT CAN'T BE TRUE, R-RIGHT?
KER-THUD
JOLT
YOU BETTER WIPE THAT SMIRK OFF YOUR FACE, HIROSE!!
YOU WANT TO CATCH THESE HANDS, BOY?! NO?! THEN SHOW SOME RESPECT!!
KER-SLAAAAM

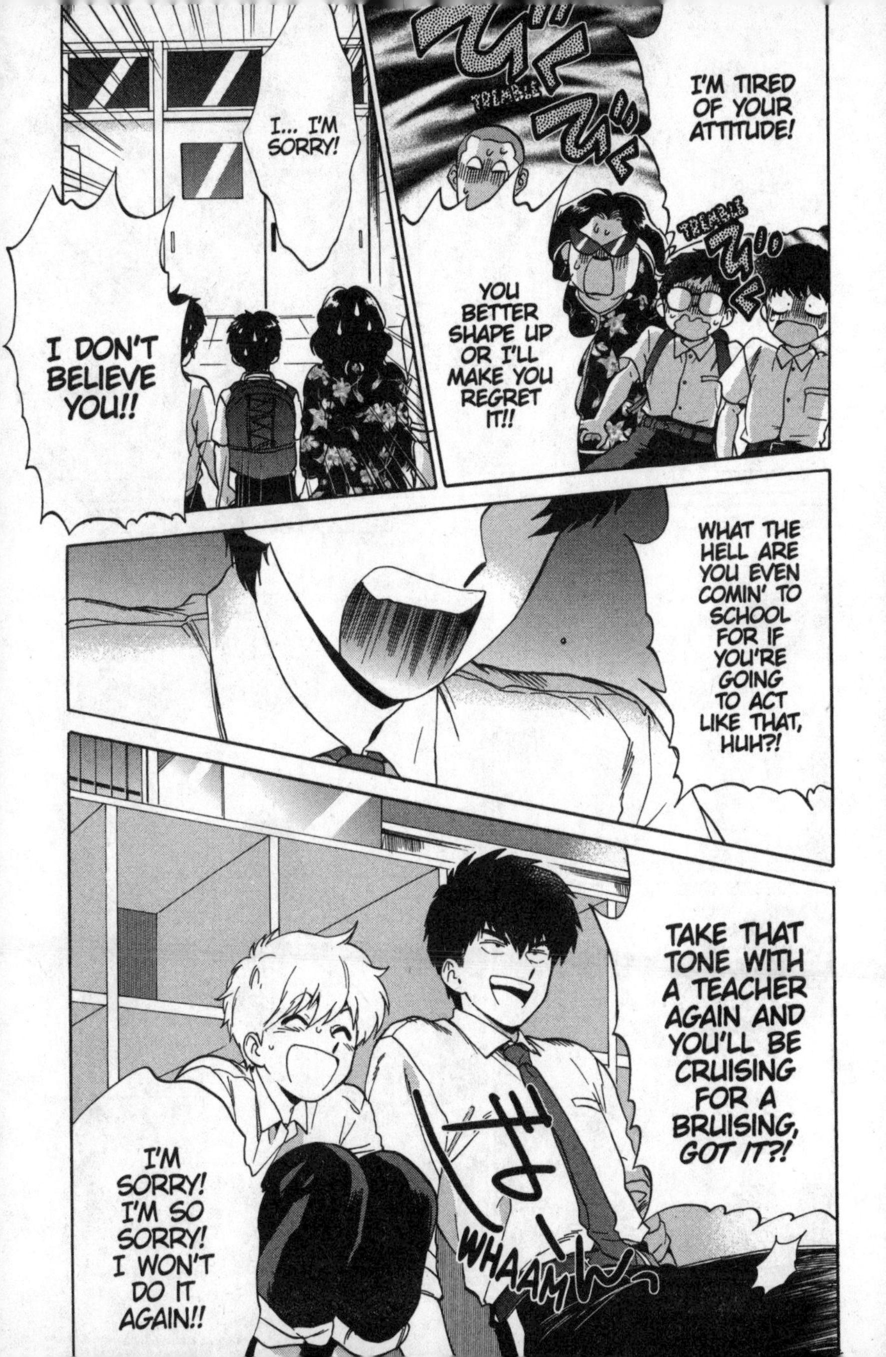
I'M TIRED OF YOUR ATTITUDE!
TREMBLE
YOU BETTER SHAPE UP OR I'LL MAKE YOU REGRET IT!!
TREMBLE
I... I'M SORRY!
I DON'T BELIEVE YOU!!
WHAT THE HELL ARE YOU EVEN COMIN' TO SCHOOL FOR IF YOU'RE GOING TO ACT LIKE THAT, HUH?!
TAKE THAT TONE WITH A TEACHER AGAIN AND YOU'LL BE CRUISING FOR A BRUISING, GOT IT?!
WHAAM
I'M SORRY! I'M SO SORRY! I WON'T DO IT AGAIN!!

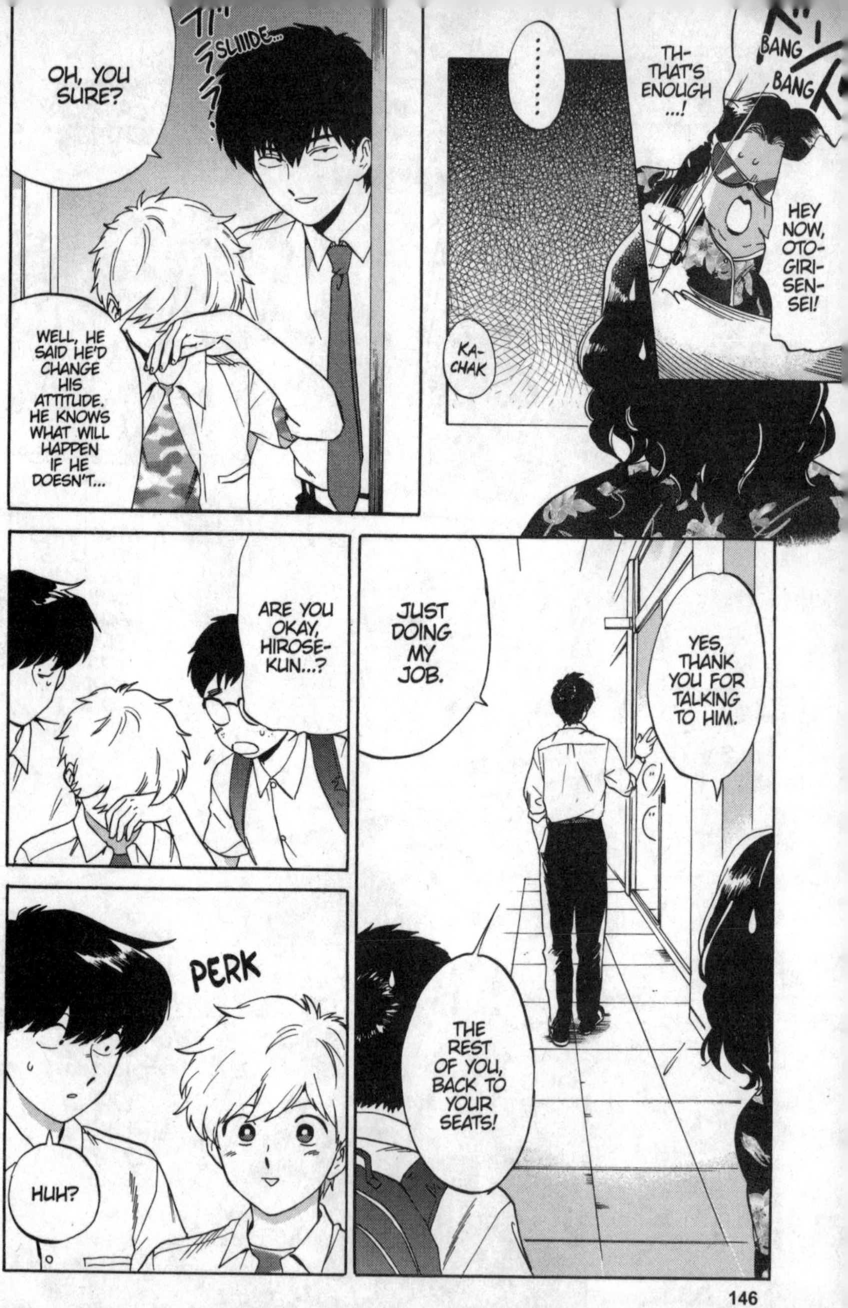
BANG
BANG
TH-THAT'S ENOUGH ...!
HEY NOW, OTO-GIRI-SEN-SEI!
......
KA-CHAK
SLIIIDE...
OH, YOU SURE?
WELL, HE SAID HE'D CHANGE HIS ATTITUDE. HE KNOWS WHAT WILL HAPPEN IF HE DOESN'T...
YES, THANK YOU FOR TALKING TO HIM.
JUST DOING MY JOB.
THE REST OF YOU, BACK TO YOUR SEATS!
ARE YOU OKAY, HIROSE-KUN...?
PERK
HUH?

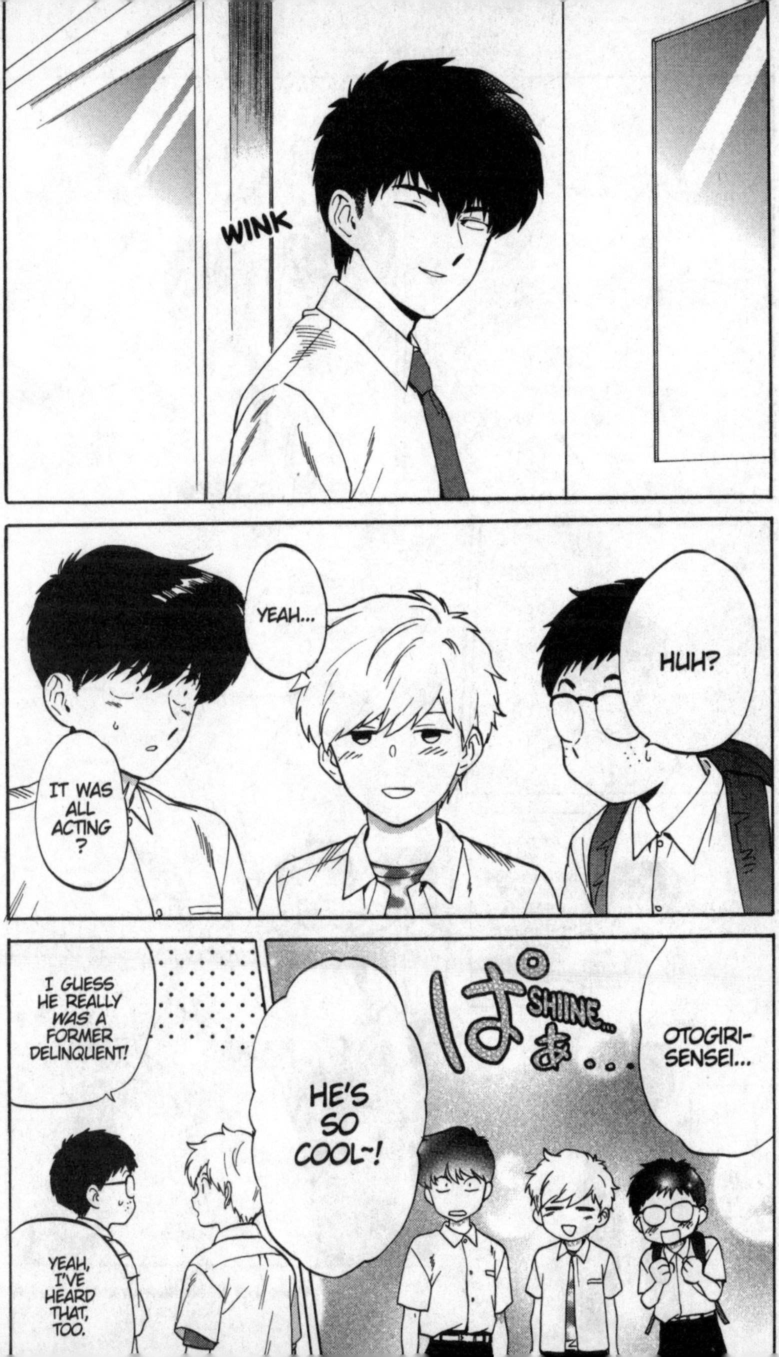
WINK
HUH?
YEAH...
IT WAS ALL ACTING?
OTOGIRI-SENSEI...
ぱぁ...
SHIINE...
HE'S SO COOL~!
I GUESS HE REALLY WAS A FORMER DELINQUENT!
YEAH, I'VE HEARD THAT, TOO.

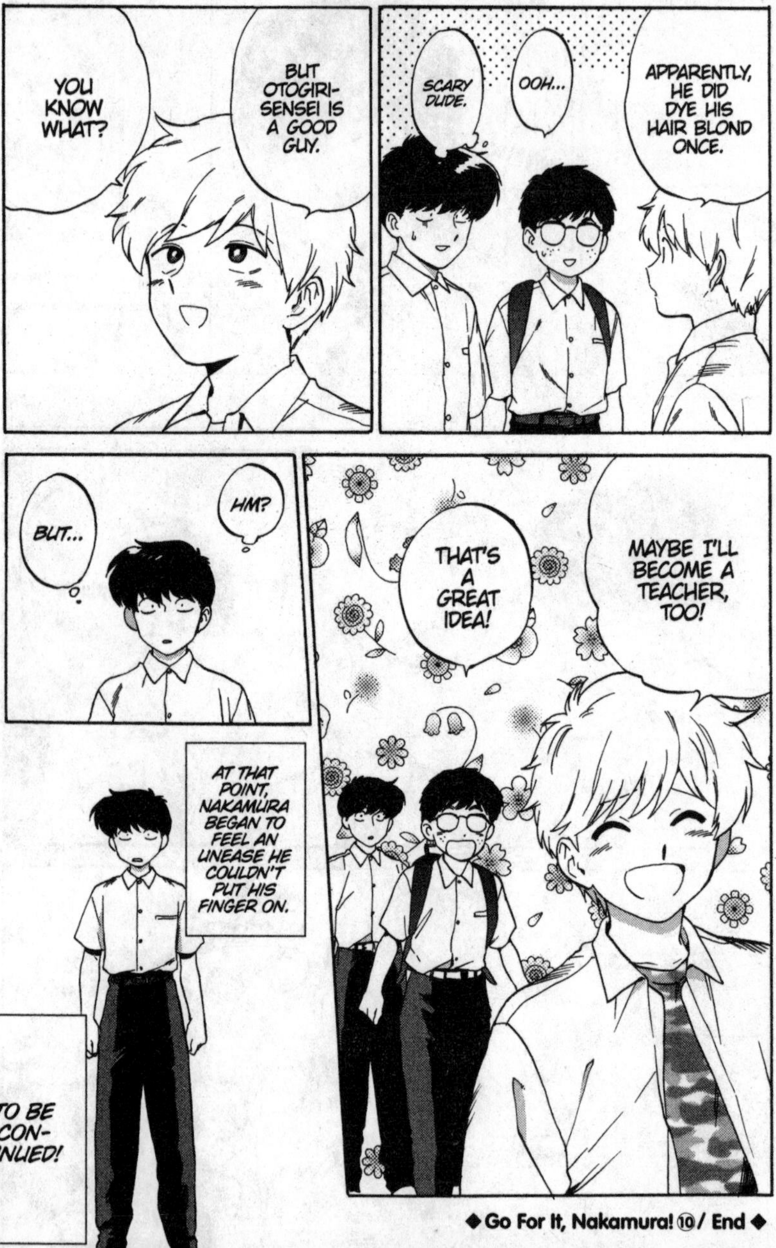
APPARENTLY, HE DID DYE HIS HAIR BLOND ONCE.
OOH...
SCARY DUDE.
BUT OTOGIRI-SENSEI IS A GOOD GUY.
YOU KNOW WHAT?
MAYBE I'LL BECOME A TEACHER, TOO!
THAT'S A GREAT IDEA!
HM?
BUT...
AT THAT POINT, NAKAMURA BEGAN TO FEEL AN UNEASE HE COULDN'T PUT HIS FINGER ON.
TO BE CON-TINUED!

◆Go For It, Nakamura! ⑩ / End◆

CHAPTER 11

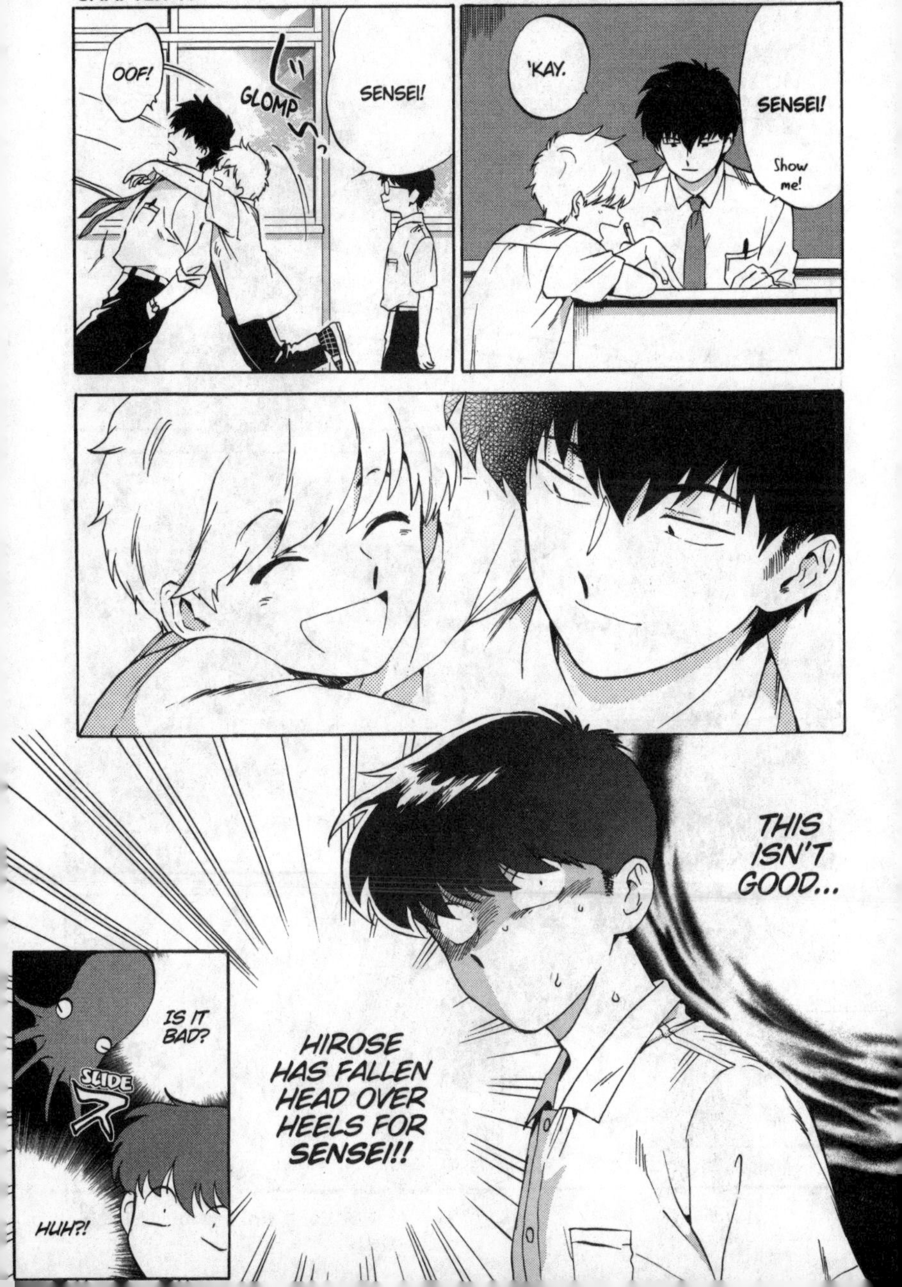
SENSEI!
Show me!
'KAY.
SENSEI!
GLOMP
OOF!
THIS ISN'T GOOD...
HIROSE HAS FALLEN HEAD OVER HEELS FOR SENSEI!!
IS IT BAD?
SLIDE
HUH?!

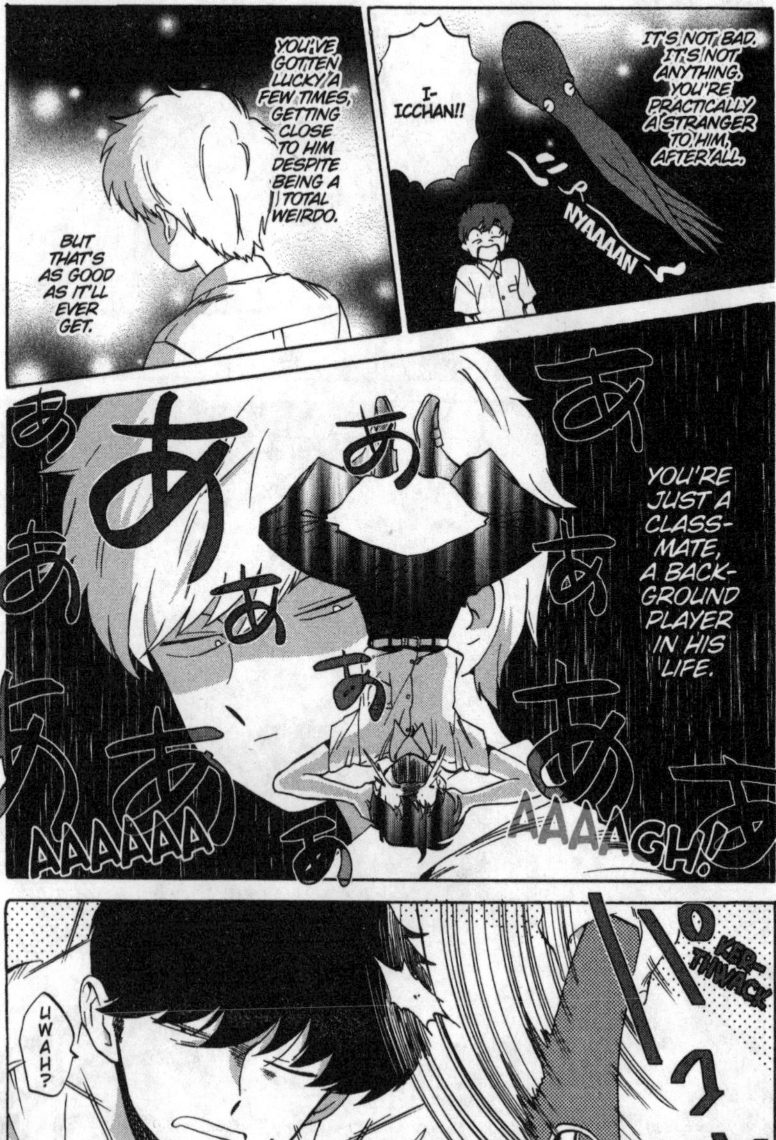
IT'S NOT BAD. IT'S NOT ANYTHING. YOU'RE PRACTICALLY A STRANGER TO HIM, AFTER ALL.
I-ICCHAN!!
NYAAAAN
YOU'VE GOTTEN LUCKY A FEW TIMES, GETTING CLOSE TO HIM DESPITE BEING A TOTAL WEIRDO.
BUT THAT'S AS GOOD AS IT'LL EVER GET.
YOU'RE JUST A CLASSMATE, A BACKGROUND PLAYER IN HIS LIFE.
AAAAGH!
AAAAAA
KER-THWACK
UWAH?

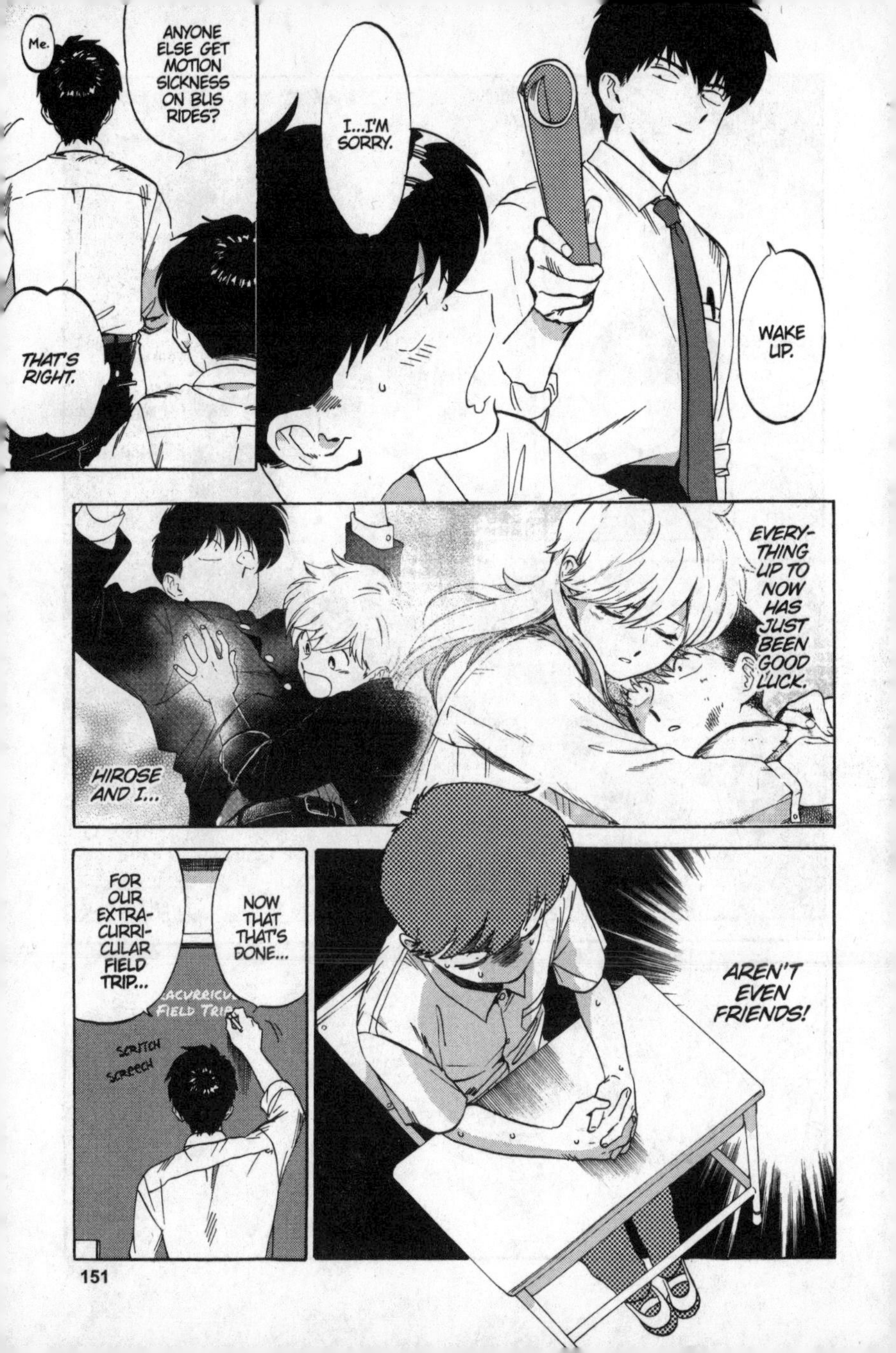

WAKE UP.
I...I'M SORRY.
ANYONE ELSE GET MOTION SICKNESS ON BUS RIDES?
Me.
THAT'S RIGHT.
EVERY-THING UP TO NOW HAS JUST BEEN GOOD LUCK.
HIROSE AND I...
AREN'T EVEN FRIENDS!
NOW THAT THAT'S DONE...
FOR OUR EXTRA-CURRI-CULAR FIELD TRIP...
SCRITCH
SCREECH

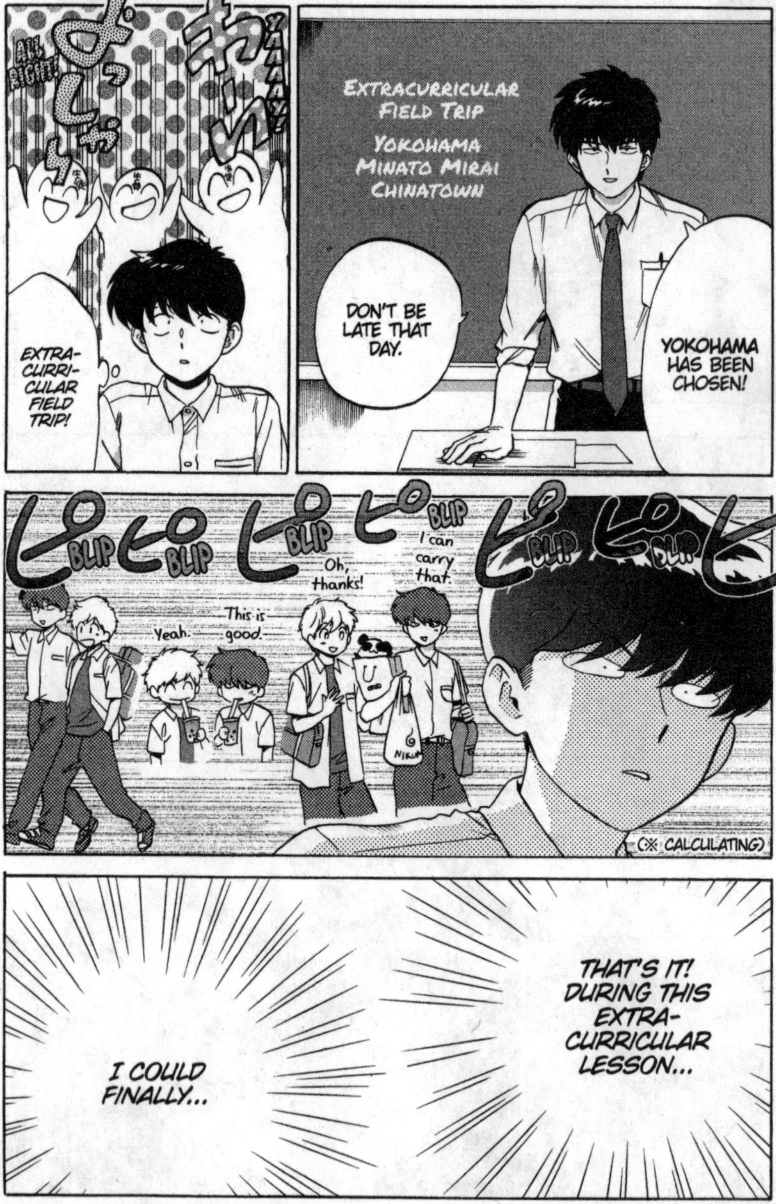
YOKOHAMA HAS BEEN CHOSEN!
EXTRACURRICULAR FIELD TRIP
YOKOHAMA MINATO MIRAI CHINATOWN
DON'T BE LATE THAT DAY.
ALL RIGHT!
EXTRA-CURRICULAR FIELD TRIP!
BLIP BLIP BLIP BLIP BLIP BLIP BLIP BLIP
I can carry that.
Oh, thanks!
This is good.
Yeah.
(※ CALCULATING)
THAT'S IT! DURING THIS EXTRA-CURRICULAR LESSON...
I COULD FINALLY...

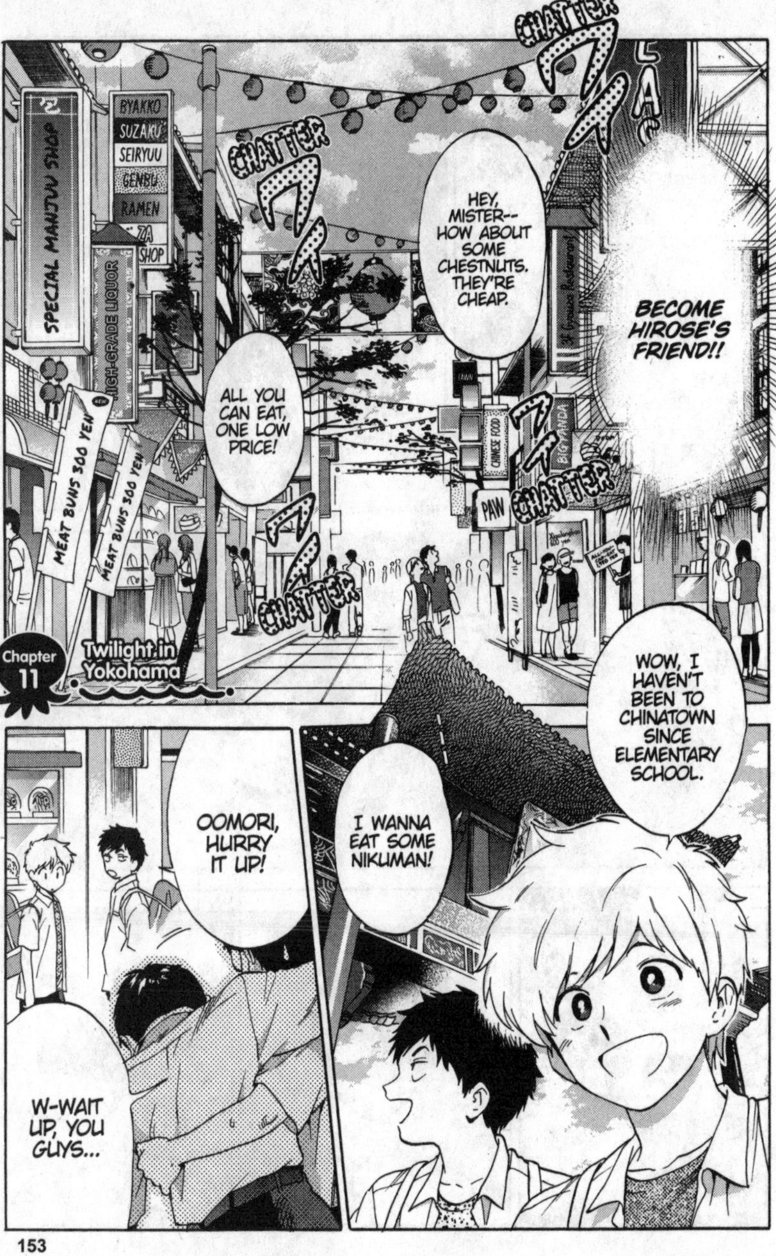
CHATTER
BECOME HIROSE'S FRIEND!!
HEY, MISTER-- HOW ABOUT SOME CHESTNUTS. THEY'RE CHEAP.
CHATTER
CHATTER
ALL YOU CAN EAT, ONE LOW PRICE!
CHATTER
BYAKKO
SUZAKU
SEIRYUU
GENBU
RAMEN
SPECIAL MANJUU SHOP
MEAT BUNS 300 YEN
MEAT BUNS 300 YEN
CHINESE FOOD
PAW
Chapter 11
Twilight in Yokohama
WOW, I HAVEN'T BEEN TO CHINATOWN SINCE ELEMENTARY SCHOOL.
I WANNA EAT SOME NIKUMAN!
OOMORI, HURRY IT UP!
W-WAIT UP, YOU GUYS...

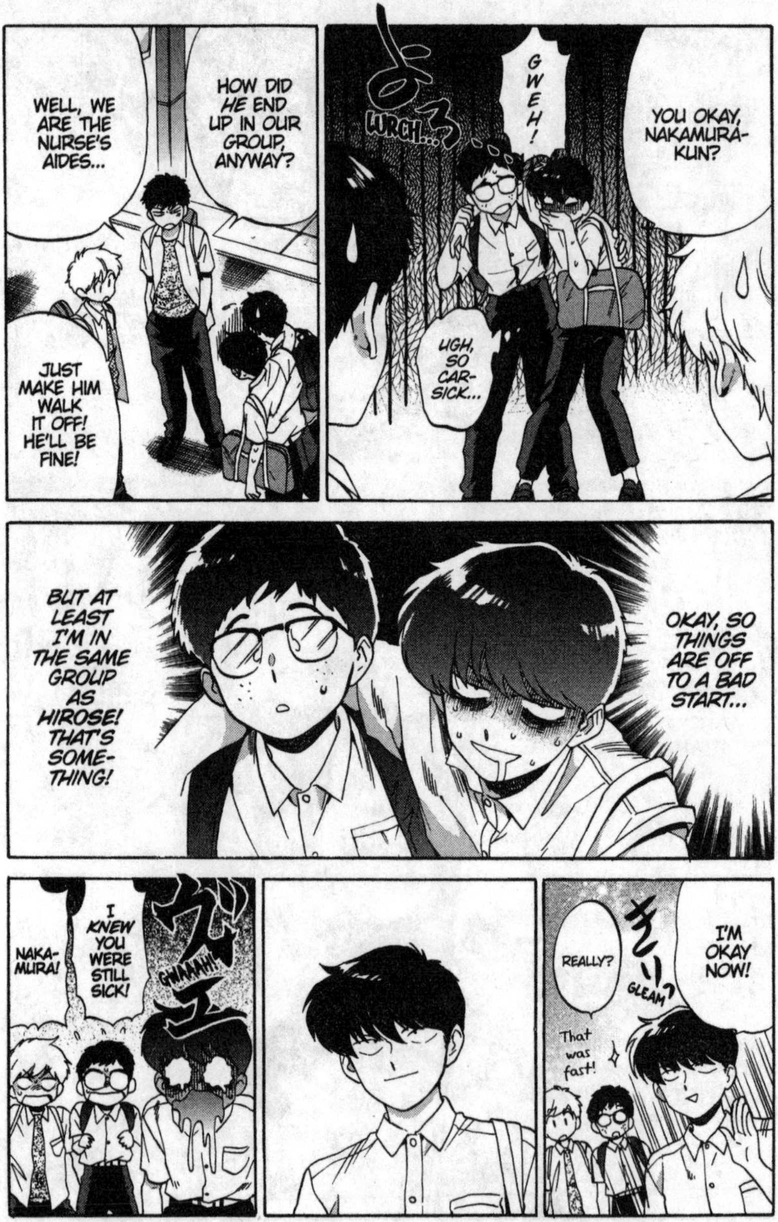
YOU OKAY, NAKAMURA-KUN?
GWEH!
LURCH...
UGH, SO CAR-SICK...
HOW DID HE END UP IN OUR GROUP, ANYWAY?
WELL, WE ARE THE NURSE'S AIDES...
JUST MAKE HIM WALK IT OFF! HE'LL BE FINE!
OKAY, SO THINGS ARE OFF TO A BAD START...
BUT AT LEAST I'M IN THE SAME GROUP AS HIROSE! THAT'S SOME-THING!
I'M OKAY NOW!
GLEAM
REALLY?
That was fast!
GWAAAH!
I KNEW YOU WERE STILL SICK!
NAKA-MURA!

Sign: Panda

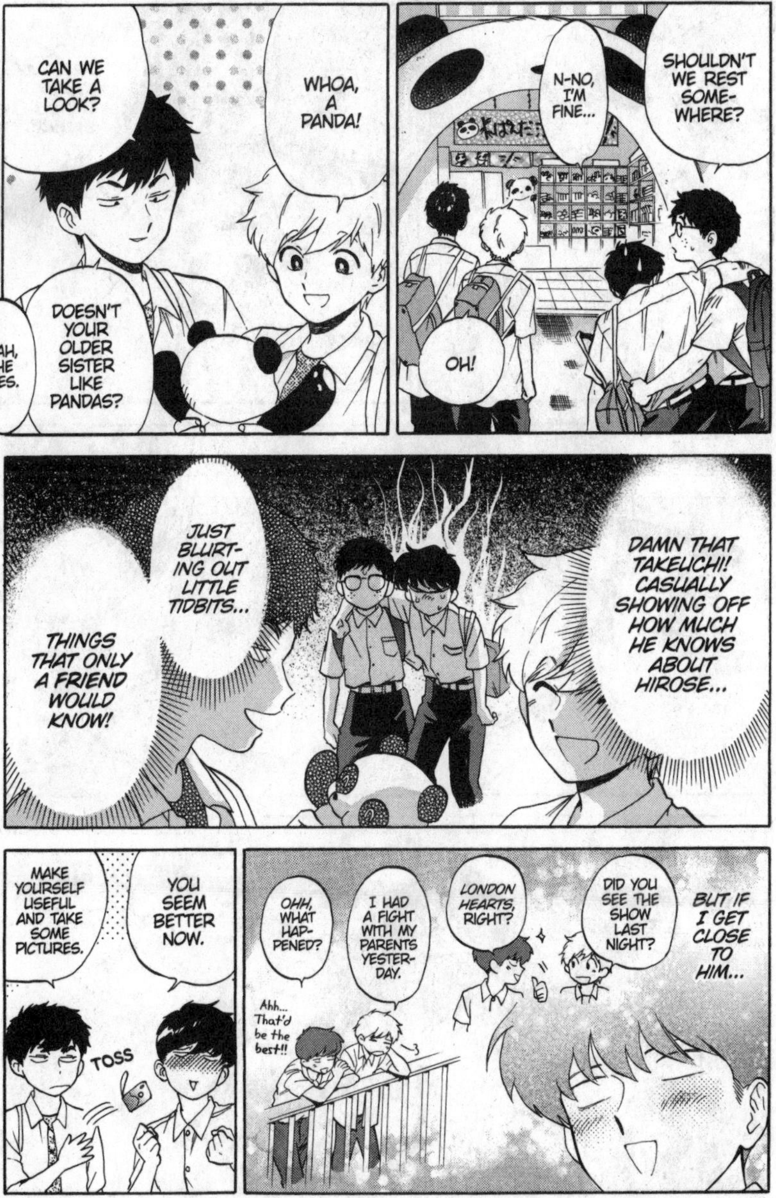
SHOULDN'T WE REST SOME-WHERE?
N-NO, I'M FINE...
OH!
WHOA, A PANDA!
CAN WE TAKE A LOOK?
DOESN'T YOUR OLDER SISTER LIKE PANDAS?
YEAH, SHE DOES.
DAMN THAT TAKEUCHI! CASUALLY SHOWING OFF HOW MUCH HE KNOWS ABOUT HIROSE...
JUST BLURT-ING OUT LITTLE TIDBITS...
THINGS THAT ONLY A FRIEND WOULD KNOW!
BUT IF I GET CLOSE TO HIM...
DID YOU SEE THE SHOW LAST NIGHT?
LONDON HEARTS, RIGHT?
I HAD A FIGHT WITH MY PARENTS YESTER-DAY.
OHH, WHAT HAP-PENED?
Ahh... That'd be the best!!
YOU SEEM BETTER NOW.
MAKE YOURSELF USEFUL AND TAKE SOME PICTURES.
TOSS

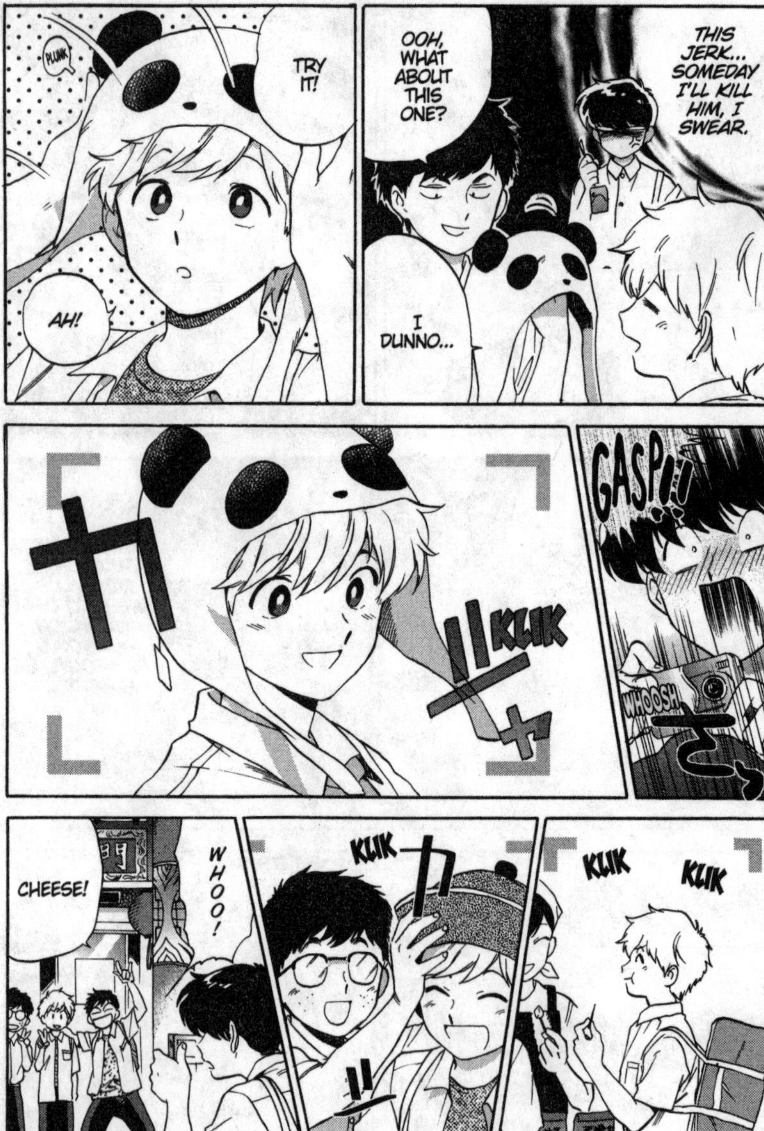
THIS JERK... SOMEDAY I'LL KILL HIM, I SWEAR.
OOH, WHAT ABOUT THIS ONE?
I DUNNO...
PLUNK
TRY IT!
AH!
GASP!!
WHOOSH
KLIK
KLIK
KLIK
KLIK
KLIK
WHOOO!
CHEESE!

Sign: mon

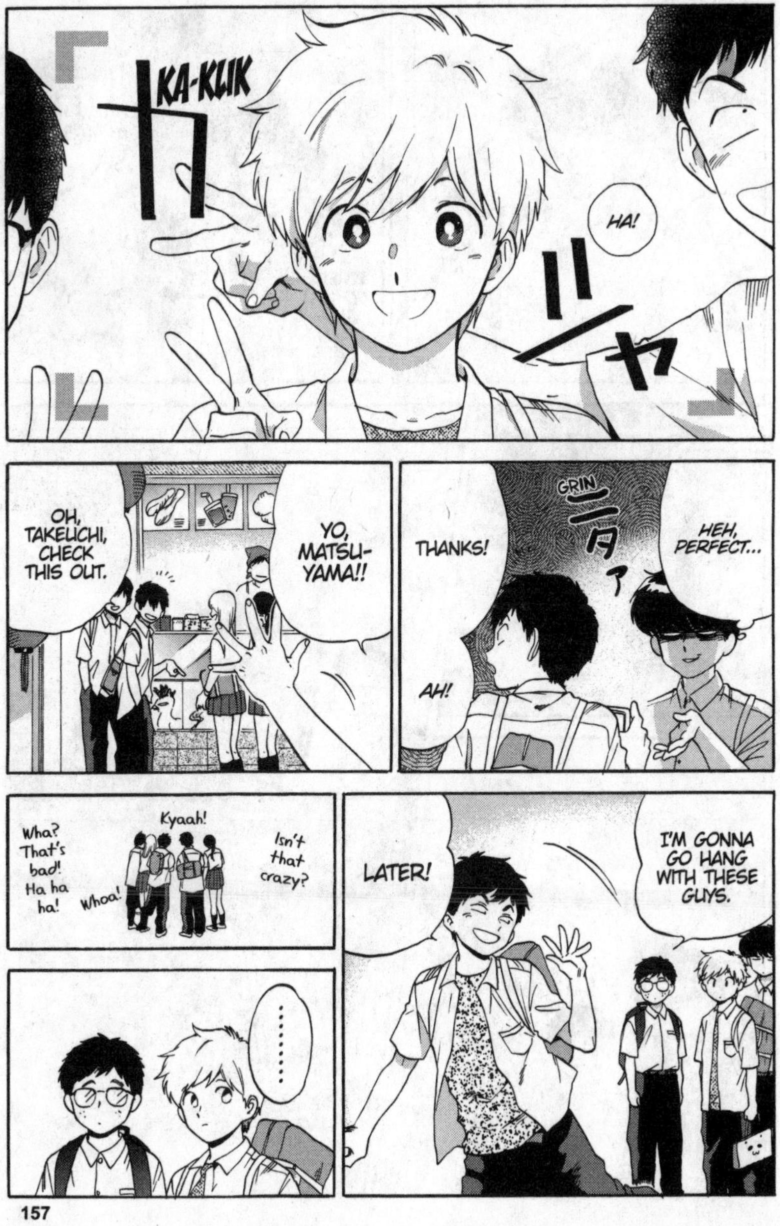

KA-KLIK
カ
HA!
HEH, PERFECT...
GRIN
ニタァ
THANKS!
AH!
YO, MATSU-YAMA!!
OH, TAKEUCHI, CHECK THIS OUT.
I'M GONNA GO HANG WITH THESE GUYS.
LATER!
Isn't that crazy?
Kyaah!
Wha? That's bad! Ha ha ha!
Whoa!
......

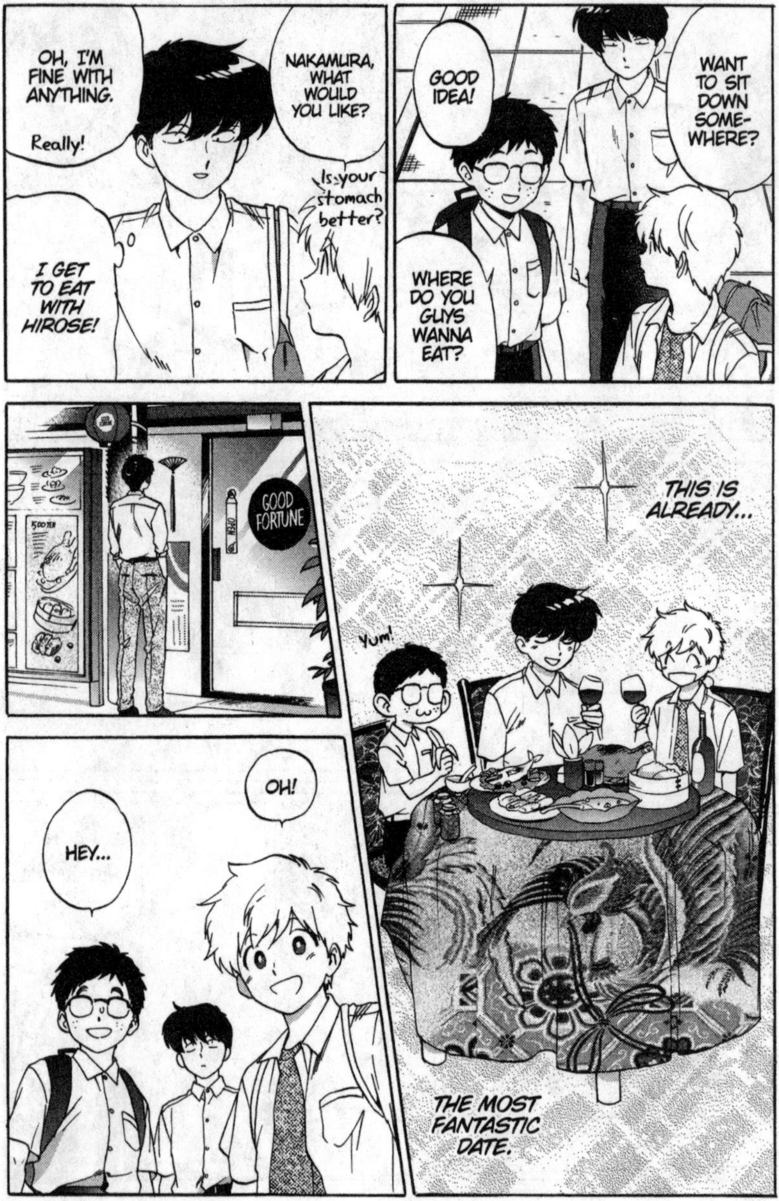
WANT TO SIT DOWN SOMEWHERE?
GOOD IDEA!
WHERE DO YOU GUYS WANNA EAT?
NAKAMURA, WHAT WOULD YOU LIKE?
Is your stomach better?
OH, I'M FINE WITH ANYTHING.
Really!
I GET TO EAT WITH HIROSE!
THIS IS ALREADY...
Yum!
THE MOST FANTASTIC DATE.
GOOD FORTUNE
OPEN
OH!
HEY...

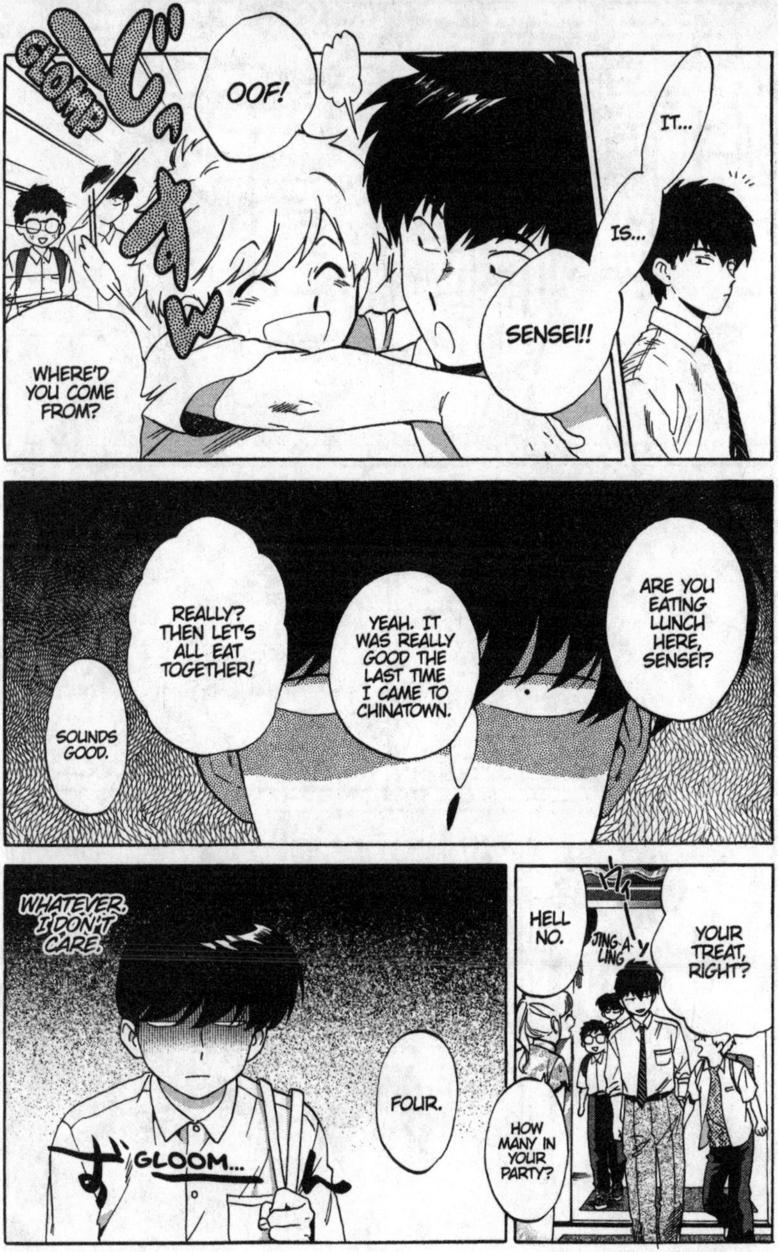
IT...
IS...
SENSEI!!
OOF!
GLOMP
WHERE'D YOU COME FROM?
ARE YOU EATING LUNCH HERE, SENSEI?
YEAH. IT WAS REALLY GOOD THE LAST TIME I CAME TO CHINATOWN.
REALLY? THEN LET'S ALL EAT TOGETHER!
SOUNDS GOOD.
YOUR TREAT, RIGHT?
JING-A-LING
HELL NO.
HOW MANY IN YOUR PARTY?
FOUR.
WHATEVER. I DON'T CARE.
GLOOM...

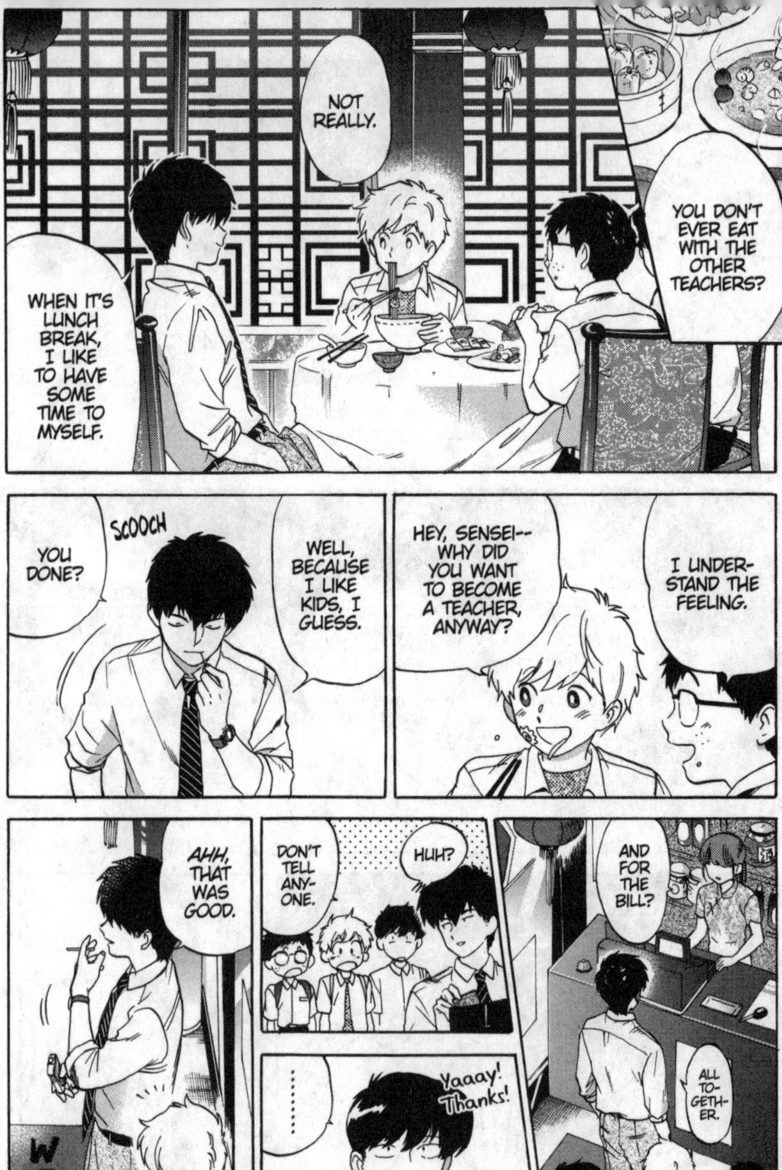
YOU DON'T EVER EAT WITH THE OTHER TEACHERS?
NOT REALLY.
WHEN IT'S LUNCH BREAK, I LIKE TO HAVE SOME TIME TO MYSELF.
I UNDER-STAND THE FEELING.
HEY, SENSEI-- WHY DID YOU WANT TO BECOME A TEACHER, ANYWAY?
WELL, BECAUSE I LIKE KIDS, I GUESS.
SCOOCH
YOU DONE?
AND FOR THE BILL?
ALL TO-GETH-ER.
HUH?
DON'T TELL ANY-ONE.
Yaaay! Thanks!
......
Whoo!
AHH, THAT WAS GOOD.
WELC

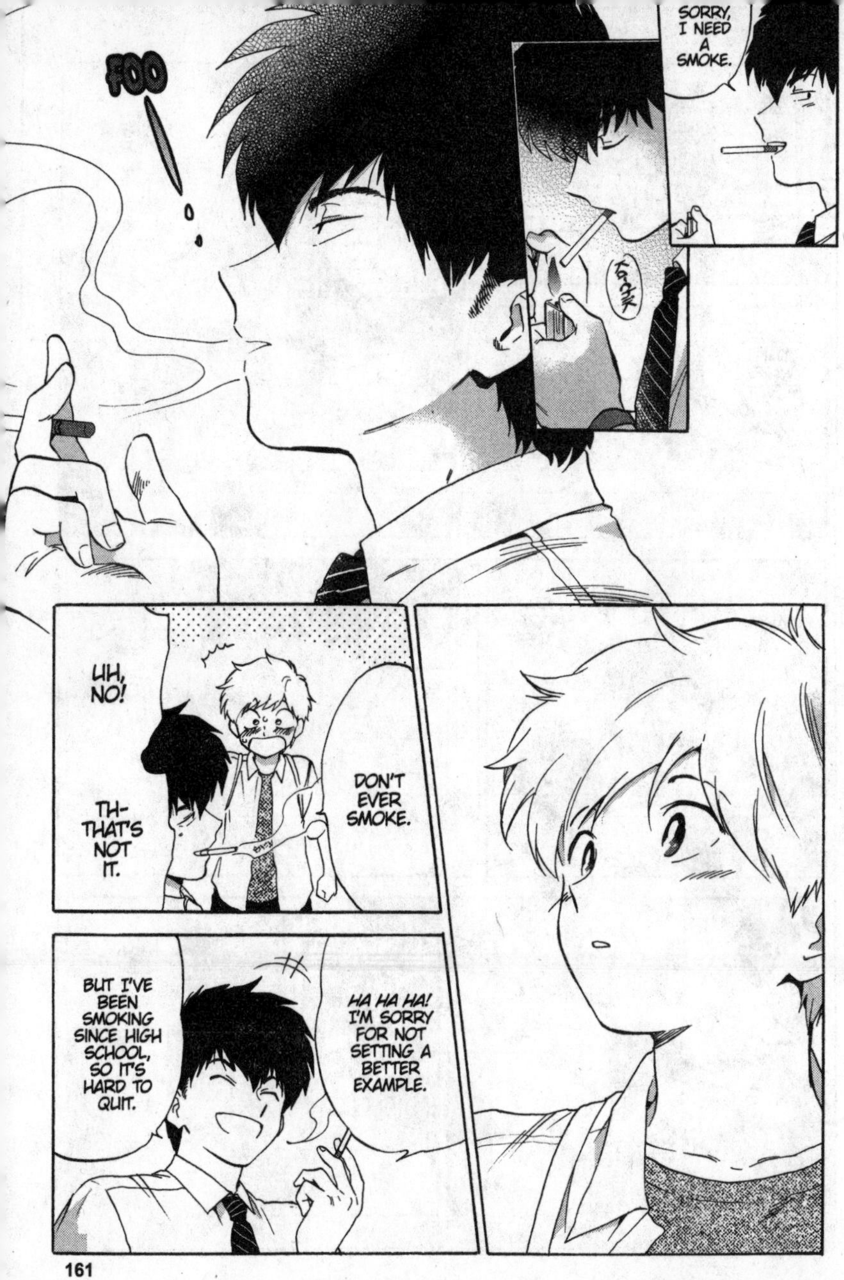
SORRY, I NEED A SMOKE.
FOO
DON'T EVER SMOKE.
UH, NO!
TH-THAT'S NOT IT.
HA HA HA! I'M SORRY FOR NOT SETTING A BETTER EXAMPLE.
BUT I'VE BEEN SMOKING SINCE HIGH SCHOOL, SO IT'S HARD TO QUIT.

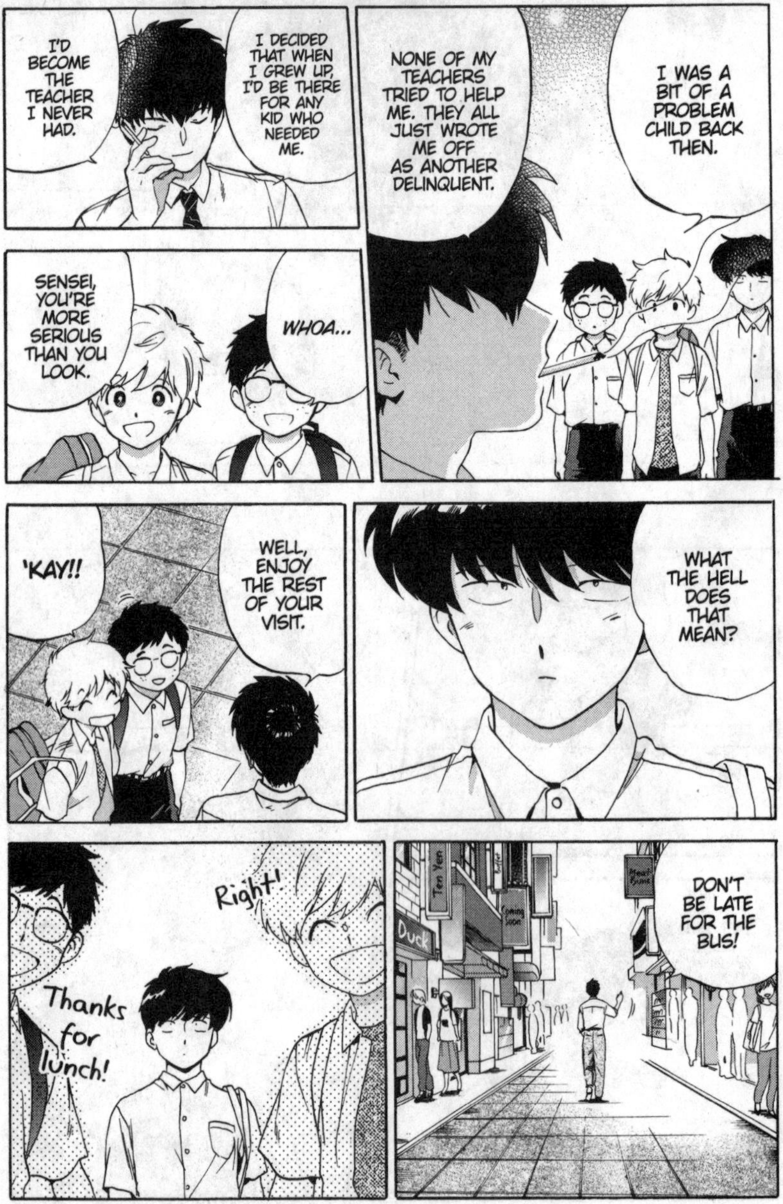
I WAS A BIT OF A PROBLEM CHILD BACK THEN.
NONE OF MY TEACHERS TRIED TO HELP ME. THEY ALL JUST WROTE ME OFF AS ANOTHER DELINQUENT.
I DECIDED THAT WHEN I GREW UP, I'D BE THERE FOR ANY KID WHO NEEDED ME.
I'D BECOME THE TEACHER I NEVER HAD.
WHOA...
SENSEI, YOU'RE MORE SERIOUS THAN YOU LOOK.
WHAT THE HELL DOES THAT MEAN?
WELL, ENJOY THE REST OF YOUR VISIT.
'KAY!!
DON'T BE LATE FOR THE BUS!
Duck
Right!
Thanks for lunch!

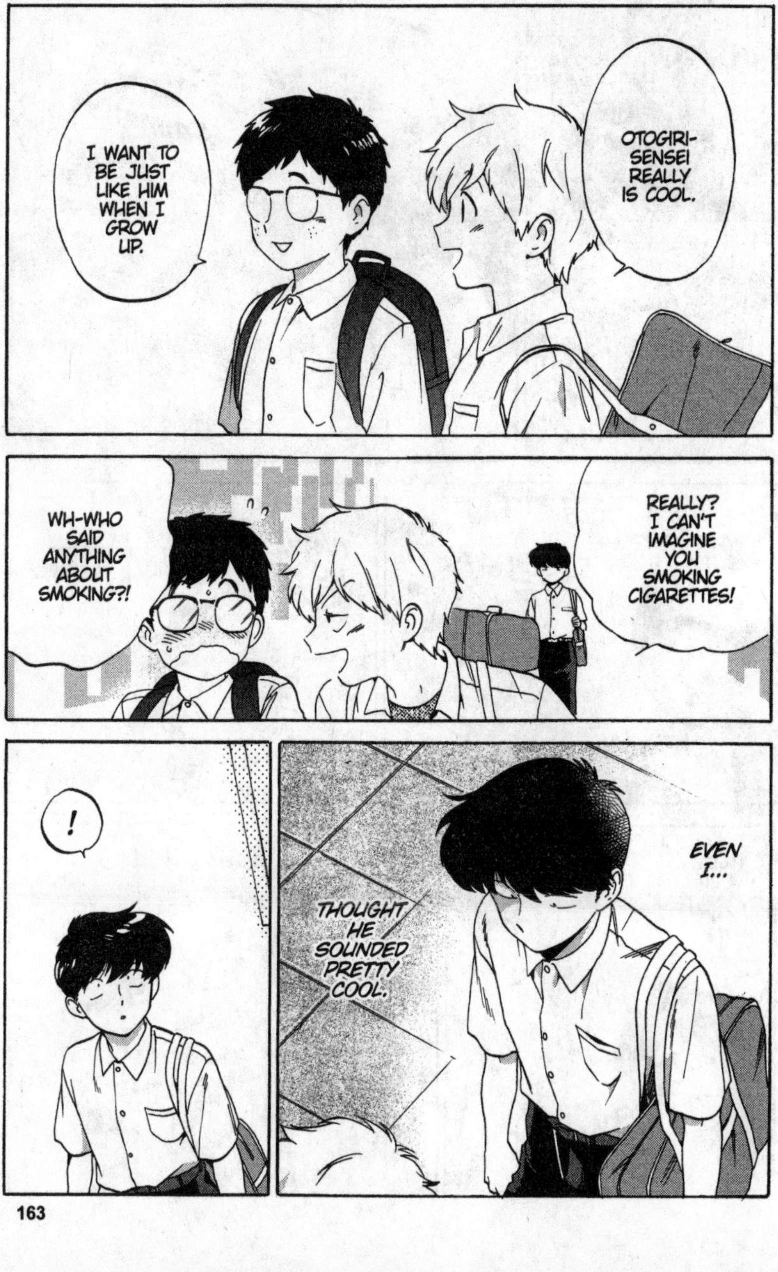
OTOGIRI-SENSEI REALLY IS COOL.
I WANT TO BE JUST LIKE HIM WHEN I GROW UP.
REALLY? I CAN'T IMAGINE YOU SMOKING CIGARETTES!
WH-WHO SAID ANYTHING ABOUT SMOKING?!
EVEN I...
THOUGHT HE SOUNDED PRETTY COOL.
!

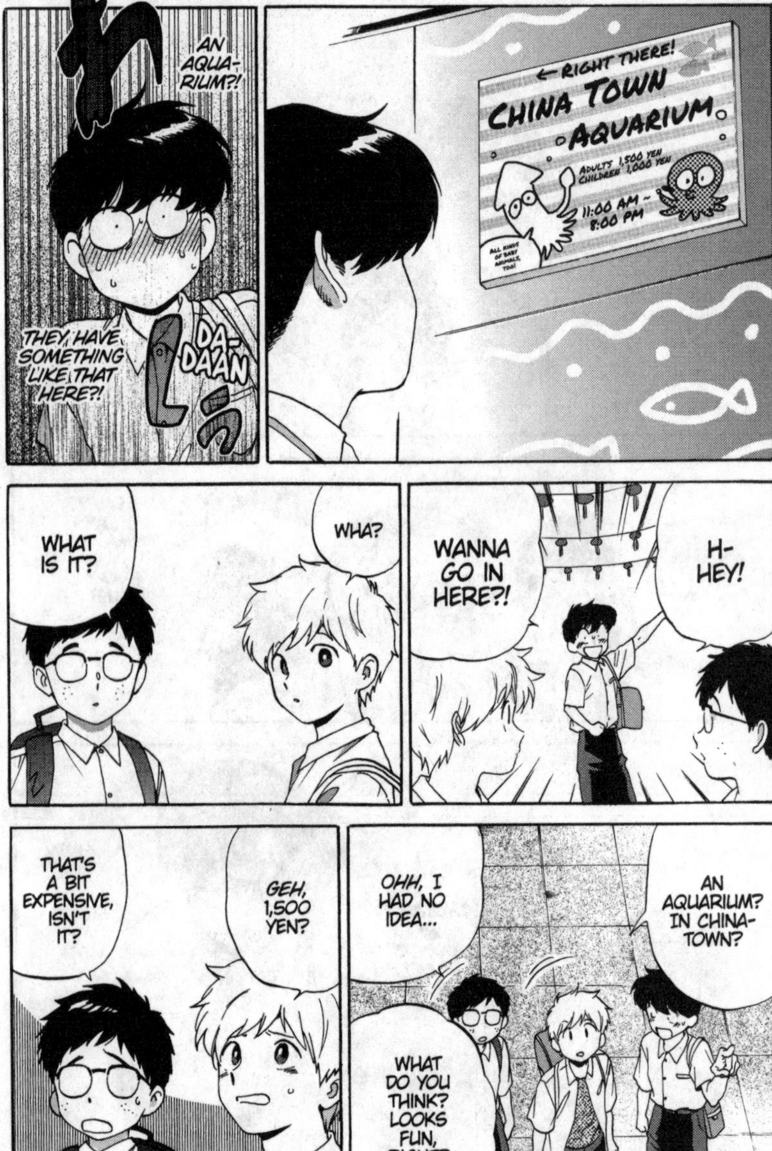
← RIGHT THERE!
CHINA TOWN AQUARIUM
ADULTS 1,500 YEN CHILDREN 1,000 YEN
11:00 AM ~ 8:00 PM
ALL KINDS OF BABY ANIMALS, TOO!
AN AQUA-RIUM?!
DA-DAAN
THEY HAVE SOMETHING LIKE THAT HERE?!
H-HEY!
WANNA GO IN HERE?!
WHA?
WHAT IS IT?
AN AQUARIUM? IN CHINA-TOWN?
OHH, I HAD NO IDEA...
WHAT DO YOU THINK? LOOKS FUN, RIGHT?
GEH, 1,500 YEN?
THAT'S A BIT EXPENSIVE, ISN'T IT?

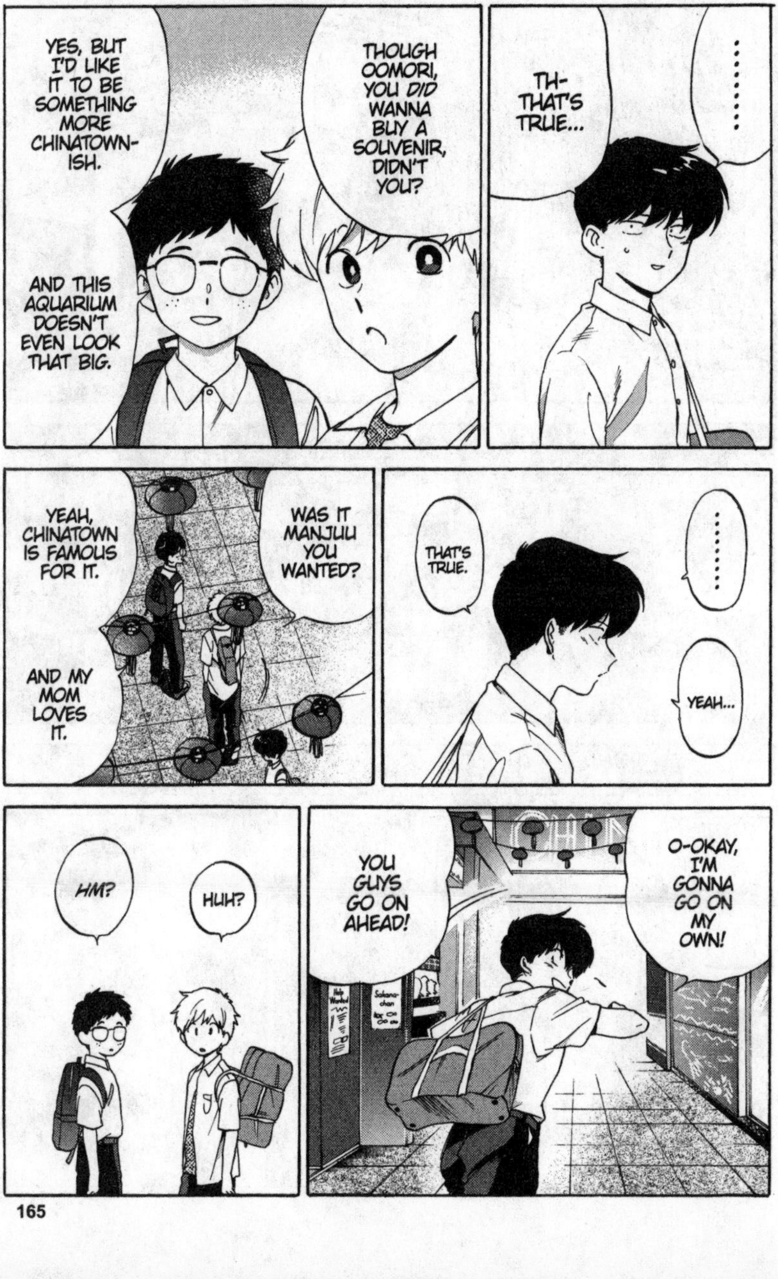
....
TH- THAT'S TRUE...
THOUGH OOMORI, YOU *DID* WANNA BUY A SOUVENIR, DIDN'T YOU?
YES, BUT I'D LIKE IT TO BE SOMETHING MORE CHINATOWN-ISH.
AND THIS AQUARIUM DOESN'T EVEN LOOK THAT BIG.
....
THAT'S TRUE.
YEAH...
WAS IT MANJUU YOU WANTED?
YEAH, CHINATOWN IS FAMOUS FOR IT.
AND MY MOM LOVES IT.
O-OKAY, I'M GONNA GO ON MY OWN!
YOU GUYS GO ON AHEAD!
HUH?
HM?

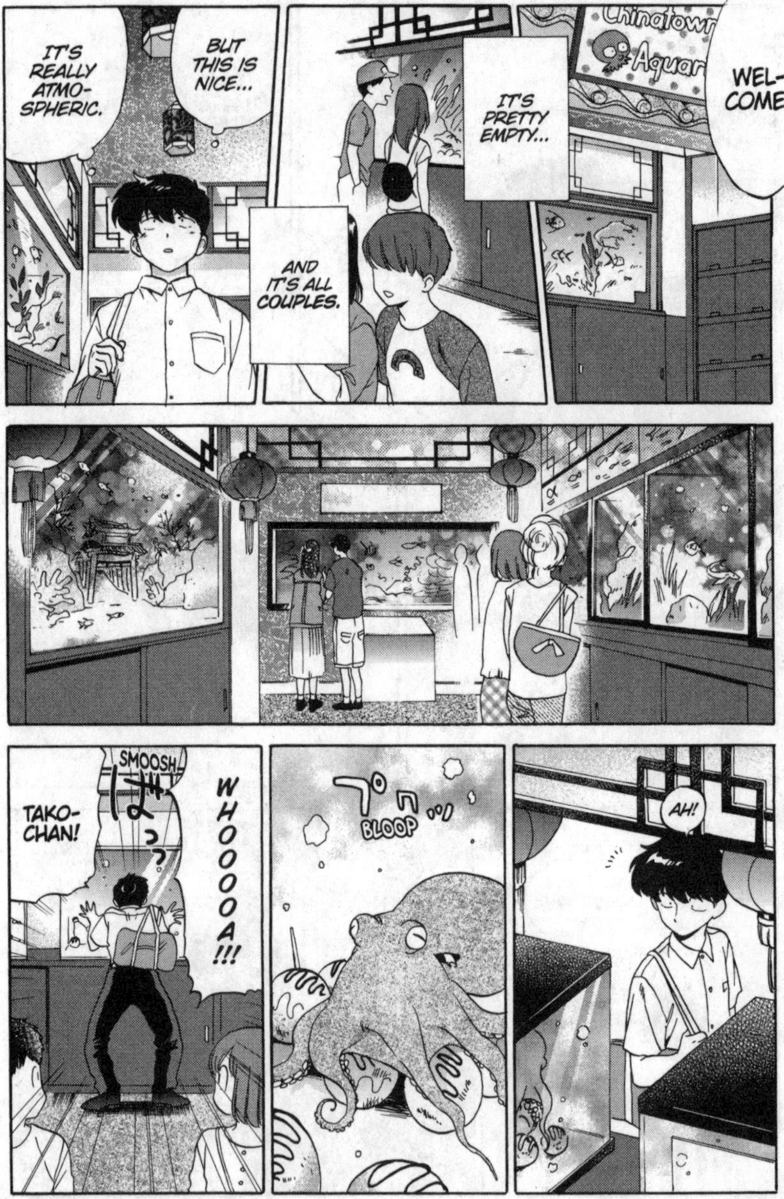
WEL-COME!
Chinatown
IT'S PRETTY EMPTY...
AND IT'S ALL COUPLES.
BUT THIS IS NICE...
IT'S REALLY ATMO-SPHERIC.
AH!
BLOOP
WHOOOOOA!!!
SMOOSH
TAKO-CHAN!

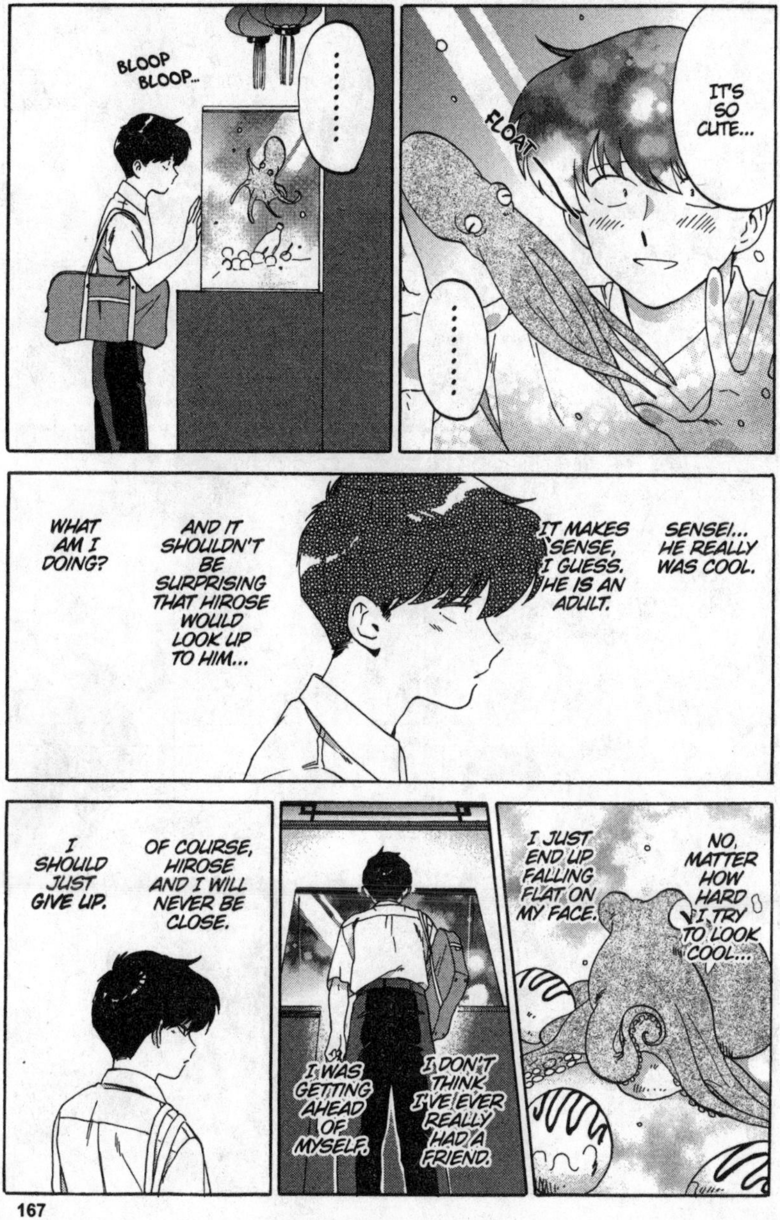
IT'S SO CUTE...
FLOAT
......
BLOOP BLOOP...
......
SENSEI... HE REALLY WAS COOL.
IT MAKES SENSE, I GUESS. HE IS AN ADULT.
AND IT SHOULDN'T BE SURPRISING THAT HIROSE WOULD LOOK UP TO HIM...
WHAT AM I DOING?
NO MATTER HOW HARD I TRY TO LOOK COOL...
I JUST END UP FALLING FLAT ON MY FACE.
I DON'T THINK I'VE EVER REALLY HAD A FRIEND.
I WAS GETTING AHEAD OF MYSELF.
OF COURSE, HIROSE AND I WILL NEVER BE CLOSE.
I SHOULD JUST GIVE UP.

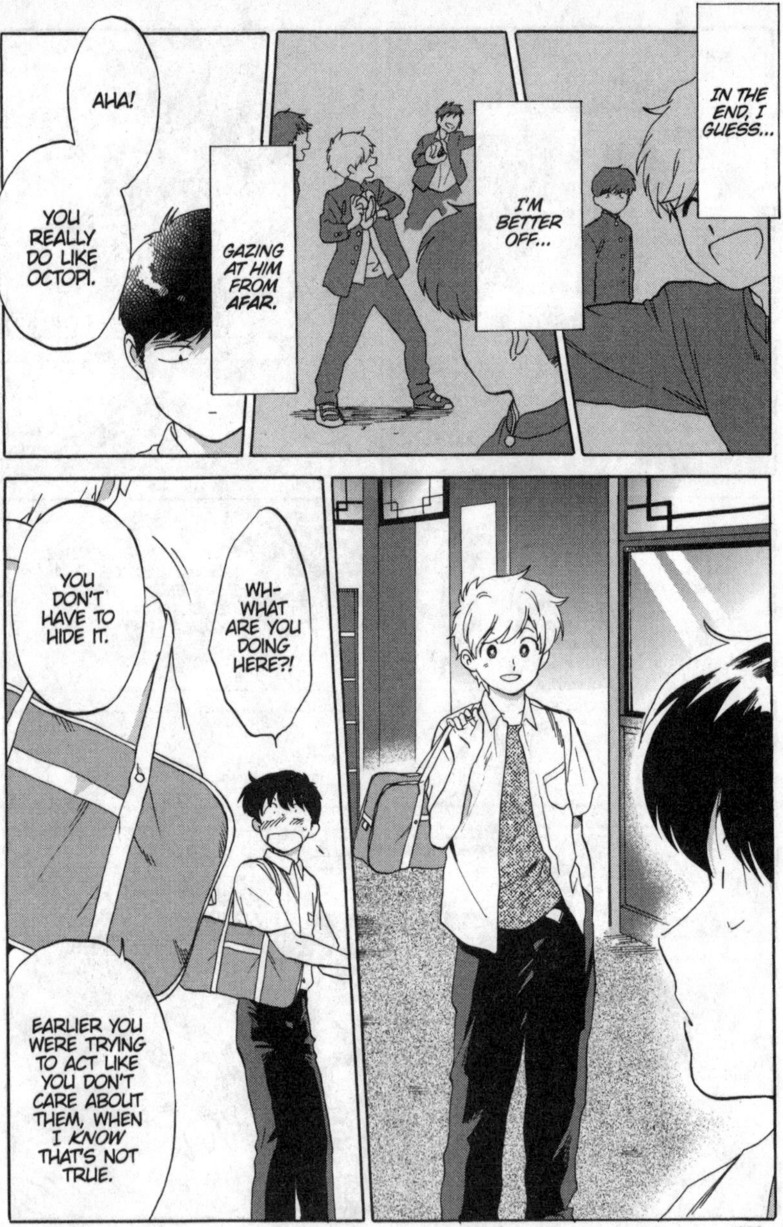
IN THE END, I GUESS...
I'M BETTER OFF...
GAZING AT HIM FROM AFAR.
AHA!
YOU REALLY DO LIKE OCTOPI.
WH-WHAT ARE YOU DOING HERE?!
YOU DON'T HAVE TO HIDE IT.
EARLIER YOU WERE TRYING TO ACT LIKE YOU DON'T CARE ABOUT THEM, WHEN I *KNOW* THAT'S NOT TRUE.

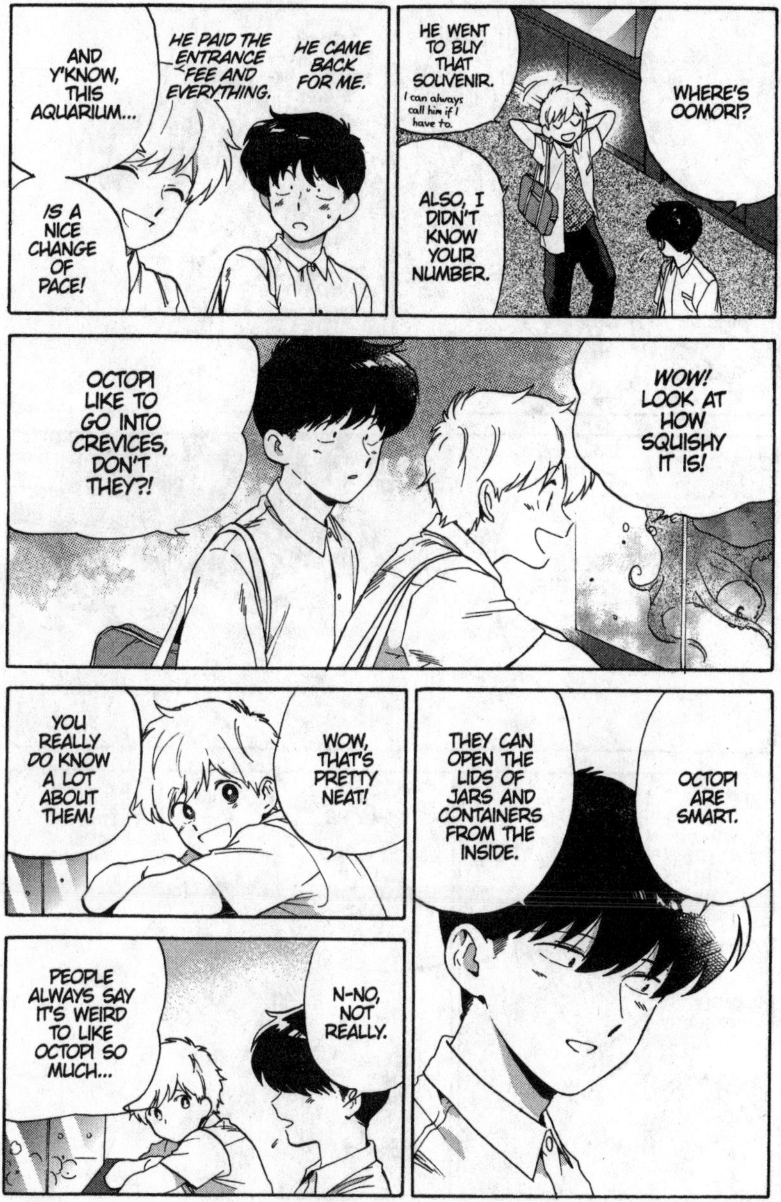
WHERE'S OOMORI?
HE WENT TO BUY THAT SOUVENIR.
I can always call him if I have to.
ALSO, I DIDN'T KNOW YOUR NUMBER.
HE CAME BACK FOR ME.
HE PAID THE ENTRANCE FEE AND EVERYTHING.
AND Y'KNOW, THIS AQUARIUM...
IS A NICE CHANGE OF PACE!
WOW! LOOK AT HOW SQUISHY IT IS!
OCTOPI LIKE TO GO INTO CREVICES, DON'T THEY?!
OCTOPI ARE SMART.
THEY CAN OPEN THE LIDS OF JARS AND CONTAINERS FROM THE INSIDE.
WOW, THAT'S PRETTY NEAT!
YOU REALLY DO KNOW A LOT ABOUT THEM!
N-NO, NOT REALLY.
PEOPLE ALWAYS SAY IT'S WEIRD TO LIKE OCTOPI SO MUCH...

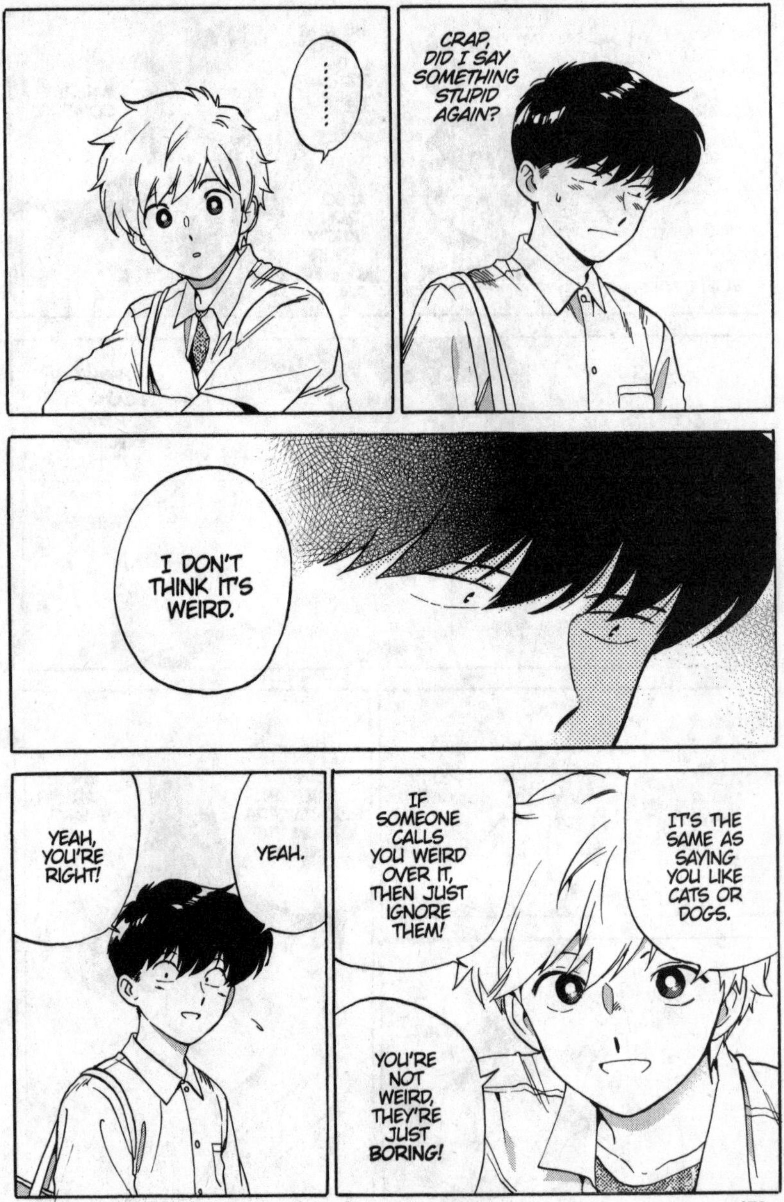
CRAP, DID I SAY SOMETHING STUPID AGAIN?
......
I DON'T THINK IT'S WEIRD.
IT'S THE SAME AS SAYING YOU LIKE CATS OR DOGS.
IF SOMEONE CALLS YOU WEIRD OVER IT, THEN JUST IGNORE THEM!
YOU'RE NOT WEIRD, THEY'RE JUST BORING!
YEAH.
YEAH, YOU'RE RIGHT!

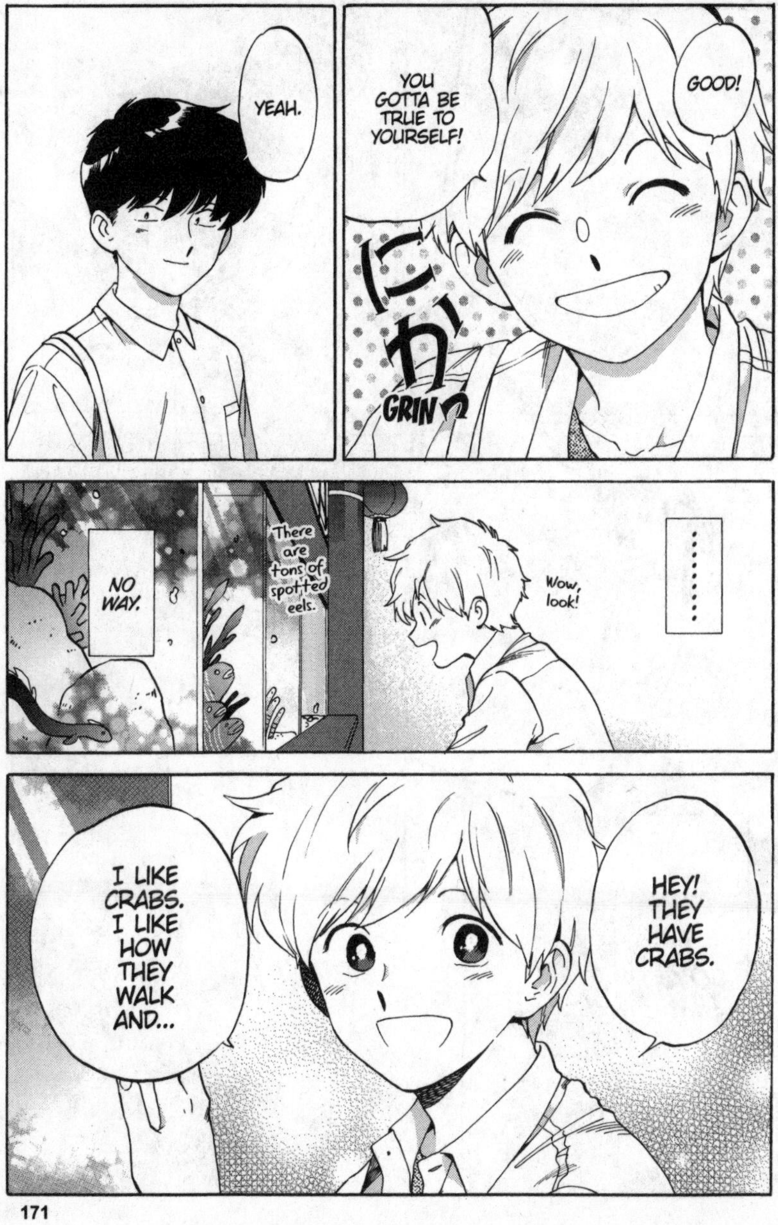
GOOD!
YOU GOTTA BE TRUE TO YOURSELF!
にか
GRIN
YEAH.
......
Wow, look!
There are tons of spotted eels.
NO WAY.
HEY! THEY HAVE CRABS.
I LIKE CRABS. I LIKE HOW THEY WALK AND...

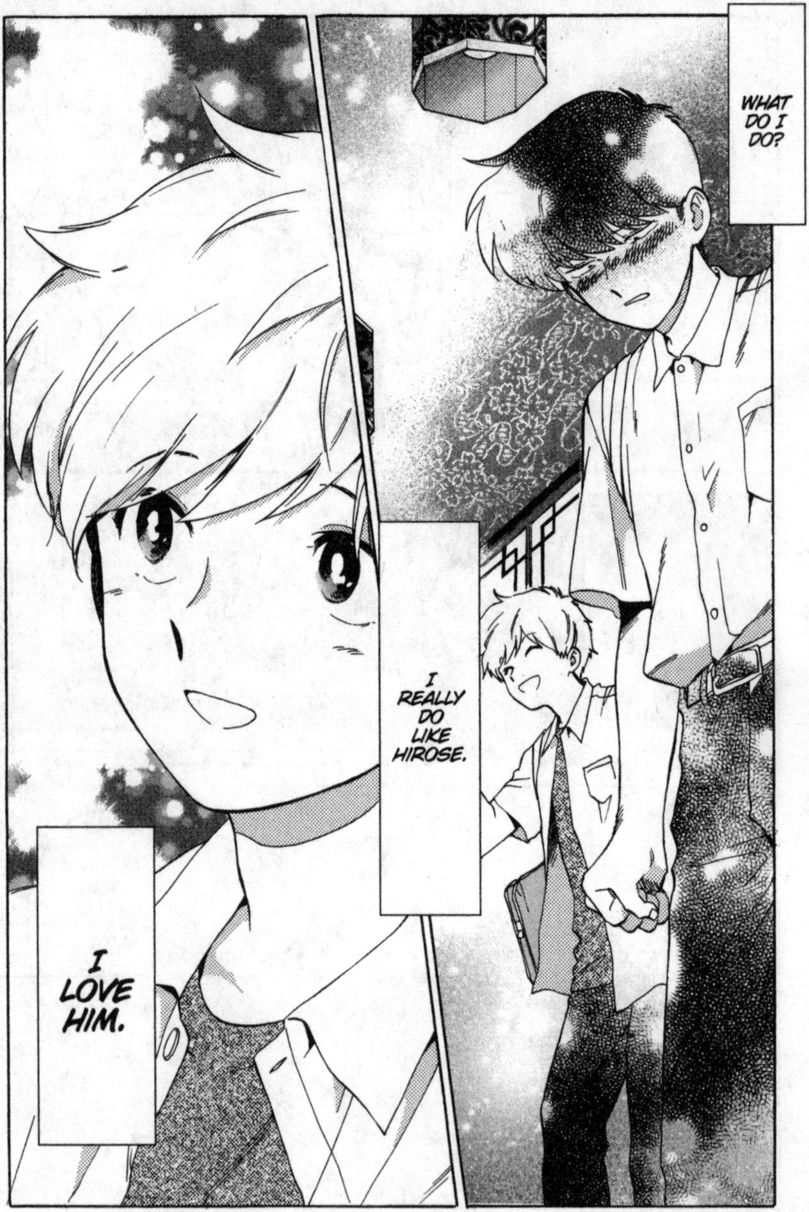
WHAT DO I DO?
I REALLY DO LIKE HIROSE.
I LOVE HIM.

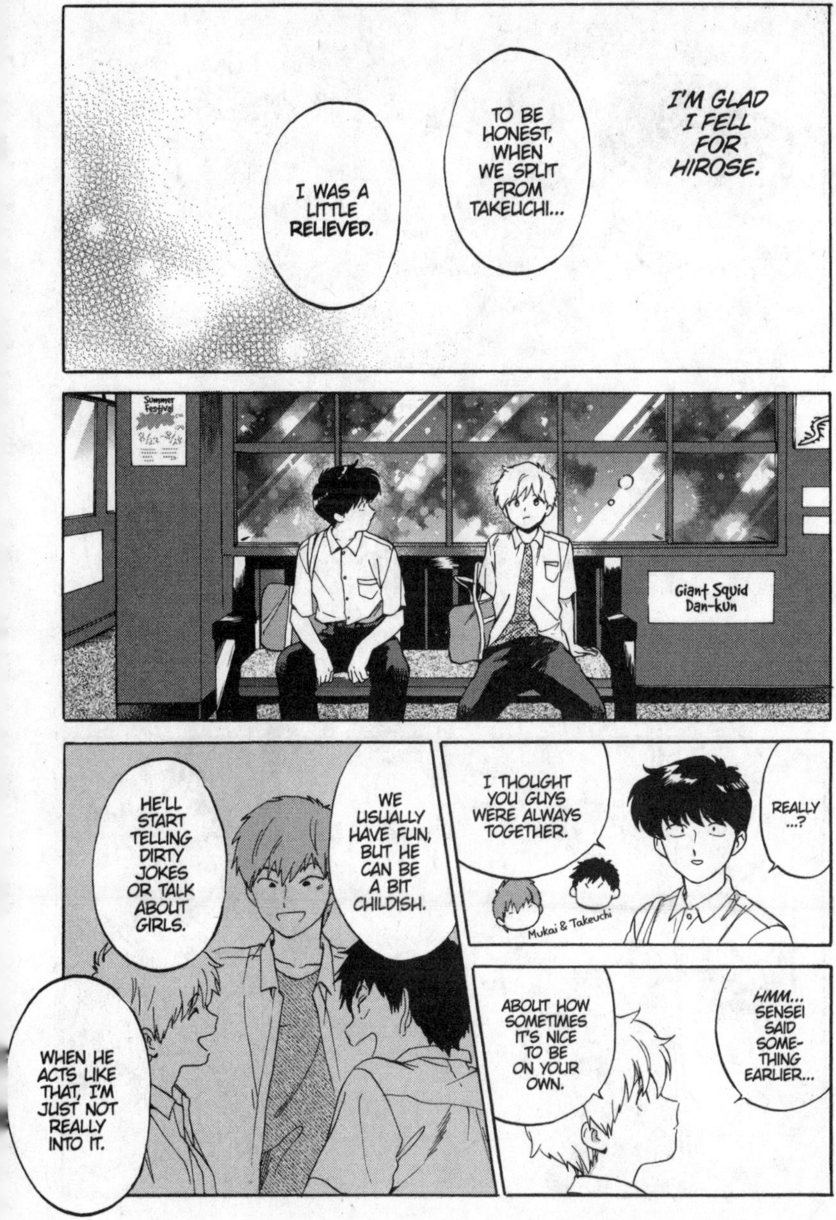
I'M GLAD I FELL FOR HIROSE.
TO BE HONEST, WHEN WE SPLIT FROM TAKEUCHI...
I WAS A LITTLE RELIEVED.
Summer Festival
Giant Squid Dan-kun
REALLY ...?
I THOUGHT YOU GUYS WERE ALWAYS TOGETHER.
Mukai & Takeuchi
HMM... SENSEI SAID SOME-THING EARLIER...
ABOUT HOW SOMETIMES IT'S NICE TO BE ON YOUR OWN.
WE USUALLY HAVE FUN, BUT HE CAN BE A BIT CHILDISH.
HE'LL START TELLING DIRTY JOKES OR TALK ABOUT GIRLS.
WHEN HE ACTS LIKE THAT, I'M JUST NOT REALLY INTO IT.

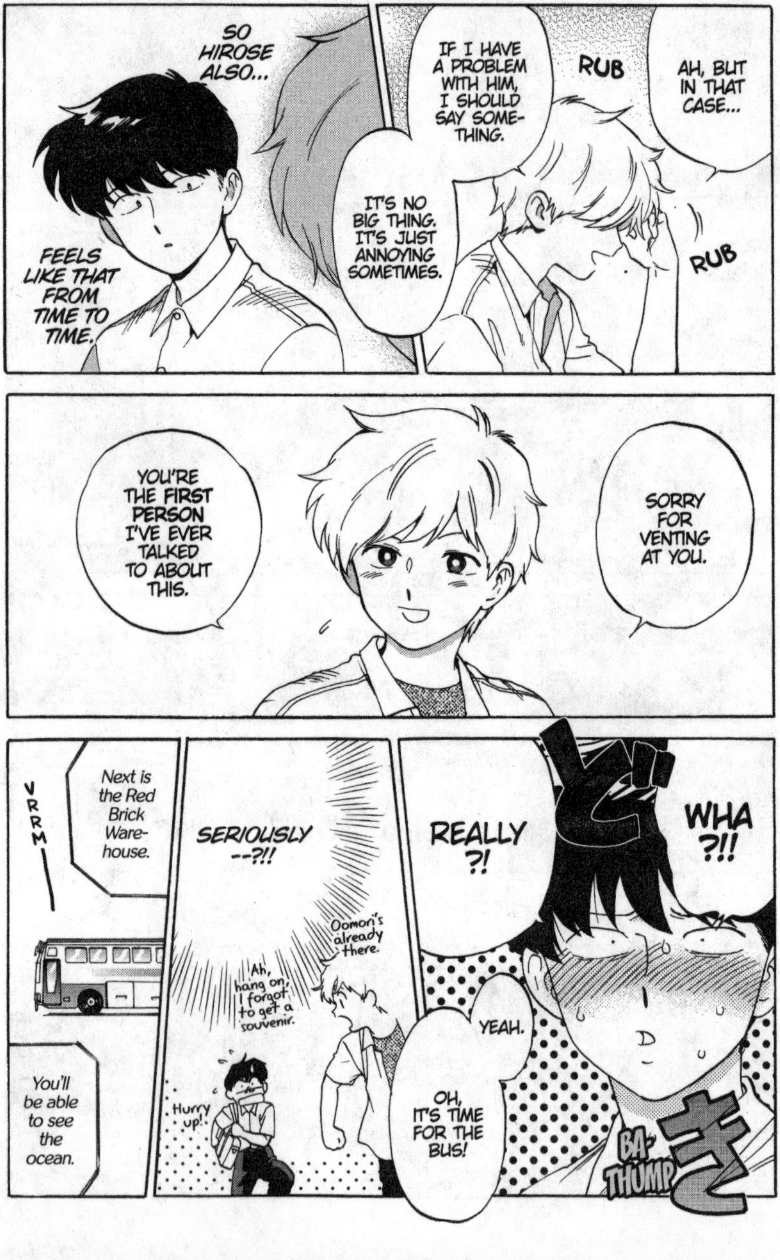
AH, BUT IN THAT CASE...
RUB
RUB
IF I HAVE A PROBLEM WITH HIM, I SHOULD SAY SOMETHING.
IT'S NO BIG THING. IT'S JUST ANNOYING SOMETIMES.
SO HIROSE ALSO...
FEELS LIKE THAT FROM TIME TO TIME.
SORRY FOR VENTING AT YOU.
YOU'RE THE FIRST PERSON I'VE EVER TALKED TO ABOUT THIS.
WHA?!!
REALLY?!
YEAH.
OH, IT'S TIME FOR THE BUS!
BA-THUMP
SERIOUSLY--?!!
Oomori's already there.
Ah, hang on, I forgot to get a souvenir.
Hurry up!
Next is the Red Brick Warehouse.
VRRM
You'll be able to see the ocean.

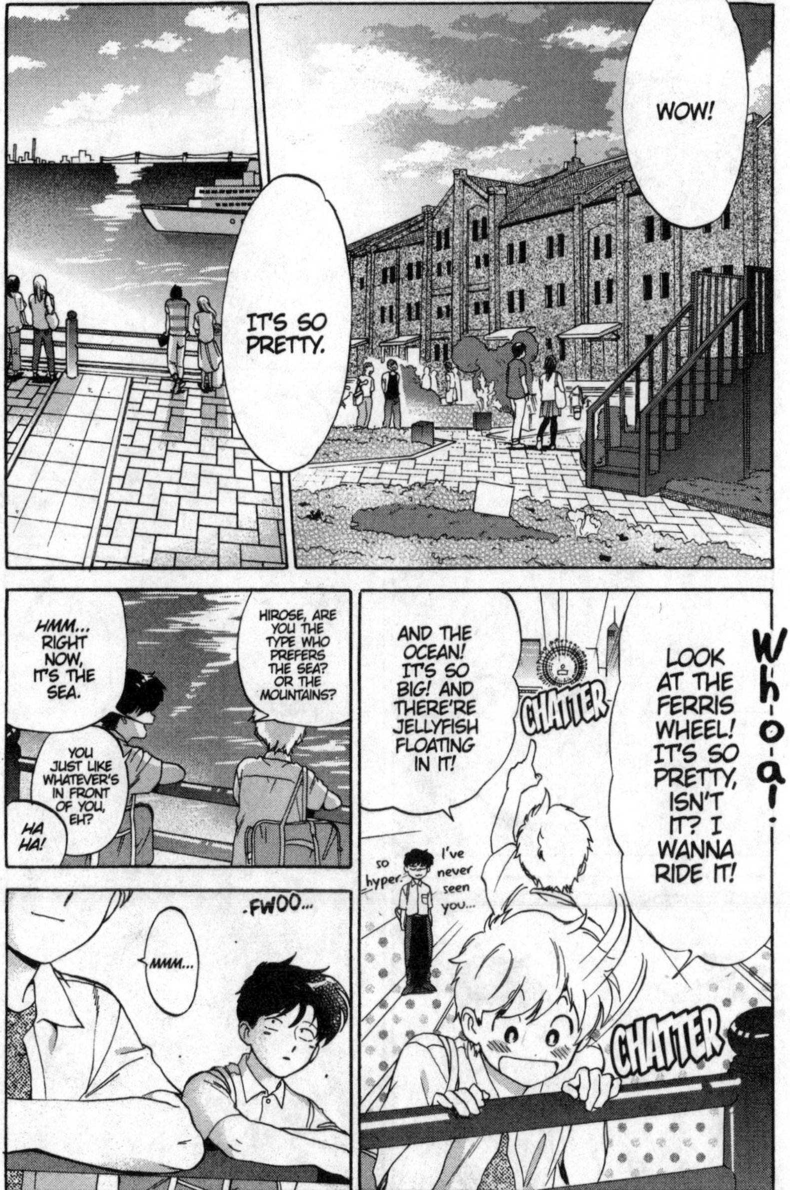
WOW!
IT'S SO PRETTY.
Whoa!
LOOK AT THE FERRIS WHEEL! IT'S SO PRETTY, ISN'T IT? I WANNA RIDE IT!
CHATTER
AND THE OCEAN! IT'S SO BIG! AND THERE'RE JELLYFISH FLOATING IN IT!
I've never seen you...
so hyper.
CHATTER
HIROSE, ARE YOU THE TYPE WHO PREFERS THE SEA? OR THE MOUNTAINS?
HMM... RIGHT NOW, IT'S THE SEA.
YOU JUST LIKE WHATEVER'S IN FRONT OF YOU, EH?
HA HA!
FWOO...
MMM...

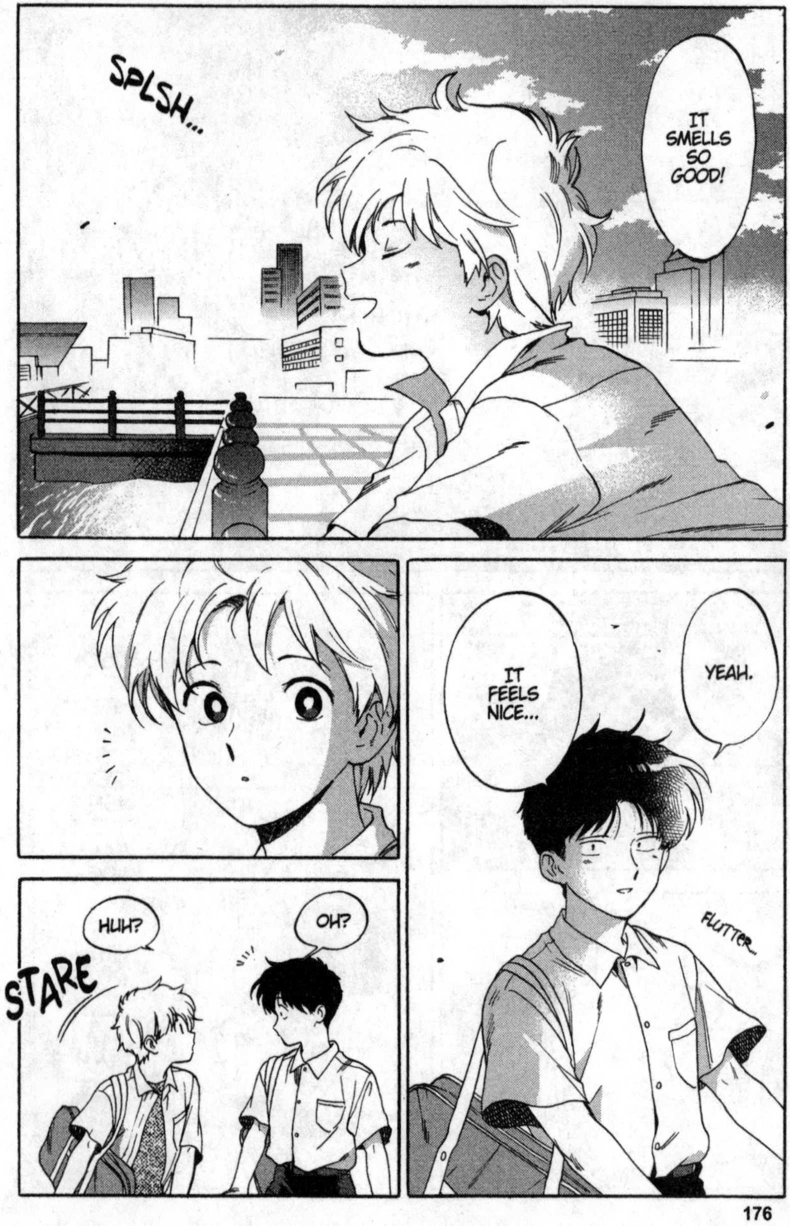
IT SMELLS SO GOOD!
SPLSH...
YEAH.
IT FEELS NICE...
FLUTTER...
OH?
HUH?
STARE

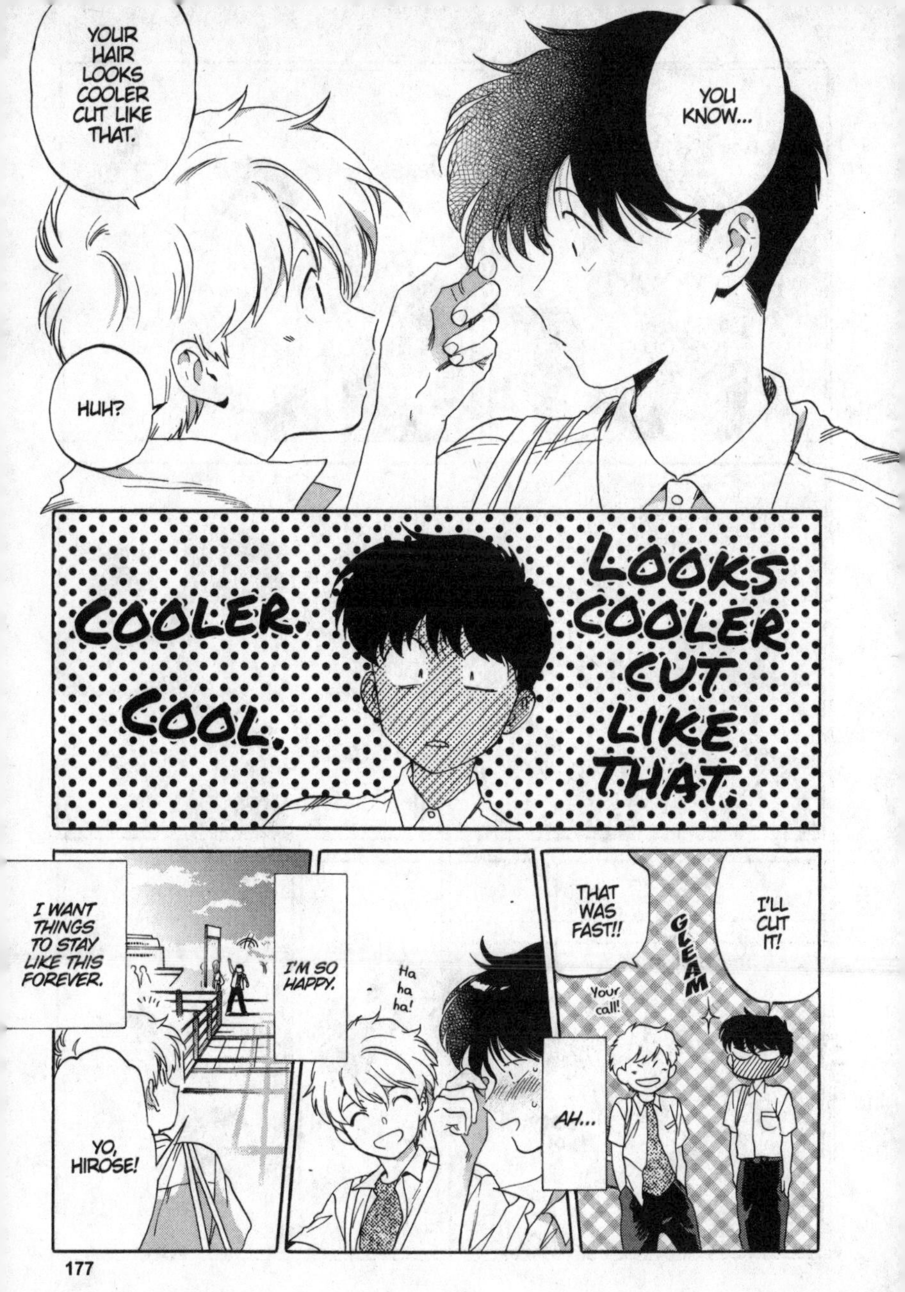
YOU KNOW...
YOUR HAIR LOOKS COOLER CUT LIKE THAT.
HUH?
LOOKS COOLER CUT LIKE THAT.
COOLER.
COOL.
I'LL CUT IT!
GLEAM
THAT WAS FAST!!
Your call!
I'M SO HAPPY.
Ha ha ha!
AH...
I WANT THINGS TO STAY LIKE THIS FOREVER.
YO, HIROSE!

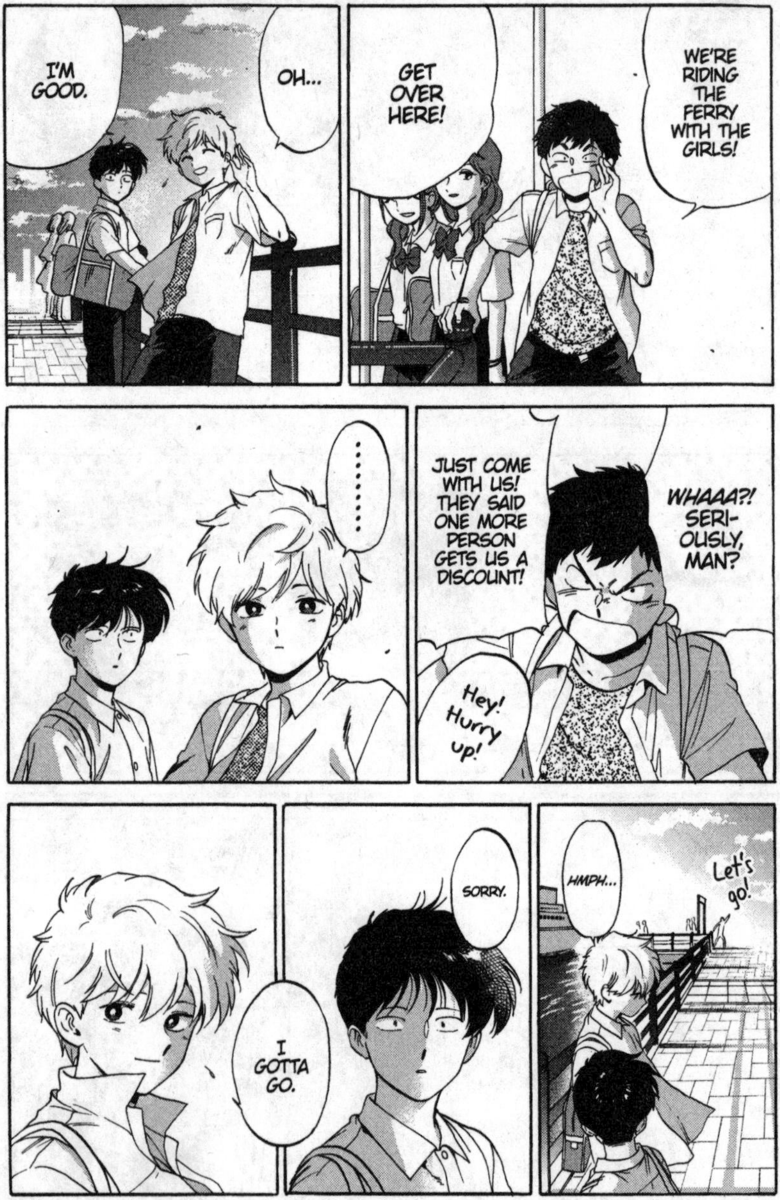
WE'RE RIDING THE FERRY WITH THE GIRLS!
GET OVER HERE!
OH...
I'M GOOD.
WHAAA?! SERI-OUSLY, MAN?
JUST COME WITH US! THEY SAID ONE MORE PERSON GETS US A DISCOUNT!
Hey! Hurry up!
......
Let's go!
HMPH...
SORRY.
I GOTTA GO.

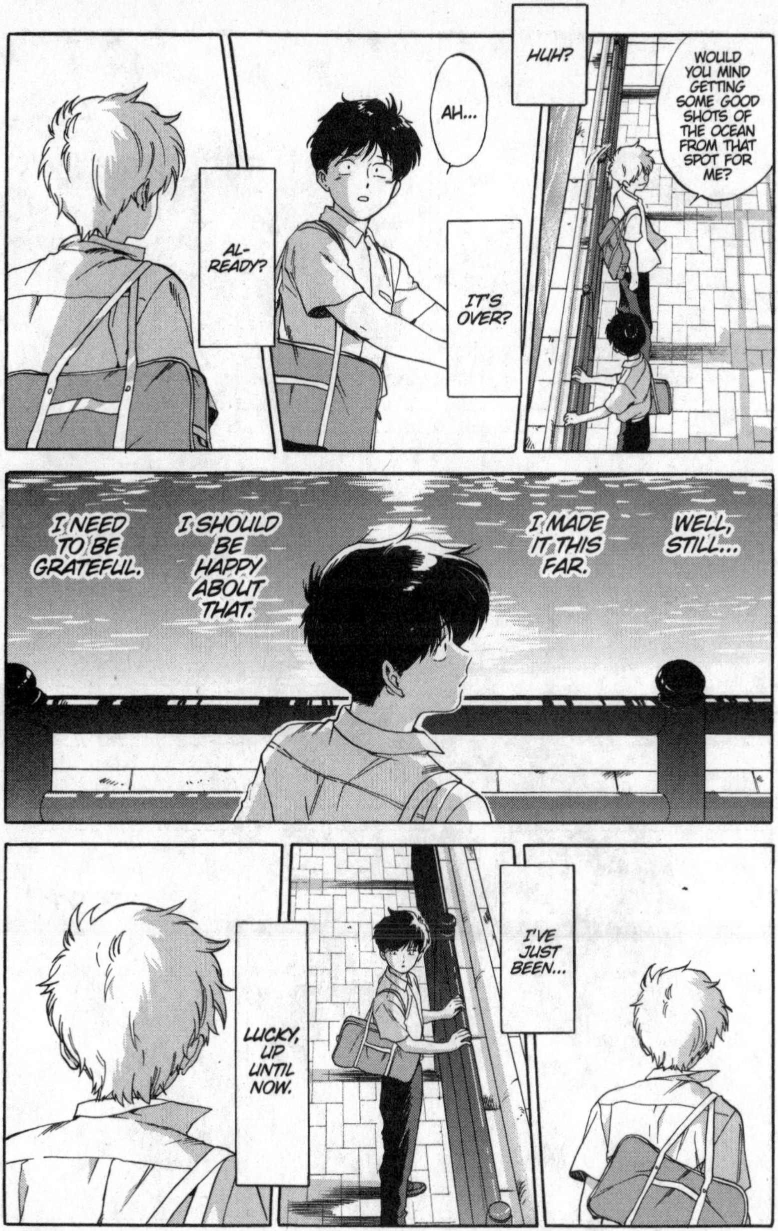
WOULD YOU MIND GETTING SOME GOOD SHOTS OF THE OCEAN FROM THAT SPOT FOR ME?
HUH?
AH...
IT'S OVER?
AL-READY?
WELL, STILL...
I MADE IT THIS FAR.
I SHOULD BE HAPPY ABOUT THAT.
I NEED TO BE GRATEFUL.
I'VE JUST BEEN...
LUCKY, UP UNTIL NOW.

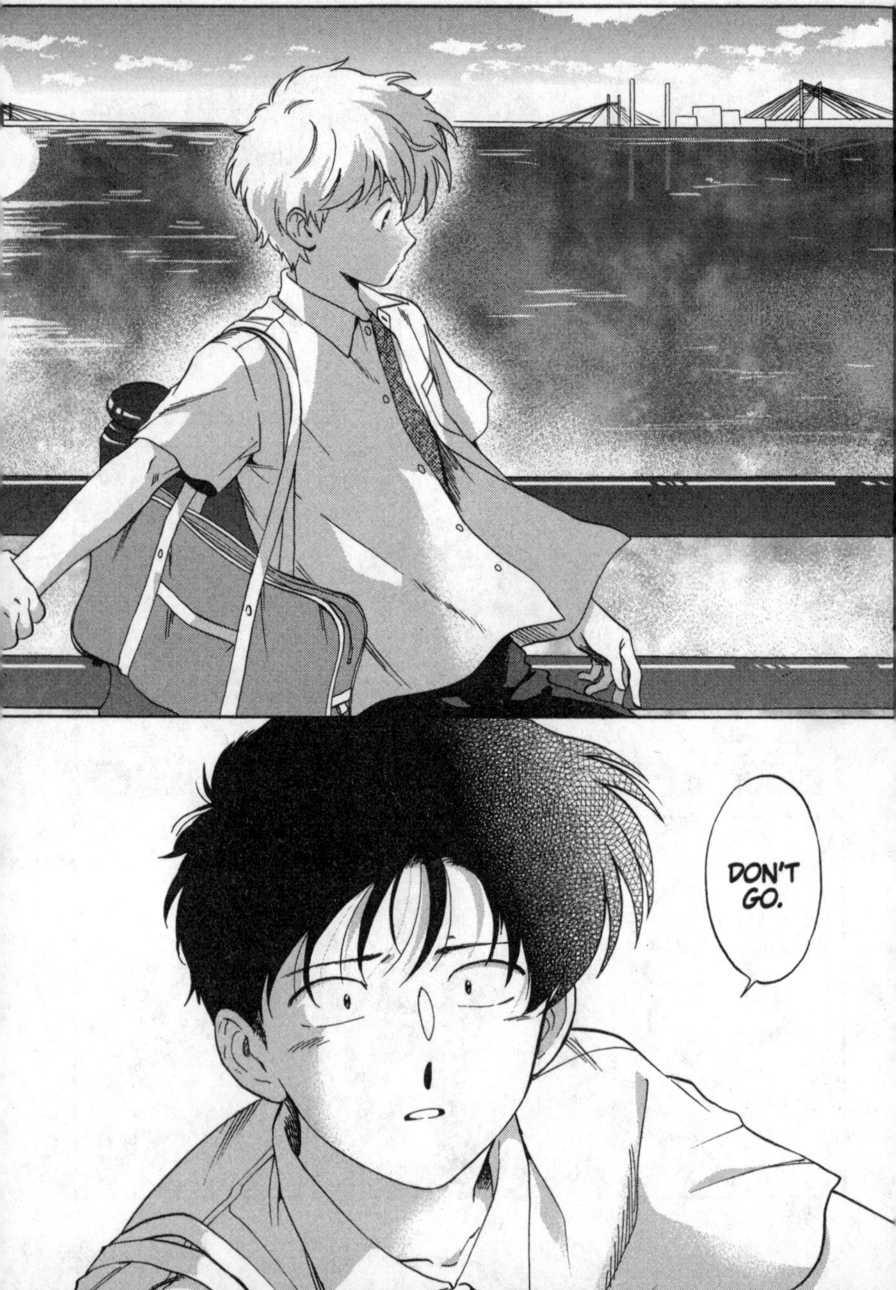
DON'T GO.

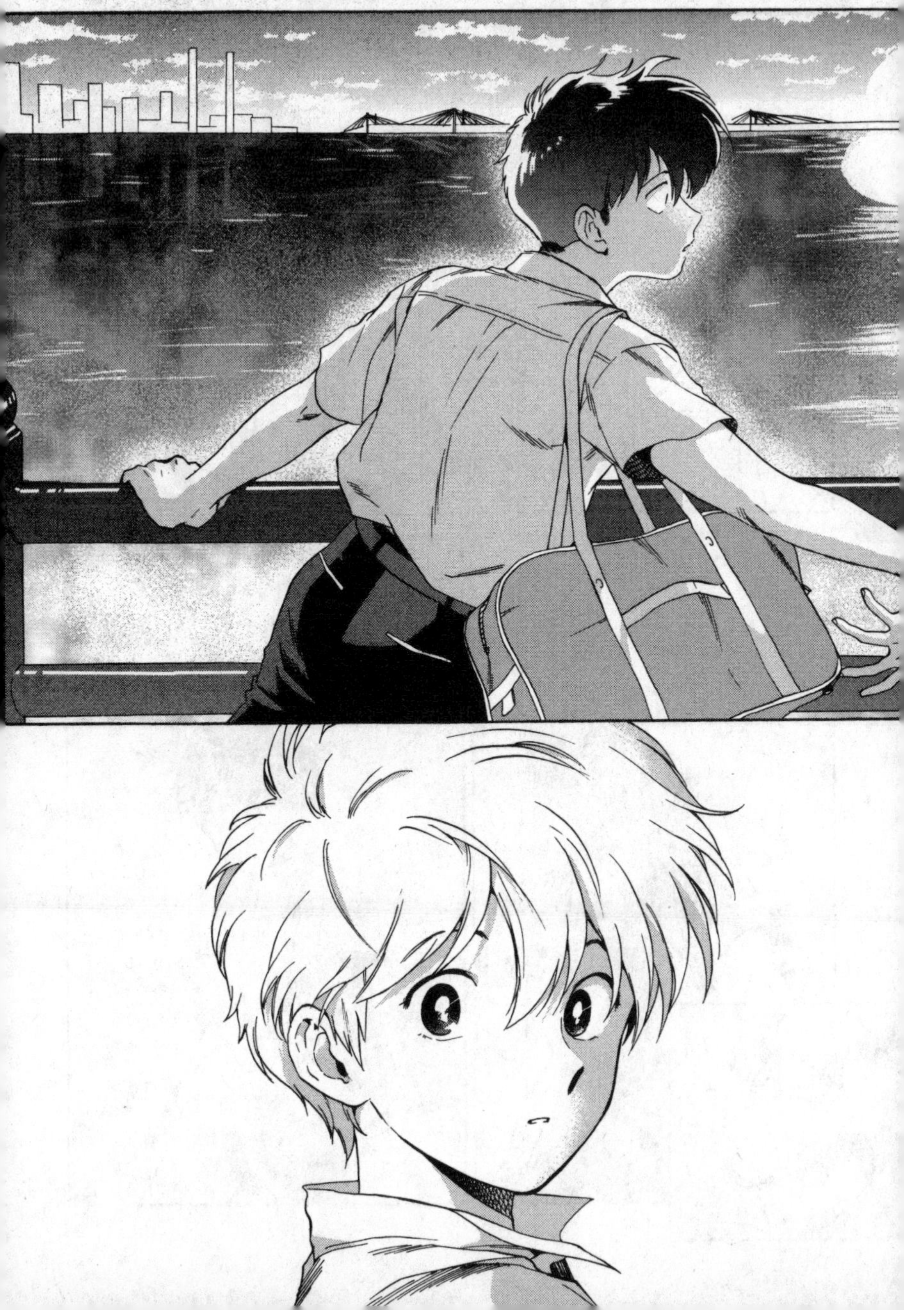

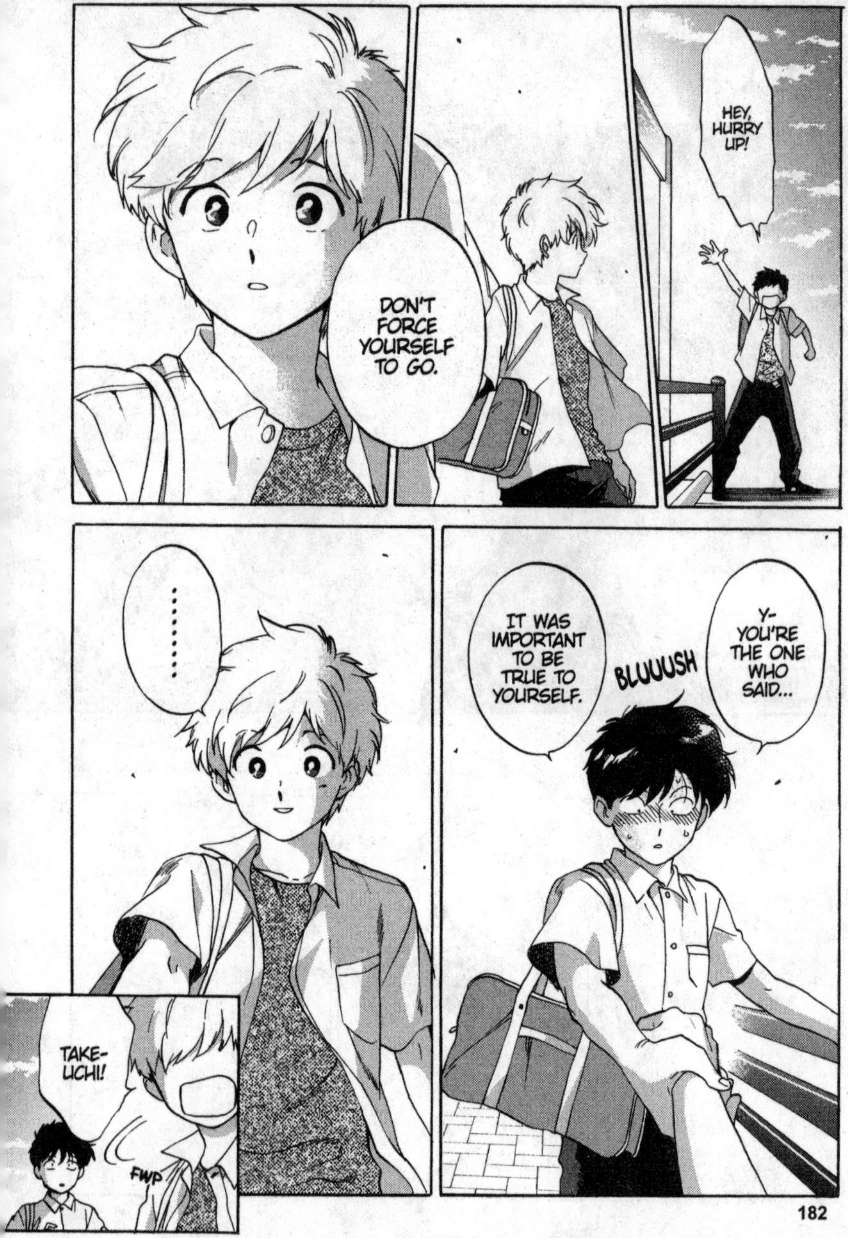
HEY, HURRY UP!
DON'T FORCE YOURSELF TO GO.
Y- YOU'RE THE ONE WHO SAID...
IT WAS IMPORTANT TO BE TRUE TO YOURSELF.
BLUUUSH
......
TAKE-UCHI!
FWP

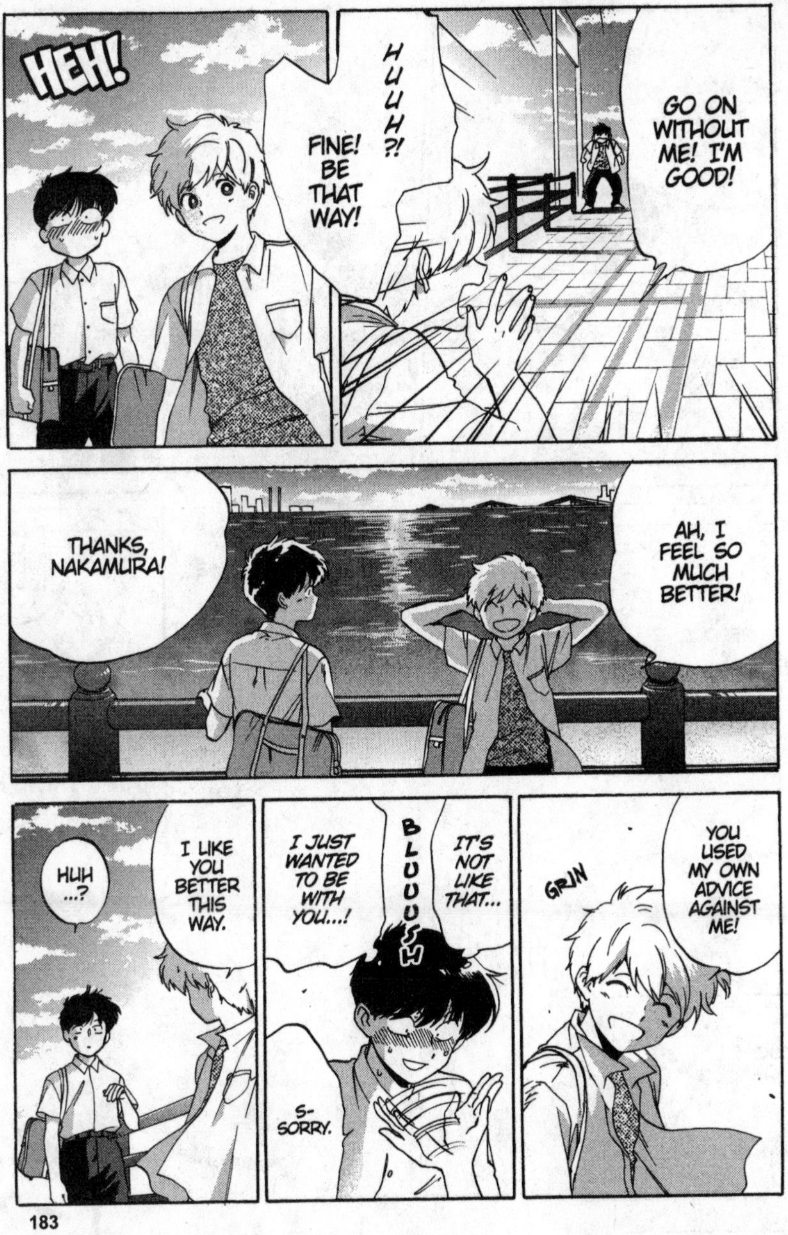
GO ON WITHOUT ME! I'M GOOD!
HUUUH?!
FINE! BE THAT WAY!
HEH!
AH, I FEEL SO MUCH BETTER!
THANKS, NAKAMURA!
YOU USED MY OWN ADVICE AGAINST ME!
GRIN
IT'S NOT LIKE THAT...
BLUUUSH
I JUST WANTED TO BE WITH YOU...!
S-SORRY.
I LIKE YOU BETTER THIS WAY.
HUH ...?

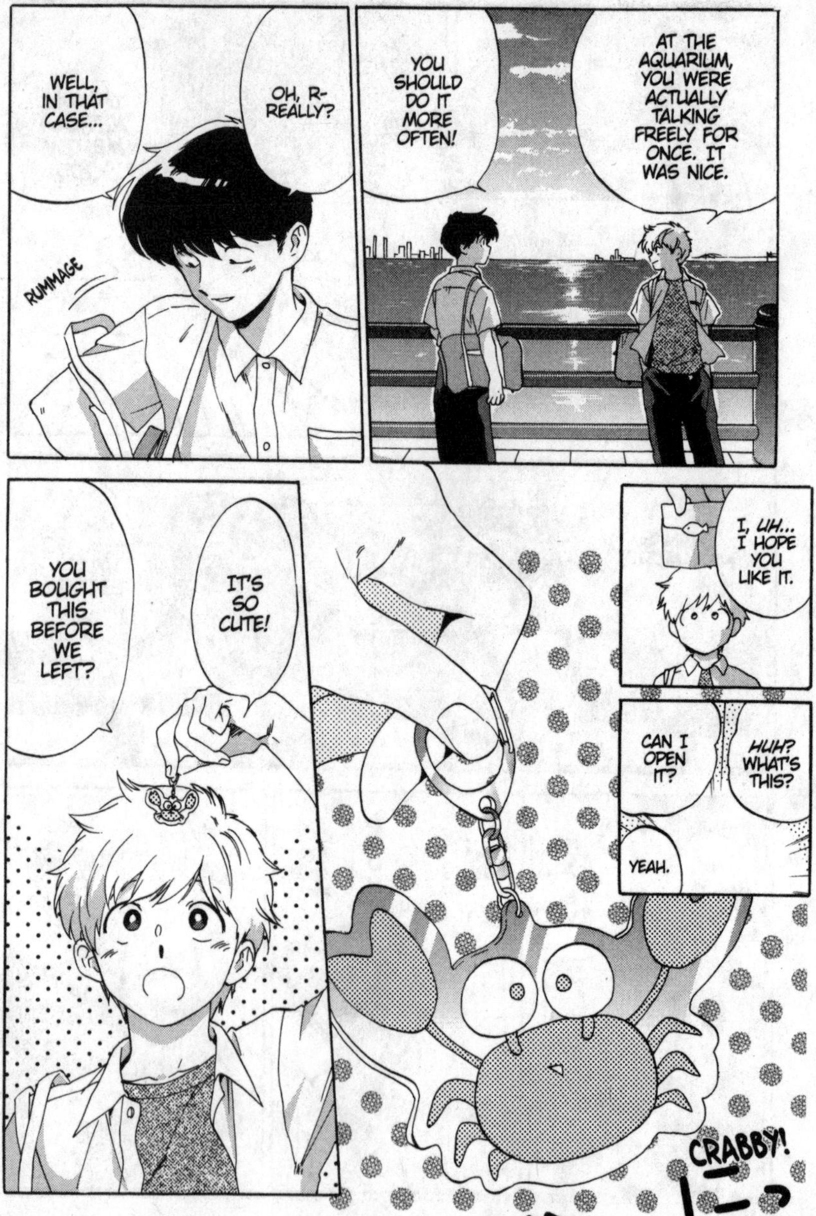
AT THE AQUARIUM, YOU WERE ACTUALLY TALKING FREELY FOR ONCE. IT WAS NICE.
YOU SHOULD DO IT MORE OFTEN!
OH, R-REALLY?
WELL, IN THAT CASE...
RUMMAGE
I, UH... I HOPE YOU LIKE IT.
HUH? WHAT'S THIS?
CAN I OPEN IT?
YEAH.
IT'S SO CUTE!
YOU BOUGHT THIS BEFORE WE LEFT?
CRABBY!
かにーっ

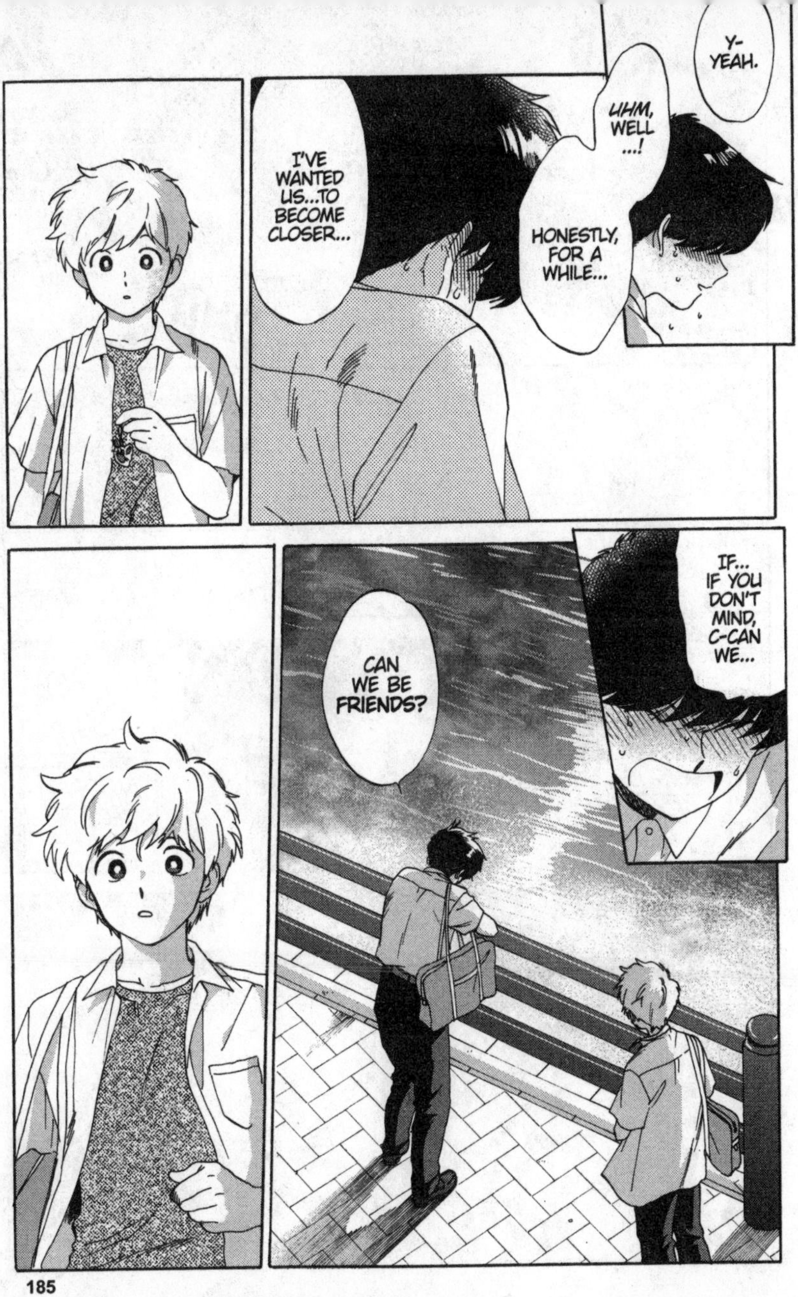
Y-YEAH.
UHM, WELL ...!
HONESTLY, FOR A WHILE...
I'VE WANTED US...TO BECOME CLOSER...
IF... IF YOU DON'T MIND, C-CAN WE...
CAN WE BE FRIENDS?

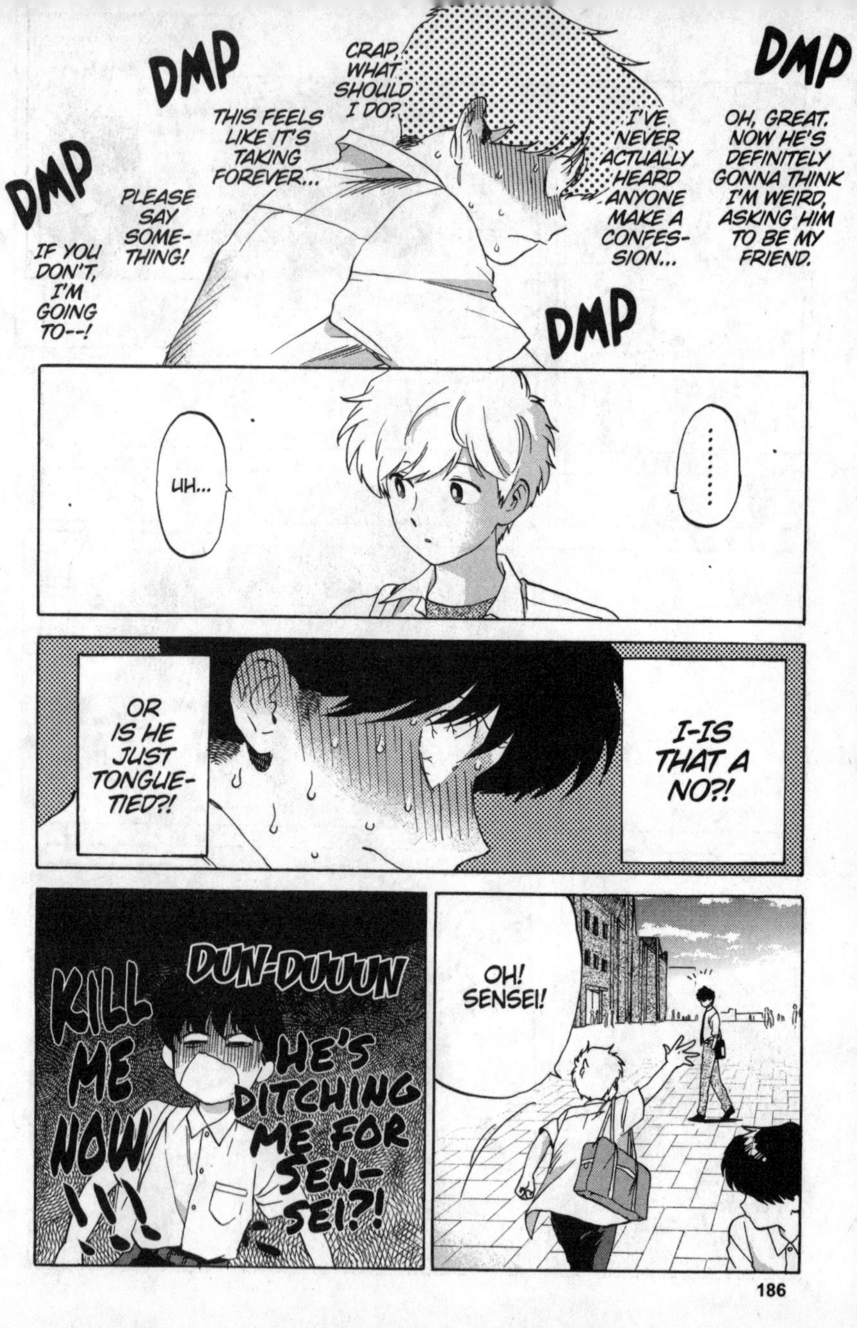
DMP
OH, GREAT. NOW HE'S DEFINITELY GONNA THINK I'M WEIRD, ASKING HIM TO BE MY FRIEND.
I'VE NEVER ACTUALLY HEARD ANYONE MAKE A CONFESSION...
CRAP, WHAT SHOULD I DO?
THIS FEELS LIKE IT'S TAKING FOREVER...
DMP
PLEASE SAY SOMETHING!
DMP
IF YOU DON'T, I'M GOING TO--!
DMP
......
UH...
I-IS THAT A NO?!
OR IS HE JUST TONGUE-TIED?!
OH! SENSEI!
DUN-DUUUN
HE'S DITCHING ME FOR SEN-SEI?!
KILL ME NOW!!!

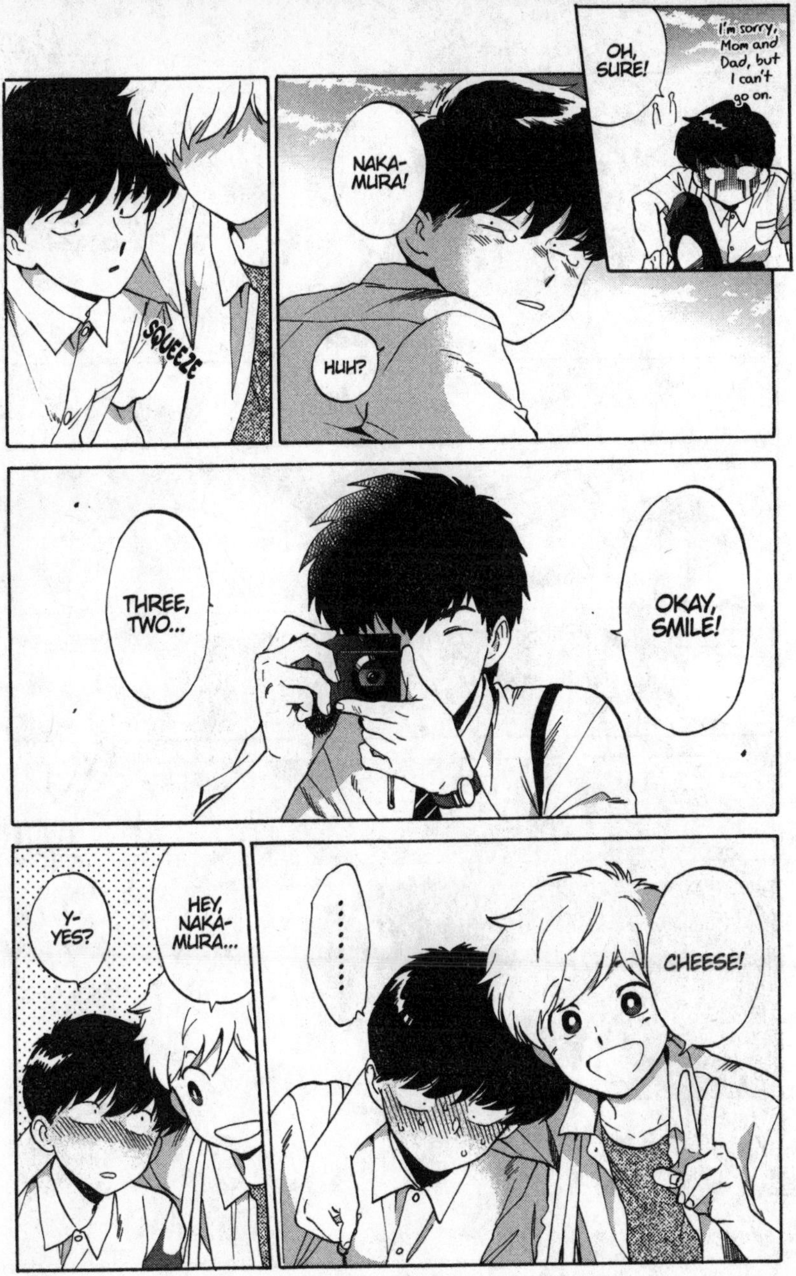
I'm sorry, Mom and Dad, but I can't go on.
OH, SURE!
NAKA-MURA!
HUH?
SQUEEZE
OKAY, SMILE!
THREE, TWO...
CHEESE!
......
HEY, NAKA-MURA...
Y-YES?

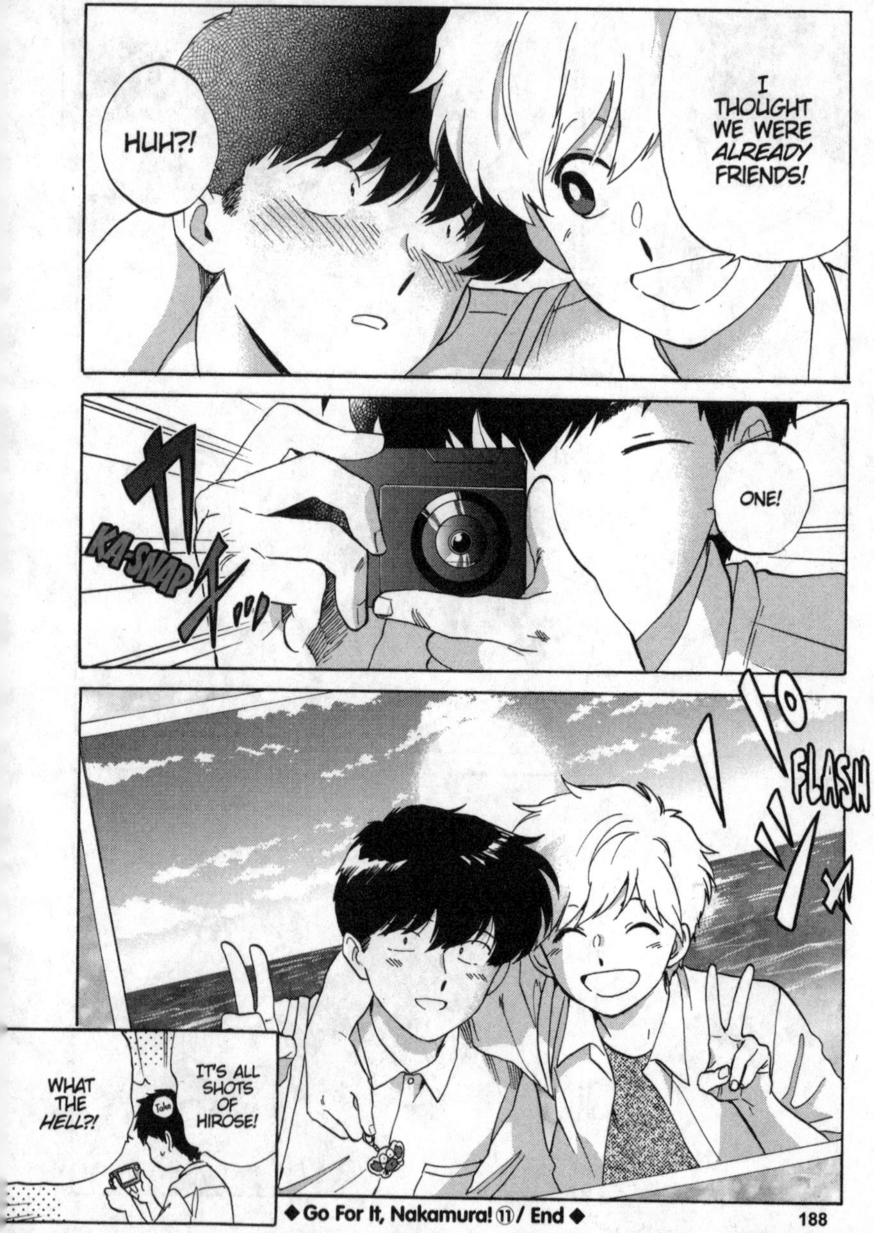
I THOUGHT WE WERE ALREADY FRIENDS!
HUH?!
ONE!
KA-SNAP
FLASH
IT'S ALL SHOTS OF HIROSE!
WHAT THE HELL?!

◆ Go For It, Nakamura! ⑪ / End ◆

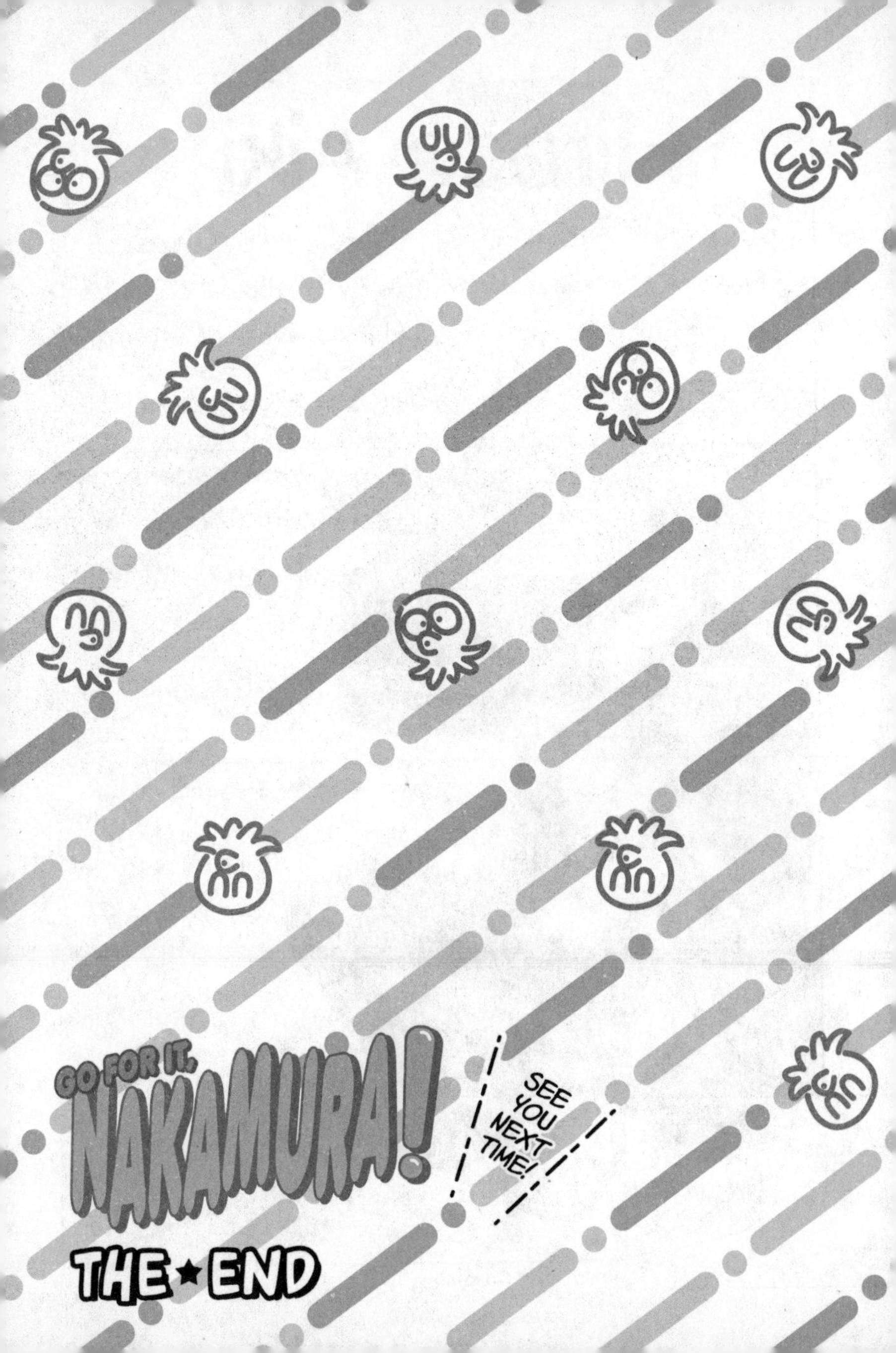
GO FOR IT, NAKAMURA!
SEE YOU NEXT TIME!
THE ★ END

Profile

Hirose Aiki

- Age: 15
- Height: 163cm
- Birthday: March 2 (Pisces)
- Blood Type: A
- Immediate Family: Father, Mother, Older Sister
- Favorite Food: Meat, potato chips
- Least Favorite: Cow or pig entrails

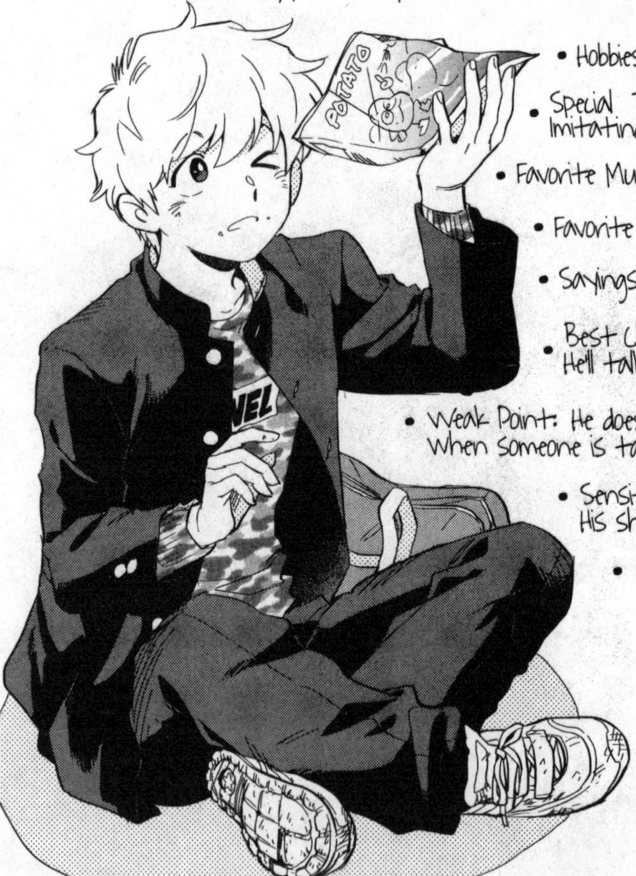
POTATO

- Hobbies: Comedy
- Special Talents: Imitating a machine gun
- Favorite Music: Western music
- Favorite Movies: Suspense
- Sayings: "Cool!" "Crap..."
- Best Characteristics: He'll talk to anyone
- Weak Point: He doesn't always listen when someone is talking to him
- Sensitive About: His short height
- Loves: Dogs

Profile

Nakamura Okuto

- Age: 16 • Height: 167cm • Birthday: October 24 (Scorpio)
- Blood Type: O • Immediate Family: Father, Mother, Younger Sister
- Favorite Food: Vegetables, Japanese food, octopus
- Least Favorite: Carbonated beverages
- Hobbies: The zoo, boys' love books
- Special Talents: Hiding his presence
- Favorite Music: Anything
- Favorite Movies: Chaplin films
- Sayings: "Ah, okay."
- Best Characteristics: Has nice fingers
- Weak Point: He can be contrary

Sensitive About: His monolid eyes

Loves: Octopi

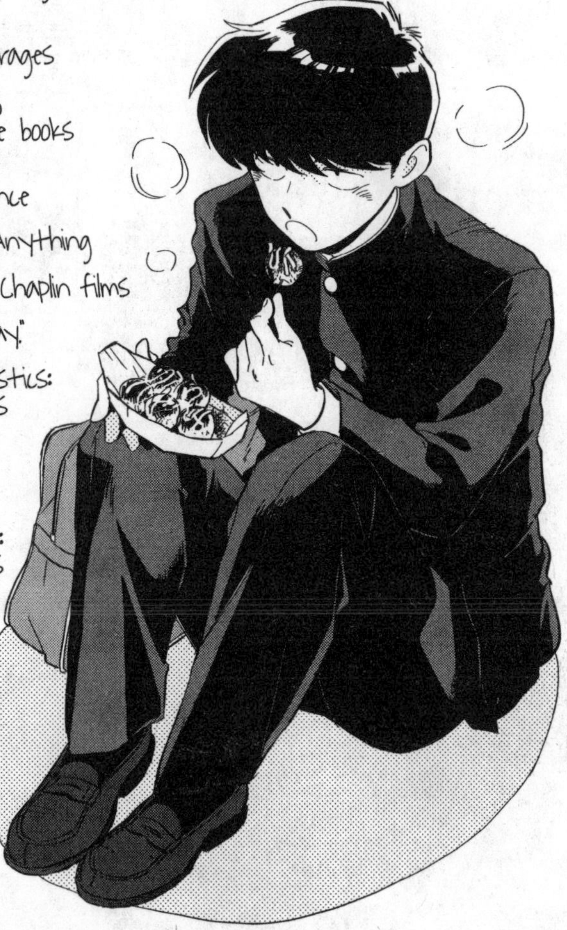

Afterword

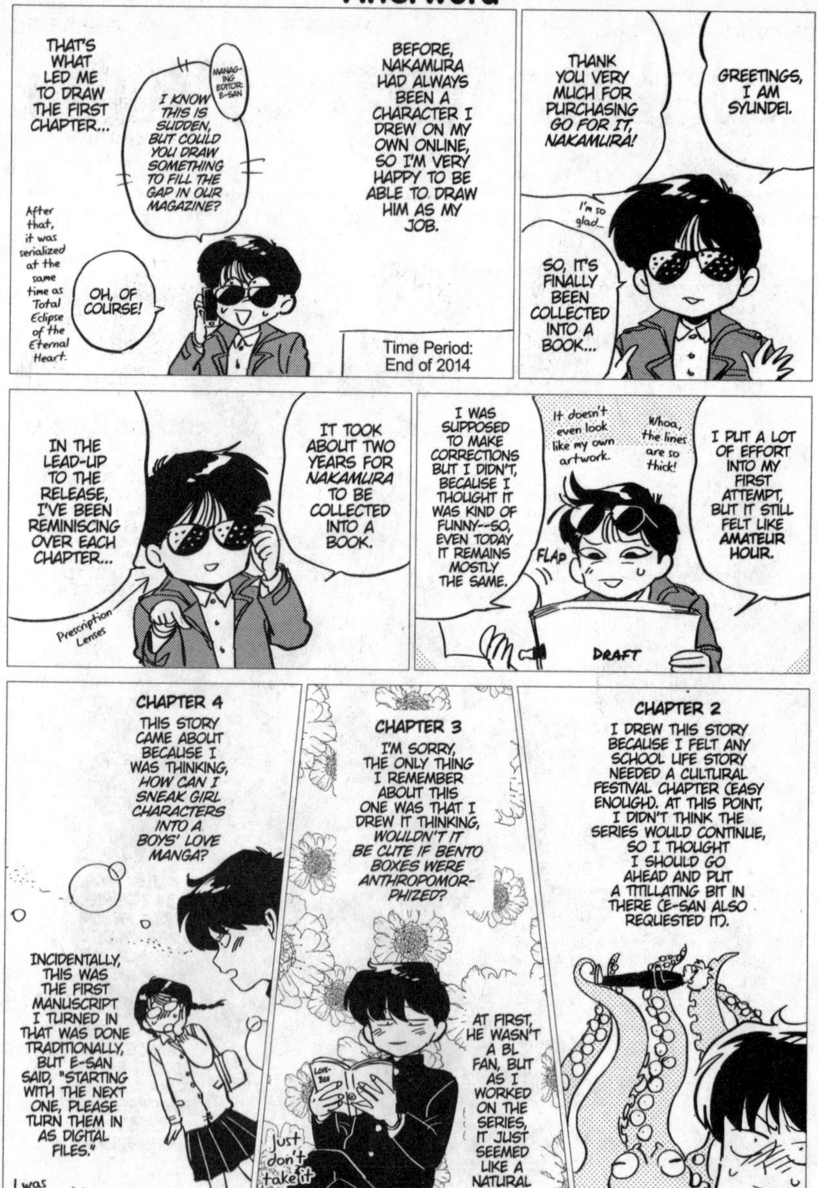
GREETINGS, I AM SYUNDEI.
THANK YOU VERY MUCH FOR PURCHASING *GO FOR IT, NAKAMURA!*
I'm so glad...
SO, IT'S FINALLY BEEN COLLECTED INTO A BOOK...
BEFORE, NAKAMURA HAD ALWAYS BEEN A CHARACTER I DREW ON MY OWN ONLINE, SO I'M VERY HAPPY TO BE ABLE TO DRAW HIM AS MY JOB.
Time Period: End of 2014
MANAGING EDITOR: E-SAN
I KNOW THIS IS SUDDEN, BUT COULD YOU DRAW SOMETHING TO FILL THE GAP IN OUR MAGAZINE?
THAT'S WHAT LED ME TO DRAW THE FIRST CHAPTER...
OH, OF COURSE!
After that, it was serialized at the same time as Total Eclipse of the Eternal Heart.
I PUT A LOT OF EFFORT INTO MY FIRST ATTEMPT, BUT IT STILL FELT LIKE AMATEUR HOUR.
Whoa, the lines are so thick!
It doesn't even look like my own artwork.
I WAS SUPPOSED TO MAKE CORRECTIONS BUT I DIDN'T, BECAUSE I THOUGHT IT WAS KIND OF FUNNY--SO, EVEN TODAY IT REMAINS MOSTLY THE SAME.
FLAP
DRAFT
IT TOOK ABOUT TWO YEARS FOR *NAKAMURA* TO BE COLLECTED INTO A BOOK.
IN THE LEAD-UP TO THE RELEASE, I'VE BEEN REMINISCING OVER EACH CHAPTER...
Prescription Lenses
CHAPTER 2
I DREW THIS STORY BECAUSE I FELT ANY SCHOOL LIFE STORY NEEDED A CULTURAL FESTIVAL CHAPTER (EASY ENOUGH). AT THIS POINT, I DIDN'T THINK THE SERIES WOULD CONTINUE, SO I THOUGHT I SHOULD GO AHEAD AND PUT A TITILLATING BIT IN THERE (E-SAN ALSO REQUESTED IT).
CHAPTER 3
I'M SORRY, THE ONLY THING I REMEMBER ABOUT THIS ONE WAS THAT I DREW IT THINKING, *WOULDN'T IT BE CUTE IF BENTO BOXES WERE ANTHROPOMORPHIZED?*
AT FIRST, HE WASN'T A BL FAN, BUT AS I WORKED ON THE SERIES, IT JUST SEEMED LIKE A NATURAL DEVELOPMENT.
LOVE-BEN
Just don't take it to school!
CHAPTER 4
THIS STORY CAME ABOUT BECAUSE I WAS THINKING, *HOW CAN I SNEAK GIRL CHARACTERS INTO A BOYS' LOVE MANGA?*
INCIDENTALLY, THIS WAS THE FIRST MANUSCRIPT I TURNED IN THAT WAS DONE TRADITIONALLY, BUT E-SAN SAID, "STARTING WITH THE NEXT ONE, PLEASE TURN THEM IN AS DIGITAL FILES."
I was so sad...

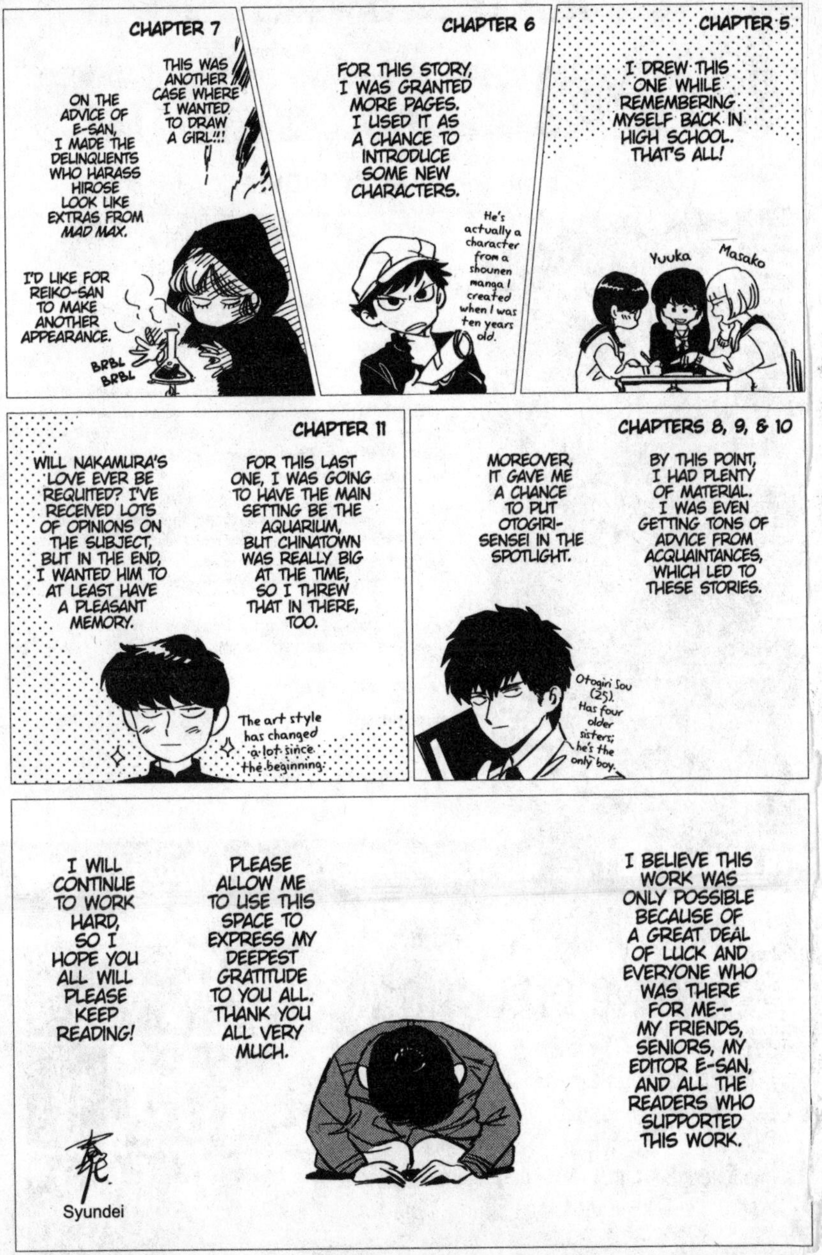
CHAPTER 5
I DREW THIS ONE WHILE REMEMBERING MYSELF BACK IN HIGH SCHOOL. THAT'S ALL!
Masako
Yuuka
CHAPTER 6
FOR THIS STORY, I WAS GRANTED MORE PAGES. I USED IT AS A CHANCE TO INTRODUCE SOME NEW CHARACTERS.
He's actually a character from a shounen manga I created when I was ten years old.
CHAPTER 7
THIS WAS ANOTHER CASE WHERE I WANTED TO DRAW A GIRL!!!
ON THE ADVICE OF E-SAN, I MADE THE DELINQUENTS WHO HARASS HIROSE LOOK LIKE EXTRAS FROM *MAD MAX*.
I'D LIKE FOR REIKO-SAN TO MAKE ANOTHER APPEARANCE.
BRBL BRBL
CHAPTERS 8, 9, & 10
BY THIS POINT, I HAD PLENTY OF MATERIAL. I WAS EVEN GETTING TONS OF ADVICE FROM ACQUAINTANCES, WHICH LED TO THESE STORIES.
MOREOVER, IT GAVE ME A CHANCE TO PUT OTOGIRI-SENSEI IN THE SPOTLIGHT.
Otogiri Sou (25). Has four older sisters; he's the only boy.
CHAPTER 11
FOR THIS LAST ONE, I WAS GOING TO HAVE THE MAIN SETTING BE THE AQUARIUM, BUT CHINATOWN WAS REALLY BIG AT THE TIME, SO I THREW THAT IN THERE, TOO.
WILL NAKAMURA'S LOVE EVER BE REQUITED? I'VE RECEIVED LOTS OF OPINIONS ON THE SUBJECT, BUT IN THE END, I WANTED HIM TO AT LEAST HAVE A PLEASANT MEMORY.
The art style has changed a lot since the beginning.
I BELIEVE THIS WORK WAS ONLY POSSIBLE BECAUSE OF A GREAT DEAL OF LUCK AND EVERYONE WHO WAS THERE FOR ME-- MY FRIENDS, SENIORS, MY EDITOR E-SAN, AND ALL THE READERS WHO SUPPORTED THIS WORK.
PLEASE ALLOW ME TO USE THIS SPACE TO EXPRESS MY DEEPEST GRATITUDE TO YOU ALL. THANK YOU ALL VERY MUCH.
I WILL CONTINUE TO WORK HARD, SO I HOPE YOU ALL WILL PLEASE KEEP READING!
Syundei

SEVEN SEAS ENTERTAINMENT PRESENTS

GO FOR IT, NAKAMURA!

story and art by SYUNDEI

TRANSLATION
Amber Tamosaitis

ADAPTATION
Shannon Fay

LETTERING AND LAYOUT
Kaitlyn Wiley

COVER DESIGN
Karis Page

PROOFREADER
Shanti Whitesides
Stephanie Cohen

ASSISTANT EDITOR
Jenn Grunigen

PRODUCTION ASSISTANT
CK Russell

PRODUCTION MANAGER
Lissa Pattillo

EDITOR IN CHIEF
Adam Arnold

PUBLISHER
Jason DeAngelis

GANBARE! NAKAMURA-KUN!!
©Syundei 2017
Originally published in Japan in 2017 by AKANESHINSHA, Tokyo.
English translation rights arranged with COMIC HOUSE, Tokyo,
through TOHAN CORPORATION, Tokyo.

No portion of this book may be reproduced or transmitted in any form without
written permission from the copyright holders. This is a work of fiction. Names,
characters, places, and incidents are the products of the author's imagination
or are used fictitiously. Any resemblance to actual events, locales, or persons,
living or dead, is entirely coincidental.

Seven Seas books may be purchased in bulk for promotional, educational, or
business use. Please contact your local bookseller or the Macmillan Corporate
and Premium Sales Department at 1-800-221-7945, extension 5442, or by
e-mail at MacmillanSpecialMarkets@macmillan.com.

Seven Seas and the Seven Seas logo are trademarks of
Seven Seas Entertainment, LLC. All rights reserved.

ISBN: 978-1-626928-87-9

Printed in Canada

First Printing: July 2018

10 9 8 7 6 5 4 3 2 1

FOLLOW US ONLINE: *www.sevenseasentertainment.com*

READING DIRECTIONS

This book reads from *right to left*, Japanese style.
If this is your first time reading manga, you start
reading from the top right panel on each page and
take it from there. If you get lost, just follow the
numbered diagram here. It may seem backwards at
first, but you'll get the hang of it! Have fun!!

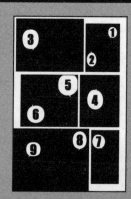